To my daughter

Foreword

From its inception, one of the A.D.C.K.'s tasks has been to "highlight the archaeological, ethnological and linguistic Kanak heritage" complemented by the duty of "defining and conducting research programmes".

It was in arranging our delegation, representing Kanak culture, to the 1992 South Pacific Arts Festival in the Cook Islands, that it was realised how very little was known, often by Kanaks themselves, about our dance heritage.

Although there has always been a living musical tradition among Kanak societies the dance heritage appears to be more difficult to preserve. It is neither written down nor made concrete in any way and it includes numerous constituents (number of dancers, costumes, music...etc.). Moreover its conservation depends essentially on the memories of the owners of each dance, who alone have the right of performance. No-one else can claim the right to present a dance or perform a piece of Kanak music. The owner clan must first give its permission. Furthermore, dances have suffered because they were performed only on certain occasions which, due to social changes and the effects of urbanisation, have become progressively rarer. Too often, performances have been restricted to occasions such as charity fetes and ministerial visits. As it had become clear that the dance heritage was particularly threatened, it was chosen as one of the subjects for our first research programme.

No-one with the necessary qualifications could be found here in the Territory so Dr. Raymond Ammann was asked to carry out the work. At that time he did not know New Caledonia but he had already observed dances and music in Papua-New Guinea and he agreed to undertake the work. His simplicity and valuable personal qualities, which quickly enabled him to be welcomed everywhere, have been greatly appreciated. Today it gives me great pleasure to thank him for the valuable work he has carried out and for the way in which he has put his heart into it. This book contains a synthesis of his research. The numerous observations he has cited together with the recordings made, bear witness to a precious part of our cultural heritage, so lively and interesting when it is seen and heard.

In order to put new life into the dance and music heritage, the A.D.C.K. has developped a second strategy, that of organising events. Along with the research programme, the number of festive and social meetings has been increased in such a way that owners are encouraged to "give" their dances, both to transmit them to their children and to perform them. Thus, each year the A.D.C.K. organises a dance festival in one of the three New Caledonian Provinces, as well as *ae-ae* concerts. Local cultural societies have also increased the number of their meetings and occasions on which performances can be given. When the time came, last year, to arrange the delegation to go to the 1996 Pacific Arts Festival in Apia, it could be seen how much easier it had become to form the dance delegation. A better identification of the different cultural regions to which the various groups of dances belong and the increase in the number of occasions for dancing and singing, had resulted in fine performances.

This heritage does not belong only to the past. So much effort has not been spent only to have the pleasure of allowing our children, and people of other ethnic groups, the joys of discovering and appreciating Kanak dance and music. It has been made, above all, to nourish cultural creativity, to offer to

Kanak dance and music

Ceremonial and intimate performance
of the Melanesians of New Caledonia,
historical and actual

by

Raymond Ammann

Photographs by David Becker

Editorial assistance for the English text :
Helena E. Reeve-Brinon

KPI

Agence
de Développement
de la Culture
Kanak

First published in April 1997 by
A.D.C.K. BP 378 - Nouméa - New Caledonia
Tel : (687) 28 32 90 - Fax : (687) 28 21 78
& Kegan Paul International UK : P.O. Box 256, London WCIB 3SW, England
Tel : (0171) 580 5511 - Fax : (0171) 436 0899
E-mail : books a keganpau.demon.co.uk
Internet : http://www.demon.co.uk/keganpaul/
USA : 562 West 113th Street, New York, Ny 10025, USA
Tel : (212) 666 1000 - Fax : (212) 316 3100

Distributed by
John Wiley & Sons Ltd
Southern Cross Trading Estate
1 Oldlands Way, Bognor Regis
West Sussex, PO22 9 SA, England
Tel : (01243) 779 777 - Fax : (01243) 820 250
Columbia University Press
562 West 113th Street
New York, NY 10025, USA
Tel : (212) 666 1000 - Fax : (212) 316 3100

Diagrams, Labanotation and music transcriptions : Raymond Ammann
Photographs : David Becker
Editorial help : Dr. Helena E. Reeve-Brinon

Layout and dummy : Synapse, Nouméa, BP 3144 - 98846 - New Caledonia
Cover photographs : David Becker/A.D.C.K. 1992-1994
Back flap : Scene from an incised bamboo (Dellenbach 1936:270)
Jacket design : Stephane Herby
Printed in New Zealand by Academy Press

ISBN 0-7103-0586-9
British Library Cataloging in Publication Data
Applied for
US Library of Congress Cataloging in Publication Data
Applied for

present-day Kanak musicians access to their cultural roots so that they are able to produce music which breathes the sounds and rhythms of our ancestors. We have greatly appreciated the capacity of Dr.Ammann to share his art and science with young musicians and help them to find and play traditional instruments in a way which is compatible with contemporary aspirations. This has been particularly important in the case of the Kanak flute where the instrumental use had been lost.

Thanks to this shared research and renewed performance, new choregraphies have appeared. Inspired by the gestures and sonorities drawn from tradition, their originality lies in their production. They are not comparable with the "modern dancing" as presented by visiting troupes which we have received during the last few years, but they demonstrate the creative capacity of Kanaks. In this way, that which Jean-Marie Tjibaou called "*une tradition dans la modernité*" ("Kanak tradition within contempory time") can be realised.

So this book is about the living heritage of a creative people, not a collection of folklore, archives of the past. It is certainly addressed to all those who wish to extend their knowlege of Kanak dance and music in depth, but I recommend it too, to all young people who dance and play *kaneka* music. I suggest that, after careful study, they will find in it, through the spirits of our ancestors, the inspiration from the begining of time and the strength necessary for the development and enrichment of their creative work. This is the way in which we should enter the third millenium.

Marie-Claude TJIBAOU

President of the Agence de
Développement de la Culture Kanak

Contents

Author's preface

During the last 150 years, Kanak culture has been exposed to enormous changes resulting in much neglect and loss of cultural values. To learn about the culture, both an analytical study of the actual situation and an examination of 18th and 19th century reports are needed.

This book brings together and discusses the ethnomusicological and ethnochoreological field-data collected in New Caledonia over a period of five years. In this time as many dances as possible have been observed and filmed and as much music as possible heard and recorded. Interviews with a large number of informants have been carried out not only to furnish needed technical details but also to try to relate the dance and music thus experienced to Kanak culture as a whole. This study also looks at the ethnographical literature and collections of artefacts in the Pacific and Europe, from the first European contact up to the present day, gleaning and presenting as much information as possible relevant to the occurrence of dance and music on the *Grande Terre* and in the Loyalty Islands

It is hoped that the book will provide a way of learning more about Kanak culture through the elegant approach of its music and dance.

Acknowledgements

The present study was carried out at the request of the 'Agence de Développement de la Culture Kanak (A.D.C.K.)' in Nouméa and is the result of collaboration with many people involved in research on Kanak society. I received practical and moral support from a large number of institutions and people whom I would like to thank here.

For general and financial support so that the research could be carried out I would like to thank the 'Centre Culturel Yeweine Yeweine', Maré ; the 'Conseil des Études des Sociétés Kanak (ESK)', Paris ; the 'Délégation aux Affaires Culturelles, Nouméa'.

For editorial help and correcting the English text I am very grateful to Dr. Helena E. Reeve-Brinon. She not only corrected and translated parts of the text but has also been a moral support and done much to keep the project going.

I would very much like to thank David Becker for his photographs and for his much appreciated collaboration in illustrating this book.

Support in the field has been so large that it is impossible to acknowlege individually all my helpers and friends in the Caledonian bush and on the Loyalty Islands.

In the Paicî region I would like to thank the Cidopwa family of Tioumidou, all the inhabitants of the *tribus* Galilé-Tioumidou, especially the *apooro cäbu* Nicaise Amo and Marcel Koaté. I would also like to thank the singers from the Tiéti *tribu* and the 'Jèèmâ Cultural Association'. From the 'Conseil d'Aire Coutumière Paici Camuki' I would like to thank Reybas Wakaceu. In the Koné area a very warm thankyou to Seraphin Mereâtu and his singer colleages and also to Antoine Goromido. In the Gohapin *tribu* I would like to thank Pierre Pouroudeu and the singers Athanace Meru and Devido Pouroudeu, and from the Nekiriai *tribu* the singer Marie-Angèle Meroudhia.

In the Hienghène region I would like to give my thanks to the whole of the Ouarap *tribu* especially to Bealo Wedoye, Benoît Boulet and Salomon Mayat.

From the south of the *Grande Terre*, I would like to thank Vincent Kamodji from St.Louis, Tito Tikoure and Alex Koteureu from the Ile of Pines and John Ouetcho and Toku Atti from Touaourou.

On Maré I was helped by my colleagues and friends Wassissi Konyi and Davel Cawa. I would also like to thank the TA.PE.NE Association, especially the President, Kaiwatr Ngaiohni together with Léon Koce, Kaloi Cawidrone, Paris Kaloi, Alexandre Wamedjo, Guéro et Jean Wahéo.

On Lifou I would like to thank the Wiliamo-Passa family who made me feel very welcome. In the Losi district I am grateful to the *chefs* Kaloié-Gope and Wahnyamalla. I would like to thank the musicians of Kirikitr, especially Kass. I owe many thanks to the Nyikeine family and Edu Wamai of Drueulu and to all the dancers of the 'Association Culturelle of Wetr', especially to Obao.

To Ouvéa goes a special thankyou to my friend Jaques Adjouhniope and his family. My thanks are due to the women singers of the group from Muli, as well as to Kas Poulawa and the *seloo* singers of the Ohnyot *tribu*, especially to the *Vieux* Eloa. Many thanks are also due to the 'Association Kerisiana' and to the Lakon Yien group.

My thanks are due to the staff of the A.D.C.K. : Marie-Claude Tjibaou, Octave Togna, Emanuel Kasarherou, Jean-Pierre Deteix, and especially to those of the Médiathèque : Odile, Sophie, Nathalie, Wadrussa, Alidi, Suzanne, Anitâ and Auguste who ensured that I was able to use the facilities so easily. My thanks are due to all the staff of the A.D.C.K. who ensured a pleasant and efficient working atmosphere : Linda, Brigitte, Vincent, Jojo, Jean-Baptiste, Philippe, Denise, Hervé, Jean-Marc, Frank, Frank-Eric, Rémy, Melchior, Charles, Marie-Paule, Danielle, Marie-Claire, Boniface, Léa, Laurent. I would like to thank the ethnologist Roger Boulay for his great help and for sharing his opinions with me so freely.

I would like to thank Stephane Herby of Synapse for his generosity in sharing his computer knowledge with me throughout the work and for the kindness and patience he has shown in dealing with the complexities of the final text. It has also been a pleasure to work with Morgan Tiphagne of Synapse to arrange the Labanotation for the computer.

I would like to thank the directors of the various museums and libraries who have allowed me access to their collections : Christian Kaufmann (Ethnographical Museum in Basel), Emanuel Kasarherou (Musée Territorial de Nouvelle-Calédonie in Nouméa), Roger Boulay (Musée des Arts d'Afrique et d'Océanie in Paris), Francois Borel (Musée d'Ethnographie in Neuchâtel (Switzerland), René Fuerst (Musée d'Ethnographie in Geneva). I would also like to thank the staff of the Cambridge University Library for sending the A.D.C.K. a copy of their Montague manuscripts.

I would like to thank Laurent Aubert and Christian Oestreicher of the 'Archives internationales de musique populaire' in Geneva for their kindness and expertise in the way in which they have dealt with the production of the CD that accompanies this book.

To Richard Moyle, Auckland, I am grateful for his freely shared opinions and advice as well as for his kindness in having me to stay with him during the research period at the Auckland University Library.

I would also like to thank here my friend Peter Crowe, for his editorial help and for sharing his experience as an ethnomusicologist in Vanuatu. I thank Barbara Smith of Honolulu and Don Niles of Port Moresby, for their interest in my work.

I would like to thank Alban Bensa and Jean-Claude Rivierre in Paris and Chris Corne and Jim Hollyman in Auckland, for helpful discussions and for answering my questions, often by mail.

For their moral support and discussions I am most grateful to the members of our small group of researchers in Anthropology, in New Caledonia : Patrice Godin, Christine Salomon-Nékiriai, Marie-Héléne Teulière-Preston, Louis Mapou, Christophe Sand and, with a very special thankyou, Lisette Babois.

NOTES

A note on the south of the *Grande Terre*

Of the 330 odd Kanak *tribus* today, only 30 or so are found in the south of the *Grande Terre* including those on the Isle of Pines. Most of New Caledonia's ultrabasic rocks are to be found in the south of the *Grande Terre* and the resulting so-called mineral soils are infertile and even toxic as far as traditional Kanak cultivation of staple food-stuffs is concerned. *Tribus* are generally found along the coastal areas and on the plains outside the mineral regions. During its prehistory the south seems to have been lightly populated and frequently people from the Loyalty Islands, particularly Maré, and even further afield had strong sea links with the coastal population. After European contact, once Nouméa was decided on as the capital in 1854, the full brunt of colonisation was experienced in the area where there was the least room for change and expansion. Post contact literary sources tell us nothing of the dance and music situation in the south of the *Grande Terre*. Today the south of the *Grande Terre* provides few clues to its traditional past. The truly *Grande Terre* people have been quite uprooted and may even be largely gone. The *tribus* with strong Loyalty Island links, in a more favorable position to defend their culture, especially on the Isle of Pines, have survived. Their dances and music reflect their participation in exchange with the Loyalty Islands.

Terms used in the study

The use of the word Kanak

The Kanak movement for political independence and cultural development that surfaced at the beginning of the1970s chose the word 'kanak' as their term for the Melanesian population of the *Grande Terre* and the Loyalty Islands. The term 'kanak' originates from the Hawai'ian word, kanaka, meaning 'man'. 19th century sailors and others since, have used this term in a pejorative way.

The French administration used the spelling 'Canaque' to refer to the Melanesian populations of New Caledonia and the New Hebrides (today Vanuatu). To demonstrate, in a symbolic way, its separation from French culture, the Kanak movement for independence adopted the bislama spelling 'kanak' which has neither an initial capital nor a plural ending. However, to make for clarity in English (which lacks, for example, a plural definite article) the plural will be indicated by the ending 's'. The use of a capital K in English seems called for because English usage demands an initial capital for all countries and peoples, a status which the translation can hardly deny the Kanaks.

The spelling of Kanak words and names

When using names and words in one of the Kanak languages, the spelling as given in the existing dictionaries will be used without taking into account any dialects within the same language. For words not found in these dictionaries, linguistic specialists have been asked for help with the spelling. The dictionaries used are the following : Belep : Dubois (1974); Nyâlayu : Ozanne-Rivierre/Mazaudon (1986); Jawe, Nemi, Fwâi, Pije : Haudricourt/Ozanne-Rivierre (1982); Cèmuhî : Rivierre (1994); Paicî : Rivierre (1983); Ajië : Leenhardt (1935); Xârâcùù : Moyse-Faurie/Nechero-Joredie (1986); Isle of Pines : Dubois (undated); Maré : Dubois (1969/1980); Drehu : Sam (1995); Fagauvea : Hollyman (1987); Iaai : Ozanne-Rivierre (1984).

Geographical names

New Caledonia, like all the Melanesian countries, is multilingual and there exist many different names and pronunciations for one geographical locality. To avoid confusion the spelling of geographical locations will follow the IGN (Institut Géographique National) maps of New Caledonia. However, well-established English names will also be used : New Caledonia, Loyalty Islands or Loyalties, Isle of Pines etc. There is no official name for the main island of New Caledonia but it is referred to locally, and by French authors, as the 'Grande Terre' which will be used here.

Dance notation

Today two dance notation systems are widely used by ethnochoreologists : the Benesh[1] movement notation system, developed by the British couple Rudolf and Joan Benesh (1956 and1977) and the Labanotation system developed by the Hungarian, Rudolf von Laban[2].

Both systems enable an experienced user to notate body movements in detail. The Labanotation system will be used in the present study because it was accepted as the official dance notation for the ICTM[3] and most researchers of Pacific dancing now use it.

Compared with complexities of Hawai'ian Hula dance and Indian or Indonesian court dances, Kanak dance consists of simple basic dance motions. Positions of head, hands and fingers are in general undefined as are the exact position of ankles. There is a difference in quality of performance from one group to another and one group may present a dance with more precision than another. In cases where synchronised motions were performed in such a rough way that the movement which they were approximating was far from obvious, and if further information was not available from informants, all the dancers were observed but only the clearest motions were notated.

[1] Rudolf Benesh (1916 - 1975) was born in London. He was educated in art and music, but was no dancer himself. In 1949 he married Joan who had studied ballet and joined the Royal Opera Company in 1950. The Benesh couple copyrighted the Benesh Movement Notation in 1957 and founded the Institute of Choreology in 1963.

[2] Rudolf von Laban (1879-1958), was an autodidactical dancer and a ballet master. He is said to be the intellectual father of European modern dance. In his reflexions and meditations on dancing, referring especially to the ballets of the 20s and 30s, he put forward not only a dance notation system but also an entire theory on human movements. His method of notating human movements, now called Labanotation, was outlined in his Kinetographie Laban (1928), but the detailed tutor of how to use this system was not published until 1973 by his scholar Ann - Guest Hutchinson.

[3] ICTM : International Council for Traditional Music, the World Organization (UNESCO 'C') for the Study, Practice, and Documentation of Music, including Dance and other Performing Arts.

Some explanatory notes on Labanotation

Labanotation or Kinetography Laban, is a system of recording all forms of human movements. For readers unfamiliar with the system a brief note is given here.

In Labanotation the vertical notation staff corresponds to the normal verticality of the dancer's body in ordinary stance and locomotion. Placement of movement indications on the staff shows which part of the body executes the movement (adapted from Hutchinson [1954/1973]).

Vertical notation staff

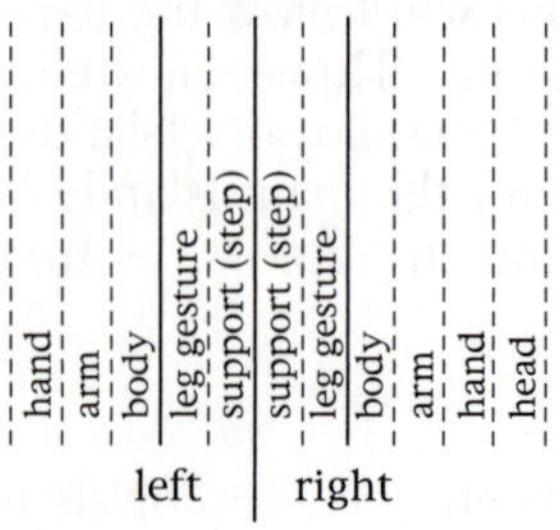

Three levels are distinguished by the different shading of the symbols.

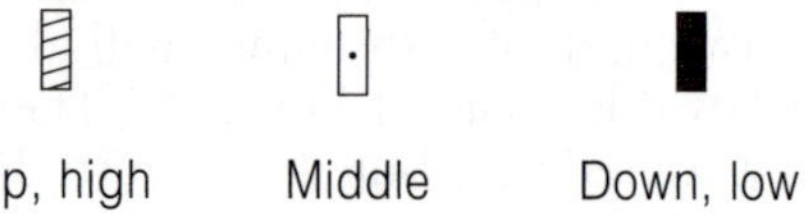

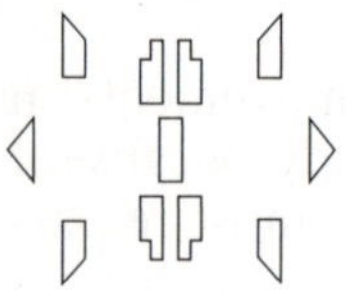

Direction of the body parts is indicated by the shape of the symbols.

The following body signs are used in this study :

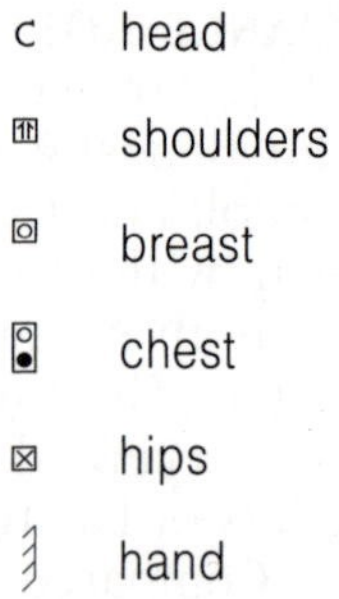

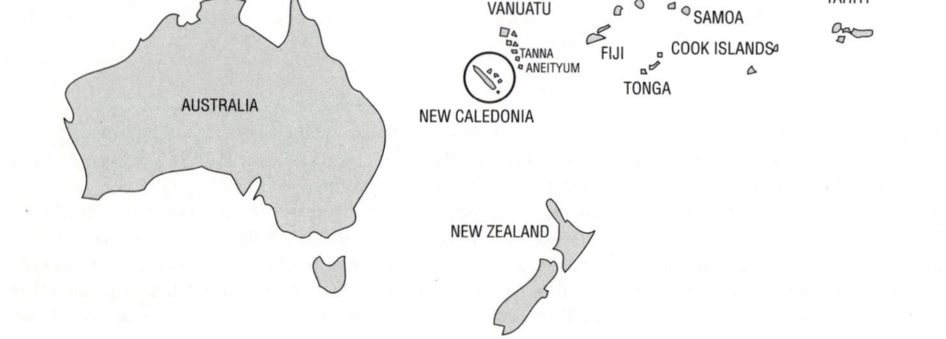

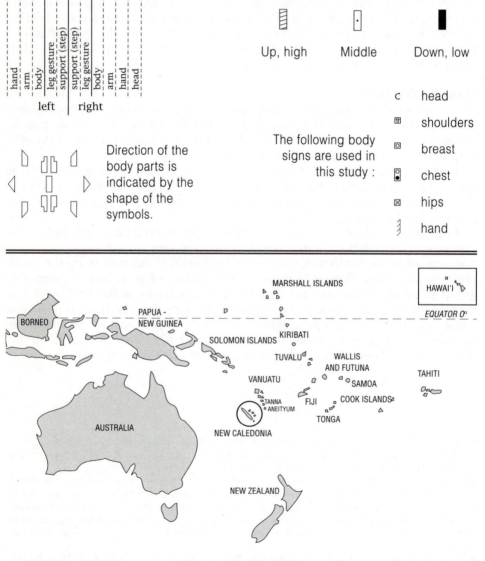

Map of the South Pacific showing the position of New Caledonia

INTRODUCTION

KANAK DANCE AND MUSIC AFTER 150 TURBULENT YEARS

Sounds which made up the aural world of ancient Oceanic societies : the roaring of the sea, the whispering of leaves in the wind, the crackle of fires, the birds, the insects, winds, rains, hurricanes, trees crashing down, floods. That world may not have seemed quiet to those who lived in it, but probably would to modern urban people who are constantly assailed by noise, especially by that of machines even inside the home. It can be difficult for urbanised folk to imagine a world where the daily sounds are those of nature and of the small noises of human work and voices. That ancient Kanak and Oceanic aural world was, nevertheless, sometimes interrupted by the sounds of huge ceremonies.

It is clear that these ceremonies, named *pilous-pilous* or *pilous* by the first French missionaries, had great importance in Kanak life, and that they were the most tremendous acoustic events to be heard in that world. The beating of bark-clappers and the rich thud of bamboo stamping-tubes were combined with part-songs by two singers, accompanied by the shouting, cries and whistles of hundreds of dancers. All this must have left an indelible mark on the aural sensations of the participants. After such ceremonies, that world returned to the sounds of nature. Today the Kanak aural world has entirely changed. People are used to the noises of cars and machines, to the wonders of modernisation, and even to those living in rural areas the presence of machine noises is so prevalent that the sounds of the seas and forests may now seem dulled. Before studying the lost acoustic world of the old Kanaks, it is worth making an effort to empathise with the time when natural sounds predominated in New Caledonia, to listen intently and to experience the sensations induced by the stamping of bamboos, the hissing of dancers and the shy sounds of the Kanak reed flute. How physical it was! And how emotional! It is in imagining the original aural world that an idea of the power and effect of the sounds which reigned during an enormous *pilou-pilou* can be appreciated.

What has happened in the last 150 years to change the Kanak world so much that to many young Kanaks today the songs of their ancestors are unfamiliar? Of the changes brought about by colonisation, many were directly responsible for the modification or abandonment of traditional values and cultural expressions, especially in dance and music.

Depopulation : a human and cultural disaster

The German naturalists, Reinhold and Georg Forster (father and son), who accompanied Captain James Cook on his second Pacific voyage in 1774, estimated the population of the *Grande Terre* at about 50.000 people. They spent only a few days on land, in the region of Balade, so their estimation could only be very approximate.

Christophe Sand, archaeologist at the Musée Territorial de Nouvelle-Calédonie, Nouméa, suggests that the population of the *Grande Terre*, in the mid-18th century (just before Cook's 'discovery'), was much higher than Georg Forster estimated. The hypothesis is based on the number of datable taro gardens in use at the time, still detectable in enough places for a viable extrapolation to be made. These gardens would have nourished far more than 50.000 people. There was a great deal of foodstuff exchange but no exportation and the total production was used for local consumption. In addition, some taro gardens were set in mountainous zones, difficult of access, implying a lack of space in the more accessible regions, which is taken to indicate population pressure (Christophe Sand pers. comm.).

Missionaries and officials estimated the population of the *Grande Terre* at between 30.000 and 70.000 for the period between 1840 and 1870 (Sand 1995:300). This was followed by the first official census of 1886, in which the figure was 26.000, based on information from *grand chefs* and including only the population living in tribal reservations. Shineberg (1983:40) corrects the figures and gives an estimation of 37.000 as the total Kanak population of the *Grande Terre*. The census of 1921 revealed that the population was down to 16.194 (the figure given in Sarasin❶ (1929:22), who obtained it from M. Leenhardt); here again, only the reservation population was counted. Christiane Kasarherou (1991:104 [unpubl.]) gives some 16.800 as the total Kanak population of that year and Shineberg (1983:41) gives 27.100 for whole of New Caledonia, including the Loyalty Islands. 1921 was the year with the lowest recorded figure for the size of the Kanak population.

The fall in population figures during the period 1850-1920 was so acute that many authors of the period feared that the Kanaks would soon become extinct (Sarasin 1929:22). When Pastor Maurice Leenhardt❷ arrived in 1902, the mayor of Nouméa asked him : "What are you going to do here? In ten years time there will be no more natives"❸ (Tchoeaoua 1982:45). The situation

❶ The Swiss, Fritz Sarasin (1859-1942), an independent and broadly educated naturalist and ethnographer had carried out research in Ceylon (Sri Lanka) and Sulawesi (Celebes). He arrived in New Caledonia in 1911 with Jean Roux, a Swiss zoologist, and spent 15 months travelling on the *Grande Terre* and the Loyalty Islands, collecting data and artefacts, which are now in the Museum für Völkerkunde (Ethnographical Museum) at Basel, Switzerland.

❷ Maurice Leenhardt (1878-1954) arrived in New Caledonia in 1902 as a French Protestant missionary, founding the Do Néva school at Houaïlou. Besides his activities as a missionary, he did extensive ethnological research. On his return to Paris, he published many books and articles and taught ethnology. Maurice Leenhardt has been called the Kanaks' ethnologist.

❸ "Que venez-vous faire ici? Dans dix ans, il n'y aura plus de Canaques".

at that period was so serious that Archambault (1908) saw the need to publish an article entitled "Sur les chances de durée de la race canaque" (Concerning the likelihood of survival of the Canaque race). Similar fears were expressed about many Oceanic societies, bearing in mind the most notorious case, that of the Tasmanian Aborigines, where an entire people had been lost. Many reasons have been put forward as to why populations decreased : epidemics of diseases against which natives of the Pacific had no immunity (for example, measles, influenza, tuberculosis), loss of morale, confiscation of traditional lands, the introduction of alcohol and firearms, and so on. The process may have started with diseases brought to New Caledonia around 1800 by European explorers, whalers, sandalwood traders and other adventurers.

In missionary records of the mid-19th century, there are reports that whole villages appeared to have been suddenly abandoned (Rouvray 1946:112) without preparations to leave : a sign of the sudden ravages of an epidemic. One reason for the first attack on a Marist station at Balade was that the Kanaks accused the missionaries of having brought a current epidemic (Monfat 1925:167). The worst of the diseases were, according Sarasin (1929:30), tuberculosis and leprosy. Tuberculosis was prevalent in New Caledonia before colonisation, probably introduced by seamen in the 1840s (C. Kasarherou 1991:261 [unpubl.]). Leprosy probably appeared after the arrival of Tonkinese indentured labour in the 1860s, certainly by 1889 cases of leprosy were to be found in almost every *tribu* (C. Kasarherou 1991:252 [unpubl.]).

The introduction of alcohol had a deadly impact on the autochthonous population and Pastor Maurice Leenhardt fought stalwartly against alcohol abuse. Certainly with the pressure of alcohol, and the alienation of land to the colons, Kanak morale was undermined. Lambert (1900/1985:250) and Sarasin (1929:24) say that many of the women indicated, around 1900, that they did not want to have any more children. Again, according to Sarasin (1929:22) the terrible revenge taken by the colonial administration after the insurrection of 1878 was another significant cause of the depopulation of a large area of the *Grande Terre.*

Taking 100.000 as the Kanak population figure on the *Grande Terre* at the time of Cook's arrival[1], and the official census of 1921 recorded a Kanak population of some 17.000, there was a population fall of about 80 per cent. This is not as brutal a fall as occurred on some other Pacific islands, for example, Tahiti, the Marquesas or Vanuatu (Rallu 1990) but nevertheless during this period, only one in five Kanaks had a successor.

Many cultural elements were lost as the population fell. In New Caledonia, as in many regions of the Pacific, most dances and music are personal property to be passed on within a family or lineage. A family wiped out in an epidemic had no time to hand on the music or the dance to someone else. Assuming the same rate of loss for culture as for population, the implication is that by the 1920s only 20 % of the original repertoire of Kanak dance and music had survived on the *Grande Terre.* This does not allow for the possibilities of regeneration and fresh creation on the basis of key cultural elements for example the revival of the Kanak flute (see p.38) or the work of the Wetr

[1] This figure lies in the middle of the various estimates available.

dance group (see p.232) in which the conditions for the maintenance of tradition as distinct from preservation and conservation play a significant role.

The situation on the Loyalty Islands was rather different. There was no expropriation or alienation of land, and the islands were declared 'reservations' from the time of French possession (1864-1865). Although alcohol and epidemics took their toll, the population drop was less than on the *Grande Terre.* The census statistics from 1860 to 1921 show a decline of about 37 % in the population on the Loyalty Islands from, 16.600 to 10.500, (C. Kasarherou 1991:56 [unpubl.]).

(A.D.C.K. collection)

People of the *tribu* ni-Bourail about 1890. Behind them is the conical roof of a *case,* judging from its height probably that of the *chef.*

Influences upon and changes within Kanak dance and music since the time of extra-Oceanian contact

Apart from explorers, such as La Pérouse (who may have visited New Caledonia before his ship sank off Vanikoro), d'Entrecasteaux and Dumont d'Urville, it was sandalwood traders and whalers who were the first Europeans after Cook to come to New Caledonia and the Loyalty Islands. Local and spontaneous exchanges of music and dances in such encounters may well have occurred, for example, by the exchange of musical instruments or by learning seafarers' songs (such as sea-shanties). This may in general have had little consequence for ongoing Kanak musical life. No precise information from these early days has been found. There is one studio photograph[1], probably taken in the 1880s, which shows a Kanak holding, possibly playing, an accordion.

Blackbirders called from 1863 onwards, ostensibly to hire labour for the sugar-cane plantations of Queensland and Fiji, but in fact often resorting to

[1] This photograph, bought from an Australian collector is in the archives of the New Caledonia Territorial Museum. From the objects in the photograph, it seems likely, that the picture was taken in the studio of the photographer Allan Hughan (see p.46) probably even by Hughan himself.

brutal kidnapping. The Kanaks who came back had probably had little contact with the world of the whites - and its music - during their sojourns. They lived with other Pacific Islanders, and probably had a kind of inter-Pacific exchange, thus contributing to the creation of Bislama (in Vanuatu) and other pidgins. It seems likely that musical interchange also took place.

The first verifiable and serious influence on Kanak dance and music came with the missionaries. There were two main churches which carried out missionary work in New Caledonia in the second half of the 19th century : the Protestant L.M.S. (London Missionary Society) was based, after a short period in the south of the *Grande Terre*, in the Loyalty Islands, whilst the Marist Brothers' Mission (French Catholic) settled in the north of the *Grande Terre*. Towards the end of the 19th century the L.M.S. was replaced by the 'Société des Missions Evangéliques de Paris', which had its headquarters at Houaïlou on the *Grande Terre*. The Marist Brothers' first station was founded at Balade in December 1843. The initial handful of French missionaries were for a time the only Europeans living permanently on the *Grande Terre*. For two years the Kanaks around the Balade mission station paid little attention to the newcomers. They did not go to the mission for services, but instead the missionaries went to the various *tribus* to bring their message, alternating amongst themselves for the visits, four times a week, armed with a crucifix and a bottle of holy water. A missionary would call at each household and attempt to explain the Christian message : first of all, how to make the sign of the cross, then trying to describe the phenomenon of the Christian god (possibly in Tahitian!) and ending with the singing of canticles (Rouvray 1946:85).

After only a few years some Kanaks learned to sing hymns. In 1844 a children's choir singing Christian canticles existed in the region of Balade (Rozier 1990:103). In 1845 *Père* Viard met a group of warriors in the Balade region. He persuaded them not to go to war but rather to sing canticles, and the good Father commented that "[they] then sing some canticles which he had already taught to the catechists of Balade"❶ (Rouvray 1946:86). The Christian Kanaks of Balade sang the litanies of the 'Holy Virgin' to welcome *Père* Rougeyron after his return from Futuna in 1846 (Rougeyron 1995:24). It took a very short time for the new music to find a place in Christian Kanak musical expression.

Meanwhile the Loyalty Islands were visited by Polynesian teachers from Rarotonga and Samoa, schooled by the L.M.S. in New Zealand. These teachers brought the portable wooden slit-gong (the *pate*) for use as a kind of church bell, as well as the (very English) game of cricket. The game in New Caledonia developed its own rules and forms. These introductions had, as will be shown, a significant impact on the dance and music of the Loyalties.

Acceptance of Christianity meant acceptance of monotheism, and this changed the whole living style of a baptised Kanak. He excluded himself as well as his family from the traditional social system in many ways. Baptised Kanaks could, for example, sing Christian songs even though they did not belong to a traditional singer's family, which may have seemed provocative to the keepers of customary traditions❷.

❶ "...[ils] chantent alors des cantiques que, déjà, il a appris aux catéchumènes de Balade".

❷ During the study it became apparent that joining a religious denomination by Kanaks can still be interpreted as a way to escape the obligations of the traditional customary system.

By the beginning of the 20th century most of the population on the *Grande Terre*, and all of the Loyalty Islanders had become nominal Christians. Leenhardt, in honouring the mission work of the *natas* (Loyalty Islander missionaries), says "In the evenings among the tribus, instead of three sad minor notes which mark the rhythm of the dances, one heard sung the alphabet, multiplication tables or hymns"❶ (Leenhardt 1922:44). A baptised Kanak explained to Leenhardt, "Since I stopped taking part in these *pilous*, which exhaust the tribu, I always have something for my family to eat and I can receive the men of God who come to see me"❷ (Leenhardt 1922:53).

Under French administration

One of the first acts of the French colonial administration was to send Tardy de Montravel with the ships 'Constantine' and 'Prony' to visit the east coast. He went from *tribu* to *tribu*, promulgating French law, and the *chefs* were invited to sign the sovereignty of New Caledonia over to Napoléon III (cf., the Treaty of Waitangi and Queen Victoria, New Zealand 1840). Each *chef* was then given a paper with the new laws written in French. In February 1854, for example, Montravel visited the *tribu* of Pouma (at Balade) where *Chef* Philippo Bouénone (his name indicates he had been baptised, and could well have had notions of English, possibly of French), signed away his sovereignty and received in return the code ('code des privations') of how to behave, containing 18 paragraphs. The first says that there should be no more killing or cannibalism. Paragraph 13 states : "All dancing at night is forbidden. Offenders will be punished by imprisonment for one to three days"❸ (cit. in Mariotti 1953:63 and Brou 1973/1992:101). This law may not have been fully implemented. No doubt the advice to forbid night-time dancing came from the Marist Brothers, at the time the only people in contact with the administration to have witnessed it, and for whom it contained the most horrible and morally offensive scenes (see p. 68).

A native reservation system had been set up in 1868, but after the insurrection of 1878, the French colonial government redefined the limits of the reservations on the *Grande Terre*. Those within a reservation were not allowed to go outside it, without official permission, which effectively caused the collapse of the *pilou-pilou* ceremonies, where people from a wide area came together (see p.56). These ceremonies were the principal occasions on which to present dances. Their extinction meant that the reasons for performing a great number of dances were gone, too. Leenhardt commented, "Under the sway of colonisation pilous became too heavy a burden, all-night dancing sustained by alcohol aggravated their mortal agony. And the society appeared to be dying out"❹ (Leenhardt 1937/1986:170). As the dances disappeared, so

❶ "Le soir, dans les tribus, au lieu de trois notes tristes et mineurs qui marquent le rythme des danses, l'on entendait chanter l'alphabet, la table de multiplication ou des cantiques".

❷ "Depuis que je ne m'occupe plus de ces pilous qui épuisent la tribu, j'ai toujours à manger pour ma famille, et je puis recevoir les hommes de Dieu qui viennent me visiter".

❸ "Toute danse nocturne est interdite. Les délinquants seront punis d'un emprisonnement de un à trois jours".

❹ "Sous l'emprise de la colonisation, les pilous sont devenus une entreprise trop lourde, les danses nocturnes soutenues par l'alcool ont exaspéré leur agonie. Et la société est apparue mourante".

did the songs that accompanied them. Once the school system reached the Kanaks from the 1870s, the prohibitions of singing Kanak songs and speaking Kanak languages were ensured by the teachers.

From the end of the 19th century it was French policy to import foreign labour for the nickel mines. Boatloads of indentured labourers came from Java, Japan, and other countries. These people formed their own ethnic communities and even today rarely intermingle with Kanaks. There appears to have been no direct influence from them on the music, dance and general creative activities of the Kanaks.

A contingent of Kanak soldiers went to join the French army for the 1914-18 war. They were at first volunteers, and as from 1916 were compensated for their service in the theatre of war. A Kanak evangelist led Christian hymns every evening on the troop-ship heading for Europe. Some of the songs composed for this historic event were in traditional style, for example *ayoii*, *ae-ae* (see p.122 and 134), and some were in the European musical style, having a structure similar to Christian songs (see *Mwà Véé* 1995 [11]: 10-40).

A group of Kanak people were invited to Paris for the Colonial Exhibition of 1931, at Vincennes. The members, from the *Grande Terre* and from each of the Loyalty Islands including *Grand Chef* Boula of Lifou with some of his people, were presented in Paris as 'cannibals' which filled the Kanaks with indignation (see *Mwà Véé* 1995[11]:10-40). However, the 'Insitut de Phonétique' took advantage of the Kanak presence in Paris to record some Kanak songs, including some traditional dance songs from the Loyalties and some speeches from the *Grande Terre*. Of the 12 items recorded, three (on discs 3973, 3974 and 3989) were in a European style. None of these recordings have been published (O'Reilly 1946:101-104).

In the late 1930s the German ethnologist Hans Nevermann wanted to record, in Nouméa, the singing of a group from Maré, which was rehearsing for a wedding. He found that all the songs had a strong European influence or were Christian songs. He asked the singers for one of the very old songs, but the group did not want to perform them : "Old songs are not good. Your compatriots might think that we are savages, when we are not. That's why it is better that we do not sing ancient songs"❶ (Nevermann 1942:142).

Another occasion to record Kanak songs in Paris occurred just after the second world war, on 8th November 1945. Some 15 Kanak soldiers of the 'Bataillon du Pacifique' were recorded in the 'Institut de Phonétique'. Jean-Albert Villard who analysed the songs musically, heard "perfect chords, dominant seventh chords, their inversions, the use of the sixth chord in parallel progression"❷ (Villard 1946:94). It was concluded that these songs "...show, in their harmonisation, very considerable European influences"❸ (O'Reilly 1946:107). From Villard's remarks, it look as if the soldiers chose to sing in a purely European style, possibly to impress French people with their adaption to European singing.

With the arrival of the American army in 1942, the Kanaks along with the

❶ "Alte Lieder sind nicht gut. Ihre Landsleute könnten dann denken, wir seien Wilde, und das sind wir nicht. Darum ist es besser, wir singen nichts Altes".

❷ "accords parfaits, accords de septième de dominante, leurs renversement; emploi de l'accord de sixte en déplacements parallèles".

❸ "...témoignent, dans leur harmonisation, de très notable influences européennes".

rest of the New Caledonians, were confronted with modern technology, and with unfamiliar activities in the construction of camps, aerodromes and port facilities. At times there were over 130.000 American soldiers in New Caledonia (an addition of more than twice the total pre-war population number). The Americans had their own music - swing, jazz, country and western - which was new to the Kanaks who found it fascinating. From then on Kanaks began to make or buy guitars and ukeleles and to copy foreign music, such as the American music of the day.

In the years after the second world war, true Kanak dances and songs slowly came to be tolerated by the colonial administration and the Catholic Church. Thus, after several decades of almost total silence, the first dance performances took place. At the time only a few elderly Kanaks remembered the traditional dances and songs, and they began to teach younger people. Many of the older people had been forced to leave their original homes in the period between 1900 and 1950 and had settled somewhere else, so that younger people in the 1950s were frequently unable to learn their own traditional dances. Furthermore, the few older people left could teach a dance only in the way that they remembered it. It is more than possible that the dances taught in the 1950s did not entirely correspond to their original forms. In general it can be said that the dances of today are strongly influenced by the personal styles of those who were available to teach traditional dancing after the second world war.

During these years, some Kanaks still felt uneasy about the sudden liberty to give traditional dance performances. In March 1949, Trans-Pacific Pictures Inc. of New York wanted to produce a short documentary film on the *tribu* of Couli, and Jean Mariotti was asked to help them to get a Kanak dance organised. The Kanaks had special permission from the Governor, and also from the 'Chef du Service des Affaires Indigènes' (Head of the Native Affaires Service), so that the *tribu* could perform a dance without suffering reprisals. The Kanaks, however, also had to be persuaded. "I have had to fight against both the fear of possible sanctions, and also, with many, against the fear of ridicule. At first the Canaques said to me with foreboding : 'We don't know how to dance any more, there is no more *pilou* amongst us'"❶ (Mariotti 1950:252).

The war in the Pacific, together with the stationing of foreign troops, also led to a new identification among the Kanaks as one of the peoples of the Pacific, even though they were under the French flag. Kanaks showed solidarity with other Pacific Islanders, which led to some neglect of their own culture, which, of course, was being weakly maintained at the time, in favour of a more 'pan-Pacific' culture. Kanaks were, for example, playing contemporary Tahitian songs with guitars and ukuleles and singing them without understanding the words. This 'pan-Pacific' movement had a major impact on dances, as will be described later on in this book.

Events of the year 1968 influenced not only Parisian students, but also the musical scene of Kanak youth. French protest songs were sung by young Kanaks at the same time as 'south seas' songs in Tahitian. The years following 1968, as Kanak graduates returned from France, marked the beginning of

❶ "J'ai eu à lutter à la fois contre la crainte de sanctions possibles, et aussi, chez beaucoup, contre la crainte de ridicule. Tout d'abord, les Canaques, pressentis, me dirent : 'Nous ne savons plus danser, il n'y a plus de pilou chez nous'".

Kanak political movements, with the main goals of a more socialistic infrastructure, and eventually a Kanak independence. Jean-Marie Tjibaou, the late charismatic Kanak leader, urged that the struggle for political independence needed to be based on an understanding of Kanak culture with its living expression going hand in hand with research into Kanak cultural roots. The slogan *Kanak et fier de l'être* (Kanak and proud of it) grew, in part, out of these ideas.

In 1972 a Kanak troupe went to the First South Pacific Festival of the Arts at Suva, Fiji, where contact was made with traditional Pacific cultures from 20 nations. Mutual exchanges with people from Malakula, Vanuatu, with Australian Aborigines, with francophones from Tahiti, and many other groups took place, and various models for the spectacular presentation of traditional cultures were observed. This was followed by the first significant modern presentation of Kanak culture, the festival 'Mélanésie 2000', in 1975. It featured Kanak dances, traditional songs and ceremonial speeches that had survived the preceding 125 years (see *Mwà Véé* 1995[10]:18-45). The political situation both in New Caledonia with the rise of the *indépendantistes*[1] and in France with the election of the socialists, gave great impetus to Kanak cultural activity especially to dance and music. Preparations for the 1984 Pacifc Arts Festival in Nouméa included much cultural activity in the *tribus*[2].

The same political and cultural movement gave rise to a new musical consciousness among young Kanaks. Some musicians, players of jazz, rock or reggae, held a meeting in 1986 to discuss the question of how to present authentic Kanak sounds with modern musical instruments. This meeting marked the birth of *kaneka*. The Kanak element in *kaneka* is found typically in the percussion group which is part of every *kaneka* band, while the songs are compositions in various international music styles. The *kaneka* of the Loyalties has more choral singing than that of the *Grande Terre*. All *kaneka* bands are electrically amplified, and all have a similar collection of musical instruments, besides the traditional Kanak percussion : a synthesiser of rudimentary quality (good ones are too expensive), electric guitars and rock-type drum kits. The song texts are not always in a Kanak language; many are in French and some even in English. The texts are often political, expressing the problems and anxieties of contemporary young Kanak people.

It is astonishing, after these 150 destructive years for Kanak culture, that there are still some traditional songs and dances in existence. The persistence of some elements of the ancient repertoire is probably due to those who deliberately kept up cultural life, possibly performing items in private, always in danger of being sent to prison if discovered by the colonial or religious police. The authenticity of the retained or re-created repertoire is open to question. It has to be asked if the dances still resemble the traditional versions, and if the songs are still performed as they used to be 150 turbulent years ago. The following study attempts to show in some detail if and how musical development has occurred.

[1] Supporter of political independence.

[2] The depth of the Kanak cultural involvement in the Festival was such that the French administration hesitated over a decision to cancel it and did so only at the last minute, after overseas visitors had begun to arrive.

CHAPTER 1

TRADITIONAL INSTRUMENTS OF THE *GRANDE TERRE* AND THE LOYALTY ISLANDS

The corpus of traditional Kanak musical instruments includes some unique items, unknown elsewhere in the Pacific. The total number of instruments, however, is somewhat less than in Northern Melanesia. Membranophones and chordophones seem never to have existed in New Caledonia. The absence of the skin drum, the typical Oceanic membranophone[1], from New Caledonia is not surprising, as it was not been reported from Vanuatu[2] (see Fischer 1958/1983:68 ; McLean 1994:4). The musical bow, a chordophone, has been reported in certain areas of Vanuatu, such as Ambrym (Fischer 1958/1983:72 ; McLean 1994:11), but appears to be unknown in New Caledonia[3].

Traditional Kanak musical instruments are either idiophones or aerophones, with the former predominant, usually found accompanying dances. Aerophones have become rare, and are either solo instruments or children's toys. During the past 150 years major changes have occurred. Some instruments have disappeared, while some others have been adopted. Esoteric knowledge surrounding the older instruments has largely been forgotten and the phenomenon of 'spirit voices', present in other parts of Melanesia (see Gourlay 1975), is no longer apparent. Musical instruments are treated as common objects, and no division into the sacred and profane is now possible.

This chapter is based on the Sachs and Hornbostel systematic classification (1914), which has the advantage of being the best available work. It is used as applied to Oceania by Fischer (1958) and translated into English by Holz-

[1] For example, the *kundu* of Papua New Guinea.

[2] Peter Crowe (pers. comm.) says that some drums known as *na olo* with woven pandanus membranes were referred to by informants on Maewo as having come from Tikopia, but were kept secret and used only for rites such as *qat baruqu*. Though not seen, Crowe has a recording (Crowe 1994:track 19[CD]).

[3] McLean (1994:11) says the distribution of the musical bow extends from New Guinea to New Caledonia. An exhaustive study of available literary sources (see bibliography) has failed to bring to light any report of the musical bow in New Caledonia and no hint of its existence has been found during fieldwork.

knecht (1983). McLean (1994), while still using the Sachs and Hornbostel terminology, groups Melanesian instruments according to function and diffusion, which is very useful in Northern Melanesia. The idiophones, which make up the larger group, are referred to first before the aerophones. There is no particular system to the order in which the different instruments are treated within each group.

Idiophones

EARLY IDIOPHONES

Significant published reports on idiophones date from the 1860s. They contain references to the use of various sorts of idiophones for accompanying dances. The older idiophones will be described first before turning to those in use today, so that traditional instruments can be identified, and possible modifications of the traditional corpus can be more clearly detected. The reliability of early descriptions is very variable, often so vague that possibilities of classification and comparison with the present situation are tenuous. An example of this comes from Lambert[1] (1900/1985:155), describing a bamboo or wood idiophone; "...the ouh-ouh...[sound] of the hollow bamboo which is made to vibrate upon a piece of sonorous wood as if it were a tom-tom"[2]. Is Lambert referring to a wooden slit-drum struck with bamboo beaters, or to a long bamboo, with its nodal cross-walls removed, stamped upon a wooden sounding-board? In either case, such an instrument is not played today.

Garnier[3] (1867/1990:206/52) mentions "hollow bamboo" ("bambou creux") which accompanied flute playing. It is unknown whether he was referring to a stamping-tube or a slit-drum but it is interesting as a unique statement about flutes accompanied by some sort of percussion. Michel (1885/1988:116) mentions "struck-bamboos" ("bambous frappés"), but her description could apply to many current idiophones, including a bamboo slit-drum or a bamboo stamping-tube. Opigez (cit. in Sarasin 1929:232) mentions "the beating of pieces of wood on parts of hollow trees..."[4], which could refer either to a slit-drum or to beating on a hollow tree-trunk. Vieillard and Deplanche[5] (1862:213) give the following description "... a board is placed horizontally on some stones. A person strikes this board with a kind of club..."[6]. Perhaps the authors saw an instrument which has not been mentioned elsewhere. Struck-

[1] Pierre Lambert (1822-1903) arrived in New Caledonia 1852 as a Marist Brothers' missionary. He spent his first years in the Belep Islands, founding the first mission station there. Later, he spent a period in Nouméa, then in the Isle of Pines, finally dying in New Caledonia. His book *Moeurs et superstitions des Néo-Calédoniens* ("Customs and superstitions of the New Caledonians") is probably the most comprehensive 19th century text on the Kanaks of the north of the *Grande Terre*.

[2] "...les ouh-ouh... du bambou creux, qu'ils font vibrer sur un bois sonore en guise de tam-tam".

[3] Jules Garnier (1839-1904) arrived in New Caledonia at the end of 1863, appointed as civil engineer at the St-Etienne mines. It was he who discovered the nickel deposits in New Caledonia. His travel reports include valuable information on the way of life of the Kanaks of the epoch.

[4] "das Schlagen von Hölzern auf Stücken hohler Bäume...".

[5] Eugène Vieillard (?-1896) was a surgeon of the French Navy, stationed twice on the *Grande Terre* : 1855-60 and 1860-67. He was also a botanist with an extensive knowledge of the flora of New Caledonia. Together with a second naval physician, Emile Deplanche, he wrote essays on New Caledonia which include ethnographic data.

[6] "... une planche est disposée horizontalement sur des pierres. Un individu frappe sur cette planche avec une espèce de casse-tête...".

bamboos have not been seen placed on stones today.

The half coconut-shell, said by Beaudet (1984:31) to be used on Ouvéa and on the Isle of Pines for clapping on the ground by singers and dancers, is not given in Dubois'[1] (undated) Kwenyii-French dictionary[2] but he does include an instrument called a *jokari* which was a concussion wooden clapper. Today *jokari* is the name of the struck-bamboo. Dubois (1984:215 and 1989:15) has described a lost idiophone from Maré. It was called *aloth* in Nengone[3] and was probably in use until a few decades ago. It was a hollowed dry calabash from the 'bottle gourd' (*Lagenaria vulgaris*[4]) with the top end cut, to be gently stamped on the ground. Dubois elsewhere (1969/1980:47) considered it a substitute for the bamboo stamping-tubes of the *Grande Terre*, used by the chorus conductor for the *kutera* dances (see p.179). The *aloth* was the principal instrument for accompanying dances at a time when the leaf-parcel (see p.26), which the conductors use today, was less important.

Hadfield[5] (1920:134) also mentions a stamping gourd with one end cut off, but does not identify the plant, nor give its name in Drehu[6]. An informant from the coastal region of Lifou said that in his *tribu* the *bua* dance was accompanied by an instrument called an *aloth*, but that it was made from a piece of a hollow tree. Socio-economic exchanges between Maré and Lifou have existed for a long time, and it is possible that these two apparently different *aloths* were localised developments from one source.

The ceremonial axes were not only prestige objects of the *grand chefs* but also idiophones. The top was a disc of highly polished jade, and the base had a covered half coconut-shell in which special stones or other magical objects could tumble about. When the axe was moved rhythmically in a speech it became a vessel-rattle (Leenhardt 1937/1986:55 ; E. Kasarherou 1990c:52). Their musical or rhetorical use has long ceased and all existing specimens are now in museums.

CONCUSSION BARK-CLAPPERS

Without doubt the most frequently mentioned instrument in early reports is the pair of concussion bark-clappers. On early incised bamboos[7] it is the only instrument shown in dance scenes. It is the most typical idiophone on the *Grande Terre*, evidently popular in traditional times, conspicuously in use in the centre and the north. It has been adopted by *kaneka* bands, and has become a frequent motif on T-shirts. It is a unique instrument and is a symbol for traditional Kanak music in general. This kind of concussion instrument is not found on any other Pacific island.

The instrument's pair of clappers are often of different sizes, shaped like long isosceles triangles and held at the pointed end. The larger of a pair has a perpendicular length of up to 50 cm and at the extremity a breadth of up to 30 cm. Among early reports Sarasin (1929:232) collected several specimens in

[1] For personal notes on Dubois see p. 174.

[2] Kwenyii is the Melanesian language spoken on the Isle of Pines.

[3] Nengone is the Melanesian language spoken on Maré.

[4] *Lagenaria vulgaris* is not a native plant of New Caledonia. It was first collected in 1855 when it was already common (MacKee 1985:48).

[5] For personal notes on Hadfield see p. 211.

[6] Drehu is the Melanesian language spoken on Lifou.

[7] Kanaks used to incise scenes of traditional daily life on pieces of bamboo, (see Boulay 1993).

the north of the *Grande Terre*, and cited the older collectors Glaumont and De Vaux. Vieillard and Deplanche (1862:212) were the first to describe the construction of the instrument. Garnier (1867/1990:67) gives a short description of the form of the instrument, adding that its sound (by onomatopoeia) may explain the origin of the term *pilou*. Leenhardt (1937/1986:169) says briefly : "... fig tree bark folded to make resonating boxes"[1]. Captain Kanappe (Courtis 1984:114) who saw them around 1880 at Hienghène refers to them as "... small sacks of banyan bark stuffed with dry grass..."[2]. Although La Hautière[3] (1869/1980:238) is referring to concussion bark-clappers when he says "....barks of coconut trees, dried, bent back on themselves and hermetically sealed"[4], his reference to the coconut palm and the sealing are not confirmed by any other writer and there was no similar finding in the field.

A popular *kaneka* band from Hienghène took up the instrument's name in their local language as their band-name Bwan-jep. Such is the popularity of this band that the expression *bwan-jep* is known all over New-Caledonia, and many young people have adopted it as a loan-term from a language not their own. Concussion bark-clappers are known in several widely spoken Kanak languages : *dööbwe* in Xârâcùù; *pédawa* in Ajië; *jepa* in Paicî; *bwajep* or *bwajé* in Cèmuhî; *duba* in Nyâlayu; *bwan-jep* in Fwâi, Nemi, Jawe and Pije. The word *bwan-jep* clearly indicates 'concussion' (*bwan*) in the horizontal way (*jep*) in contrast to the vertical movement of the stamping-tube (*bwan-thai*). The names *bwan-jep, jepa* and *dööbwe* may be onomatopoeic, inspired by the rhythms and timbres of the instrument which is played in a double-beat rhythmic pattern (see p. 115) where each pair of beats may represent the two syllables of these names. The individual beats of a pair are characterised by their timbres. While the names vary from region to region, the instrument is consistent in its form and size, playing and construction.

Construction

Vieillard and Deplanche (1862:212) offer an abridged description of the construction of the instrument, as they observed it in the 1860s, which does not entirely correspond with present practice. They give the name as "domboês", which indicates that their observations were made in the Xârâcùù-speaking area. Weiri (1986:15-18) briefly describes the construction and some sequences were filmed for *Jemââ* (Lalié 1992 [film]) and for *Ayoii-cada* (Dagneau 1995b [film]).

The making of bark-clappers was observed several times in the field and the following description comes from notes made at Tiéti (24. April 1993) where a group was getting ready to perform traditional songs at the forthcoming Mayday celebrations in Nouméa.

The bark of a fig-tree (*Ficus habrophylla*) is preferred, but if not available there are substitutes. Vieillard and Deplanche (1862:212) may be referring to *Hibiscus tiliaceus* while Opigez (cit. in Sarasin 1929:232) names the banyan. A tree is selected that has sufficient circumference to permit the excision of a

[1] "...les écorces de figuier rabattus pour former des caisses de résonance".

[2] "... petits sacs en écorce de banian bourrées d'herbe sèche...".

[3] Ulysse de La Hautière, accompanied Governor Guillain on his travels along the east coast of the *Grande Terre*, to verify the extent of the submission of the Kanaks in 1863.

[4] "...d'écorces de cocotiers, desséchées, repliées sur elles-mêmes et fermées hermétiquement".

(David Becker/A.D.C.K.1994, Nouméa)

Salomon Mayat from Hienghène playing the bark-clappers (*bwan-jep*, in Salomon's language fwâi). He is wearing a headdress made of a band of a coconut leaf base to which feathers from the big Notu Pigeon (*Ducula goliath*) are attached.

piece of bark 10-30 cm in width and 60-100 cm in length. The maker (usually the musician who will use the instrument) marks the measured rectangle with the tip of a bush-knife, cuts in, then slips the bush knife under the bark to prise the piece away. One such piece of fig-bark will make one clapper. The bark piece is wet with sap on its inner side and begins to roll inwards. It is taken to a fire, and there the middle part, which is where the fold will be, is made to lie flat by heating and drying, while the rest remains curled. The next step is to cut off the unneeded width in the curled area so that when the two halves come together and roll one over the other a convenient grip is made. After that, it is stuffed.

Fibre from the husk of the coconut fruit found between the shiny outer skin and the hard interior shell is preferred for the filling. Other material may be used as a substitute, such as dry leaves, dry grass, crushed newspaper, or bark from the *niaouli* tree (*Melaleuca quinquenervia*). Experience is needed to know how much material to insert, and where to place it. The clapper is tested by hand claps for its sonority, and when the musician is satisfied, it is closed up tightly. If it is not satisfactory the clapper will be re-opened and stuffing added or withdrawn in various places.

Strangely, the concussion bark-clappers examined by Sarasin (1929:232) appeared to him to have been hollow. He wrongly concluded "...this is necessary, for then they are able to give out a sound"❶. Sarasin's instruments were held together by cords going through holes in the instruments. Today a length of liana, or even a rubber band cut from a tyre's inner tube, may be wound around the clapper to keep it together, but most instruments do not need a band as the edges have rolled over each other and are giving adequate solidity. To assemble a pair of bark-clappers, the timbre is tested by hand slapping. Clappers with two contrasting sounds are chosen although when the pair is struck together the resulting sound is different again. A number of clappers are usually made at one time, and an experienced person will need 15 to 30 minutes to make a specimen. A relic of esoteric knowledge indicates that if the stuffing of a clapper includes magical stones or bones it will have an irresistible sound that will induce all who hear it to dance (Marie-Louise Ouindia pers.comm.).

Variations

Sarasin (1929:232) cites Glaumont's description of the concussion bark-clapper as a stick of wood coated with a piece of fabric and stuffed with straw, and declares this to be "certainly incorrect" ("sicher unrichtig"). Perhaps Glaumont observed a variation of the typical instrument, made for spontaneous performance when no standard specimens were to hand. One variation is made from the inflorescence axis of the so called 'agave' (or American aloe) plant (*Agave* or *Furcraea*). This instrument does not have a distinct name, but is referred to with the same term as the standard instrument for which it is temporarily a substitute. The interior of the 'agave' consists of long fibres and is rather soft. The construction is simple : a piece about 40 cm in length and 7 to 10 cm in diameter is stripped of its outer green bark and then cut to a thin end for the grip. When two such clappers are struck one on the other, the size of them makes little apparent acoustic difference. A casual variation is the use of common sandal-like footwear❷ made of rubber or plastic material which are simply taken off the feet and clapped together.

Playing techniques

The manner of clapping is individual, and many different ways may be observed. It takes considerable stamina to keep up the beating for a whole night as is usually necessary during a dance festival. The larger clapper may be held stationary and horizontal while the smaller one concusses on the downward movement. Musicians often change the hand holding the clapper

❶ "...das ist auch nötig, damit sie einen Klang von sich geben sollen".

❷ known as 'flip-flops' or 'thongs' or 'open sandals'.

Photo published in Lennier (1896:Planche VII)

Lennier gives the following caption : "Group of women, children and men, meeting for a feast (Pilou-Pilou) at Hienghène (New Caledonia)" ("Groupe de femmes, d'enfants et d'hommes, réunis pour une fête [Pilou-Pilou] à Hienghène [Nouvelle-Calédonie]"). The picture could have been taken in the 1880s. Most of the women are wearing traditional skirts and some are beating bark-clappers.

for relief. Sometimes a stick will be used instead of the smaller concussing bark-clappers. It is lighter and easier to handle, but lacks the typical sonority. A pair of standard concussion bark-clappers, used with vigour throughout a night, may be so worn by morning that it is thrown away.

Symbolism

There is some doubt about the existence of gender specificity in bark-clapper playing. The illustration in Garnier (1867/1990:58) (see p. 73) shows women beating clappers while men dance. This is corroborated by Patouillet from the same period (1873:177).Vermast (1902:35) refers to women playing them in the 1870s and a photograph taken in the Hienghène region ca. 1880s (Lennier 1896:plate VII) also shows only women playing the instrument. Leenhardt, too (1930/1980:52) in his male-female division of daily-life activities, ascribes the bark-clappers to the feminine side. However in the first decade of the 20th century in Bopope (centre of the *Grande Terre*), the instrument was being played by men and boys (Sarasin 1917:52) and on an incised bamboo probably from the late 19th century, in the Geneva collection, it can be seen that the bark-clappers are played by men (Dellenbach 1936:269). Recently Beaudet (1984:31) asserted that the instrument could be played only by men (or boys).

When asked about this informants gave various replies. The dance-leader of the *cèto* dance, from the region between Koné and Poyes, Mme Marie Louise

Ouindia (Mani) gave a customary interpretation. The *cèto*❶ dance is one of the very few remaining traditional female dances on the *Grande Terre*, in which women do indeed (still) play the bark-clappers. Mme Ouindia said that in ancient (probably mythical) times, women struck their breasts together, thereby making a comparison with the form of the bark-clapper. These days, the instrument may be played by either men or women, but most often by men to accompany singing and dancing of either mixed-sex or gender-specific groups.

There is a legend about the origin of the instrument reported by Beaudet (1984:32) in which the clappers in the region of Canala were formerly made with the shells of large crabs. The name *dööbwe* (which is the name of the crab and the name of the instrument) refers to this origin.

Diffusion

Bark clappers are found in the centre and north of the *Grande Terre*. Only Bourgey (cit. in Sarasin 1929:232) reports seeing them in the south. They are not present in the Loyalty Islands, although suitable trees that could provide the bark do indeed grow there. Overall in Oceania there are many varieties of concussion idiophones, such as the use of dance paddles on Wallis Island or the clap-sticks and boomerangs of Australia. The importance of the concussion bark-clapper is its originality, nothing quite comparable is to be found outside the *Grande Terre*. No information is available as to whether the instrument was invented there or whether it was imported long ago and its use subsequently discontinued except in New Caledonia.

Bamboo stamping-tubes (stamping-bamboos)

The bamboo stamping-tube (stamping-bamboo) is today the second most commonly found Kanak idiophone, usually played as a complementary instrument to the bark-clappers. Frequently, only these two instruments accompany dances on the *Grande Terre*.

The instrument is made from a section of a bamboo trunk from 100 to 140 cm in length, while diameters vary from 5 to 25 cm. There are few precise descriptions in early reports. Besides Patouillet (1873:177), Vieillard and Deplanche (1862:213) mention "striking the ground with bamboo trunks..."❷, and Durand (1900:501) "... to beat the soil with bamboos..."❸. Sarasin (1929:232) collected two stamping-tubes. He gives their measurements, and refers to a specimen mentioned by Edge-Partington (1895:65+68). Names for the instrument are seldom specified beyond the local word for bamboo as a plant. In Xârâcùù the name for bamboo as a plant is different from the name given to the instrument, *wau*. These names for the instrument have been collected : *tee wau* in Aijë; *jö* in Paicî; *ju-o* in Cèmuhî; *byavic* or *bwan thai* in Pije, Fwâi and Nemi; *go* in Jawe. Most people simply use the French name *bambou*.

Construction

Only the small reed-like *Greslania* genus of bamboos (*Gramineae; Bambuseae*) is native to New Caledonia (Schmidt 1981/1992:140). Of the

❶ *cèto* is the Cèmuhî spelling; *céto* is the Paicî spelling.

❷ "... frappant la terre avec des troncs de bambous...".

❸ "... battre le sol de bambous...".

A musician from Hienghène playing the stamping-bamboo at the first concert of 'Kanak classical music' at the Territorial Museum in Nouméa in June1994.

introduced giant bamboos only one is used to make stamping-tubes. This bamboo is characterised by its long internodes with thin elastic walls, allowing the tubes to vibrate when stamped on the ground❶. As an instrument the property of elasticity means both that it will not split with repeated stamping and that resonance is enhanced. The following description of construction comes from observations of the Ti.Ga.❷ dance group, and of the musicians of the Ouarap *tribu* near Hienghène. No significant variation has been observed in its construction elsewhere.

To make the instrument, a straight piece of bamboo of the desired diameter is selected. The stem is cut off a short distance beneath a node with a bush knife. The length of a stamping-bamboo is decided by the length of its internodes. The instrument usually consists of three internodes, but when possible those of two are preferred. At the upper end the bamboo piece is cut just below the third or fourth node, in order to leave an internode as long as possible at the top. All the cross-walls at the nodes, except the bottom one, are pierced with a hard wooden rod. It is not necessary to remove the wall completely, sometimes only the centre of the wall is pierced. The part of the internode left below the bottom node is filled with a piece of *niaouli* (*Melaleuca quinquenervia*) bark, to protect the last nodal cross-wall, when the tube is stamped on the ground. A stamping-tube may split and crack when

❶ The elasticity also makes it sought after for fishing-rods (in Paicî this variety is called *jö iri pwô* "bamboo for fishing").

❷ The cultural association Ti.Ga., near Poindimié, derived its name from the first two letters of the names of the two *tribus*, Tioumidou and Galilée, to which the members belong.

A scene of a round-dance during the 'Pwolu Jenaa' dance festival in 1994. A boy is holding a stamping-bamboo with both hands, stamping it on the ground after each step. The dancer in front of him adds whistling to the *rythme du pilou*. Many people have joined in the dance.

used during a long night so that new instruments are often made before a performance.

The dancers of the Ti.Ga. group always make their stamping-tubes in pairs and they are played in pairs. A critical acoustic decision is needed to decide which two tubes should be played together. In general the two tubes of a pair are of unequal size and the acoustic difference is more in the timbre than in the pitch. The longer tube gives a more rounded sound than the shorter tube which has a sharper tone.

Playing technique

The bamboo stamping-tube is usually held with both hands, less frequently with one tube in each hand. The tube can be stamped against the soil, or it is dropped from a distance of 20 to 30 cm above the ground. The most perfect 'dull' sound is obtained when the soil is slightly wet. Sometimes the musician holds his free hand with the open palm facing downwards above the tube. When the tube is lifted up, it stamps gently on the palm of this hand and gives a second, lower sound more or less on the offbeat. In some performances of the round-dance dancers themselves may play a stamping-tube while walking. In this case a dancer holds the tube with both hands in front of him and stamps the tube after each step.

Variations

Today on the Loyalty Islands stamping-tubes of aluminium or polyester are sometimes used. The sound of such stamping-tubes is different from that made by the bamboo tubes. The particular sound quality of the aluminium stamping-tube can be heard on track 21 of Ammann (1997 [CD]), and compared with that of the bamboo stamping-tube on, for example, track 7.

Symbolism

There is little information in the early reports about which gender was playing the instrument. Around the year 1911 it was played by women and boys in the north of the *Grande Terre*, according to Sarasin (1929:232). This is confirmed at the end of the 19th century by Durand (1900:501) who says that the instrument was played by women "...then the women crouch down together in a group and begin to strike the ground with hollow bamboo..."❶. In Leenhardt's (1937/1986:52) list in which he separates the activities of daily life into either men's or women's duties, the stamping-tube is not mentioned. Today the bark-clapper and the stamping-bamboo are, as described by Patouillet (1873:205) over a hundred years ago, the only instruments to accompany many dances. The rule that the stamping-tubes are to be played in pairs is often ignored today.

In New Caledonia, the stamping-tube may not be as old as the concussion bark-clapper. It lacks specific names, while the concussion clappers have a rich local nomenclature. The stamping-tubes are not shown in 19th century engravings of dance scenes, although they are described in the literature of the period. They were perhaps rarer than the bark-clappers. The same considerations have to be taken into account for the age of the struck-bamboo and the bamboo slit-drum (see below).

Diffusion

There are no early reports of the instrument on the Loyalty Islands where the bamboo used to make it is not found. Loyalty Islanders have to use a substitute material or import the instruments. Leenhardt (1946:452 note 7) reports the existence of imported instruments on the Loyalty Islands and Guiart (1953:4) saw them at the beginning of the 1950s on Ouvéa, where they were played by both men and women.

The stamping-tube was widely known in Melanesia and Polynesia. In Melanesia they exist in Vanuatu on East-Santo and on Ureparapara. On Ureparapara the bamboo tubes were stamped on a board covering a hole in the ground. Speiser gives a photograph (Speiser 1923/1990:plate 105 picture 5) of such an ensemble accompanied with small bamboo slit-drums. The 'Are'are of Malaita in the Solomon Islands have not only stamping-tubes of the same size as those from New Caledonia, but also a whole orchestra of small stamping-tubes which are tuned in relation to each other (Zemp 1972:7 and 1979 [film]). In Polynesia they were known on Samoa and Tonga (Moyle 1988:42) and the Marquesas (Moulin 1994:24). The size of the instruments varied from island to island. Today it is only played on the islands of Fiji and Hawai'i (Kaeppler 198O:144 ; Moyle 1990:24).

Slit-drums and struck-bamboos

In New Caledonia slit-drums and struck-bamboos are played in the same way and they are both used to accompany dances. Here they are presented together. Several forms of slit-drums made of either bamboo or wood exist in

❶ "...puis les popinés s'accroupirent en un groupe et se mirent à battre le sol de bambou creux...".

(David Becker/A.D.C.K.1994, Touho)

A dance group presenting their costumes and musical instruments, bark-clappers, bamboo stamping-tubes and a wooden slit-drum, at the 'Pwolu Jenaa' dance festival at Touho in 1994.

New Caledonia. All are of such a size that they can be transported. The wooden slit-drums are 40 to 50 cm long and 30 to 40 cm in diameter. The length of bamboo slit-drums varies greatly. Some are short, consisting of one or two internodes only, measuring around 40 cm, others are longer than 150 cm and consist of several internodes.

The groups using these instruments have no specific names for them. They may refer to the bamboo slit-drum and the struck-bamboo by using the generic name for bamboo in the same way as they do with bamboo stamping-tubes. The people who speak Fwâi refer to the instrument as *bwan-jep* which is primarily the name of the concussion bark-clapper. In the Nyâlayu language the wooden instrument is called *wouadu-a* which is a generic term that covers all percussion instruments. On Ouvéa the wooden slit-drum is called *patee* which may well indicate the instrument's origin (see below). The bamboo slit-drum is never clearly described in the literature of the 19th century. There are only some confusing statements about the *bambou creux* (see p.11) which could refer either to the stamping-tube or to the slit-drum.

Construction

No specific wood is needed to make the wooden slit-drum but part of the trunk of a coconut palm is often used. A piece of wood with a suitable diameter is cut to the required length; it is hollowed out with an axe and a chisel. The side walls of the hole are vertical without any widening to reduce wall thickness. The slit ends a few centimetres above the bottom of the drum. Wooden slit-drums are neither decorated nor polished.

The bamboo slit-drum and the struck-bamboo are made from the same sort

(David Becker/A.D.C.K.1994,Touho)

A dance group making music with stamping-bamboos and a slit-drum during their arrival at the 'Pwolu Jenaa' dance-ground.

of giant bamboo that is used to make the stamping-tubes. A length of stem is cut and usually both ends of the instruments are closed by a nodal cross-wall although there is no fixed rule. Struck-bamboos are not modified after they are cut out of the tree. The bamboo slit-drums have a rectangular slit made with a chisel or a knife cut into the internode and ending a few centimetres before the nodes at each side. slit-drums consisting of several internodes have a separate slit for each internode.

Playing Technique

The slit-drum and the struck-bamboo generally lie directly on the ground with musicians sitting behind them. Undecorated wooden drumsticks, 30 to 40 cm long and 3 to 4 cm in diameter are used to strike the drum not to stamp on it, as is done in northern Melanesia on the big wooden slit-drums.

Long bamboo slit-drums and long struck-bamboos can be played by two musicians together, either in the same rhythmic pattern or in complementary rhythms, each musician holding a drumstick in each hand. When these instruments are played while making an entrance for dances, the slit-drum may be held by two people walking while a musician strikes as he walks.

Variations

A mixed form, partly slit-drum, partly struck-bamboo, consisting of two internodes, only one of which has a slit is used by some groups. Wooden boxes played with sticks or cardboard boxes beaten with the hand are used as substitutes. Even an old oil barrel, covered with a piece of fabric to dampen the sound may be used for dance rehearsals. All these various forms are beaten in the same rhythm as the slit-drum and the struck-bamboo (see p.117).

Symbolism

The instruments are not decorated and there are no visible signs of symbols. Leenhardt does not mention the instruments in his list where he distinguishes between men's and women's duties. Today these instruments can be played by women but they are usually played by men.

Diffusion

The slit-drum and the struck-bamboo are used by the dance groups from Belep, Pouébo, Oubatche, Ouaré and Muli (Ouvéa), among others.

Bamboo slit-drums and struck-bamboos are widely known in Oceania. Bamboo slit-drums exist in isolated places along the north coast of New Guinea, in the Bismarck Archipelago, on the Solomon Islands and in Vanuatu (Fischer 1958/1983:17) ; on Polynesian outlier islands like Futuna in Vanuatu (A. Thomas/Takaroga 1992) as well as on Polynesian islands such as Samoa (Moyle 1988), the Cook Islands (Jonassen 1991) and others. The bamboo slit-drum and the struck-bamboo, or the idea of the instruments, may have come to New Caledonia from southern Vanuatu, or from Polynesia. On the *Grande Terre* bamboo slit-drums and struck-bamboos are well-established, while in the Loyalties the bamboo instruments have to be imported because of the absence of the bamboo plant.

New Caledonian wooden slit-drums are very different from those of Northern Melanesia. The New Caledonian ones are much smaller and without any decoration. Their origin does not lie in the huge Melanesian slit-drums which are not found even in southern Vanuatu, Efate marking the most southerly point where these slit-drums exist (Crowe 1995:24)[1].

There is a similarity in form between the New Caledonian slit-drums and the *pate*. The *pate*, from Rarotonga, was introduced by teachers of the London Missionary Society (L.M.S.) to Samoa between 1830 and 1870 (Moyle 1988:38). There it was first used as a substitute for a church bell[2], and later made its entry into dance music ensembles on Samoa. There are even sets of different sized *pate* playing together (Moyle 1988:40).

The expansion of the L.M.S. from Tahiti started in 1797 and reached Rarotonga in 1821, Samoa in 1830, southern Vanuatu in 1835 and the south of the *Grande Terre* and the Loyalty Islands at the beginning of the 1840s. The first Polynesian teachers who stayed at Kaaji on the Isle of Pines were the Samoans, Taniela and Noa. The first L.M.S. teachers in Touaourou in 1842 were the Rarotongan, Mataio, and (another) Taniela from Samoa. Two missionaries from Rarotonga reached Lifou from Maré in 1845 and finally Ouvéa in 1856 (Ta'unga cit. in Pisier 1980:42). The first Polynesian L.M.S. teachers introduced the habit of calling people to church using a drum and it seems likely that they would use one like that already in use in Samoa or Rarotonga. Ta'unga, one of the first Polynesian L.M.S. teachers in New Caledonia, wrote in his diary on the 24.7.1842 that he went to strike the drum to announce the beginning of worship (Ta'unga cit. in Pisier 1980:56).

Sarasin (1929:229) reports the usage of the slit-drum as a way of calling people to church in the first decade of the 20th century. The slit-drum is

[1] Codrington's (1891/1972:337) statement that vertical slit-drums exist in southern Vanuatu has not been confirmed.

[2] On Samoa slit-drum church bells were made of either wood or bamboo.

(Bouge collection in the Museum of Chartres, France, date unknown, published in Boulard [1992:59])

An engraving of a Lifou scene : three women are striking a slit-drum in a particular way probably to call the population to a Christian service. The way in which the instrument is being played and its position on a stand, are unknown today.

described from Lifou by Ray (cit. in Fischer 1958/1983:34) as imported and he states that it was a recent importation.

An old engraving, see above, shows a rather big slit-drum, judging from the picture about 130 cm long, placed on a wooden stand. It is struck by three women one of whom (possibly two but one of them is partly hidden) is holding a stick in one hand and is beating on the drum next to the slit. The third woman on the other side of the drum is holding a longer stick with the end reaching inside the drum and striking the drum on the inside. This way of striking the drum is not used today. Behind the drummers people are going into a building, very probably a church because there is light beaming out of it.

The slit-drum could have existed on Ouvéa before the arrival of the L.M.S. teachers. The Polynesian migration which reached the island in the 18th century may have brought it or the idea of it. If so, the instrument was also used to call the community to church. In the Iaai❶ language the drum is called *ut paate* and the church bell is called *paate*. In Drehu the church bell is called *pate* and even in the Protestant villages of the Paicî region on the *Grande Terre* the church bell is called *paaté*.

❶ Iaai is the Melanesian language spoken in the centre of Ouvéa.

Until a few decades ago the slit-drum was often played by a teams' supporters at a cricket match. As their team made runs the musicians struck the drum and several people started dancing. This is rather rare today and has been observed in the field only once. Cricket, brought by the L.M.S. missionaries, has had an important influence on Kanak dances (see p. 173).

Voyages were made frequently between the Loyalty Islands and the *Grande Terre* and the wooden slit-drum may have reached the *Grande Terre* by this route. The French Evangelical Church employed converted Loyalty Islanders on missions to the *Grande Terre.* These missionaries were called *natas* from a Nengone word meaning 'mature'. It seems very likely that the *natas*❶ would have brought the slit-drum with them unless it had already been introduced. In the Hienghène region wooden slit-drums were used not only to accompany cricket matches but also to accompany trade-dances (see p. 63) and sometimes even to accompany Christian religious songs, something that it would never have been possible to do with the concussion bark-clappers because they are too strongly associated with traditional Kanak music.

Palm spathes

This instrument from native palms (*Palmae : Arecoideae*) was common until the 1980s, but it is rarely played now, only a decade later. The instrument is mentioned in the literature of the second half of the 19th century : Patouillet (1873:205) says that it was the instrument which accompanied dances which were performed inside houses, Durand (1900:501) says that it was struck only by women, Michel (1885/1988:116) mentions the way of playing it and Leenhardt (1937/1986:26 and 1930/1980:152) says it accompanied the "sitting dances" ("dances assisses").

The instrument consists of the spathe a structure which encloses the young inflorescence of a palm tree and which drops to the ground later. It is used without any modification, except that it can be filled with dry grass. The instrument is called *pulijié* in Paicî and *kombara kimwâ* in Xârâcùù (Beaudet 1984:31). According to Beaudet the instrument was kept dry inside the house and then, on the evening it was to be used, it was exposed to dew so that it became damp and expanded.

The instrument is reported only from the *Grande Terre.* The trade-dances (see p. 61) carried on inside houses are not performed any more so that this use of the instrument has gone, but the instrument has been observed being played as an accompaniment to *ae-ae* singing, for example in the Gohapin *tribu.* The musician, in this case a woman, was sitting on the ground with the instrument across her outstretched legs. She struck on the instrument with the finger tip of one hand, and scratched with the fingers of the other hand. Exactly the same way of playing was described by Patouillet (1873:205) but Michel (1885/1988:116) mentions only the friction of the instrument while Leenhardt (1930/1980:152) just mentions striking the instrument. There may have been several ways of playing it, perhaps with regional differences too. Striking the palm spathe with two sticks was seen quite often in the in the course of this study. Such a way of playing the instrument is not reported in the literature. The instrument can be played while walking, for example to accompany the

❶ *Nata* - mature, ripe : a mature man or a ripe fruit. It was wrongly interpreted by Garrett (1992:111) who sees its origin in *uanata* - telling a story.

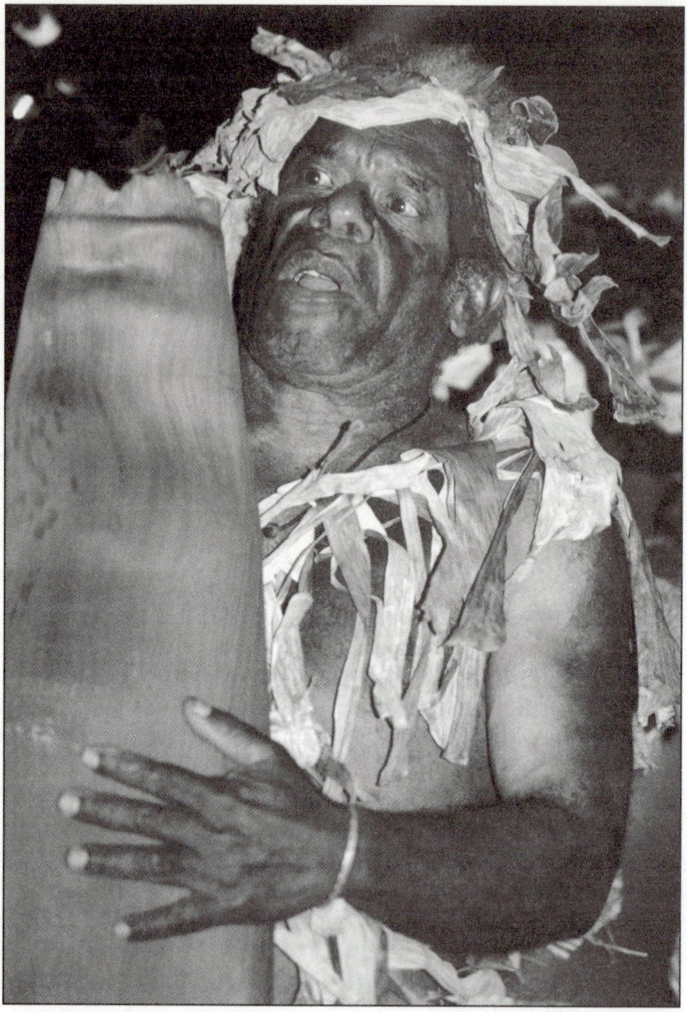

A singer from Moméa accompanying his song by tapping and scratching on a leaf base from a palm crownshaft. This is a possible alternative instrument to the palm spathe.

ae-ae songs for the entry of a group of dancers on to the dance-ground; a shoulder strap is made by attaching a piece of string to the instrument so that the musician can walk while playing it.

Leaf parcels

The leaf parcel (see front cover) is the typical musical instrument of the Loyalty Islands. It is used in most of the choral singing which accompanies mimetic dances on the Loyalty Islands. The leaf parcel consists of coconut fibres covered by leaves held together by a string wound around it.

It is disc-shaped 20 to 30 cm in diameter and 10 to 15 cm thick. The leaf parcel is known on all four inhabited Loyalty Islands.

The names of the instrument reflect the ideas associated with 'bringing together' or 'being struck'. It is called *ae-be* : *be* 'to strike' in Nengone (Maré) ; *itra pë* : *itra* 'accumulation' in Drehu (Lifou) ; *bwinj-bet* : *bwin* 'accumulation in Iaai (Ouvéa). The Fagauvea speaking population on Ouvéa refer to it by the Iaai name.

Construction

The following description of the construction of a leaf parcel corresponds exactly to the procedure observed at Mu, Lifou in 1994 and filmed by Whaap and Ravel (1994c [film]), other observations of construction made during the study showed no essential differences.

The large (up to 20 cm diameter) heart-shaped leaves of the tree *Macaranga vedeliana (*called *be*, *ye-be* or *eruma* in Nengone, *elu* in Drehu and *be* in Iaai) are used to envelop fibres from the mature coconut fruit. The fibres are found between the outer brown skin and the hard shell surrounding the seed, and make up the filling of the parcel. The construction is not limited to these plants, other plants giving material with similar qualities can also be used. To make the string to hold the instrument in shape, the upper layer of the midrib of a coconut frond is sliced off. This thin layer is sliced longitudinally into narrow strips using the finger nails. The strips are attached one to the other to form a long string. The string is laid out on the floor. The leaves, largely overlapping one another, are placed over the string making a disc-shape of 40 - 50 cm diameter so that the centre of the disc lies on the middle of the string. The coconut fibres which are arranged in a loose, round pile of about 30 cm in diameter are placed on top in the middle of the leaves. The leaves at the periphery are bent to wrap around the pile. More leaves are added on top so that the pile is entirely enveloped. The string is fixed first on top of the bundle to hold the parcel together. As more leaves are added to the parcel, the string is passed enough times around the parcel to keep all the leaves tightly held. This work is better done by two people. A 'nice' leaf parcel has the sinews going through the centre and at the periphery the distance between the sinews is about 2 cm. Lastly a separate string goes around the parcel's sides. In the centre of the upper side of the instrument a loop made out of the string, so that the musician can pass a finger through it and the instrument can be held while it is being struck.

Playing technique

The leaf parcel is held in one hand and is struck with the open palm of the other hand. Sometimes the leaf parcel is struck against the thigh.

Variations

The leaves that are used to build the instrument dry out after a few days and the instrument can no longer be played. A leaf parcel generally lasts for only one performance. A dance group from Lifou which was performing in Australia for two weeks made their leaf parcels last by replacing the leaves with the wide fibrous bases of coconut fronds, which are more resistant and do not dry out as quickly.

To avoid the complicated construction of the instrument for only one evening's use, several modifications have been developed. For example instead of the coconut fibre in the centre of the parcel, old newspapers are used. Or, even easier, the instrument consists of a pile of crushed newspaper, held together with sticky brown 'scotch' tape.

Symbolism

No information has been received concerning any symbolic importance of the leaf parcel and no myth concerning its origin has been encountered. The instrument is played by men and women and, according to informants, it always has been.

Diffusion

The leaf parcel is not played on the *Grande Terre*. Besides the Loyalty Islands, it is used in similar forms on Tanna in Vanuatu and it is known in the southern half of Malaita (Zemp 1972:38). It is possible that it is known elsewhere in Vanuatu or on the Solomon Islands. The instrument is not mentioned in Fischer (1958/1983) nor in McLean (1994).

Jew's-harps

According to De Rochas (1862:189) in the 1850s there was a jew's-harp in every woman's hand and according to Mencelon (cit. in Sarasin 1929:231) it is the only women's instrument. It is possible that these jew's harps were of European origin because during these decades the instruments were imported in large quantities (Garnier cit. in Sarasin 1929:231). Unfortunatly there is no information about the sort of jew's-harp in use at the time.

There are jew's harps other than the European metal ones in New Caledonia, although they are very rarely played today. These jew's harps are heteroglott, made of a length from a coconut leaflet about 20 cm long. A coconut frond midrib slightly longer is set longitudinally against the leaflet. At one end the two parts are pressed together with the thumb and the index finger. The leaflet part is held horizontally in front of the slightly open mouth touching the teeth; the midrib is snapped on the leaflet, producing a sound which can be modulated by changes in the mouth cavity.

The instrument seems to have been played throughout New Caledonia but it may have been especially popular in the Loyalty Islands. Sarasin quotes one specimen of a jew's harp in the collection of the 'Museum Umlauf' in Hamburg, which is made of one piece of bamboo 18 cm long. This is the only report of a monoglott jew's harp from New Caledonia.

Friction leaves

Quite common today but not reported in the literature, is the use made of the sound of two small dry leaves rubbed together. The musician holds one leaf in each hand and slides one over the other. All kinds of leaves can be used for this sound production. An example of the sound quality of friction leaves can be heard on track 6 of Ammann (1997 [CD]).

Costume parts as friction-idiophones

The costume that the dancers wear these days consists mostly of dry vegetable material. Parts of the costumes produce sounds during dancing. This may seem to be a very low and negligible sound production, but when motions are synchronised and especially in regions where the dances are carried out without musical instruments, these sounds are completely perceptible.

Wearing coconut frond anklets is common all over the *Grande Terre* and the Loyalty Islands. The following description is based on observations of their construction on Lifou, at Xepenehe in 1993 and at Jozip in 1994 (see Whaap/Ravel 1994d[film]). On Lifou these idiophones are called *otrene-ca*.

The youngest yellow leaves (those which grow straight up from the top of

a)

(David Becker/A.D.C.K. 1992, Lifou)

Tim, musician and dancer, from the Wetr dance group, Lifou, demonstrating the fabrication of anklets, called *otrene-ca* in Drehu, from immature coconut fronds.

a) Binding the two exposed leaflet midribs together.

b) Tying several times around the shinbone, with the knot at the front.

c - e) Three anklets in place on each leg.

b)

c)

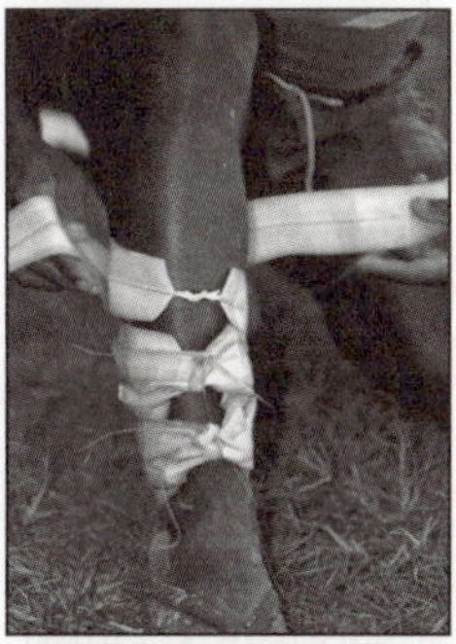

d)

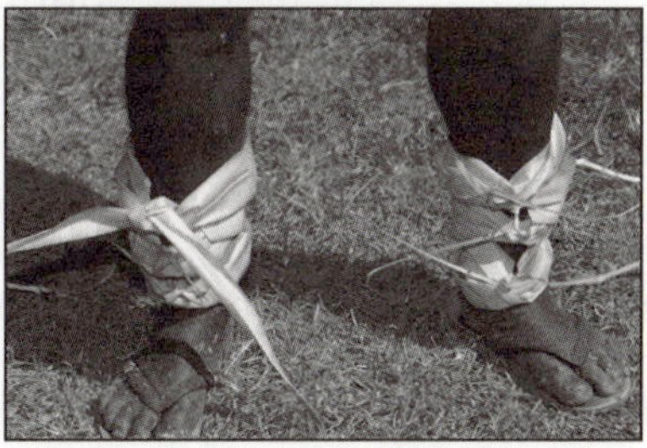

e)

the coconut crown) are used to make the instrument. The leaves which are still rolled-up are quickly heated over a fire, to flatten them. Of the approximately 70 cm long leaf, the basal 5 to 7 cm is cut longitudinally on both sides so that only the midrib is left. The leaf can be folded several times in an accordion way. In front of the shinbone, two leaves are knotted together with the midrib left over at the end. The leaves are wrapped around the ankle, each in the opposite direction, and the ends of the leaves are knotted together in front of the shinbone. Some dancers have the whole shinbone covered with these leaves, others wear only two or three.

Another part of the costume that functions as a kind of friction Idiophone is what is known as a skirt. In Paicî it is called *nä coo kärä cäbu* and in Drehu it is called *iut*. It is made either of dry grass or of fibres from the aerial roots of the screwpine (*Pandanus)*. These fibres or the dry grass, about 50 cm long hang loosely from a string that is tied around the dancer's waist. Small lengths of about 20 cm can be fixed around the upper arms and just below the knees. In Paicî these are called *pwiâ*.

Other possible sound producing objects make a kind of vessel rattle. A number of dry cycad seeds (*Cycas circinalis*) containing loose kernels are set on a string and tied around the dancers' ankles.

Sarasin states that dance rattles ("Tanzrasseln") do not exist. Today dancers do wear them around their ankles but this is a rather recent development. Originally the dancers did not wear the sort of costumes which are worn today and therefore there were no costume sounds. More information on costume is given in the chapter on dance costumes and body paint (see p. 105).

Aerophones

With the notable exception of modern umpires' metal whistles, aerophones do not accompany the present forms of Kanak dance. Most aerophones today are children's sound-makers, often mere toys. However, only a few children still make and play some of the traditional instruments in this class.

A curious aerophone observed in the 18th century will be discussed first. With few exceptions, the aerophones mentioned in 19th century reports are the flute and the conch. The unique Kanak flute was of the transverse type, although mistaken by some authors for a nose-flute. It had already nearly fallen into disuse when, in the 1930s, cheap harmonicas were imported from Japan. They became popular because of their price, ease of playing and lack of taboo, and virtually completed the flute's demise. The conch was, as well as a musical instrument, a ritual and decorative object. A description is given of all the miscellaneous aerophones found today, including children's instruments and toys, before dealing fully with the conch shell trumpet. The final section concerns flutes and includes the reconstruction and playing of the Kanak flute which was carried out in the course of the present study.

A CURIOUS AEROPHONE OF THE 18TH CENTURY

'Curious' because the 18th century popularised the 'cabinet of curiosities' which in turn developed into modern museums. At that time, after several centuries of exploration during which vast numbers of items had accumulated, Europeans had little idea of the context in which to situate them, and the term 'curiosity' would have had a neutral connotation.

The first quotation is from Georg Forster, who spent a few days on land in the region of Balade in 1774, in the north of the *Grande Terre*, and who remarked on what seemed to him to be the only musical instrument of the natives : "Among the objects that were exchanged today was also a small musical instrument, namely a kind of whistle, which was made of a piece of wood of approximately two 'zoll' [2 zoll = about 5 cm], in the form of a bell but it was not hollow and at the narrow end there was a little string. Close to the flat bottom part were two holes and not far from the string a third, all of them must be joined inside because, while blowing into the upper hole, a kind of penetrating sound emerges from the others. Excluding this whistle, we did not see another instrument with them that could have been said to be even somewhat musical"❶ (Forster ed. in Steiner 1966:306).

There is no subsequent mention of such an instrument in the literature. Did it fall into disuse? Could it have been a unique specimen brought from overseas? Following Forster's description the instrument may have resembled this sketch :

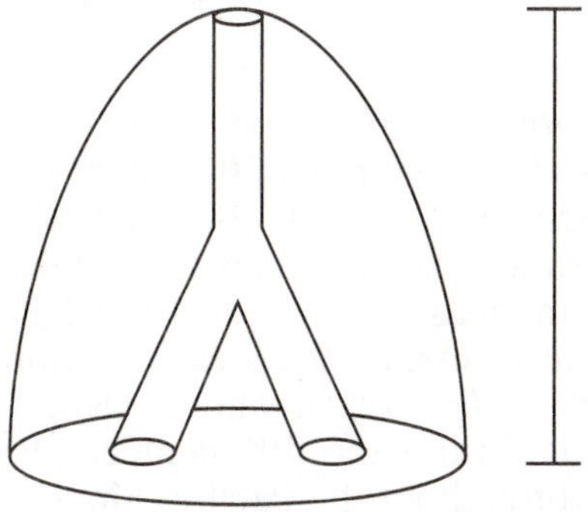

It would be possible to produce sounds while blowing in the upper hole if, at the joint there were an edge or lip (as in a recorder, or fipple-flute) to cut the air stream coming in. This joint would have been very difficult - if at all possible - to make. Forster says that the instrument was not hollow. If he was mistaken on this point, the instrument could have been a kind of ocarina and Sarasin (1929:230) interprets Forster's instrument in this way. The use of the dried seed of a cycad palm (*Cycas circinalis*❷) as a kind of ocarina was common in the region of Balade, where it was called the *juuyuu*. The use of this fruit as an ocarina is also common in other parts of the *Grande Terre*, as well as on the islands of Vanuatu. Similar instruments were widely known in the Pacific (Andersen 1934:294-296).

❶ "Unter den Sachen, die heute eingetauscht wurden, befand sich auch ein musikalisches Instrument, nämlich eine Art Pfeife, die aus einem ohngefähr zween Zoll langem Stück Holz gemacht, glockenförmig gestaltet, aber nicht hohl, und an dem schmalen Ende mit einer kleinen Schnur versehen war. Dicht an dem platten Unterteil hatte sie zwey Löcher, und ohnweit der Schnurr ein drittes, die sämtlich innerhalb zusammen laufen mussten, in dem durch Blasen auf dem oberen Loch, aus den anderen ein durchdringender Ton hervorkam. Ausser dieser Pfeife, haben wir aber kein anderes Instrument, das nur einigermassen musikalisch genannt werden könnte, bey ihnen angetroffen".

❷ The genus *Cycas* is to be found from East-Africa and Madagascar through India, Southeast-Asia to Japan, Australia and the Pacific. It was first formally published by Linnaeus in 1737 and the species *Cycas circinalis* in 1753. By the time the German scientists, the Forsters, left with the English explorer Cook, Linnaeus' work was famous throughout Europe. It seems safe to assume that Georg Forster would have been able to recognise a *Cycas* ocarina. However, it needs to be stressed that the wise and botanically literate Fritz Sarasin did not make this assumption in 1929.

Clarinets

A rudimentary clarinet is made from part of a leaf (grass leaf or any other suitable leaf), being folded in the middle and set between the lips. By blowing out and then drawing breath in, two fundamental notes may be sounded. The construction seems known mostly to older people, but they obviously pass on the techniques to children. Still, it is rare to hear the instrument. On Maré the instrument is made from the fern, identified as *Phymatosorus grossus* in Dubois' dictionary, called *shukeli* in the Nengone language, and the instrument is called *wa-shukeli* meaning "who speaks without knowing the language well"[1] (Dubois 1969/1980:983). Michel (1885/1988:116) reports seeing the leaf instrument in the years around 1870 on the *Grande Terre.*

Additionally, a leaf may be pressed between the thumbs and blown so that periodic vibrations are set up. This has apparently been spontaneously and separately invented all over the world. Dubois (1984:214) says that a leaf of *watehnid* (*Dianella intermedia*), when pressed between the thumbs, was used by lovers on Maré to send signals to each other[2].

Oboes

A simple oboe can be made with an oval, hollow stem (of grass, for example) blown at one of the ends. Two strips of coconut leaflets may also be put together to form a double reed. The leaflets so joined are then surrounded by a third leaf, wrapped around a number of times to form a cone or a 'bell', which can measure between 10 and 30 cm in overall length.

This instrument, with local variations, is known on the Loyalty Islands and on the *Grande Terre* (Beaudet 1984:29). It is one of the few small instruments described during the 19th century (Patouillet 1873:206). The instrument is known throughout the Pacific; Moyle (1988:53) saw it on Samoa and McLean (1994:48) gives a list of localities to indicate its diffusion.

Whirrers, leaf whizzers

Dried cycad palm (*Cycas circinalis*) seeds, in the form of small ovoid calabashes, may be used to construct an instrument with a sound resembling spinning or whirring perforated discs. Two holes are drilled, eccentrically placed on the seed, and a string passes through to an overall length of 40 to 60 cm. By pulling and relaxing on the ends of the string, the player makes the suspended instrument oscillate, so that the holes on the seed set up periodic vibrations according to the speed thus engendered. The instrument is known on both the *Grande Terre* and the Loyalty Islands and at least one group (Wetr) uses it today during dance performances.

A sound somewhat similar to the cycad whirrer is made by a leaf whizzer. A 15 cm piece of a folded up coconut leaflet is spanned by a bowed coconut leaflet midrib. A longer piece of the midrib attached to the bow is used to whirl the instrument in a circle. The instrument is called *maguk* in the Pije language, meaning 'bee', and refers to the quality of the sound produced (Beaudet 1984:27). Exactly the same instrument exists on the Southern Marquesas Islands, where it is called *pinao* (Moulin 1994:20). McLean

[1] "qui parle sans bien savoir la langue".

[2] In the north of the *Grande Terre*, older people say that when they were young and in love they used harmonicas to give signals to a secret lover (Ronny Phadom pers. comm.).

(1994:39) indicates its presence in many places in Melanesia and Micronesia. The wooden bullroarer appears to be unknown in New Caledonia[1], and there is no reference to it in the historical ethnographic literature. The non-existence of the device has already been remarked on by Sarasin (1929:229).

Metal whistles

In many dances today, the performers hold such whistles in their mouths, blowing short rhythmical patterns. They are said to have originated in the umpiring of cricket matches. They are mostly used by Loyalty Islands dance groups, and are called *ne-wa pon* in Nengone (Dubois 1984:214). The whistles used are, however, particular. They consist of a few small tubes that are blown together, so that the sound resembles a chord and it is not one high pitched note.

(David Becker/A.D.C.K. 1992, Nouville)

A dancer from Belep with the typical metal whistle used today by many dancers, to add whistling patterns to the overall sound of the *rythme du pilou.*

Conch shells

The conch is a widespread instrument, found wherever there is access to the warmer seas where such shells live. In Oceania its role as a traditional trade item has ensured further diffusion.

Conch shells used as signalling trumpets are reported in early ethnographic notes for the *Grande Terre* and the Loyalties (for example : Patouillet 1873:206 ; Hadfield 1920:135). The conch was not merely a signalling instrument, but, on the *Grande Terre*, also a decorative object with powerful symbolism.

(David Becker/A.D.C.K.1993, Tioumidou)

Salomon Koaté from the Tioumidou *tribu,* Poindimié, blowing the conch shell. During the 'Month of Mary' (May) he blows the instrument every evening to call the population to prayers.

Sea shells used as signalling trumpets are widespread in the Pacific. They are either side-blown, into a hole made near the small conical-spiral end, with or without an added embouchure, or they are end-blown instruments. Fischer (1958/1983:136) mentions side- and end-blown conch shells for New Caledonia. However, side blown

[1] The bullroarer is known on Ambrym (Vanuatu) (Speiser 1923/1990:220).

instruments may have been very rare in New Caldeonia for none have been found during the present study. Hadfield (1920:135) includes the use of *Stramonita* as well as *Triton tritonis* in the Loyalties, but the former has not been observed, and may have fallen into disuse❶. On the *Grande Terre*, only *Triton tritonis* is used. In Kanak languages, the onomatopoeic terms *tutu* or *cucu*, are frequently found and it might be thought that this is a European borrowing. In the Paicî language, however, the conch is called *tuu* and this name also refers to the sound of the big Notu Pigeon, *déa tuu*, (*Ducula goliath*). When listening from a distance, the sound of the pigeon and that of the conch shell are so similar that they can hardly be distinguished❷.

Fabrication

The construction of a conch shell trumpet was observed in the region of Poindimié. The shell had been collected from the beach, presumably as a washed up dead shellfish, and a kitchen knife was used to drill the hole for the embouchure, at the small conical end. The instrument was tested by blowing from time to time to check the quality of the sound. The shape or form of the hole did not make a noticeable difference, but its size for the player's comfort was gradually enlarged until it suited❸. Without an adequate embouchure a player can not achieve the sonorous tone desired. This particular conch was then used to call people to prayers.

Playing techniques

The player uses his lips in exactly the same manner as is done when blowing a metal trumpet, pressed tight, with strong air-pressure. A player who has perfected his embouchure will need less air-pressure than an apprentice for a given volume of sound. The single pitch normally obtainable can vary slightly with the air-pressure, but the production of overtones is not normally possible because of the steep conical form of the shell's air column. In Vanuatu the pitch of a conch can be varied by the insertion of a fist in the bell end (Speiser 1923/1990:377), lowering the pitch by about a whole tone. In present-day New Caledonia no such musical variations are practised and a simple long-held note is most often heard, similar to the sounding of a horn. In modern Tonga, with ensembles conch shells of different sizes, fanfares of rhythmic variety have been developed (Moyle 1991:22). However, while in Tonga there is an established brass-band tradition, such a model is not well known in New Caledonia.

Symbolism

Leenhardt (1937/1986:52), describes conch-blowing as an exclusively masculine activity. As a signalling instrument, the conch in New Caledonia has been (and often still is) used to signal shipping movements, and to call meetings. The latter function is the most commonly found, often on a daily

❶ Fischer (1958/1983:136, 214-17) lists three types for the Pacific : *Triton, Strombus* and *Fusus* as well as cassis shells, *Cassis madagascarensis* and other unidentified species, calling them "cassis-conch".

❷ Hunters of the Notu blow across the top of a 33cl local beer bottle to imitate the pigeon's deep voice as they walk silently along forest paths (Marcel Brinon pers. comm.).

❸ Peter Crowe (pers. comm.) saw a conch trumpet on Maewo (Vanuatu) said to have belonged to the culture-hero Tagaro, amidst a number of other alleged relics. Informants claimed its antiquity by the way the embouchure had been pierced, being jagged and percussed, not drilled.

basis for prayers or church services.

Apart from profane uses of the conch, the *chefferie* would have the conch blown to announce a death. Lambert (1900/1985:155) mentions the death of a *chef*, and Leenhardt (1930/1980:160) in a description of a *pilou-pilou* reports its use by members of a mourning group to announce their arrival at the celebration. In his dictionary Ajië-French, Leenhardt (1935:86) discusses important moments in yam cultivation when the conch was blown, for example, at the beginning of a new harvest, or at the ending of an old harvest. In this way, conch-blowing was associated with renewals, births and deaths, with harvests, human mortality, initiation, seasonality in relation to yam cultivation and to human lives. It raises the possibility of a connection between the sound of the conch and the essence of life.

The conch as a decorative artefact may give some clues. In a traditional *tribu,* the *chef's* house stood at the highest point, above the rest, at the end of the central alley. The *chef's* house was thus already elevated, and moreover, it was the tallest construction, with its carved wooden roof sculpture upon which conches were placed, referred to by Leenhardt (1937/1986:28) as "the glory of the clan" ("la gloire du clan"). It appears that such conches were not for playing, because the long, thin pole at the top of the sculpture had to pass through a large hole made in the side of the shell. Some *chefs* had several conches which were arranged in a particular order according to the region. Leenhardt mentions (1930/1980:154) that they can be stuffed with special herbs, which he called "totemic". In a speech that Leenhardt (1930/1980:154), wrote down : "You will prepare it [the yam] so that its vapour will

Wooden roof sculpture from a *chef's case*. The conch shells are set alternately along the sides. This particular sculpture was purchased by Fritz Sarasin in 1911. It has been stuck into the ground only in order to be photographed.

(Fritz Sarasin 1911. Gondé is given on the back of the photograph)

rise in benediction to the conch on high (the conch containing totemic herbs). All these yams [...] they are here in part for you. Our grandchildren will eat some, and tomorrow will think of the life that comes down from the conch up there..."❶.

It seems that in taking into account the very varied characteristics of the conch, its origin in water, the spiral form of its tube, its use as a container for magic herbs and its possibilities as a musical instrument, the Kanaks have obtained from it a metaphor for their conception of life.

FLUTES

End-blown flutes

Père Dubois (1984:214) records a 30 cm long end-blown flute from Maré, made from a reed locally called *thel* or *thela*. The lower end (when held in playing position) was closed by a node, with two finger-holes nearby. The instrument seems to have been abandoned. In 1945 some women from La Roche, began using pawpaw (*Carica papaya*) petioles❷ to make end-blown flutes, but this is rarely seen today❸. The pawpaw petiole is blown at one end, the other end being open, and there are no finger holes. In Nengone the name of the pawpaw-stem flute is *guesi,* and in Drehu it is called *cane waniapo*. On Lifou, Hadfield (1920:135) saw children with a pawpaw petiole flute "with a small trumpet formation at the end, made out of the green leaf of a coconut palm". On Lifou, Samek Makë, the *chef* from Kumo (a *tribu* of the Wetr *chefferie*), has made the pawpaw flute quite famous recently, by presenting it during the dance performances of the group from Wetr. He made his instrument by taking a petiole of 40 to 50 cm, and holding the slightly wider end in his right hand, covered that end with his middle finger. Holding the instrument at a slight angle, and downwards, with the lips at the smaller end, it is possible to play a fundamental and several overtones❹.

There is another pawpaw flute found on the Isle of Pines. A block or fipple is inserted at one end leaving a small opening, presumably to aid the edge-blown sound production, but there is no vent with a lip below this block (as with a recorder), and no finger-holes. Like the Lifou example, the bottom end is closed with the right hand middle finger and it has the same sound quality. This type of flute was played while walking to work, and in the gardens, where the sound is said to help the plants grow. There is no mention of pawpaw-stem flutes in the 19th and early 20th century literature. Whether or not it was a spontaneous invention is unknown. Due to the fragile nature of the material, a specimen was probably not imported, but the idea could have been (Tito Tikouré pers. comm.).

❶ "Vous la cuirez pour que sa vapeur monte en bénédictions vers la conque là-haut (la conque aux herbes totémiques). Toutes ces ignames [...] elles sont ici en partie pour vous. Nos petits-enfants en mangeront, et demain penseront à la vie descendant de la conque là-haut...".

❷ Petiole = 'leaf stalk' : those of the pawpaw are hollow and up to about one metre in length.

❸ The pawpaw is a tree bearing very large and delicious fruits, native to tropical America, but now found in many tropical regions. It was introduced into New Caledonia around 1845 by French missionaries (Mackee 1985:29). Pawpaw petioles are used world wide to make flutes. For example, the Aka pygmies of the Central African Republic make a kind of voice/flute hocketting music.

❹ Beaudet (1984b:20) gives a transcription of a song from the island of Tiga, called *muto muto* (my little sheep) played with such a flute.

Transverse flutes

Dubois (1984:214) mentions a flute called the *wekon* on Maré. It was 40 to 50 cm in length, had an embouchure and was blown with the instrument held sideways. The shorter end near the embouchure was stopped and the far end was left open, to be covered with a finger to modulate the sound. A legend is quoted by Dubois : "It is the flute of two sisters Hnaxelen and Hnameleon, *yaac* [spiritual beings] of the si Gurewo(e) at Pakad(a) who by their playing attract Wabudina a yaac from Pic Nga on the Isle of Pines"[1]. This flute was normally played by men. The *Vieux* Eloa of Ouvéa said that there was formerly a side-blown flute with no finger holes, but in which the open end could be stopped for modulation of the pitch. It could be similar to that mentioned by Dubois, but it is no longer found on Ouvéa.

Water-flutes

Hadfield (1920:134) reports a water-flute from Lifou : "Smaller pieces of cane, made up at one end, and filled, or partly filled, with water, according to the pitch of the tone desired, were blown; these (*hobo*) produced a sound somewhat resembling that of a Pan's pipes"[2]. But on Lifou today there are no more water-flutes. The *Vieux* Eloa said that a water-flute had once existed on Ouvéa and was played by two men facing each other, blowing in alternation. The instruments were made from a kind of reed, which grew until about 30 years ago in one place in the region of Gossanah, in the north of Ouvéa. The plant was destroyed by a fire, putting an end to the construction of the musical instrument on Ouvéa. In the Iaai language it was called *bloowe*. There is no mention of a water-flute on Maré by Dubois, and no indications of its existence on the *Grande Terre*; perhaps water flutes were confined to Lifou and Ouvéa.

Panpipes

Glaumont (1888 cit. in Sarasin 1929:229) reports the existence of panpipes, but Sarasin maintains that panpipes were not known in New Caledonia. It is possible that some specimen (or the idea of it) had been introduced towards the end of the 19th century by immigrant indentured labourers who came to work in the nickel mines. Beaudet (1984:29) says that he received information about the former existence of panpipes made of two tubes in the region of Canala, played by children. Panpipes from the Solomon Islands are very famous (Zemp 1972). In 1986 a panpipe group from Malaita toured in New Caledonia and was very popular with all sections of the New Caledonian public. Panpipes have since been adopted by some *kaneka* bands.

Piston-flute

Beaudet (1984:28) reports that in some places in the Loyalty Islands Kanak children make a piston-flute from a piece of branch from the oleander

[1] "C'est la flûte de deux soeurs, Hnaxelen et Hnameleon, yaac des si Gurewo(e) à Pakad(a) qui attirèrent par leur jeu Wabudina, yaac de l'île des Pins, du Pic Nga".

[2] The name *hobo*, as given for the water-flute by Hadfield, refers on Lifou today to the harmonica. It is likely that the introduction of harmonicas caused flutes to disappear, as happened with the Kanak flute (see p. 30). In this case the harmonica took over the generic name of the ancient flutes. Hadfield elsewhere (1920:133) notes a song, accompanied with a 'fife', which she also calls *hobo*.

(*Nerium oleander*)[1]. It is operated by shifting the wooden part while blowing into its bark tube covering. It was not encountered during the field work.

A notched-flute

The notched-flute (with a V-cut to make a lip) in the Sarasin collection, discussed by Beaudet (1984:29), is most unlikely to be a Kanak instrument, as Sarasin himself said (1929:230). The specimen probably came from Vanuatu, where such flutes are widespread. It is decorated with incisions like those on the notched-flutes from Vanuatu (see for example Huffman 1996:152-155). Although the Kanaks were very familiar with this technique, using it for incised bamboos, known in French as *bambous gravés*, Kanak flutes were not incised, except for the carving of the owner's name on some flutes[2].

The Kanak flute[3]

Only a few of the older Kanaks still remember this flute, which had once played a significant role in their traditional culture. Its characteristic is that some flutes were strongly bent, others less so and some were left straight. The length of the instrument (measuring the whole arc of the curve) varied between 1 and 1,5 metres, with a diameter of up to 2 cm. The overall length depended on the length of the player's arms, those with shorter arms requiring either shorter or more strongly curved instruments. There are specimens of old Kanak flutes in museums in Nouméa, Sydney, Paris, Basel, Rome, Cambridge and elsewhere.

The plant used for making this flute is the cosmopolitan tall grass known as Common Reed (*Phragmites communis*). The plant is known in Fwâi as *hago,* which is at the same time the name of the reed species and that of the instrument itself. However, there are some old people in the Hienghène region who recall the flute's name as *womi,* and in this case it was also the name of the place where the reed was collected. In the Nenemâ language (northern tip of the *Grande Terre*) the reed is also called *hago,* but the flute itself called *pwêlô* (Ronny Phadom pers. comm.). On Belep Island the flute was known as *hââgu,* in Cèmuhî as *apwêê,* in Paicî as *kuruö* or *kurö* (with the name of the plant being *waty*), and in Ajië as *hndor.* For the period around 1913 (Montague ms.V) the most common name was clearly the Ajië word *hndor,* in both the north and the centre, and in Ajië the word also refers to the conch shell. In the Xârâcùù language - the most southerly part of the flute's distribution - the instrument is called *bèchöö,* made up of '*bè-*', a piece of something cut longitudinally, and '*-chöö*', the name of the reed.

Construction

Benoît Boulet, an elderly Kanak from the north of the *Grande Terre*, never learned to play this flute but he had, as a young man, observed the flute

[1] This decorative poisonous bush is not native to New Caledonia, but was already in cultivation on the *Grande Terre* in 1883 (MacKee 1985:17).

[2] In the article "Deux flûtes néo-calédoniennes" (Lobsiger-Dellenbach 1951) the carving on this particular flute is examined and Dellenbach-Lobsiger suggest that the flute was incised in New Caledonia, because the carving is similar to that on Kanak incised bamboos.

[3] The term Kanak flute is used here because the instrument was certainly once the main Kanak flute and is very probably an autochthonous invention. A vernacular term has been avoided because it would have only regional application.

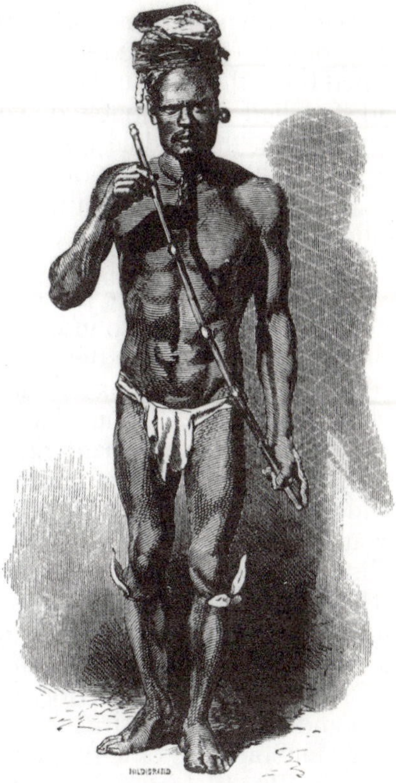

A Kanak holding a slightly curved Kanak flute. Picture published in Garnier (1867/1990:54), entitled : "Flute player. - Drawing from A. De Neuville after a photograph" ("Joueur de flûte. - Dessin de A. De Neuville d'après une photographie").

players of his family making their instruments. As they are now all deceased, the *Vieux* Benoît seems to be the last person who remembers the flute's construction, and in April 1994 he agreed to make several flutes according to the way he had seen it done in his youth and to answer questions.

The reed *hago* grows only in marshy areas on the *Grande Terre*, but it seems likely that where *Phragmites communis* was unavailable another plant was used. Captain Kanappe (Courtis 1984:115) described a flute he saw in the 1880s in the region of Hienghène as made of "a strong reed" ("fort roseau"), which may well have been *Phragmites communis.* Sarasin (1929:229-30) explained that flutes could be made of bamboo or of another kind of "tube" ("Rohr"). Vieillard and Deplanche (1862:219), who studied the New Calendonian flora, say that the plant used to make the flute was one of the *Erianthus* grasses. Thus, though *Phragmites communis* may have been the preferred plant, there is evidence that others were used where it was not available❶.

The *Vieux* Benoît proceeded, in his demonstration of construction, to chose *Phragmites communis* reeds with a diameter of at least 2 cm at the base, and a height of at least 150 cm. He said the reeds needed to be green when cut, for this would allow bending without cracking in the next steps. Once the reed was cut off, all side leaves were removed. As indicated above, the final length of a flute and the exact position of the finger holes were determined by

❶ In Australia termite-hollowed trunks of a Eucalyptus species are preferred for the didjeridu, but bamboo or other trees are used if necessary, and in modern times even PVC or metal pipes.

the player's own body measurements, for each musician built his own instrument. For the length, the reed is held in the same position as when playing a finished flute, the left hand on the thicker end just below the mouth, the right hand stretched out obliquely downwards at about 45° to bend the reed slightly when held, the middle finger of the right hand seeking the middle of an internode. The ideal position for the embouchure is also at mid-internode. This often requires some juggling and bending, and although the precise position of the finger hole may be slightly below or above the centre of an internode, the maker must take care, because any piercing near a node can lead to splitting. Once the places for the two holes, the embouchure and the finger hole, have been found, with more or less bending, the reed is again trimmed, this time beside the nodes determining the length of the flute.

The embouchure is burned into place with a red-hot tip of an iron rod or thick wire, to about 7 mm diameter, this technique permitting a perfectly rounded hole with some hardening of the surrounding plant tissue. The *Vieux* Benoît thought that before metal rods or thick wire were available, the hole would have been made with a shell drill. The finger hole was made in a similar way and of the same size. The orientation of the finger hole is about 90° from the line of the embouchure (i.e. quarter-circle).

Then the interior nodal cross-walls have to be pierced, which is done with a thin stick of hard wood, or an iron rod or wire, introduced from the wider end, but not piercing the distal end, so that the flute is end-stopped. The next process is to clean the interior of the reed's stem of all debris from broken nodes and any other obstructions, which can be done by blowing vigorously into the embouchure or letting water flow through, or both. Finally, the upper end of the flute is closed with rolled up pieces of bark from the paperbark tree (*Melaleuca quinquenervia*) known as *niaouli* in French or as *hyoonik* in Fwâi. Some flutes have the nodes at both ends pierced, as described by Patouillet (1873:206) and then cleaning the inside by blowing through the tube is more efficient. Both ends are then closed with pieces of rolled up bark. One flute in the Sarasin collection (Museum für Völkerkunde [Ethnographical museum] in Basel, Switzerland) has its distal end closed with resin.

The flute is bent to the desired degree with a cord fixed under tension to both ends. Because the reed is slightly conical, the distal end curves more, and the result is an oval arc, the typical form. There will have been loss of strength in the reed after the piercing of the internal nodes, and budding points may develop small holes. To prevent this, a special sticky paste is spread around each node, but not all museum specimens of the flute have this. The paste may be made from the flowers of the tree *Macaranga vedeliana*, known in Fwâi as *hwiip*. The flowers are chewed and then spat out as a sticky paste which is mixed with pulverised charcoal.

Other substances used to produce a suitable paste are the resin of the kaori tree (*Agathis*) in Fwâi *dayu*, and the latex of the banian tree (*Ficus*), *thilic*. This juice needs to be heated and is then mixed with pulverised charcoal. The charcoal causes the juice to solidify. The flowers of the *hwiip*, are collected in season and can be stored until they are needed. The resin of the kaori and the latex of the banian can be collected the whole year through. The construction of a flute is thus not limited to a particular season. Once the paste is spread around the nodes, the flute, still under tension with the cord, is hung under the ceiling in the *case*. There it is constantly in the smoke from the cooking

a)

b)

c)

d)

a) Two participants, Alex Koteureu and Tuko Atti, collecting the reeds for making the flute.
b) Benoît using an iron rod to pierce the nodal cross-walls.
c) With a hot iron rod, the embouchure and the hole are burnt into the reed.
d) The flute is kept bent like a bow for several weeks while it dries out, thus acquiring its permanent form.

(Ammann/Konyii 1994, Hienghène)

In 1994 a workshop was organised in which the abandoned Kanak flute was revived. Each of the participants made several flutes and learned the rudiments of how to play the instrument. The person in the centre is blowing through the flute in order to get rid of fragments of the pierced nodal cross-walls.

fire, which helps to dry the reed, and eventually the cord can be removed, for the flute is now permanently in its required shape. Knowledge and experience are needed to reshape the embouchure by cutting it accurately before the flute is ready to be played.

There has been some misinterpretation of the function of the paste found covering the nodes of many flutes. De Rochas (1862:189) said that the flute consists of individual bamboo internodes glued one to the other, lengthwise, with a kind of resin❶. All the museum specimens that have been inspected, however, were made of only one piece. The *Vieux* Benoît and other informants all declared they had never seen or heard of a flute made of several bamboo pieces. Indeed, such a flute would be extremely difficult to construct with natural materials.

The manuscripts of Paul Montague❷ contain the only contemporary and comprehensive description of the Kanak flute, observed in the region of Houaïlou, and there is a close correspondence with the *Vieux* Benoît's method : "The *bndor* is a bamboo flute, usually but not always bent nearly into a semi-circle. It is made of a species of slender bamboo called by the natives *Undovi*. A piece suitably curved is chosen and bent subsequently by the application of heat. The septa [❸] are burned or broken through with a flexible stick, and the open ends plugged with njaouli-bark. A mouth-hole is burned through them at four inches from the thicker end. It is rather elongated, and on the inside of the curve. A smaller hole is burned through very near to the thinner end, usually but not always on the outer curve of the bamboo. This is the fingering hole, and is covered or uncovered with the index finger of the right hand. The nodes of the bamboo are often covered with a black waxy substance called *O-ro*, obtained from the Banyan" (Montague ms.V:15).

Playing the flute

A person wanting to play the Kanak flute could only hope to be chosen as an apprentice. Accredited players chose the apprentices and would normally choose one of their own sons, or a man from the extended family circle. There were family lines which had a system of regulated inheritance of flute playing, which is perhaps paralleled today with regard to the transmission of knowledge of how to sing traditional songs, or how to be responsible for a dance. The flute apprentice had to memorise the repertoire and develop the skills of construction of the instrument, and at proper points of indocrination learn the taboos and customs, such as ingesting plant 'medicines', before playing.

An apprentice of the flute was in general a married man with a number of children, already possessing some personal prestige. The *Vieux* Benoît said

❶ This error became so entrenched that the staff in the 'musée territorial de Nouvelle-Calédonie' described their flute as being made of several pieces. When examined, it became clear that it was made of only one piece - although with an exceptionally wide diameter. This specimen may have been the reason why Beaudet (1984:28 + 30) declared that there were two flutes :"the side blown flute : hago" and "the side blown flute of bamboo" made of several pieces. Other writers and non-specialists referring to flutes took this information over (Ohlen 1987:13; Boulay 1993:14 and others).

❷Paul D. Montague, a British naturalist, spent 1913 - 14 in New Caledonia. Montague's accounts are of great importance, with much unique information, and are in the University Library at Cambridge, UK. He also made what are probably the first cylinder recordings in New Caledonia.

❸ The septa (singular : septum) are cross-walls at each node, the internodes being hollow.

that some middle-aged women could learn to play the instrument, but there is no mention of this in the literature, and no illustrations. His information is in contradiction to Leenhardt's (1937/1986:52), who, in his division of male and female cultural activities, sets flute-playing on the masculine side. According to Ronny Phadom (pers. comm.) in his home region of Poum in the north of the *Grande Terre*, an apprentice flautist had the responsibility of keeping all secrets and taboos of the instrument strictly and there is a legend saying that a whole nuclear family would have to die for the error of 'a child who did not respect his father's flute'.

Symbolism

The flute was much more than a musical instrument, it was an outward and visible sign of prestige. In some 19th century photographs, Kanaks hold their flutes beside their traditional arms which may well indicate their importance[1]. Guiart (1963:87) cites a legend from the Cèmuhî language area in the north of the *Grande Terre*. A she-oak tree ('bois de fer') (*Casuarinaceae*) was planted on the central alley of the *chefferie*. A child came out of the tree, leaned against it and played the flute *hago*. When people approached him and asked 'who are you' he told them his name, and he was given the status of the *chef's* servant, a very high position in the traditional Kanak social system. In fact it seems that the flute was reserved for an élite, for *chefs* and others of considerable prestige.

Occasions for playing the flute

According to Ulysse de La Hautière (1869/1980:113), the flute could be played while travelling in the bush (where it was accompanied by the singing of a second person), for personal solace, or for a group of people. Garnier (1867/1991:121) saw it being accompanied with the beating of a struck-bamboo. Sarasin (1929:230) comments that on occasions a Kanak would play his flute for hours on end. Again, Montague (ms.V:16) says that the flute could be played as a dance accompaniment : "The hndor was played in the *Quie*[2], both as a solo instrument and in dances". Montague (ms.V:16) also mentions the use of the flute in yam cultivation : "The sound has the magical property of making the young yams grow quickly, so it was employed extensively for this purpose at the season of planting". Other writers confirm this : Sarasin (1929:230) says it was played while going to the yam gardens, as well as while working there. Leenhardt (1930/1980:132) further states that flute music was played to the yams only at particular points of the growing season. The *Vieux* Benoît recalled a game when flute music was being played to the growing yams : a piece of reed (but not the same species as the flute) would be launched along the ditches between two yam beds, to fly as close to the ground as possible.

Playing techniques

Some writers have claimed that the Kanak flute could be played with breath from either the mouth or the nostrils. According to De Rochas

[1] Studio photos and those posed for outside seldom reflect authentic Kanak scenes so that data obtained from them have to be treated with caution.

[2] Montague explains the *quie* as a ceremony. *Quie is* probably *koe* an ancient Ajië term used in relation to dances and ceremonies (Leenhardt 1935).

Studio picture by Allan Hughan (probably 1872)

The face of the flute player shows that he was not blowing into the flute at the moment when the picture was taken and his right hand is not in a playing position.

(1862:189), "... the natives play it equally easily with the mouth or with the nose, by closing one of the nostrils with the thumb"❶. Ulysse de La Hautière (1869/1980:113) indicates something very similar : "... our flautist blew, with visible satisfaction, in one of the holes, now with the mouth, now with one of the nostrils, while the middle finger, placed on the second hole, helped the modulation..."❷. And Leenhardt who lived more than 20 years among the Kanaks, commented on one of Hughan's studio pictures (published in Leenhardt 1930/1980:PlancheXI,n°2) : "Flute player. He blows it with the nose"❸. Other writers repeated these remarks. The pictures in the Hughan collection in the Musée de l'Homme in Paris, France, were captioned "nose flute"❹.

There are very good reasons to believe that the Kanak flute was played only with the mouth, and never with the nose. Apart from those writers who said that the instrument is played with either the mouth or nose, there are many others who report it as played with the mouth and make no mention of the nose. To mention only a few : Captain Kanappe (cit. in Courtis 1984:115), Patouillet (1873:206), Baudoux (1952[II]:70), and Lambert (1900/1985:156). If it had been a fact, why not mention it? The most informative and comprehensive text comes, once again, from Montague's manuscripts (V:15) : "This instrument is *not*, as often stated, played by the nose. It is sounded by gently blowing through the nearly closed lips...", the word 'not' is underlined in Montague's own handwriting. It may be added that in the field, every elderly Kanak who spoke about flute playing said, without exception, and sometimes with a slight smile, that the flute was only played with the mouth❺.

What made people think that the Kanak flute could be nose-blown? It's embouchure is about 10 cm from the stopped end, so that when held at a steep downward angle for playing, the tip of the instrument may touch the nose of the musician. it looks like this, for example, in the pictures in Leenhardt (1930/1980:planche XI,n° 2) and on some of Hughan's unpublished studio photographs. The photographer Allan Hughan lived in New Caledonia in the 1870s. He made many glass negatives of Kanak people, singly and in small groups, usually in studio conditions. Exposure periods for each plate were fairly long; it was usual for sitters to be asked to hold an immobile

❶ "...les indigènes en jouent avec une égale facilité par la bouche ou par le nez, en se bouchant l'une des narines avec le pouce".

❷ "...notre tibicien soufflait, avec une satisfaction visible, dans l'un des trous, tantôt de la bouche, tantôt de l'une des narines, pendant que le médium, placé sur le second trou, aidait à la modulation;...".

❸ "Joueur de flûte. Il souffle par le nez".

❹ A Polynesian nose flute, however, had been introduced to Ouvéa by Tongans according to Foy (cit. in Sarasin 1929:230). It was probably a single instrument and was not adopted by the Ouvéans. It is not found there any more, and the present population does not remember such a flute. Polynesian nose flutes have a completely different form from the Kanak flute, being typically one internode of bamboo 20 to 40 cm long, stopped by nodes at each end, of a diameter that the thumb and middle finger can encircle, and a variable number of finger holes, often four (see for example Andersen 1934:215-266; Emerson 1909:145).

❺ There is a manuscript of Waïa Gorode which contains a wide ranging account of Kanak culture taken from his own experiences. This has not yet been the subject of a comprehensive study and conclusions drawn from isolated parts of it would be premature. However it can be said that in talking about the Kanak flute he does say that it was blown with the mouth. The idea of nose-playing seems to have entered European mythology about the Pacific, perhaps because of its exotic character. McLean (1974:79-94) in a very detailed article concerning the oft-supposed nose-blown Maori flute (in fact blown with the mouth), scotches the 'observations' of early reporters, and the persistence of fairy-tales.

Detail from an incised bamboo, published in Boulay (1993:15). A man is shown playing a curved flute with his mouth. Passing the flute underneath the right knee is quite unusual.

position for several minutes, hidden supports for the head (to stop any nodding) being common. A photographer was something of a stage director, with decor for his mise en scène installed, and he arranged the human figures into various postures. In some of Hughan's plates the Kanak flute is among the decorative paraphernalia, but in others the flute appears to be held in position for playing. From the position of the lips it can be concluded that in no case is the flute actually being played during the length of the exposure for the photographic plate. While it can be deduced that Hughan's photographs do not give reliable evidence of blowing techniques, it is more important that there is absolutely no suggestion that the Kanak flute was nose-blown[1], even though such a posture would open up dramatic possibilities.

Incised bamboos were a popular art form among the Kanaks in the second half of the 19th century. They are an important pictorial and narrative resource for they recorded many facets of the contemporary scene. The artists would certainly have known how the flute was played. In Roger Boulay's book *Le Bambou gravé kanak* (1993:16) there is a picture (see above) showing a man with a flute where the instrument appears to be held in a playing position and it is clearly mouth-blown.

In Montague's manuscript (p.16) he says : "While performing, the player hums a deep base"[2] and he adds in the footnote : "This practice may have given rise to the idea that the instrument is played with the nose, for it might seem as though the man were blowing with his nose while he sang with his mouth".

[1] The lack of authenticity in Hughan's pictures is demonsrated in the catalogue (Ammann 1996:18) of the exhibition "Studio canaque, Histoire kanak; Exotisme et photographie de studio en Nouvelle-Calédonie de 1867 à 1900" (Canaques in the studio, Kanaks in History : Exotism and Studio Photography in New Caledonia from 1867 to 1900) in the 'musée territorial de Nouvelle-Calédonie' (4th April - 3rd June 1996). The photographers of the time preferred to show the Kanaks as 'beau' (handsome) and the curios savage, than to search for authenticity.

[2] "Base : the spelling of 'bass' till the 19th century" (The Shorter Oxford English Dictionary on Historical Principles 1933:150-152).

The intrinsic musicological argument against nasal blowing is the fact that all the flute's notes are harmonics within a restricted range. A certain number can be obtained when the finger hole is closed and a complementary number when the hole is open. With a thin, long (up to 150 cm) tube of reed, the Kanak flute demands fine shades of blowing angles and pressures, with constant adaptation of lip position. This is virtually impossible with the nose. The nose flutes of the Pacific build their melodies by stopping finger holes to alter the air column. Nobody has yet found a flute that certainly doubles as mouth- and nose-blown, which is part of a standard cultural repertoire.

Leenhardt (1930/1980:132) describes the music of the flute as being composed of only two notes : "At the extremity of the flute, a single hole, which, stopped or opened by the finger, gives two sounds incessantly repeated..."[1]. Lambert (1900/1985:156) describes the flute music as compositions of only two tones. It seems as though these writers took notice of what they saw rather than what they heard : a flute with only one hole could only have two notes. Montague (ms.V: 15) comes to the rescue here : "...by means of harmonics a scale of six notes is easily obtained. There is no definitive pitch or scale for this instrument. The bamboo is simply cut 'the length of a man's arm', and as the bone varies, its pitch varies accordingly. Some give a scale almost of whole tones, whereas others give less than semi-tones. Some are very much higher than others".

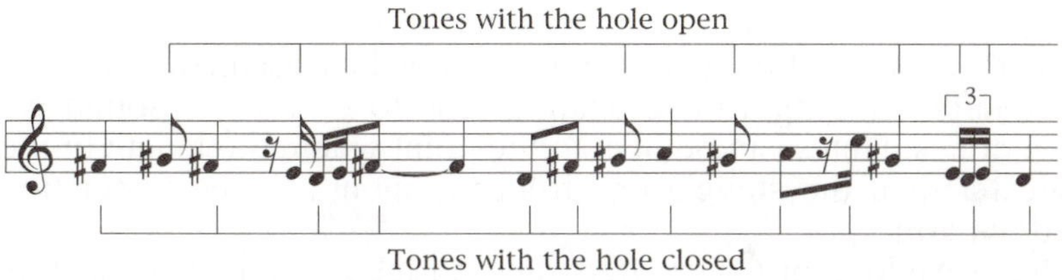

Montague's report of six notes corresponds with the only (at present) known recording of the flute, a short melody of 47 seconds taped by the linguist A. Haudricourt in 1963. It was played by Kallen Bova at Tiouaé, a small settlement in the northeast of the *Grande Terre*, close to Touho, and he was at that time the last traditional Kanak flautist (Jean-Claude Rivierre pers. comm.). Although Kallen is long dead, his daughter (born in the 1940s), and his cousin, both remembered the melody when they listened to the tape in 1994, and they were both certain that the music was played on a slightly curved transverse flute.

Now, with the *Vieux* Benoît's help, a flute has been reconstructed with a length of 107 cm, a diameter of 2 cm or less, an embouchure 6 cm from the upper end, and a finger-hole 5 cm from the distal end. On this instrument it is possible to play overtones (except the 'e' with the open hole) at nearly the same pitches as on the Kallen recording, and this indicates that it is close to the size of Kallen's flute.

Six notes can be played easily on the reconstructed instrument, and a seventh is sometimes possible, but never very clear. With the finger hole

[1] "À l'extremité de la flûte, un seul trou, qui, bouché ou ouvert par le doigt, donne deux sons sans cesse répetés...".

closed, the instrument resonating along its whole length upon the fundamental of D, the harmonics 4, 5, 6, 7 give d, f♯, a, c ; if the 8th harmonic sounds, it is d. When the finger hole is open, the resonating length is shorter, with a fundamental slightly higher than E upon which the harmonics 5 and 6 give g♯ and b (Kallen played, with the hole open, the harmonics 4 and 5).

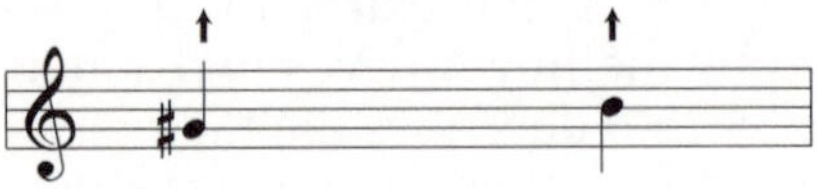

These two series of harmonics thus produce the flute's scale :

The curved shape of the instrument can now be explained. It is a matter of having a sufficient length of resonating tube to be able to sound precisely these overtones. Flutes can be bent to the point where the length of the arc is 50 % greater than the straight-line from the mouth to the finger tip of the streched out arm.

M. Bealo Wedoye of Ouarap recorded an interview in 1986 with the late Paul Bwerou of Haut Coulna with some intriguing information which it has not so far been possible to confirm. Prior to the appearance of the *ayoii* repertoire (see p. 134), said to have been in the second half of the 19th century, people of the Hienghène region sang songs with the *bago* flute in antiphony, having repeated alternations of sung verse, and the same melody played on the flute. The traditional songs of this region have intervals from semi-tones to major thirds. It is likely that the pre-*ayoii* songs had similar intervals. The *bago* flute could presumably play all these intervals. If the flute were not curved and therefore shorter, the intervals of the overtones would be wider : octaves and fifths. Perhaps the fact that the length of the flute is so great that it is often curved for all but the tallest players, is determined by the spectrum of overtones that were present in this kind of antiphonal singing.

This would be a case of the modification of an instrument in order to obtain the intervals of pre-existing singing and not that the intervals of the singing were adopted from the instrument. The idea that a people sings according to the tones obtained on its instruments (for example the 'alphorn fa' that is also found in the *yodel*) has been widely held but the information about the Kanak flute seems to run counter to it. However, this suggestion is based on only one interview about the musical situation of more than 100 years ago and is therefore far from established. Still, it may contribute to reflection about the interaction over time between singing and instrumental music.

The timbre of the Kanak flute is often rather 'breathy', and the boundaries of the harmonics sounded are often unstable. Pauses in performance are for taking in breath, and there is no evidence of the practice of circular breathing (which permits continous sounding, as with the *didjeridu*). Montague's reference to the players humming a deep bass❶ is most interesting. The hummed drone is found as part of various musical traditions all over the world and is not a unique Kanak flute playing technique.

Distribution

Most museum flute specimens are from the centre and northern regions of the *Grande Terre.* One flute, in the Sarasin collection was purchased at Canala, but none come from further south. Hadfield (1920:134) mentions a curved flute from Lifou, but her information is insufficient to say whether it was the same kind as the one on the *Grande Terre.*

Relations with the Pacific

In its sound producing and playing technique, the Kanak flute is comparable with the mouth-blown transverse flute *'au porare* of the 'Are'are (Coppet/Zemp 1978:22), which has one finger-hole at the end, and is long and thin, but not curved. In Zemp's film (1979[film]) the musician plays two pieces on the instrument, using an over-blowing technique (to obtain harmonics), as with the Kanak flute. McLean (1994:59) says the only Melanesian nose-blown flute was the Kanak one (but it has been demonstrated above that this is a mistake), with a vague reference to such flutes in northern New Guinea. In the Pacific, the established distribution of nose flutes is in Micronesia and Polynesia (excluding New Zealand), but not in Melanesia❷.

In the alternation of overtones with different fundamentals the Kanak flute may be related to the paired flutes of New Guinea. Ceremonial flutes of the middle Sepik, are made of bamboo up to more than two metres in length, without finger holes, but a range of 4 to 6 or more harmonics can be easily obtained with such a length. Such flutes are commonly played in pairs of different lengths typically producing fundamentals about a whole tone apart. There is thus some resemblance to the musical structure obtainable on the Kanak flute. The flutes are often played in hocket (alternation) but also simultaneously. With the finger-hole of the Kanak flute it is also possible for a solo performer to play upon two interlocking harmonic series as shown above.

The Kanak choice of musical instruments

The corpus of traditional Kanak instruments has two unique members : the concussion bark-clapper and the Kanak flute, and one, the palm spathe, which is found in only one other place, the Banks Islands of northern Vanuatu. These

❶ On the recording of Kallen Bova this bass cannot be heard. It is possible that the music played by Kallen was just an improvised piece for the recording, to demonstrate the instrument.

❷ Fischer (1958/1983:200, plate XXI, fig.322) illustrates a transverse flute supposed to be from New Caledonia, in Zürich (Universitäts Sammlung), with the holes offset. There has been no corroboration in New Caledonia of the Zürich flute, which is straight and appears to be made of wood (nodes, which would indicate bamboo, are not shown). It seems quite possible this specimen was wrongly labelled.

(David Becker/A.D.C.K.1992, Nouville)

The bark-clapper and the stamping-bamboo are the instruments most commonly used to accompany mimetic dances on the *Grande Terre*.

seem to be the oldest instruments of the Kanaks. Besides these, the leaf parcel, thought to come from southern Vanuatu, may have have been in use on the Loyalty Islands for a considerable time. In each case, these are the instruments where traditional vernacular names are still in use. Of course, there could have been others, exclusively Kanak, which have fallen into disuse, such as the 'curious' aerophone described by Forster in 1774.

Other sound-makers or 'small' instruments, such as the simple oboes, clarinets and the leaf-whizzer, may well have been a part of Kanak culture for a very long time. However, some of them are widely known throughout the Pacific and could have been introduced at any time, from many centuries ago to just a few decades ago. On the *Grande Terre*, instruments made of bamboo, such as stamping-tubes, struck-bamboos and slit-drums, could have been imported as ideas or instruments. The bamboo slit-drum may have developed from the struck-bamboo at any time. As for wooden slit-drums, it seems their use for dance began in the second half of the 19th century, although Polynesians, from Tonga, Samoa, Wallis etc. may well have introduced the notion of these instruments earlier. The manufacture of smallish portable wooden slit-drums was always feasible but it is not certain that the wooden slit-drum existed in New Caledonia before the arrival of the L.M.S. At any rate it is not mentioned in the earliest literature. The huge slit-drums well known in Melanesia, as well as the giant upright slit-drums of Central Vanuatu were not imported into New Caledonia. Furthermore, such instruments were unknown south of Efate Island, and most pre-European contacts between Vanuatu and New Caledonia are presumed to have been between the southern islands of Erromango, Tanna and Anatom with the Loyalties.

Much of the esoteric lore connected with the manufacture and utilisation of Kanak instruments appears to have been forgotten. Some taboos connected with the flute are known through legends, as well as the general restrictions concerning the player's gender (which do not seem, to have been absolute).

The design of traditional Kanak idiophones seems to indicate an aesthetic preference for muffled rather than clear sounds, especially in accompanying dancing. The concussion bark-clapper is a case in point. A pair of simple wooden clap-sticks would have been easy to make, and have been durable but their sound tends to be clear and sharp. The dull thudding of the bark-clappers represented a distinct aural quality. Bark clappers would leave preferential aural space open to vocal production, whereas clap-sticks might have interfered with desired vocal registers. The whistles, shouts and repertoire of Kanak vocalisations were important, and the dull thudding of bark-clappers may have been like an aural carpet against which human noises could stand out. It is supposed that the aesthetic of the timbre for Kanak instruments was a matter of deliberate choice.

One may speculate on why certain instruments were not found among the Kanaks, such as the musical bow and various membranophones. Shark skins, parts of the sea-turtle, the wings and skin of the flying fox would give the necessary material and those are all animals known and hunted for food by the Kanaks. One might also ask why the people of the Loyalty Islands did not adopt the concussion bark-clappers as a substitute for the leaf parcel, as the material was available. They do appear to have replaced the stamping-gourd with the stamping-bamboo, although the bamboo plant does not grow on the Loyalties and the stamping-tubes have to be introduced from the *Grande Terre.* On the other hand the people of the *Grande Terre* appear never to have made leaf parcels although the tree with suitable leaves grows along the coast.

From the great selection of world instruments that a modern Kanak could buy from a store in Nouméa, the choices made in relation to traditional music are restrained; so far only the harmonica is played with traditional rhythm instruments to accompany dances and while playing, the musician snaps his finger against it, following the rhythm instruments. Thus ancient modes of selectivity appear to be still operating in the Kanak aesthetic world. It may be concluded that Kanaks, like other peoples, choose their musical instruments carefully, today from those commercially available and in the past from the natural world, to express the sound in their minds.

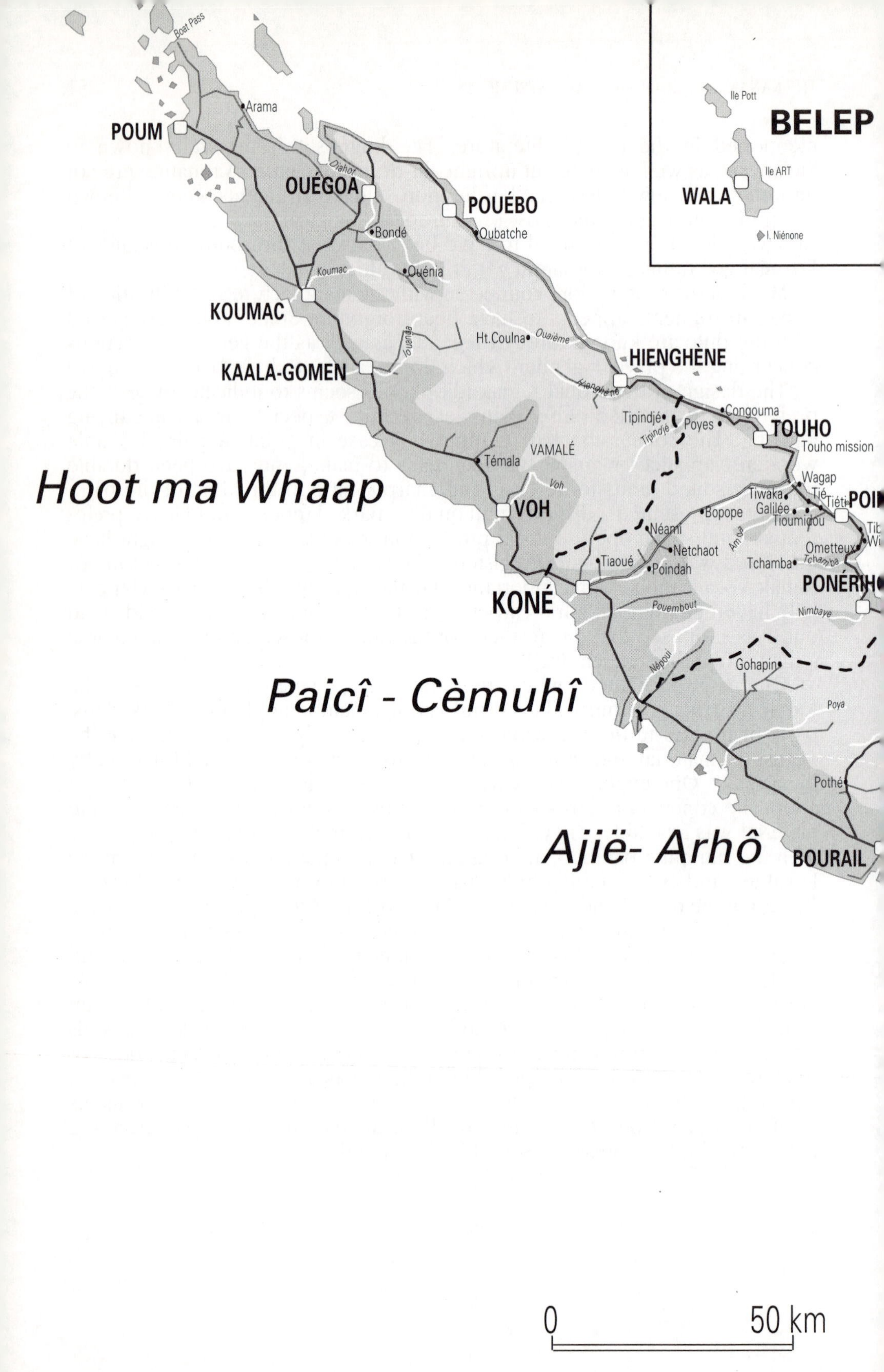

Boat Pass
Arama
POUM
Diahot
OUÉGOA
POUÉBO
Oubatche
Bondé
Koumac
Ouénia
KOUMAC
Iouanga
Ht.Coulna
Ouaième
KAALA-GOMEN
HIENGHÈNE
Hienghène
Tipindjé
Poyes
Congouma
TOUHO
Touho mission
Tipindjé
VAMALÉ
Témala
Hoot ma Whaap
Voh
VOH
Wagap
Tiwaka
Tié
Tiéti
Galilée
Tioumidou
Bopope
Néami
Netchaot
Tiaoué
Poindah
Am oa
Ometteux
Tchamba
Tchamba
KONÉ
PONÉRIH
Pouembout
Nimbaye
Népoui
Gohapin
Paicî - Cèmuhî
Poya
Pothé
Ajië- Arhô
BOURAIL
Ile Pott
BELEP
Ile ART
WALA
I. Niénone
0
50 km

The *GRANDE TERRE*

SHOWING LINGUISTIC REGIONS

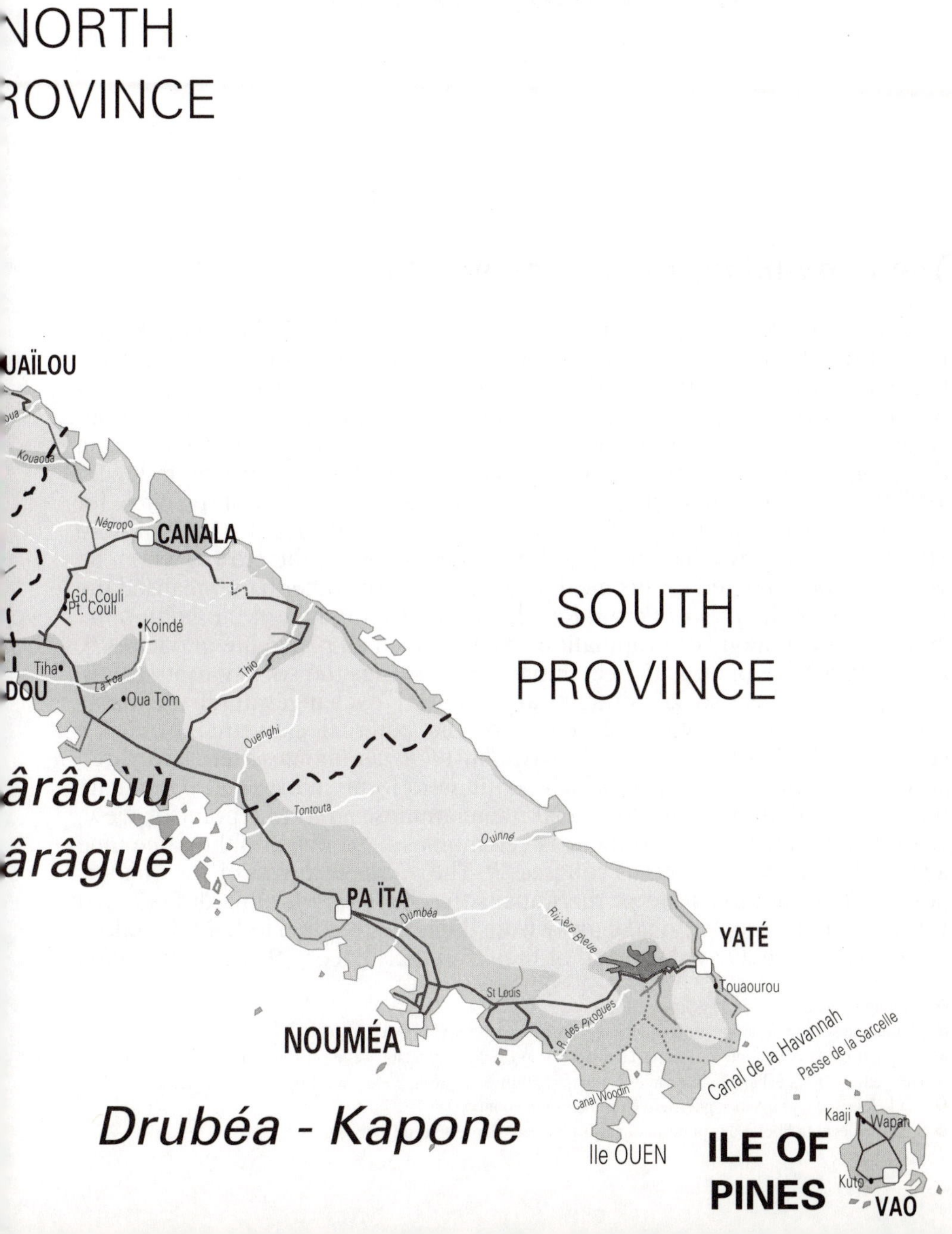

CHAPTER 2

EARLY DANCE AND MUSIC OF THE *GRANDE TERRE*

The *pilou-pilou*, a Kanak ceremony

The diverse Kanak ceremonies which continued to be held until the beginning of the 20th century, when bans upon their practice were enforced, have become known under the single generic term *pilou-pilou*. They are frequently mentioned in early ethnographic literature. Whosoever saw the former ceremonies was never untouched by them. Some were frightened and saw in the *pilou-pilou* only "a big meeting of thieves…"❶ (Mgr. Douarre cit. in Rozier 1990:97) or a feast where "the intended victims are carried out of the circle [of dancers] to be prepared for the pot" (Lainé 1942:28). La Hautière (1869/1980:238) says that the *chef* chose a person out of the crowd, whom he wanted to be prepared for his meal. Leenhardt, on the other hand, realised the importance of the *pilou-pilou* in Kanak society. He thought of the *pilou-pilou* as a "social ceremony of propitiation around which all native life gravitates"❷, also stating "The pilou is the ceremony which brings the society to its culminating point, where social contracts are renewed, exchanges are made, debts settled, and the prestige and power of the paternal clan are affirmed"❸ (Leenhardt 1937/1986:162). The early *pilou-pilou* ceremonies were structured according to the mechanisms which continue to form, inform and perpetuate the social and spiritual life of Kanak communities. From this point of view, Lemire (1884:110) described them as ceremonies… "at one and the same time a martial festivity and a trades congress"❹. The *pilou-pilou* was of such importance to the traditional life of the Kanaks that Raymond Leenhardt (1978:23) was moved to write, "…to take away from them the freedom to hold the pilou-pilous, is to take away the sense of their very existence…"❺. The *pilou-pilou*

❶ "un grand rassemblement de voleurs…".

❷ "cérémonie sociale de propitiation autour de laquelle gravite toute la vie indigène".

❸ "Le pilou est la cérémonie qui porte la société à son point culminant, celle où sont renouvellés les contrats sociaux, effectués les échanges, acquittées les dettes, affirmés le prestige et la puissance du clan paternel".

❹ "...à la fois une rejouissance guerrière et une réunion commerciale".

❺ "…leur enlever la liberté des pilou-pilous, c'est leur enlever le sens de leur existence…".

can be seen as the New Caledonian set of variants upon the great exchange ceremonies found all over the Pacific, including the Trobriand exchange cycles, *moka* of highland Papua New Guinea, and *na huqe* of Ambae in Vanuatu, etc.

The principal procedure of such ceremonies was a meeting of matrilineal and patrilineal clans, with the exchange of foodstuffs and materials, combined with celebrations in dance. Although these ceremonies have been curtailed in their former style and scope, the idea behind them continues today in the large-scale distributions that occur at weddings or funeral wakes said to be held traditionally.

The origin of the word *pilou-pilou*

There are several interpretations of the expression *pilou-pilou* and there is no single accepted definition. Jim Hollyman (pers. comm.), says that the origin of the word *pilou-pilou*, as it was first used by the French *colons* in the north of the *Grande Terre*, derives from the old French verb 'pilouter', meaning dancing. French immigrants saw the impressive Kanak dances, and applied the term both indiscriminately to every kind of Kanak dance, and especially, to the culminating dances of exchange ceremonies which are considered in this book to be variants of the round-dance.

At the present time the terme *pilou* or *pilou-pilou* has several meanings, to both Kanak and European groups in New Caledonia. It may well refer to ancient and vast ceremonies but in the sense of *pars pro toto*[1]. Leenhardt (1937/1986:169) wrote, "Travellers have enlarged a detail [the dance] of the immense ceremony, as if with a magnifying glass, and the sense of the whole has been forgotten"[2].

In a number of Kanak languages, terms similar to the word *pilou* can be related to words used for dance, but not necessarily to the names of the ceremonies themselves. *Philu*, with aspirated *p*, belongs to two of the far northern group of languages, namely Caac (Pouébo) and Nyâlayu (Balade) with its dialect Belep (for Belep Dubois [1973-1974:250] writes *phiilu*) where it refers to 'dance' and 'to dance'. The first use of the term *pilou-pilou* is thought to have been by Marist missionaries in 1846 (Gasser 1992:124). There is a widespread opinion in New Caledonia that the Nyâlayu word *philu* is the origin of the term *pilou-pilou,* since the Marist Mgr. Douarre was mainly in contact with Nyâlayu speakers. However, it is not known if the Marists, in the early years of their mission, knew any Nyâlayu words.

Garnier (1867/1990:67) saw a different origin for the word *pilou-pilou*. By onomatopoeia, he thought that the sound of the concussion bark-clapper as heard from a distance would sound like either *pelou-pelou-pelou*... or *pilou-pilou-pilou*... This hypothesis was taken up by Vermast (1902:35) and was not excluded by Leenhardt (1930/1980:143). Leenhardt refers particularly to the reduplication, associating it with the 'monotony' of the bark-clappers' music. On the other hand, *colons* may have reduplicated *pilou* to make it sound 'more native'. There were a number of Bislama speakers in New Caledonia during this period and they too could have used reduplication.

After the period (from about 1900 to 1950) during which Kanak dancing

[1] 'part in place of the whole'.

[2] "Les voyageurs ont grossi comme à la loupe un détail de l'immense fête, et le sens de l'ensemble en a été oublié".

was hardly performed, there was much confusion about the places of origin of dances. Terms referring to dances also seem to have been confused. In earlier years more terms referring to specific dancing and specific dances are likely to have existed. Today generic terms are used for various kinds of dances, *pila* in the languages Pije, Fwâi, Nemi and Jawe ; *pwölu* in Cèmuhî or *cäbu* in Paicî. Then again the term *hwâi* in Pije, Fwâi, Nemi and Jawe, besides being the name of a dance rhythm (see p.117) also means 'dancing with singing' ; the term *pila,* meaning 'dance in general', seems to have been introduced, perhaps from Ouvéa ; in Iaai 'dance' is *biâ,* in Fagauvea it is *pia ;* in Nengone the term *pia* refers to 'dancing in general', and the traditional dance of Nengone is called *kutera* (see p. 179).

When Kanaks from different language areas come together, they use the term *pilou* or *pilou-pilou,* but if they speak the same Kanak language they may, if they know their own local vocabulary, use a local expression. In the languages of the north, as listed in Haudricourt and Ozanne, the big exchange ceremony with dancing is called *genaman.* In Cèmuhî, the ceremonies are called *bwénaado* and in Paicî, they are called *gé.* In the Ajië language the generic term for the ceremony is *boê,* and the same word is used for the yam (*Dioscorea* spp.), which is an important item of exchange in the ceremony. In the Ajië language there are several names which refer to the ceremony according to the season in which it is held. Finally, in Xârâcùù this festival is called *xiti,* which also stands for religion or for the idea of the sacred.

Pilou is used today by the general public to refer to what is called in this book the round-dance. One reads on printed programmes for festivities, for example, '20 Heures : Pilou' (8 o'clock : Pilou) and everybody knows that this will be the start of the round-dance. In the 19th century all kinds of Kanak dances were referred to by a single generic term which has made the literature difficult to understand. To avoid such confusion, from here on the following terms will be used :

- *pilou-pilou* — for the whole ceremony of exchanges, dancing, etc.
- *pilou* — (without reduplication) for the round-dance itself

FUNCTION OF THE *PILOU-PILOU*

In traditional Kanak life, several forms of material exchange worked together. Leenhardt (1937/1986:92-96) distinguished four formalised exchange systems. The *piré*, the trade-dance (see p. 61), the 'jade cycle' ('*cycle du jade*')❶ and the *pilou-pilou.* The *pilou-pilou* was the most important of all these formal exchanges, not only because of its economic functions, but also because it was the occasion when changes in social status were made, and the moment for significant public announcements such as the birth of a high-ranking child, weddings, deaths, the end of mourning periods, the elevation of a new *chef,* male initiations, newly established alliances (for economic reasons or for warfare), the placing of new sculptures such as the vertical sculpture on a *chef's* roof, and so on. During a single *pilou-pilou,* several of

❶ A specific New Caledonian trade-cycle, which touched the southern Vanuatu islands, involving jade (nephrite) objects such as the *haches ostensoires* (ceremonial axes). There is now doubt about the reality of the 'jade cycle', especially since the discovery in 1994 of jade together with traces of quarrying in the north of the *Grande Terre* (Christophe Sand pers. comm.). Until then it had been thought that jade existed only on the island of Ouen in the south of the *Grande Terre* and that it was traded northwards, while treated shells (*nacre*) mainly from the Loyalties, were traded southwards.

(photo Allan Hughan1880)

A post-card, showing a *tribu,* at Canala, prepared and ready to hold an exchange ceremony (*pilou-pilou*) where a number of dances will be performed.

these actions and announcements could take place.

The number of persons attending a *pilou-pilou* varied enormously. De Vaux (cit. in Sarasin 1929:219) wrote of a *pilou-pilou* with five to six thousand people present. For huge events, the invited groups were members of the hosts' matrilineal clans, friends and allies. The accommodation and feeding of such numbers imposed colossal burdens on the hosts. Vast *pilous-pilous* would have had to be prepared several growing seasons in advance, with considerable stockage of yam harvests to have enough on hand (yams are vegetatively reproduced, so that the first harvest can be used for 'seedlings' in the following season). Many new houses or shelters would have had to be constructed to lodge guests. The usual time for the *pilou-pilou* was in the cool season after the yam harvests (Leenhardt 1930/1980:146) which varies according to local climate and soils.

When ethnologists write about the former *pilous-pilous,* they are at pains to emphasise their scale and importance. However, some *pilous-pilous* were more modest in scope, and were held much more frequently than the giant feasts. Leenhardt's (1930/1980:143-178) well-known passage describing a *pilou-pilou* which was held principally to end a mourning period, will be followed here. The description is certainly very detailed, but it may have been idealised, including more characteristic elements brought together than would have occurred during one ceremony. It refers to the region of Houaïlou.

According to Leenhardt, before the ceremony proper began, the hosts made offerings for the inauguration of newly-built houses. Dances took place, with the yam offerings, and at the end of this period there would be a very big dance. Leenhardt also states that the dancing and singing would be accompanied by the sounds of friction upon palm spathes. He divides the *pilou-pilou* into several sequences, for the duration of a large ceremony could go on for as long as three weeks. A ceremony was held in the central alley of the *tribu*. In the first of the sequences, allied patrilineal groups came together and presented yams and other prepared foods such as sugar cane, coconuts etc. These would be piled up along the alley, to make as fine and impressive a display as possible. This sequence closed with speech-making, in which lessons were repeated on the reasons for holding the ceremony, the yams were formally handed over, and the alliances of those present satisfactorily confirmed.

In the following sequence invited matrilineal groups came and offered their artefacts and food. During both these sequences individual trade-dances could take place inside various houses.

In the next sequence there were fresh piles of food, one for each invited group having been prepared in advance, and persons in mourning, who had been wearing big turbans since the death of a relative, arrived with those young men who had been recently initiated by incision. The mourners cleaned the skulls of the dead and assisted the newly initiated. The women performed the *kare* dance (unique to the Houaïlou region), which seems to have been performed in one long line, with very gymnastic steps. This was followed by the *vikai* dance, suggesting war-games, in which the mourners and the newly initiated danced one behind the other in a line that led from the matrilineal groups to the patrilineal, who were placed on either side of the central alley.

(photograph in the Serge Kakou collection, Brignoles, France ; date and place are not given)

During *pilou-pilou* ceremonies food is arranged in impressive piles. This pile, mainly of yams and sugar cane, is ready to offer to guests accompanied by an eloquent speech.

Food was distributed with eloquent speeches in which the past was recalled. The round-dance *boria* took place at night. Finally, some mimetic dances specially prepared by the young men of the matrilineal group(s) were presented to the hosts. At the very end, some warlike or competitive games, as well as individual 'sales' and exchanges could take place. Such a feast closed with the official proclamation of the end of the mourning period, and all those who had been affected were then able to take up their normal lives once again.

Smaller ceremonies were also called *pilou-pilou* by the *colons*. Rozier (1990:89) says that they were a way of welcoming strangers and could consist of a simple meal followed by dances, and last for only an afternoon. Vermast (1902:34-40) writes about a small *pilou-pilou* like this which was held in the 1870s for a family of settlers. The *colon* built his house at Koné and, when it was finished, *Chef* Galiaté❶ of the neighbouring *tribu* invited the whole French family to attend a *pilou-pilou*. The ceremony lasted an afternoon and there were dances, speeches, a meal and an exchange of presents.

The *pilou-pilou* : scene of exchange and a way of making concrete the notion of exchange

For Leenhardt (1930/1980:146) "Every gathering for family reasons which includes a meal is a pilou-pilou"❷. Apart from dancing, the most important factor was the offering of exchange items. Exchanges could consist not only of material things or goods, but also of speeches and ideas. In this latter sense, the dance was also an exchange item. The *boria* dance was a spiritual exchange between the living and the dead (the ancestors). The mimetic dances prepared by young men of the matrilineages were equally exchanged for they were 'given' to the patrilineages and in following *pilous-pilous,* the reciprocity of exchange continued.

Speech given from a tree

In the centre and north of the *Grande Terre* some ritual speeches are delivered with the speaker standing on a small tree or on a wooden structure. While the speaker utters his speech, a group of kinsmen perform a specific dance. The act of such ritual speech-making became popularly known to the *colons* as a '*discours sur la perche*' (speech from a pole). In the Fwâi language of the north, such a speech is known as *di cuut ge ceek* (beginning on the tree) because it was performed at the beginning of ceremonies. The dance performed during the speech is called in Fwâi *pila le hwan hoot* 'the dance of the speech' *(la danse du discours).* In Paicî the speech is called *popai görö upwârâ* (speech from a tree), and the dance is called *câbu pi têê*, (to dance with sliding steps).

The speech

The speech given from a tree formed an important part of the traditional *pilou-pilou* because each invited group provided a speaker who spoke of the group's origin and its relation to other social groups in a poetical language

❶ Vermast's writing is in novel-form and the names he uses are fictitious.

❷ "Toute réunion pour une circonstance de famille et comportant un repas est un pilou-pilou".

rich in symbols. These speeches were so important that the speaker was not allowed to stand on the ground but needed to be above the people present. A small tree with a forked branch or a wooden pole with notches for toeholds was therefore set in the ground in the lower part of the alley (*goroaupwatêê* in Paicî), where later on the dances took place (W. Gorode 1990:184).

Although in each language region the vernacular is used for the speech from a tree, they all begin with the same *urere* or cry, which is *uaka riririri-ri, uaka*...[1]. This cry is not performed by the speaker, but by a person, whom Leenhardt (1930/1980:151) calls "le crieur" ("the crier"), who had the duty of calling together and preparing those present for the speech.

The speech has a kind of rhythm, in the form of verses of eight steps or "lines" (Bensa 1990:47). The speaker on the pole rotates torso and head to the rhythm of the speech's steps, addressing all the people standing around[2]. The ideal is that a speech should be continuous, uninterrupted, except for the shortest pauses for respiration, in which the dancers hiss, whistle and shout in order to cover the silence and to encourage the speaker to continue. Such speeches may have lasted up to half an hour. Today only a few elderly men know these speeches, they are performed very rarely and do not last as long as the ancient speeches.

The subject of the speech is always historical recounting events concerning the group which owns the speech and various other matters. The language is rich in allusions and symbols, quasi-poetic. There could be narrations of weddings, adoptions, former wars and alliances. At the outset of a speech from a tree, the names and relationships of various social groups are recited, so that the supporting dance-group is formally presented to other people present as spectators.

The dance

The dancers, exclusively men[3], stand on the ground in a circle around the speaker, watching him, carrying their traditional weapons : a spear or a club over the shoulder. The dancers make long backwards sliding steps staying on the spot (see opposite). They turn their shoulders slightly in synchronisation with the steps. The Paicî name *câbu pi têê* refers to the foot motions. Montague (ms.V:10) describes this kind of dancing : "While thus speaking, the audience danced around him in characteristic fashion, with

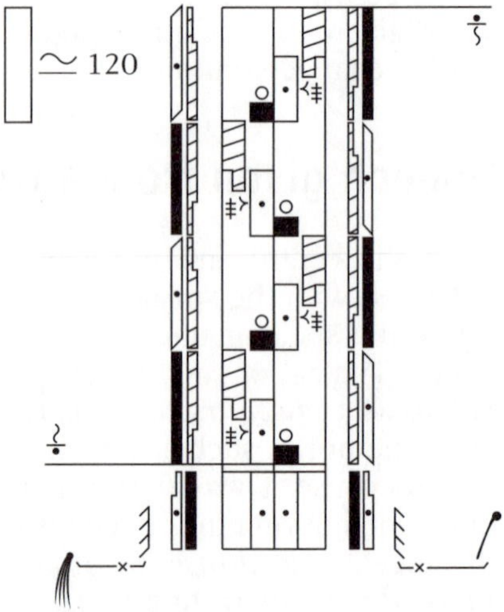

Extract from the dance as performed in anonymous (1954[film]).

[1] Compare Beaudet (1990:track1[CD]).

[2] Track 2 on Ammann (1997[CD]) presents a *popai görö upwârâ*. The stereo microphone (Sony ECM-737) was in front of the speaker. The rotating of his head results in having the sound arriving alternately from the left and right channels.

[3] In a film, in the archives of the A.D.C.K. (anonymous 1954) there is a short sequence of a speech given from a tree, possibly somewhere in the northeast of the *Grande Terre*. There is a group of men and also of women dancers around the speaker. This is the only report of women dancing at a speech given from a tree.

a springy step, the knees bent and toes turned outwards, the arms rather bent at the elbows and held away from the sides, rhythmically snapping their fingers, and making a noise with the mouth, which can be written as sh-sh sh-sh sh-sh sh-sh..., the accented 'sh' accompanied by a finger-snap. At various points they whistled and shouted and the whole while a soft beating was kept up upon dry coconut leaf-bases[❶], and the tapping together of objects of folded Bourao stuffed with Njauli-bark". The 'sh-sh' sounds are still common today, however the finger snapping has not been seen in the field during a speech given from the tree.

Trade-dances

Within traditional Kanak economic systems, there were several forms of institutionalised procedures, or rituals of exchange, of which, as described above, the *pilou-pilou* was the largest and most impressive. A 'silent' exchange system existed between coastal people and those living in the mountain ranges, called *piré* by Leenhardt (1937/1986:92). A mound of goods from the coast, mainly sea-food, would be placed at a recognised point on the track leading from the coast to the interior. Those who took the goods would replace them with specific mountain vegetable crops (for example, particular varieties of taro) and the coastal initiator of the exchange could then go and collect his reciprocal mound, without face to face contact between the groups being mandatory. The exchange point was, of course, kept under surveillance by each side.

In contrast to these 'quiet' or 'silent' procedures, there were others accompanied by music and dances, which are called trade-dances in this book. The oldest people among informants well remember ritualised exchanges, but even when they were young the exchanges were no longer accompanied by dancing or singing. They remember two main types : those carried out within a *case* and those made outside on open ground.

In-house trade-dances

Exchange dances held in the interior of houses did not need special ceremonial preparation, and appear to have been organised spontaneously. According to Lambert (1900/1985:160) women would dance in one *case* and men in another.

The trade-dance that Lambert calls the *tsianda* was performed frequently, even at times on a daily basis (Vieillard/Deplanche 1862:209). Participants sat in a circle, the leader started a song and the others joined in. The accompaniment was "the sound of hollow bamboo" ("le son du bambou creux") (Lambert 1900/1985:158). A man would dance to the rhythm of the music up to the centre post of the house, and there place the item he wished to exchange. The leader would stop the dancer at that point with the musical signal of a prolonged note. Then, anyone who wanted the item placed on offer could stand and propose his own item as an exchange. Upon agreement, the goods would change hands, the dance would then resume, and the next person with

❶ The beating of coconut leaf-bases has not been found today; however it could easily reappear as an ad hoc percussion instrument, a substitute for the bark-clapper.

Detail from a 19th century engraving showing a dance scene. Published in Godard : 1978:292 (no further information is available).

something to exchange would dance with it to the centre post.

Unfortunately, Lambert gives no indications of the movements of this dance and neither does Rau (1944:180). Rau compared the scene in the house to a theatrical spectacle. The man who set down his exchange item would declare its fine qualities in a loud voice, and only after he had left it would he start to dance. It is not known if Lambert and Rau witnessed variants of the same genre❶. Lambert's description of the *tsianda* seems to correspond with Leenhardt's (1937/1986:94) decription of the trade-dance which he calls "a sitting-dance" ("une danse assise")❷: "In a case seated men mark the rhythm of a dance. One of them gets up, presents an item, and dances, while he praises the value of the item on offer, (...) ...supported by the sympathy of the audience who, in a circle, mark rhythmically the cadence of his movements..."❸.

❶ Rau stayed in New Caledonia in the 1930s. According to the oldest informants today in-house trade-dances had probably been abandoned by that time. Rau's description may be based on interviews with old Kanaks of the time.
❷ Although sitting dances are well known on many Pacific islands (for example, Samoa and Hawai'i), there may be no link with Leenhardt's "sitting dance". That people perform in-house dancing seated may well be explained by the fact that there is a very high smoke density in the air above the door, which is about 100 and 120 cm high, and standing is possible for only a few moments at a time.
❸ "Dans une case, les hommes assis rythment une danse. L'un d'eux se lève, présentant un object, et danse, tandis qu'il vante la qualité de l'objet offert, (...)...soutenu par la sympathie des auditeurs qui, en cercle, rythment la cadence de ses mouvements...".

Leenhardt goes on to say that it was not only material objects which were exchanged, but also ideas and recitations of victories or war plans.

These in-house trade-dances were very popular and were held frequently. At times they were conducted during big meetings such as the *pilou-pilou*, when people from different regions came together. Leenhardt (1937/1986:94) adds that when the full, traditional ceremonies of *pilou-pilou* were forbidden, in-house trade-dances became even more popular and frequent, out of sight of missionaries and officials.

Lambert (1900/1985:159) describes a second type of trade-dance, the *ouaï*, referring to it as a "danse de secours" ("helping-dance"). Lambert's dance *ouaï*, is probably the dance *hwâi*, a word that in the northern languages Pije, Fwâi, Nemi and Jawe means a 'dance accompanied by singing' (see also p. 117). Lambert does not indicate the form of the dance but explains the reason why it was held. He says that a person whose resources were depleted, might be offered material gifts and food. It was also a method of repayment for labour in the construction of a *case* or a boat. From his description it is not clear as to whether the dance happened in-house or outside (or both). Today the *hwâi* dance, which is no longer performed as a trade-dance is danced outside the *case*.

Open-air trade-dances

Sarasin (1929:58) quotes Patouillet and Opigez to say that Kanak women did not hold markets of the passive kind, where vendors sit with their products and wait for clients to arrive and then to barter. Sarasin (1929:58) then cites Atkinson, who reported that the women would sit on the ground, in two rows, one facing the other, with each woman behind her products. Actual exchange would then take place in dancing. A woman who stood up would dance towards the other group, seeking to exchange her produce[1].

An open-air trade-dance was described by M. Bealo Wedoye of the Ouarap *tribu* (near Hienghène), of a type that was performed up to a few decades ago. Two stout poles would be planted in the ground, to which would be fixed either a cross-bar or a rope, upon which goods offered for exchange would be hung. A person who wished to have the offered goods, would dance up to them, take the goods down and replace them with their own trade-goods. There was accompaniment by slit-drums or bamboo stamping-tubes and songs. Hanging exchange items on a transversally fixed rope, was also mentioned by an informant of the Paicî region, but there the exchange was done without music and dancing, at the time when the informant was a young man. It may well be that earlier on in this region the exchange was accompanied by music and dances.

The open-air trade-dance took place under the watchful eyes of the assembled group, acting as witnesses of the relative values of exchanged items. The taker of the offered items might not have items of equivalent value, hence he or she was putting himself or herself in debt. On the other hand, to take a smallish item and replace it with something of greater value created credit. This kind of public ritual depended for its eventual accounting on the memories of participants.

[1] A similar arrangement for a ritualised exchange is reported from Ambae Island (Vanuatu) (Peter Crowe pers. comm.).

DANCE AS A DISTINGUISHED FORM OF WALKING

Trade-dances involve, as shown, the offering and exchange of customary and economic items, in which the presentations are made with dancing movements : not walking, nor marching, nor running but, always, dancing steps.

The combination of dance and trade was most evident in the former huge *pilou-pilou* ceremonies, as well as for smaller events such as in-house and open-air trade-dancing. It is consistently seen from the literature that arriving at the ceremonial area, bringing goods, and carrying them away, is all done with dancing. It has also been noted that today arrivals of goods to be offered at a dance-ground are accompaned by dances. Further on in the study it will be shown that mimetic dances themselves were exchange 'objects' at huge *pilou-pilou* ceremonies.

It is suggested here that the carrying out of exchanges is the major surviving elixir of traditional Kanak culture, that the acts of presentation are so respected, that nothing like a daily manner of walking about is good enough and dancing could be regarded in this light as a distinguished form of walking.

The round-dance

As there are some 28 separate Kanak languages spoken today in New Caledonia, it is not very surprising that there is no term common to all of them for the round-dance. Even so, the round-dance is performed in the same manner all over the northern half of the *Grande Terre*. Leenhardt (1930/1980:171) refers to the round-dance by the Ajië name of *boria* and uses it for the northern half of the *Grande Terre*, but in fact each language in the centre and north of the *Grande Terre* has its own name for this dance. In Paicî it is *cäbu tabéâ*, in Cèmuhî it is *pwölu tabéè*, in some languages of the Hoot ma Whaap region, namely Fwâi, Nemi and Jawe, the dance is called *pilaa-pije-paac*. In everyday language Kanaks will refer to this dance as *pilou*. It is sometimes called *danse autour du mât* (dance around the pole), making reference to the central symbol of the dance.

The round-dance is public property, it is not in the possession of a person or a family, and to hold this dances requires no special permission. It makes up a part of almost every feast or festival, everyone may participate in it and there is no choreography to be learned. Sometimes, it is cheerfully called *le tour du monde*❶. The dancers walk or lope to percussion rhythms around the central pole - when there is one. If there is no wooden pole, the musicians themselves take its place as the pivotal centre or hub of the dance. Originally, there would have been two leading male singers, performing *ae-ae* songs (see p. 122) accompanied by percussion instruments but now only a few older men know how to sing these songs, and so today the round-dance is frequently accompanied by percussion instruments only❷.

The largest dances these days attract several hundred people, and the circle moves either clockwise or anticlockwise. At the periphery of the circle a group

❶ *'Le tour du monde'*, in the sense of the 'everybody going round in a circle' and also in the sense of 'a voyage around the world'.

❷ See tracks 1 and 3 to 7 on Ammann (1997[CD]) and tracks 2 to 8 on Beaudet (1990[CD]).

may proceed in opposite direction to the main group, and perhaps again another group can proceed in opposite direction to its neighbour (The usefulness of some groups proceeding in a contrary direction will be explained below, see p. 66). However, in all old engravings and photos, the centre group of dancers are consistently moving anticlockwise. Crowe (1990) in his article "Dancing Backwards?" points out that most Melanesian round-dances move 'backwards', that is in the anticlockwise direction. Crowe explains this by the fact that Melanesia is in the southern hemisphere, and the anticlockwise direction is the apparent direction of movement of the sun, moon and shadows. He sees also a natural element in that the anticlockwise direction places the left-hand side to the centre, for protection by the stronger right-hand side, on the outside[1].

At festivals and feasts everyone waits with passionate impatience for the beginning of the round-dance, which is usually the final attraction. It will not begin until dusk has ended and, at last, night has come and it continues until sunrise. It is only rarely that a dance finishes before dawn for lack of dancers. The atmosphere is exuberantly happy, with shouting and laughing.

MUSIC AND CHOREOGRAPHY OF THE ROUND-DANCE

In traditional times musicians were stationed around the pole, at the hub of the circle, playing concussion bark-clappers and stamping-bamboos while two men sang *ae-ae* songs. Vieillard and Deplanche (1862:213) said that the ensemble of the singers was "... usually composed of strapping young men with powerful lungs"[2]. Today, such singing is rare, and the rhythm ensemble is often the only musical accompaniment, apart from the vocal and body sounds of the dancers themselves. When the dance is accompanied by singing, the musical passages between two pauses are shorter, as singers need to rest more often than percussionists. When the singers pause for breath and recuperation, the dancers rest on the spot, stationary, waiting for the music to start again. The dancers add to the overall sonic complexity with hisses, whistles, whoops and all kinds of original vocalisations, not to mention the sounds of their bodies being slapped or their feet pounding the ground.

The lead-singers received with traditional 'Kanak money' (*monnaie kanak*), and the contract was that they would sing the whole night through. Such singers were recognised specialists, to be paid for their services. A singer with a reputation would be asked to perform for dances at places very distant from his home (Montague ms.V:12)[3]. These days, when there are no singers, the percussionists play the same kind of rhythm as the one which accompanies the *ae-ae* songs, and such beats have become known as the *rythme du pilou* (rhythm of the *pilou*)(see p. 115).

Without a fixed choreography, dancers move freely in the general direction that has been chosen, arms often dangling or perhaps the hands clapping in time with the rhythm. The positions and motions of dancers in earlier days

[1] In general human beings are naturally right-handed, have more strength and flexibility on the right side of the body and make longer steps with the right foot so that ice-skaters move anticlockwise and people lost in the desert turn in anticlockwise circles.

[2] "... composé ordinairement de gaillards doués de solides poumons".

[3] To hire singers by contract is a widespread Melanesian custom.

were different. Sarasin (1929:219) said of a round-dance he saw at Oubatche, "Single or in lines of two or three tiptoeing men and youths, with their knees slightly bent and separated, the hips slighty undulating and hissing at the same time, an axe or a club held over the shoulder"❶.

Very similar dancing was described by Captain Kanappe (Courtis 1984:114) in the region of Hienghène at the beginning of the 1880s, where people danced in this way to carry the yam for presentation : "When the right foot taps the ground, the left shoulder is projected foward, and then vice versa"❷. Montague (ms.V:14) describes the actions for the round-dance as follows : "Knees and toes bent out and elbows away from the sides, snapping a finger rhythmically, and carrying over their shoulders ornamented lances or hatchets; decorated specially for the occasion".

The round-dance is described above in the way it is held on occasions when everybody can participate for example at dance festivals. During ceremonies where matrilineal and patrilineal clans come together, such as marriages or in earlier days the *pilous-pilous,* the round-dance includes a particular ritual.

The following description concerns the manner in which it is performed in the Paicî region. In other regions of the north of the *Grande Terre* the same procedure apparently takes place. The round-dance starts, but the adult men (20 to 40 years old) stay away and wait. The men of the matrilineage, who have been invited to the feast, prepare gifts for their cross-cousins. Once the matrilineal 'brothers'❸ have decided on and prepared a good number of presents (lengths of fabric, shirts, mats etc.) they join the dance. They dance in the general direction of and on the periphery of the round, holding the presents ready. Their patrilineal 'brothers', the hosts, observe the gifts their cross-cousins are carrying, and prepare a larger number of gifts. The hosts then, carrying their presents, join the dance by forming a group on the periphery but dancing in contrary-direction. When they cross for the first time, the front man of the host group, shows his open hand, a gesture indicating 'give me your presents'. The matrilineal men don't yet give their presents, but continue to dance. There will be breaks in the dancing, because the singers and the musicians need to rest for a while. Only after the third break does the exchange of presents take place while dancing.

In the morning when the dance ends, the matrilineal group takes the pole from the centre : on its upper part branches have been left to which ribbons have been attached. These ribbons represent the piece of fabric which is used as an exchange item in the *coutume.* The matrilineal 'brothers' carry the pole to the patrilineal group as the final gift of *coutume,* before they start their journey home.

This ritual added to the round-dance was not described in 19th and early 20th century reports. However, it seems that up to the banning of the *pilous-pilous* different kinds of round-dances existed.

❶ "Einzeln oder in Reihen von zwei und drei trippelten Männer und Jünglinge, mit leicht gebogenen Knien etwas gespreizt gehend, die Hüften leicht schaukelnd und Zischlaute ausstossend; Axt oder Keule trugen sie geschultert".

❷ "Lorsque le pied droit frappe le sol, l'épaule gauche est projetée en avant, puis inversement".

❸ 'brothers' means here both brothers and parallel-cousins, for which in the Kanak languages there is only one word.

The round-dance in the 19th century

While the round-dance is a joyful communal dance today, some hundred years ago and more it was neither trivial nor facile. It was the culmination of the *pilou-pilou*. The round-dance was a means of contact with the ancestors, and of dancing with their spirits, and it was performed only at night. Baudoux (1952:30) says no fire and no light at all was allowed, whereas Patouillet (1873:178) and Sarasin (1929:219) state that at least a few torches did illuminate the dance. The central pole was essential to relate the living dancers with the dead ancestors. It was not merely the hub of the dance but also its spiritual centre. Leenhardt (1930/1980:171) refers to the pole as "*le corps de la danse*" ("the body of the dance") and goes on to say that it is the dance of the gods, the spirits of the dead, and in the minds of the dancers it is the ghostly ancestors themselves who dance. In the Paicî language the pole is called *iri cäbu*, *iri* is from *ie* the basic form of the word referring to the pole to which branches of the climbing yam plant are fixed and is a very important object loaded with symbols of the cycle of life.

Leenhardt (1937/1986:169) also writes : "For, in the invisible world, the deified ancestors are still dancing; those newly arrived in the after-world join in the round in the same way as one joins in that around the pole with the ribbons. The gods are dancing, carrying all of nature with them. Trees, stones, turn and dance with them. The Canaque knows all these things when he dances at night"❶.

Taking into consideration all the reports and descriptions available, it becomes apparent, that the form of the round-dance as it exists today was, up to the late 19th century, the basic form of quite a number of different dances. Each of these dances, perhaps with a specific name that is forgotten today, had its own formal particularities, for example Leenhardt (1935:64) mentions a particular stone erected for the *boria* dance ; the *colon* Pannetrat saw a round-dance in the 1850s performed by women who were holding weapons while they were dancing (Pannetrat 1857/1993:27); Patouillet (1873:177) saw the round-dance performed in front of the deceased person for whom the ceremony was held ; Garnier (1867/1990:239) saw a round-dance performed by women separately and at a distance from the men and, finally, Michel (1885/1988:115) says that women danced separately and sometimes in the opposite direction from the men.

Dellenbach (1936:268-272) analysed a scene of a round-dance carved on a bamboo. The two people in the centre, very probably the singers, are holding the centre pole. The musicians form a circle, facing the centre, around the singers. The musicians play only the bark-clappers and stamping-bamboos are not shown. Women and men dance in an anti-clockwise direction. Dellenbach's interpretation that the dancers are arranged along spokes, may not be true although this form of a round-dance is mentioned in Sarasin (1917:52), but may be the result of the medium's limitations in showing hundreds of dancers moving in a circle. The women seem to be young for their breasts are shown by circles, while on other incised bamboos women's breasts are shown

❶ "Car dans le monde invisible, les ancêtres déifiés dansent toujours, les nouveaux venus dans l'au-delà se joignent à la ronde comme on se joint à celle qui tourne autour du mât aux banderoles. Les dieux dansent, et ils entraînent la nature avec eux. Arbres, pierres, tournent et dansent avec eux. Le Canaque sait toutes les choses quand il danse, la nuit".

by a triangular shape, and they hold a particular dance stick (see p. 108). It seems that three women are holding hands, which does not exist in any Kanak dance today. Two rows of warriors make up the audience for this dance. The interpretation of the picture is not certain for the Kanak artist may have merely drawn the round-dance in an idealised way, but it could well represent one of the now forgotten variants of the round-dance.

'EXCESSES' DURING THE ROUND-DANCE

The early missionaries to the *Grande Terre* declared that the round-dance (which they called the night-dance [*danse nocturne*]) was the most debauched feast of Bacchus imaginable. "Those [dances] performed at night, especially when both sexes are present, are bad, not exactly in themselves, but in their consequences"❶ (letter of Pierre Rougeyron of the 3rd September 1846 quoted in Rozier 1990:175). Not merely were missionaries offended, but colonial officials also had difficulties accepting what they considered to be excesses. Vieillard and Deplanche (1862:213) wrote : "These dances are always followed by the most revoltingly lewd scenes"❷. Turner (1861/1984:249) reports, "The singing increases with the dance, and then follow the orgies of a night of unbridled liberty, which, drinking excepted, would compare with some of the worst of the ancient bacchanalia". For La Hautière (1869/1980:239) these impressions were so strong that all he wrote was that his quill-pen refused to write down such things.

The women who participated in the dancing were not married women. The married women sat aside from the dance with their children. If Baudoux (1952:32) whose writings are legends and not ethnographic reports can be believed, those women who joined in the dance were : "...repudiated women, after they had ceased to please, and they were numerous... ; ...those guilty of adultery...; ...disparaged girls, nearly always victims of violence... ; ...young girls punished for having failed to give public marks of respect to men... ; ...those who had broken the rules of morality... ; ...young girls abducted from other tribus..."❸. Baudoux still in his legend Kaavo says : "This crowd of young women swarming in the pilou, at the disposition of the throng of men, where nonetheless there were rules of precedence : 'To you the honour, Chef' ; or, 'After you, valiant warrior - you are stronger than I am'"❹. It must be repeated that this is an Extract from a legend and not an ethnographic report❺. However, the remarks of missionaries and officials as well as a declaration of the *colon* M. Bouge, who repeated to Sarasin (1929:28) what had been explained to him by the *chef* of Poyes, confirm that sexual acts took place during the round-dance. A legend from the region of Koné (Guiart 1957:64) gives a hint

❶ "Celles [les danses] qui s'exécutent la nuit, surtout lorsqu'il y a réunion des deux sexes, sont mauvaises, non pas précisement en elles-mêmes, mais dans leurs conséquences".

❷ "Ces danses sont toujours suivies de scènes de luxure les plus révoltantes".

❸ "...les femmes répudiées, quand elles avaient cessée de plaire, et elles étaient nombreuses...;...celles coupables d'adultère,..;...les filles dépréciées, presque toujours victimes de la violence...;...les popinées punies pour avoir failli aux marques ostensibles de respect dues aux hommes...;...celles qui avaient manqué aux règles de la morale...;...les popinées volées aux autres tribus".

❹"Ce monde de popinées grouillaient dans le pilou, à la disposition de la foule masculine, toutefois en se conformant à certains usages de préséances.'À vous l'honneur, Monsieur le Chef' ; ou 'Après vous, guerrier vaillant vous êtes plus fort que moi'".

❺ The authenthicity of Baudoux' legends is dicussed in Gasser (1993).

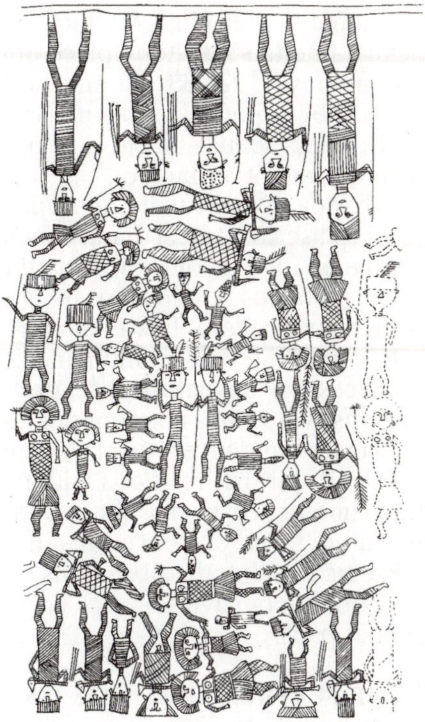

A dance scene during a *pilou-pilou* based on an incised bamboo. Dellenbach (1936:270) made a detailed drawing of a dance scene in perspective. The two singers in the centre are surounded by a circle of percussionists beating bark-clappers. Women and men are dancing around the musicians.

of the existence of such liberties during the round-dance. The hero of the legend "... is dancing the *pilou,* and is dancing with two women in one hand and three in the other"❶, which was so offensive to his wife that she left him. Sexual liberties also took place during dances at the *toka* ceremony on Tanna (Humphreys 1926:88; Bonnemaison 1986:398), to which the Kanak *pilou-pilou* shows quite a lot of similarities.

Besides sexual licence, long-suppressed interpersonal or inter-group disputes might surface on the occasion of the round-dance. While everyone was happy to come to a *pilou-pilou* for a big meal of the best quality food, and to socialise and meet family members, if there had been an undiplomatic choice of a guest, old rows could flare up again. Indeed, groups dealing with open problems, could find living side by side difficult, even in the generally festive atmosphere. It was often reported that, at the conclusion of the *pilou-pilou,* with the final round-dance, fights broke out, which were often deadly.

Excessive sexual license and dangerous fighting may have been the reasons why the missionaries wanted the round-dance to be stopped. However, the dance was of fundamental importance to the Kanaks because it involved spiritual relations with their ancestors who were thought to perform the same dance in the afterworld. In the event, the round-dance was never given up, but it was emasculated and became a far more sedate affair. Seen in a Pacific context, the objections to Kanak dances on account of licentiousness and riotous behaviour were echoed in many places, and were followed by similar bans.

Some further thoughts on the round-dance

According to Curt Sachs (1933:99), dancing in a circle is a global dance form. It is the earliest form, existing long before line dances. Sachs' approach to questions of antiquity and of the sequence of forms is purely speculative. Nevertheless, the round-dance is a widespread form throughout Melanesia, and, strangely, very rare in Polynesia (Moulin 1979:70; Kaeppler 1983:9)❷. The island nearest to New Caledonia where similar round-dances are found is Tanna in the south of Vanuatu where they are performed during the *toka* ceremony. Tanna and New Caledonia are culturally connected by ancient paths of immigration and former trading routes.

In New Caledonia dancing around a pole, or mast, seems specific to the *Grande Terre* and this symbol can have several interpretations. It can represent the power of the chief, it can connect the living with the dead, it can be a phallic symbol. It can be all or some of these - and yet more. It can also refer to the centre post of a Kanak *case* where the dancers who move around the pole in a circle represent the round floor of a *case.* Sachs (1937:146) refers to this idea, but gives no sources. In fact an example can be seen today among members of the Tiéti *tribu,* near Poindimié. They have a mimetic dance followed by a round-dance in which some dancers on the periphery hold up long bamboo poles tilted to the centre-post, symbolising the beams of the roof, and then the other dancers perform inside this '*case*'.

❶ "...danse le pilou, et danse avec deux femmes dans une main et trois femmes dans l'autre".

❷ Poort (1975:12) says, "The one circle dance is widely spread over the Polynesian area but is lacking in New Zealand and Hawai'i". He gives no more precise information.

Mimetic dances on the *Grande Terre* : a selection of early reports

It was the Kanaks' mimetic (or imitative, or pantomime) dances, the most spectacular dances in the Kanak repertoire, which were the most appreciated by early travellers and so they remain. To illustrate the change and development of such dances over the past 150 years, a chronological selection of quotations is given below concerning the *Grande Terre.* Information on early mimetic dances in the Loyalty Islands is sparse, and will be considered in the chapters on the region. The choice presented here has been governed by the clarity and detail of the authors' descriptions

1774 to 1850

The first ethnographic documentation of the Kanak people was written by the German naturalists Georg and Reinhold Forster, two of the scientists on Captain James Cook's second Pacific voyage. After visiting the Friendly Islands (now the Kingdom of Tonga) and charting and naming the New Hebrides (Vanuatu), where some of Bougainville's 'discoveries' of 1768 were confirmed, Cook sailed southwards to find and name New Caledonia.

The expedition's ships stayed in the waters of Balade from the 4th to the 13th September 1774, before heading south along the east coast of the *Grande Terre.* Georg Forster (the son of Reinhold) made notes on the natural surroundings as well as on the people encountered, during the seven days he spent on land. An oblique reference (Forster 1966:328) to music and dance says : "Except for the little whistle [see p. 31], which I mentioned above, we did not see even one musical instrument among them. Equally, we do not know if or to what extent they know dancing and singing"[1]. This remark is not surprising, given that Forster stayed for only a few days on land and that this stay did not coincide with ceremonies of any kind.

Sixty-seven years later, Captain Cheyne called at the Isle of Pines to load sandalwood, and his travel book (published in Pisier 1975:19) refers to a feast, where "The evening entertainment consists of dances and songs"[2]. In the same year, 1841, in the south of the *Grande Terre*, at Touaourou, the Rarotongan teacher Ta'unga[3] of the L.M.S. (London Missionary Society) saw dances and mentioned them in his diary, writing "Their celebrations are accompanied by dances"[4] (cit. in Pisier 1980:56).

Commander Julien-Laferrière, master of the 'Bucéphale', with the first Marist missionaries to New Caledonia on board, put ashore at Balade in December 1843, and described a feast given in his honour by the *Grand Chef* Paliki-Pouma. After the speeches of welcome, Paliki-Pouma started to sing a "wild" ("sauvage") song which was repeated by the chorus of dancers, and was accompanied by whistles (preseumably whistling with the mouth), hand-

[1] "Ausser der kleinen Pfeife [...], deren ich oben erwähnt, sahen wir nicht ein einziges musikalisches Instrument bey ihnen. Eben so wenig wissen wir, ob, und in welchem Maasse sie Tanz und Gesang kennen".

[2] "Les divertissements du soir consistent en danses et chants".

[3] Ta'unga (1820-1898) was a Rarotongan catechist for the L.M.S. He was not the first, but he was the only one of the period who kept a journal with notes on the way of life of the Kanaks.

[4] "Leur fêtes sont accompagnées de danses".

clapping and foot stamping. During the dance, two black masked figures appeared, and ran furiously about in the space between the dancers and the audience (Julien-Laferrière cit. in Rozier 1990:71).

Although Julien-Laferrière described the dances with admiration, the newly arrived missionaries did not like them at all. One of the first Marist missionaries wrote these remarks in 1846 (cit. in Rozier 1990:175) to his superior : "The dances of the New Caledonians are the most trivial and the most boring that I have seen. They consist simply of making a regular movement of the whole body, on the spot, accompanied by a certain kind of cry, as unpleasant as is the dance"❶.

1850 TO 1880

After the Act of Possession by France in 1853, colonial officers and administrators toured the *Grande Terre* to inspect and record the nature and extent of their new acquisition. Their descriptions were in general less prejudiced than those of the Marist missionaries. Vieillard and Deplanche saw dances on several occasions, and reported (Vieillard/Deplanche 1862:209) that they watched a *pilou-pilou* at Canala, where 500 to 600 dancers were present, all of them armed. "In an open space next to the chef's house they got into three or four rows, according to their number. In the middle of the first row, the dance-leader indicated each figure [section] with a special call,..."❷. The dancers moved with synchronised movements : "They mark the beat with shrill whistling, which they call tonu. When the end is reached they let out an appalling cry and all crouch down on the ground at the same time"❸. Later in this ceremony, masked figures appeared, then there was a women's dance, followed by a war dance (Vieillard/Deplanche 1862:210). The same authors (1862:212) continue the description of the Kanak mimetic dance : "The dancers dance on the spot, jumping from one leg to the other, while making a thousand contortions; voices and cries animate them and, little by little, quicken the beat. During this time, spectators, women and children, turn around the dancers in the glimmer of numerous torches, and as the beat quickens the pace, they walk, faster and faster ending up by running"❹.

Ulysse de La Hautière (1869/1980:115) observed a ceremony held by the two *Chefs*, Gelima and Kaké, in the Canala region in 1863 : "The venerable men, thrashing about as if truly possessed, heads crowned with fern, clubs in hands, yelling at the tops of their lungs, ran about in sham rage before the warriors"❺. During this performance, two masked figures also appeared, dancing in front of the warriors.

❶ "Les danses des Nouveaux-Calédoniens sont les plus insignifiantes et les plus ennuyeuses que j'ai vues. Elles consistent simplement à faire, sans changer de place, avec l'ensemble du corps un mouvement régulier, accompagné d'un certain cri aussi désagréable que leur danse".

❷ "Sur une esplanade voisine de la case du chef ils se rangeaient suivant le nombre, sur trois ou quatre rangs. Au milieu du premier rang, le directeur de la danse, indiquait chaque figure par un cri particulier,...".

❸ "Ils marquent la mesure par des sifflements aigus, auxquels ils donnent le nom de tonu. Lorsque arrive la fin, ils poussent un cri épouvantable et s'accroupissent tous à terre en même temps".

❹ "Les danseurs dansent sur place en sautant d'une jambe sur l'autre et en faisant mille contorsions; les voix, les cris les animent et peu à peu pressent la mesure. Pendant ce temps, les spectateurs, femmes, enfants tournent autour des danseurs aux lueur de torches nombreuses et suivant que la mesure presse le pas, ils marchent, marchent et finissent par courir".

❺ "Des vénérables, se démenant en vrais possédés, la tête ornée de fougère, le casse-tête à la main, criant de toute la force de leurs poumons, parcouraient, avec une fureur simulée, le front des guerriers".

A dance-scene from Garnier (1868/1990:58) with the caption : "A *pilou-pilou* at night. - Drawing by L. Crépon after a sketch by Mr. Garnier" ("Un pilou-pilou la nuit. - Dessin de L. Crépon d'après un croquis de M. Garnier"). Women and children holding torches are moving around a group of dancers. A dance of this form is mentioned by Vieillard and Deplanche (see p. 72) and La Hautière (see below). Only women are playing the bark-clappers in this engraving.

In 1865 La Hautière was present at a *pilou-pilou* near Païta given by *Chef* Ouatton at Naniouni, which lasted for three days, with 2000 people in attendance. On arrival at the dance-ground, the men of the invited *tribus* of Ounia, Bouloupari and Touaourou were painted black, wearing huge *bagayous* (penis sheaths), while the women wore traditional Kanak skirts. The men were armed and there was absolute silence as the groups arrived, until the people from Poindé came with loud shouting, imitating an attack. After the ceremonial speeches, which were accompanied by shouts and whistles, the general dancing began, in which there were synchronised jumps, again accompanied by cries and whistling. The dances continued : "On a dark night, around an immense bonfire, several lines of warriors, packed closely together, backs turned to the fire, made the ground tremble under the shock of their stamping feet"❶ and "All the rest of the natives, men, women, children, were running or walking, around the warriors alligned as we have said"❷.

❶ "Par une nuit obscure, autour d'un immense foyer, plusieurs lignes de guerriers, serrés les uns contre les autres, tournant le dos au feu, faisaient trembler le sol sous le choc alternatif de leurs pieds".

❷ "Tout le reste des indigènes, hommes, femmes, enfants courant ou marchant, tournaient autour les guerriers alignés comme nous l'avons dit".

La Hautière seems to be describing the same dance or one similar to that reported by Vieillard and Deplanche, as above (probably also from Canala), with women turning around the dancers having their backs to a fire. This dance however, is never mentioned later on in ethnological reports nor is it still performed, either in Canala or in other regions, but it appears to correspond to the scene illustrating Jules Garnier's report (see p. 73) although Garnier does not mention a dance in which women and children move around the stationary warrior-dancers. Rivière's illustration (1881:192-193) may be derived from the same picture and even a part of the illustration published, for example in O'Reilly and Poirrier (1959:ill.80), seems to have the same origin as Garnier's sketch.

La Hautière (1869/1980:240-241) spent four years in New Caledonia, and, having observed several dances, attempted a choreology of the different regions : "..., we should say, that the pilou varies according to the tribus, not in its general form nor in its ceremonial, but in the motions, the miming of the dancers"[1]. He distinguished the dances of the north of the *Grande Terre* from those of the Loyalty Islands. In the north of the *Grande Terre*, he observed that "... , the movements are more abrupt, more lively; the actors rehearse more and put more spirit, we would say with pleasure, more thunder, into their act"[2]. He thought that the dances of the north are more symbolic, for example enacting the character of the sea, the fish trying to escape from the thrown spear, and so on. On the Loyalty Islands, where "behaviour is more sensual"[3], dances are more poetic, representing people's passions, lusts, appetites, their laziness or vindictiveness.

In 1869 Patouillet watched a *pilou-pilou* at Wagap, where people from all over the east coast were among the guests. The first dance was a women's one. Then, he says "the only real dance" ("la seule vraie danse") followed, accompanied by the singing of a "monotonous" song. The masked figure called Apouéma appeared, which seemed, together with a sorcerer, to be exercising some cult magic (Patouillet 1873:183). He describes (1873:185) the following dance with some precision and admiration : "... the troupe carrying dance tassels and whistling an accompaniment, performed a kind of ballet, danced with a rhythm and steadyness that one would not expect to find among savages. The beat had five slow steps, followed by five quick ones. Upon each renewed warble of the leader, their hands changed movement and position, always in time and in perfect ensemble. After having mimed in their choreography the planting and tending of yams for 15 to 20 minutes [there followed], episodes of a war or other matters of importance to the tribu, ..."[4]. After the men's dance, another women's dance took place. The women came

[1] "...; mais, nous devons le dire, le pilou varie, suivant les tribus, non dans ses formes générales, dans son cérémonial, mais par les gestes, la pantomime des danseurs".

[2] "...,les mouvements sont plus saccadés, plus vifs; les acteurs mettent plus d'entraînement, de brio, nous dirions volontiers, d'orage, dans leur jeu".

[3] "moeurs sont plus lascives".

[4] "...la troupe qui, armée de houppes et s'accompagnant de sifflements, exécute une sorte de ballet, dansé avec une mesure et une régularité qu'on ne s'atendrait pas à trouver chez des sauvages. La mesure est de cinq pas marqués lentement, et suivis de cinq autres précipités. À chaque roucoulement nouveau du chef, les mains changent de mouvement et de position, mais en même temps et avec un ensemble parfait. Après avoir simulé pendant quinze à vingt minutes, dans leur chorégraphie, la plantation et la culture des ignames, les épisodes d'une guerre ou toute autre action importante pour la tribu,...".

in front of the *chef,* club in the right hand, and each hit an invisible enemy. In their left hands each held a shell-knife.

Patouillet's description corresponds in general to the way in which dances in this region are still performed. His indication of five slow and quick steps, does not however correspond to any of the region's dances now known. Unfortunately Patouillet does not say which group was dancing this particular dance, nor even if it was the host group or a guest group.

During the period of the 1878 insurrection, an Australian writer named Julian Thomas accompanied *Commandant* Levan, along with allied Kanaks. On their way to Oua Tom (south of the *Grande Terre)* where they expected to find the enemy, they had to spend the night at Koindé, between Canala and La Foa. Thomas describes the war dance of their troops, that was held on the night before the expected war. "Standing in line, the male savages beat time with their feet, with a swaying of their bodies, and gesticulating of their arms, singing a loud chorus. Through the dim smoke, flashing eyes shone out of the dusky mass. Louder and louder grew the strains, quicker and quicker became the motions of the bodies. They advanced, retreated, mingled together, then surrounded me. All the chiefs were now yelling and dancing" (J. Thomas 1886:107). This description of dancers in line and stamping their feet corresponds to the mimetic dances of today.

A few days later, after a battle, they presented the severed heads of the fallen enemy to the French officer and the Australian writer. They brought on their trophies in a dance-like way, and the warriors, full of joy over their victory, performed a round-dance which was accompanied by singing. "They were right upon us, they surrounded us, their spears at our breasts, their clubs and tomahawks over our heads. Then suddenly diverged into a circle, and threw some ghastly human heads at our feet, raising a song of triumph and dancing the pilou-pilou" (J. Thomas 1886:108-109).

During the first part of the 1878 insurrection a French official named J. Mauger witnessed a dance at Houaïlou, and described it thus (cit. in Hollyman 1966:113) : "A multitude of natives are gathered at this point. An immense circle of warriors, clubs over their shoulders, turn in gymnastic steps around another circle, made up of groups of three other warriors who perform, while following the [direction of the] outer circle, a kind of frightening waltz; some bend to escape the clubs which others are brandishing, pretending to hit them; they stoop, dodge, rise again, threaten each other, while still turning in groups, all the groups staying within the bigger outer circle of dancers. It is like fencing, but with clubs. The performance is led by an orchestra composed of young men in a line; six pound the ground, keeping time, with large decorated bamboos in which the lower ends let in air which compressed in the hollowed section creates a strange sound; others also strike bamboos with sticks. The warrior-dancers, naked, but with heads crowned with Kanak turbans, adorned with feathers and flowers, [their skin] well-oiled, shining and painted, have a ferocious appearance, which impresses everyone, whoever he is"[1] (see p. 76).

[1] "Une multitude d'indigènes sont réunis sur ce point. Un immense cercle de guerriers, le casse-tête à l'épaule, tourne au pas gymnastique autour d'un autre cercle composé de groupes par trois d'autres guerriers qui se livrent, tout en suivant la première ronde extérieure, à une sorte de valse effrayante ; les uns se baissent pour éviter le casse-tête que d'autres brandissent en simulant de frapper ; ils se penchent, s'esquivent, se relèvent, se menacent, tournant

The percussion instruments described by Mauger correspond to the present day stamping-bamboo and struck-bamboo. Mauger made a 'croquis de voyage' (traveller's sketch) of this scene (in O'Reilly/Poirrier 1959:illus.80). In front of what is probably the *chef*'s house there are groups of warriors who appear to be fighting with clubs. Other dancers, with clubs over their shoulders, walk or dance behind each other in a larger circle with a diameter about 50 metres, enclosing the warrior-dancers in the centre. A number of people (probably men) are watching from nearby, while other people (particularly women and children) are watching from further back in the forest. This form of dance is not known today.

A particular dance painted in 1878. The same kind of dance is described by J. Mauger (cit. in Hollyman 1966:113). Picture in Victor (1883) entitled : "War dance during the insurrection". ("Danse de guerre pendant l'insurrection").

In 1880 Captain Kanappe was invited to a *pilou-pilou* in the Hienghène region. He noted that, after the presentation of yams which was done in a dance-like action of the whole group, "... a strange and monotonous dance accompanied by singing..."[1] took place (cit. in Courtis 1984:114). The singing so often mentioned as accompanying traditional dances had in this case also accompanied the yam offering.

Lambert (1900/1985:156-161) describes several dances (see p. 77) pointing out the connections between war and dance, and considers reasons for the appearance of masked figures during dances. He indicates that first-row dancers were members of the *chef*'s immediate family or close kin. This is a rare instance in the literature of the relationship between the position of a dancer in the formation and his status in the social system. Lambert mentions the *pilou-ten*, a mimetic dance with synchronised movements, carried out with the dance tassel which makes motions more graceful, and beginning with the dancers in a kneeling position. "It is in this position that the mime begins, to the sound of soft whistling. As the momentum builds up the group rises as one man to full height; legs, bodies, all move with unequalled precision"[2] (Lambert 1900/1985:161). A

toujours en groupes et tous les groupes restant encadrés dans le grand cercle extérieur des danseurs. C'est une sorte d'escrime au casse-tête. L'exercice est conduit par un orchestre composé de jeunes gens rangés sur une ligne; six frappent sur la terre en cadence avec de gros bambous ornés, dont l'extremité inférieure donne accès à l'air qui refoulé dans la partie creuse produit un son étrange, d'autres frappent aussi des bambous avec des bâtons. Les guerrier danseurs, nus, mais la tête ornée de turbans canaques, de plumes et fleurs, bien huilés, luisants et peints, ont un aspect féroce qui impressionne quoi qu'on en ait".

[1] "...une danse curieuse et monotone, accompagnée de 'chants'...".

[2] "C'est dans cette position que commence la mimique, au bruit de doux sifflements. Sous l'action de l'élan donné, cette masse d'hommes se trouve soulevée pour évoluer en grand; jambes, corps, bras, tout fonctionne avec une précision sans égale".

An engraving of a dance scene from the Bouge collection in the Museum of Chartres (France) (date unknown, published in Boulard [1992:57]). On the right side of the engraving there may be an illustration of the laxity that seems to have existed during night-time dancing. The mask on the left is peculiar, because it shows no similarities to known traditional Kanak masks.

close correspondence of the *pilou-ten* may lie with the dance called *hneen,* which is still known in the region of Hienghène. Lambert indicates that each *tribu* has its own dances, each with its own name, such as the *aout* (waves ; La Hautière [1869/1980:241] writes "ast"), representing the sea's rolling, or the *tsiaouna* (storm) imitating the effects of cyclones. He mentions an in-house dance called the *mendo,* performed by women in one *case,* and men in another. When the same dance takes place in the open air its name is changed to *boura,* and is danced by both men and women together, but without any holding or touching between the sexes. Frequently there were fights and a show of bad feelings after a *boura.* It is possible that Lambert is refering here to the round-dance. *Boura* may be a variation in the spelling of *boria,* the Ajië name for the round-dance.

Garnier reports three different kinds of dances that he attended. What he saw at Arama he describes as "... New Caledonian dances in which everyone stamps in cadence, shaking their weapons in time, while a gasping whistie comes out of their chests"❶. On this occasion there were masked figures which appeared (Garnier 1867/1990:52). Next, Garnier was at a *pilou-pilou* in honour of a brother of the *Grand Chef* Bouarate, but he only describes the round-dance (Garnier 1867/1990:67). A *pilou-pilou* at Wiidö, was interrupted by a real battle between the people of Wiidö and Ponérihouen. Garnier's article in *Le tour du monde*, is illustrated with an engraving, showing a scene of this tribal war.

Besides these descriptions of dances from the period between 1860 and 1880 there is an engraving published in O'Reilly/Poirrier (1959:illus.80) giving a general view of a *pilou-pilou,* but it seems to be composite, not of a particular dance. There are some spectators sitting on a huge tree watching the scene and it is odd that the mask shown bears no resemblance to a Kanak mask. The engraver was probably inspired by other sketches and engravings and wanted to reproduce the atmosphere that sometimes reigned during a *pilou-pilou* rather than to show a particular scene accurately.

1880 TO 1900

Jules Durand attended a *pilou-pilou* at Ouébia in 1898. He describes (Durand 1900:501) the dance as "a real battle" ("un véritable combat") : "At first the Ouébias came foreword with raised clubs, their spears ready, striking a thousand blows at an invisible enemy. They were seen to retreat, to return, to show suspicion, presently dividing into enemy camps, uttering raucous cries, hurling threats, or appearing to greet each other, to recognise one another, to draw nearer to one another, bowed towards the ground; this was a general melee, a fantastic stamping of feet, with mouths open, whites of the eyes showing, frenzied legs, bodies streaming with sweat, a band of warriors making convulsive gestures like those of demons stirred in a furnace, in the glare of a blazing inferno, in spirals of smoke and dust. Then, suddenly, after a final and dreadful cry, they stood up straight, all motionless at the same time"❷.

Turpin de Morel (1949:33) describes a dance performed around 1900 at a *pilou-pilou* at Nenema, to which people from Koumac were invited. Besides the aggressive, warlike behaviour as illustrated above, he depicted a mimetic dance, apparently in the way it is still known in the Hoot ma Whaap region, of a bird that flies to a tree to sing and hops from branch to branch. "After one or two bars for nothing, given by clapping, the rhythm of a sweetly melancholic air came from this body [of an old man sitting off side] used by the passage of years. Immediately the white pompoms [dance tassels] swayed, rose, dipped down passed back and forth, from underneath a flexed arm. Heads [of the dancers] nodded and followed the supple movements of the whole body. To these gestures worthy of, the most beautiful theatrical perfor-

❶ "...danses néo-calédoniennes, dans lesquelles tous trépignent en cadence, en agitant leurs armes en mesure pendant qu'un sifflement haletant sort de leurs poitrines".

❷ "Les Ouébias d'abord s'avancèrent la hache levée, la sagaie tendue, portant mille coups à un adversaire invisible. On les voyait reculer, revenir, se défier, tantôt partagés en camps ennemis, poussant les appels rauques, lançant des menaces, ou ayant l'air de se saluer, de se reconnaître, et se rapprochaient baissés vers la terre; ce fut une mêlée générale, un trépignement fantastique, des bouches ouvertes, des yeux chavirés, des jambes frénétiques, des corps ruisselants, une troupe de guerriers ayant des gestes convulsifs, pareils à des démons remués dans la fournaise, dans l'éclat du brasier qui flambait, dans les spirales de fumée et de poussière. Et voilà que subitement, ils se redressent, tous immobiles à la fois, après un dernier et horrible cri".

mances, short shrill cries were uttered; all this in synchronisation, as if made by the same movement of an automaton. Then to finish, [there was] a strident cry, and all these immaculate white pompoms were thrown into the crowd"❶.

After 1900

Fritz Sarasin (1929:219) twice had the opportunity to observe Kanak dances on the *Grande Terre* : once at Oubatche and once at Bopope. At Oubatche he saw a round-dance, in its common form, and at Bopope he saw what he called an "artistic dance" ("Kunsttanz"). In the latter, the dancers' spectacular entrance was accompanied by a man singing. Sarasin saw that with each step, the dancers touch first the ground with the toe before setting down the foot. Sarasin was then presented with yams and fowl, the dancers carried out a sham attack against him and then the dance proper began, with 10 young men performing four figures (sections). At the beginning, the dancers were seated in two lines of five. With dance tassels they alternately swept the ground, then jumped up and made movements in all directions with turns and bends, all with the greatest precision. The dance leader gave signals, by whistles and hisses, to change to particular motions. One figure consisted of sitting, then standing, with graceful waving of the dance tassels; at the finale they were walking one behind the other in an ellipse, finishing by tossing the dance tassels in the air simultaneously (Sarasin 1929:221). According to this description, Sarasin may have seen the *bèèmä* dance, the present state of the dance of Bopope is given on page 162. After the dance presentation at Bopope, a masked figure appeared and feinted an attack on two warriors.

Pastor Maurice Leenhardt's works include frequent references to dances. In a description of a *pilou-pilou* he refers to mimetic dances, as they were done, according to his description (Leenhardt 1930/1980:143-178), in the last period of the classic *pilou-pilou* and where they "...constitute the most remarkable part of the *pilou*"❷ (Leenhardt 1930/1980:174). The dancers, each with the dance tassel in his hands, are led by the "maître de danse" ("dance-leader"). "They come forward, bent over, hiding under some branches that they are carrying. On the dance-leader's order, they stand up straight and get into lines : 'Sweep with your poeti [dance tassel]!' and all, with wide motions, swing their straw on level with the ground, 'Sleep!', 'Cry!',... "❸. At the end of the dance, the dance tassels were placed at the feet of the young men of the matrilineal group with the following speech: "Poeti [dance tassel] that you have bound... and have sent to us. It remained far away for a long time, while you were thinking that : they will come and bring a dance which will strengthen our bond..."❹ (Leenhardt 1930/1980:174). This quotation refers to the

❶ "Après une ou deux mesures pour rien, données par battements de main, un rythme d'un air mélancoliquement doux sortit de ce corps délabré par les ans. Aussitôt les pompons blancs se balancèrent, s'élevèrent, s'abaissèrent, passèrent et repassèrent d'un bras arrondi dessous. Les têtes dodelinaient et suivaient ces mouvement souples de tout le corps. A ces gestes dignes des plus belles représentations théâtrales, des petits cris aigus étaient poussés; tous cela avec ensemble, comme mu par un même mouvement d'automate. Et pour finir, un cri strident et tous ces pompons d'une blancheur immaculée étaient jetés à la foule".

❷ "...constituent la partie la plus remarquable du pilou".

❸ "Ils avancent, courbés, se dissimulant sous des branches qu'ils portent. Le maître commande, ils se redressent, se disposent en rangs : 'Balayez de vos poeti!', et tous, en gestes amples, balancent leur paille au ras du sol, 'Dormez!', 'Pleurez!',...".

❹ "Poeti que vous avez noué... et nous avez envoyé. Il reste longtemps loin, tandis que vous songiez : Qu'ils viennent et apportent une danse qui lie les solives...".

Two dancers from Bopope photographed by Fritz Sarasin in 1911. Both are wearing short *manous* and the dancer on the left is also wearing a *bagayou.*

symbolic value of the dance tassel and on page 108 this dance accessory will be considered further. Leenhardt then mentions a different dance, carried out without weapons but where the dancers imitate a combat, and says that this dance was introduced from the Loyalty Islands, where the mimetic dance was actually developed. He mentions at the same time, that the dance can become a theatrical play and is then called *wasai*. This name might be related to *wahai,* the women's dances of the Loyalties. The relation between the Loyalty dances and those of the *Grande Terre*, will be considered later.

Millet (cit. in Mayet ['1959':45]) called the dances he saw on the *Grande Terre* "ballets of mourning" ("ballets de deuil"), saying that the dancers arrived in stealthy silence. Suddenly a cry would be heard, and some 30 or 40 dancers, with torsos painted black, burst from the surrounding bush. They had dance tassels in their hands, and took up a position in front of the *chef,* at the far end of the central alley of the village. The subsequent mimetic dance lasted for about half an hour, consisting of sections lasting three or four minutes each, with short pauses in between. The dancers mimed hunting, sailing, fishing, war and copulation, and carried out all of it in perfect synchronisation. Another group followed and performed the dance of "the large buzzard" ("le grand buse"), in which the sounds of the great bird were also imitated.

This selection of reports from the 19th and early 20th centuries on the mimetic dances of the *Grande Terre* gives a very different picture from that of today. Many of the descriptions do not correspond to any dances known and performed today. For example, the dance with small groups simulating battle in the huge dance circle, is extinct. Those dances where women and children circle the warriors on the periphery have disappeared, but then so have the warriors. Most of the reports say that the mimetic dances were accompanied by singing. Today the round-dances are accompanied by singing, but only a few mimetic dances, in the north of the *Grande Terre*, are known that have a part accompanied by singing. The precision in synchronisation of the dance motions, so surprising to the early travellers, may not be as perfect today as it was in the 19th century.

On the other hand, certain elements of the old dances have retained their presence and importance in modern Kanak festivities. The resemblances between dance performances and the former tribal wars are still acutely felt. Many reports, from Canala and proceeding northwards to Hienghène, speak of the appearance of masked figures. Were the masked figures part of the dance itself, or were they seizing an opportunity? This question is dealt with below. It is important to note that masked figures no longer appear during dances on the *Grande Terre*. There are contradictory statements about the participation of women in dances during the *pilou-pilou*. For women to be allowed to participate at all in ceremonial life would have been quite exceptional in a Melanesian society. A discussion of these questions may also help us to understand the situation of the dances today.

CHAPTER 3

EARLY KANAK DANCES OF THE *GRANDE TERRE* AND MELANESIAN CULTURE

Kanak dance and its relationship to tribal warfare

The most obvious factor to emerge from the early reports about mimetic dances is their intimate relationship with tribal warfare. Inter-tribal war was frequent before, and for many decades after, the arrival of missionaries. The L.M.S. missionary George Turner (1861/1984:421), who stayed in Touaourou, says that before the arrival of the missionaries "...it is war, war, war, incessant war!" And Ta'unga wrote in 1846 from Maré : "The most important issue is war. The inhabitants do not stop fighting amongst themselves, night and day, month after month. Fighting is so frequent in order to satisfy their keen taste for human flesh"❶ (cit. in Rozier 1990:120). Leenhardt (1930/1980:41) confirms that cannibalism was often a sufficient reason to go to war. Anthropophagy was one reason to go on a war party, other reasons were over disputes about land or about captured women etc. Above all, war gave by far the best opportunity for a man to win prestige, the winning of which was a major theme in the life of a Melanesian❷ (Keitsch 1967:79). Anyone able to watch tribal war in Melanesia might first be reminded of a Melanesian dance. Inter-tribal war scenes are shown in the film *Black Harvest* (Connolly/Anderson 1992 [film], see also Gardner/Heider 1968) where the warriors, positioned in several rows, duck down in the tall grass, then stand up quickly to send their arrows or spears. Once they have stood up and can have been seen by the enemy, they move constantly to make it more difficult for the enemy to aim their spears or

❶ "La première question est la guerre. Les habitants ne cessent de se battre, jour et nuit, mois après mois. S'ils se battent si fréquemment, c'est pour assouvrir leur goût très vif pour la chair humaine".

❷ Winning prestige in war was a man's obligation not limited to New Caledonia. All over Melanesia this was the most important task in a man's life. For example, in the region of the Sepik (Papua New Guinea) a man's prestige rose after a succesful headhunt. Most of the songs and music recorded during a short visit in the Middle Sepik were originally performed to celebrate the return of successful headhunters (Ammann 1989 [unpubl.]).

arrows accurately. The warriors move in a rhythmically coordinated way. The coordination of movements takes place while the warrior is very alert and in absolute control of himself, ready to escape the arrows and spears with quick movements.

Kirk Huffman, an ethnologist who had many occasions to observe tribal warfare in Vanuatu in the 1960s, has said that the performance of the ni-Vanuatu warriors in battle reminded him first and foremost of their dancing (Kirk Huffman pers. comm.).

Apart from the published engraving of a Kanak tribal war scene in (Garnier 1867/1990:63) there exist only two published pictures, both taken by Leenhardt, (1930/1980:Pl.XI) showing war scenes. These two pictures are reported by one of Leenhardt's last students as 'arranged' pictures which do not show actual war scenes (Guiart 1992:137). It can be seen that there is little information available to make possible a visual comparison between traditional Kanak dancing and Kanak warfare. Most Kanaks class their mimetic dance as a war dance (*danse de guerre*) and the nature of the relationship between dance and war in traditional Kanak culture will now be examined.

The tribal war scene published in Garnier (1868/1990:9/63), with the caption : "Battle on the river of the Ponérihouens. - Drawing by Emile Bayard after a sketch by M. Garnier" ("Combat sur la rivière des Ponérihouens. - Dessin d'Emile Bayard d'après un croquis de M.Garnier"). The illustration shows a scene typical for those found in colonial literature of the period, it is not specifically Kanak (see p.144 and 181).

Dance and war are formally related on several levels. The dances are so conceptualised that dancing is a way of training for warfare, where a warrior learns how to handle his weapons and how to move appropriately. A dance both symbolically represents tribal warfare and strongly imitates it. Dance also prepares a warrior psychologically for war. Finally, joy after a sucessful battle is expressed in dance.

PREPARATION AND TRAINING FOR WAR

The appearance of the dancer in the 19th century was the same as that of a warrior. "Welcoming ceremonies in the pilous are made displaying full battle array"❶ (Leenhardt 1930/1980:39). The carrying of weapons in itself does not mean that war is being prepared because in the 19th century a Kanak man never put aside his spears and clubs and he always wore the sling around his head. But the black painted body of the dancer is a clear indication that he is now a warrior.

The most significant dance accessory is the dance tassel or *pwêêti* in Paicî which is part of nearly every Kanak mimetic dancer's equipment. Such an object is used nowhere else in Kanak culture except for the preparation of war. The 'war tassel' was sent by a courier to ask another *tribu* for a war alliance (Leenhardt 1922:257 and 1930/1980:41 ; Saussol 1979:308).

The captain's wife, Mary Wallis, kept a journal during her stay in New Caledonia in the early 1850s. In the chapter about tribal wars she says that a sort of soothsayer called the Pueaearing is consulted. "He sends women to procure a certain kind of grass which he ties in several bunches…". When war is finally decided on "the bunches of grass receive their blessing from the *Pueaearing*. These are then sent, without any message, to those friends whom they wish to join them […]. On receiving the grass the warriors lose no time in joining their friends. On arrival they are feasted, after which all paint and decorate themselves, hold a dance and go and fight their enemies" (Wallis 1994:146). The presence of the *pwêêti* in the mimetic dances demonstrates beyond all doubt the existence of a relationship between dance and war.

Not all, but quite a number of dancers, especially those from the Loyalty Islands, wear dance belts. These too, are used either in war or in dance. Leenhardt (1930/1980:40) says : "This belt is found in the equipment for dances and Canaques never say what its true significance is"❷.

There are other parallels between dance and war besides paint and equipment. For example both demand the incorporation of a 'medicine' to bring success. The 'medicines' that had to be incorporated are various and may differ from region to region. Furthermore there is secrecy surounding these 'medicines' so that most of the early reporters did not see what was being used. Besides plant 'medicine' there were special stones that the "priest" (Leenhardt uses the word "prêtre") had to touch. A special leaf was prepared by the 'priest' and all the warriors had to eat it before a battle started (Leenhardt 1930/1980:41). Lambert (1900/1985:173-175) says that Kanaks from

❶ "Les réceptions dans les pilous se font avec le grand apparat de guerre".

❷ "On retrouve cette ceinture dans l'accoutrement des danses, et jamais les Canaques ne disent quelle est sa signification véritable". Leenhardt is refering to a special belt, which is different from the belt in use today. The belt was so strongly linked to war that in Paicî people translate the expression *tôwa karapuu* which means literally 'to put on the belt', as 'going to war'.

Dancer and warrior were one and the same up to the end of the 19th century. These two postcards, show the same picture, but have different descriptions. One says that it is of a war party, the other that it is of a dance group of which the members are employees on the coffee plantation advertised on the card.

Belep came by boat to Pouébo to fight alongside the warriors there. The Belep warriors had taken a 'medicine' on Belep, which allows the personal outcome in the war to be known. If it showed that the warrior was going to be wounded, a sort of antidote was taken. Before going to war warriors and their weapons were passed through fire smoke (Lambert 1900/1985:173-175 ; Leenhardt 1930/1980:39). This may have been a preparation exclusive to war; no field observations were made nor information collected about the passage of dancers through smoke. The dance was performed regularly for training in the movements necessary for war : attack, retreat, defence etc. Apart from the dances there was no special group training for the warriors, at least on the *Grande Terre* (Leenhardt 1930/1980:39). In war each warrior could depend only on himself (Hadfield [1920:164] reports the same for Lifou).

Before leaving the *tribu* to go to war, the 'war dance' had to be performed, and this is still respected today by the performance given in the *tribu* before a dance is performed outside. In earlier times this was to show the older men of the *tribu* the total manpower and the individual capacities of each dancer/warrior. The elders were able to make a final selection : if a dancer was not good enough, he was not allowed to go to war. At the same time the elders observed the weak points of the warriors. It was the duty of the elders who stayed at home to take, in place of the warriors themselves, the special 'medecine' for the dancers' weaknesses (Seraphin Mererâtu pers. comm.). Warriors danced immediately before going to a tribal war in order to engender a war-making mood. The repetitive rhythm on the *Grande Terre* and the heroic legends told in the dance songs on the Loyalty Islands excited and encouraged the warriors. A confirmation of the statement made by Laville and Berkowitz (1944:107), that before a war the "rythme" was beaten faster than normal has not been found in the literature.

In 1917 Kanak warriors danced as the French military arrived at Tiamou. (Tchoeaoua 1982:50) and *Grand Chef* Amane first danced and then defined the frontier between his territory and that of the French with their tribal allies. By using this gesture he signaled his readiness to go to war over the issue (R. Leenhardt 1978:24).

In a dance performed just before a war the enemy might be represented in a ridiculous way as puppets which are attacked during the dance and destroyed. Sarasin (1929:224) says "...that the enemy is presented as old people, with broken spears and useless clubs or in other ridiculous and mean ways, that the enemy is attacked and declared to be subdued. By this analogy-magic, they believed that they would have an easier time in the real battle"❶.

FORMAL COMPARISON BETWEEN DANCE AND TRIBAL WAR

Most writers compare the dancing they have observed with warfar. Even on its arrival at the dance area a dance group gives the impression of being a band of attacking warriors. In general two ways of arrival can be distinguished. In the first the dancers are hidden behind branches, which is exactly the way in which, as warriors, they approach the enemy : "One sneaks along

❶ "... dass man den Feind darstelle durch alte Leute mit zerbrochenen Lanzen und wertlosen Keulen oder sonst auf eine lächerliche Weise, dass man sich auf diesen Feind stürzte und ihn für besiegt erklärte. Durch diesen Analogiezauber glaubten sie, in der wirklichen Schlacht leichteres Spiel zu haben".

quietly on little used, tracks preferably during rain; in exposed places [to enemy observation] one covered oneself with branches; warriors marching in front and at the side of the army protect it against surprises"❶ (Sarasin 1929:209).

In the second when two dancing troupes are facing each other, a dancer jumps and runs in front of the approaching dancers, with quick unexpected movements. This behaviour corresponds exactly with Garnier's description of the way in which a war chief proceeds when marching against the enemy (Garnier (1868/1990:6-11/60-65), trying to escape the spears thrown by the enemy and stones from their slings. Christine Salomon-Nékiriai (1993:81) says that "... he who marched at the head of the warriors brandishing a spear in his right hand..."❷ had the power to heal, for he carried powerful objects on his left arm.

In most of the mimetic dances of the centre and north of the *Grande Terre*, the dancers form a square which J. Thomas referred to as "standing in line" (see p.75). A square was also the position taken up by an army of warriors. Pannetrat (1857/1993:41-43) describes a feast from about the 1850s from the region of Houaïlou where the warriors were positioned in several squares.

The dance sections of a mimetic dance may themselves present war scenes : attacks, defences, retreats etc. These provide direct practice of the motions necessary for successful warfare. These actions were so lifelike, carried out with such authenticity and precision, that Vieillard and Deplanche (1862:210) were astonished that no-one was wounded. Besides the sections which provide direct training in the martial arts there are other sequences where the subject, for example fishing, is apparently far removed from warfare but which in fact contains an encrypted link with the notion of war. More information on such hidden war dance subjects are considered when describing the *bua* dance (see p. 216) and the *nêêkiipâ* dance (see p. 148)

To lead a successful tribal war discipline is necessary. Discipline is expressed in the marvellous synchronisation of the dance motions. Laville and Berkowitz (1944:107) say that a mistake in the synchronisation would only be detectable by means of photography. It will be seen that many of the Kanak dances are performed today with a fine precision in the synchronisation of the dance motions.

Each section is separated from the next by a short pause, where the dancers kneel on the ground. In effective ambushes the same tactics are used : hiding, attacking quickly and precisely, and retreating to hide again. Quick precise movements and motionless pauses still make up many parts of a mimetic dance in the centre and north of the *Grande Terre.*

Dancing after a war is won

For the celebration of a successful war all the people danced, together with the warriors. Garnier (1867/1990:60-65) describes the tribal war between the people from Wiindö and Ponérihouen. When the successful Wiindö warriors came back to their village, where at the time a *pilou-pilou* was being held, a round-dance was performed. The celebration of the successful war with a

❶ "Man schleicht sich auf selten betretenen Pfaden stille an, gerne bei Regenwetter, an offenen Stellen sich mit Baumzweigen deckend; Krieger, vorne zu den Seiten der Hauptmacht marschierend schützen vor Ueberraschung".
❷ "... celui qui marchait en tête des guerriers brandissant une sagaie de la main droite...".

round-dance is also reported by Julian Thomas. During the 1878 insurrection Thomas reports that a group of French and Australian officials stood together when suddenly a group of allied Kanaks ran towards them pretending to attack them. He says that they presented the captured heads and expressed the joy of victory in a round-dance. Thomas describes the dance performed on the evening before the war as a line dance. Both dances were accompanied by singing (J. Thomas 1886:107). It can be said that before war, a mimetic dance prepared the warriors, and afterwards the round-dance was a dance of joy, celebrating a succesful fight and the feast of the captured enemies❶.

The fact that dancing is so close to fighting and warfare may have been a reason why, at the end of a *pilou-pilou,* dances changed into a real war, as is so often described. Competitive games were also held during the last few days of the *pilou-pilou.* These games were competitions in arms, often spear throwing. In 1880 for example, during a *pilou-pilou* in the region of Hienghène, spears were thrown against a coconut on top of a post❷ (Kanappe cit. in Courtis 1984:115). Also during *pilous-pilous,* spears were thrown over the heads of people present (Boulay 1984:105 ; Pannetrat 1857/1993:41-43). These games can show the war-power of an invited group, and can also be part of a paticular ritual. For example, feinted spear throwing had a symbolic meaning, which can be interpreted in different ways. During the *pilous-pilous* for the ending of a mourning period the warriors of the matrilineal line had the right to make sham attacks on their cross-cousins. Traditional Kanak belief holds that the blood which came from the matrilineal line has been wasted through a death which occurred in the patrilineal line.

THE WAR DANCE IN THEORY

It is obvious that a war dance performed at a *pilou-pilou* had the function of declaring the manpower of a *tribu* to the people present. The aesthetic of the dance was therefore linked with the function of impressing those present who were potential allies or enemies. The aesthetic of the dance lies in a firm, fast and powerful performance. Impressing people present by a show of strong manpower is a worldwide function of this kind of war dance. Lynne (1987:180) in referring to African war dances says "Dance, and especially warrior dance, may be a symbol of power representing, expressing, and communicating self-control and dominance". She also says that "evidence from the oral histories reported in the ethnographic literature suggests that, in the precolonial period, warrior dances were status markers for groups and individuals ; vehicles for sexual display, physical preparation for war ; affective readying for violent encounters [incitement, communion, we/they distancing] ; religious behavior, displacement ; and political behaviour" (Lynne 1987:181). Performing dances which express the war power of the group during ceremonies appears in several places in Melanesia.

However, a war dance does not always mean exclusively a men's dance and an exhibition of power. War dances can be performed without weapons (Sachs 1937:76) and at first sight appear to have no link with the subject of

❶ A similar procedure is reported from Lifou. Hadfield (1920:170) reports that if a war were succesful, there was a feast where the enemies were eaten and this was followed by dancing and singing.

❷ Spear throwing into a coconut palm trunk is a common boys' game today all over New Caledonia, but it does not have the status of an institutionalised martial game.

war, as in some mimetic dances of the *Grande Terre* for example the *hneen* dance (see p. 165) or the *bèèmä* dance (see p. 160). It must be said that, as there are no detailed descriptions of this dance before the establishment of the missions, it is not impossible that dancing with weapons was abandoned under missionary influence.

Sachs gives examples from North America, and Madagascar where women performed war dances. He explains that their function is to support the warriors in the form of 'telemagical power'. Sachs also gives an example of the Thompson Indians where, in a women's war dance, the dancers point outwards in the direction of the enemy's land (Sachs 1937:76). There are no observations of a women's war dance in New Caledonia. However, that they participated in the dance celebrating a succesful war (Garnier 1867/1990:65) was quite probable.

Among all the dance forms that are given above diverse functions are evident. Trade was carried out with dancing, the offering of yams during the *pilou-pilou* was carried out with dance-like movements. Then war is danced and dance comes close to war. These are very important times in the traditional life of the Kanaks. They can be interpreted as part of the complex exchange system which is one of the bases of Kanak culture into modern times. Dance celebrates the moment when two partners come together : the heart of the exchange whether in offering, in trading or in war. This moment of meeting is not carried out with ordinary walking steps : only dancing, very probably accompanied by singing rather than speaking, is an adequate manifestation of its importance. Sadly, so many dances have been lost, that further study possibly leading to different interpretations cannot be made. A partial repertoire cannot furnish the data for a complete interpretation.

Dances and masks of the *Grande Terre*

The frequent appearance of a masked figure during Kanak festivities raises the question as to the origin of the Kanak mask in an ancient secret club system, as is known in other places in Melanesia, for example : Vanuatu (McKesson 1990) or New Guinea (Leenhardt 1945:33-35). Other ethnologists say that the New Caledonian mask is an autonomous development from the north of the *Grande Terre* (Guiart 1966/1987:147-150) and that in this region an ancient mask cult did exist. In this study only the relation of the mask to Kanak dancing will be considered.

Reports from the 19th century mention dances where one, or several masked figures appeared. The mask has been referred to as a 'dance mask' ('*masque de danse*') and also as 'war mask' ('*masque de guerre*'). E. Kasarherou (1993:54) states that it is possible that masks were carried along with war parties, as was done with the 'ceremonial axe' ('*hache ostensoir*'). It seems unlikely that the war chief wore a mask during the fighting as suggested by Moncelon, Vincent and others cited in Sarasin (1929:239), because it would restrict his movements and therefore his capacity as a warrior.

What was the function of the appearances of the masked figure? Opigez (1886:433) interprets the role of the masks during dancing as a simple attrac-

A very early engraving of a Kanak mask published in Patouillet (1873:168a) entitled "Le masque de guerre" ("war mask").

tion without a significant function. To Rochas (1862:272) the mask's function was so modest that he called it the "clown of the dance". These explanations do not go far enough. According to other reports the mask had a special task to fulfil that could vary from region to region. Garnier (1867/1990:52) observed a masked figure appear at a feast in Arama, in the 1860s. The mask, named Dagnat, came from the sea shore, just before the actual performance of the dances. At the feast in the Tia *tribu*, where Marthe Lion was present the masked figure appeared before the dance (Lovreglio 1989:149). In 1911 in Bopope where Sarasin (1917:127-128) was present, the mask appeared after the mimetic dances, and so did the masked figure at Balade at a feast reported in Rozier (1990:71). The fact that the masked figure could appear either before or after a dance, may show that there is no direct link between the mask and the content of a dance.

E. Kasarherou (1993:40) was informed by an elderly woman in the region of Hienghène, that the masked figure appeared during a feast. There the mask did not dance but frightened and hit people, especially children. In the year 1911 and from the *tribu* of Bopope, Sarasin says that a mask, armed with spear and club, carried out feinted attacks. In this period, the mask only frightened children (Sarasin 1917:127) but earlier reports show that in the north of the *Grande Terre* there were dances or scenic plays in which the audience was in awe of the mask.

Masked figures played a special role in a dance in the region of Nenema. At the end of the mourning period a group of dancers called *pumdagak,* which might have been a secret club, performed a dance called *den*. The dancing was actually limited to carrying out feinted attacks against the parental relatives of the dead person, pretending to harm them with their lances (Leenhardt 1945:32). A second dance called *hia,* from the region of Gomen, also performed with a mask is reported as a complementary dance to the *den*. For the *hia* dance, the carrier of the mask held a piece of wood in his mouth on which the mask was fixed[1].

From the region of Houaïlou Leenhardt (1953:764) reports a dance where

[1] If this was the usual way of holding the mask, Garnier's remark quoted by Waldemar Stöhr (1987:289) that the masked dancer sang cannot be correct.

one of the dancers wears a mask, the same dance is given in Guiart in the foreword to *Mythologie du masque en Nouvelle Caledonie.* "The Boewa once performed a mimetic dance for the Misikoeo, during a *pilou* at Meboeijeu, at Porodiva, country of origin of Aru Jemi Kavisoibanu"[1]. The dance was as follows : one of the dancers cut some reeds and planted them in the dance-ground, tying them together to imitate the binding of sugar cane. The other dancers were waiting there, singing. A second dancer (Nekoiko, father of old Poma, the grandfather of Kakuruino Boewa) went up to the bunch of reeds and, like a thief, cut it and carried it away, thus showing that he thought that the reeds were sugar cane. The first dancer, the one who planted the reeds, on seeing what had happened ran after the thief and beat him. The victim called to his father for help. From the nearby bush, a masked figure appeared representing the victim's father (the *Vieux* Meja, master of Nekoe's residence, a member of the senior Boewa clan) carrying lances and a club. He ran to the dance-ground and held himself upright in a threatening manner. The mask made such a terrifying impression on the audience, who thought it was a spiritual being or "god" ("dieu"), that they fled. Some men who knew all about it ran after the crowd and stopped them, calling out that it was not a god but a mask of bird feathers. (Leenhardt cit. in Guiart 1966/1987: XVIII).

(Fritz Sarasin 1911/Bopope)

Sarasin's photograph of the mask he saw in Bopope.

That the mask was regarded as a personification of a spiritual being is confirmed in the names that some masks had which were identical with those of spiritual beings. The dance described here by Leenhardt can also be interpreted by taking into account the parental and clan relationships of the dancers, so that the mask not only represented the 'father' but also a spiritual being, an ancestor or a 'totem'. The idea of a relation between the mask and the dead ancestors is supported by a mask named Pidjeuva or Pidjeupatch from the centre of the *Grande Terre.* It is known that this spiritual being, or god, is the leader of the *boria* dance in the world of the ancestor spirits (Leenhardt 1947/1985:111).

A particular scene including a masked figure is described by Patouillet. The

[1] "Les Boewa dansèrent autrefois une danse d'imitation pour les Misikoeo, lors d'un pilou à Meboeijeu, à Porodiva, pays d'origine d'Aru Jemi Kavisoibanu".

mask, Apouéma, (which is the Cèmuhî word for 'mask' and has often been used as a general name for the New Caledonian mask [E. Kasarherou 1993:15]), entered the dance-ground before the dancers. It made sham attacks on the dancers as they arrived with their faces hidden behind banana leaves. The masked figure went to get a "sorcerer", who sprinkled the dancers with black water and the mask beat each one of the dancers with a stick. According to Patouillet (1873:183-185) this part represents the burning of the dead chief's house and the black water the tears of mourning women. The rest of the black water is thrown on the ground by the family members of the dead *chef*. Then a warrior drives his spear into a coconut, representing the destruction of the coconut trees after the death of the *chef*. Only after this does the mimetic dance take place, and there is no direct link between the mask's appearance and the dance.

The reports given here concerning the appearance of a masked figure, all come from the centre and north of the *Grande Terre*. They are from the period 1862 to 1911. The two accounts from the beginning of the 20th century show that the masked figure 'only frightened' children. At this time, when most of the Kanaks of the *Grande Terre* were Christian, only children did not know that the masked figure was a man in disguise and were afraid. The particular dance described by Leenhardt, must date from the end of the 19th century. Leenhardt himself had not seen the dance but he was told about it by his informant Boeseu Erisyi[1].

But some 50 years earlier the appearance of a mask did frighten all non-initiated persons, so that they fled on its appearance. Or at least they behaved as if they were afraid in order to show their good customary manners while in reality they may have known that a man was under the mask[2]. In the 19th century, before the Kanak mask ceased to be revered, most appearances of a masked figure were just before a dance performance. An important part of its activities was to carry out sham attacks against particular persons. These attacks could have been performed in a dance-like style for, as already mentioned, sham attacking during a *pilou-pilou* is quite comparable with dancing. However, there is no report of the masked figure having any role in a mimetic dance except for the scenic play from Houaïlou, where the masked figure is a protagonist of the story performed in the dance. However, the mask was particularly made for this play and it may have been an isolated event.

There were rituals carried out by the masked figure that seem to have been very symbolic and although the dancers played a role in the ritual described by Patouillet, they actually performed the dance only after the masked figure had retreated. While the masked figure took advantage of the presence of a crowd which had come to watch dancing, it seems that, in general, it did not take part in the mimetic dances in the centre and north of the *Grande Terre*.

A mask from Lifou can be seen on photgraphs from the 1950s (Collection Fonbonne, A.D.C.K.) and on a film from 1931 (Rouel 1931[film]); it was not

[1] Leenhardt says that in his time the mask rituals were already lost (Leenhardt 1933:3).

[2] To pretend to be made a fool of by traditional beliefs makes up quite a part of the traditional belief system in Melanesia. For example, in the Sepik region the sacred flutes played behind a wall of branches and hidden from the women are supposed to be the voice of a spirit. All the women present do, of course, know that men are performing on the flutes, but they play the game and show themselves astonished by the sound of the flutes. They also tell their children that the sound that they hear is that of spiritual beings (Ammann 1989 [unpubl.]; Dean 1958:109-111; Hauser-Schäublin 1977:146; Mead 1934:226).

reported in the literature until the 1990s. The only dance today in which a masked figure appears is the *drui* dance from Lifou. This mask, which has a very different form from those of the *Grande Terre*, will be treated separately (see p. 225).

The role of women in Kanak dance

As a generalisation it can be stated that in Melanesia women are excluded from war and from ceremonial life. This is only partly true of the venerated mimetic dances from the *Grande Terre* which were ceremonial dances very closely related to war, and danced only by men but in which the participation of women was possible, even if very limited indeed. On the Loyalty Islands women participate in the choir of such dances, and women may have specific roles in men's dances.

Laville and Berkowitz (1944:197) say that women never danced with men and Lambert (1900/1985:15) and Lemire (1884:115) say that, in the northern half of the *Grande Terre*, "Women only rarely dance with men"❶. According to other observers in the 19th century, women had a specific role during dancing, for example, they ran around the group of dancers with torches, they beat the bark-clappers while the men danced and they held the branches to hide the dancers as they arrived. The dances, performed during the *pilou-pilou* ceremony, for example for the offering of the yams, were mixed dances.

Although there is no longer any direct information available on the function of women in the old dances, it seems very likely that, for example, in the dance in which women run around the dancers with torches, there is significant symbolism in the dance, even though it cannot be understood any more. In contrast to the participation of women in some men's dances are the taboos which do not allow the dancer/warrior to approach women during the period of preparation for a dance performance or, in the past, a war.

The situation of the exclusively women's mimetic dance found today in the centre and north of the *Grande Terre*, does not reflect that of the 19th century, when women's dances were much more numerous. There are only a very few women's dances in this region today, for example the *cèto* dance (see p. 163). Leenhardt (1946:450-452) gives a list with names in 36 languages that he translates as "dances of the women of the maternal clan" ("danses des femmes du clan maternel"), which shows that during the *pilou-pilou* the women on the hosts' side performed a dance.

Curt Sachs says of a women's dance, without indicating his source, "...women of New Caledonia after a birth lift their skirts high in the dance." Sachs interprets this gesture as an argument for the "disrobing dance" where "the bosom of the earth shall open to receive the new seed" (Sachs 1937:91). This interpretation cannot be followed up without knowledge of the source and more detail about the dance itself. To describe the place of the Kanak woman in general Kanak dancing from the centre and north of the *Grande Terre*, it must be kept in mind that the dances are symbolically and formally linked with war and exchange, the two activities which kept Kanak culture

❶ "Les femmes ne dansent que rarement avec des hommes".

going. In traditional Kanak culture women had several roles to fulfil. Only two are mentioned here : that of the life giver, assuring the next generation, and the role of the married woman, guaranteeing the establishment or confirmation of an alliance between two lineages.

On the Loyalty Islands the role of women in dances is different from that on the *Grande Terre.* Firstly, women take part in the many dance choirs. Even for the most venerated dances of the *feboa* genre women sing in the choir. According to observers the women's dances of the 19th and early 20th century on the Loyalty Islands had an erotic expression. Woman was the guarantee of the continuation of the lineage and of life. In this case the woman, and therefore the substance of life, might have been being celebrated in these dances. There are no such dances any more; they were probably undermined by the missionaries. The participation of women as singers or dancers, as well as the erotic side of the woman dancer on the Loyalty Islands, raises the question of Polynsesian influence which will be considered further during this study.

CHAPTER 4

THE CURRENT SITUATION OF KANAK DANCES

Since there are no more *pilou-pilou* ceremonies of the traditional kind, dances associated with them cannot be performed as they once were❶. Dances today performed at a dance festival or on other occasions, take place in a different cultural sphere. Many elements of traditional choreography appear to have been retained, but the precision of movement and synchronisation of the corps of dancers, as mentioned in 19th century reports and even to be seen in fragments of early films (Rouel 1931[film] and anonymous 1954 [film]) is no longer the norm, and is only to be seen in performances by those dance groups who work seriously at their rehearsals. There have also been

(David Becker/A.D.C.K.1994, Touho)

At the beginning of a dance festival a particular set of presents, the *coutume*, is given to the owner of the land where the festival is held. For the 'Pwolu Jenaa' dance festival the *coutume* shown here consisted of lengths of material, cigarettes, some bank notes and yam tubers.

❶ As a continuation of research into lost traditional values the A.D.C.K. in collaboration with R.F.O. (Radio France Outremer) produced a film (Dagneau 1995[film]) showing the celebration marking the end of the mourning period, one year after his death, for Paul Napoarea which took place respecting traditional rules and customs at Tiaoué. This has been criticised in some quarters as "portraying culture as theatre" ("mettre en scène de la culture").

enormous changes in dance costume, with the introduction of calico and the imposition of Christian standards of modesty.

On many Pacific islands, the performance of indigenous dances as tourist attractions is common, for example in hotels and resorts. In Tahiti this has become a profession for groups. What can be seen in New Caledonian hotels are mostly Polynesian dances by groups from the Tahitian or Wallisian communities of Nouméa. Without serious preparation Kanak dances are not immediately interesting to tourists[1]. There are occasional 'Melanesian evenings' arranged for tourists, who travel by coach to a cultural centre for a 'traditional dinner' to be followed by a dance, and tourists have complained to organising agencies, that the spectacles are 'not authentic' on such grounds as that the dancers are not in 'native' costume, but wear T-shirts bearing advertisements for Coca-cola, jeans, wristwatches and Nike-running shoes[2].

Occasions to present dances

The occasions which now most resemble the former *pilou-pilou* are weddings and *chefs*' birthday celebrations. At such celebrations the affirmation of Kanak life-style is still marked by exchanges. The dances are familiar and furthermore, here, everybody knows one another, those who are dancing will be known to the audience, and vice-versa, everybody is at ease.

There is also a number of locally important Kanak cultural associations spread throughout New Caledonia, which occasionally organise cultural days where local handicrafts, such as women's basketry or men's wooden sculptures are on exhibition, as well as for sale. The local school may have prepared a play or a concert of choral singing. Meals will be prepared in earth-ovens or on barbecues, coffee and tea are in urns, available at very reasonable prices. There may be a bingo session in the evening. Usually there will also be traditional Kanak dancing performed by either the local dance group, or another group specially invited.

Kanak dances may also be performed for the inauguration of new buildings of any consequence, especially public facilities such as a dispensary (local hospital and pharmacy), at memorial celebrations and at receptions to welcome VIPs, and so on. In these cases there is usually an official programme on posters, in which dances will be numbered among the items. The general public does not necessarily come for the dances as cultural manifestations, they are there for the celebration as a whole, and it is taken for granted that the dances are a part of it. Normally it is a local dance group which performs, and for events of lesser importance a junior dance group may be invited to gain experience of performing in public.

Sometimes there are festivals organised by provincial authorities specifically to present Kanak dances mostly with the aid of the Agence de Développement de la Culture Kanak (A.D.C.K.). The first major festival in New Caledonia, which awoke interest and gave rise to succeding festivals, was 'Mélanésie 2000', held in Nouméa in September 1975 when there was no official body like the A.D.C.K. to encourage Kanak culture. It was largely Kanak-inspired and was the first time that Kanak culture was shown to an ethnically mixed public

[1] At present (end of 1996) a group of young Kanaks is being trained to present Kanak dances for tourists.

[2] A letter from Amac-Tours [undated] was discussed in a meeting with several persons involved in traditional dancing during the 'Pwolu Jeena' festival.

in Nouméa. A number of publications and recordings were also issued (see : Misotte (1976/1978 and 1976/1984) ; Mwà Véé 1995 [10] ; Musiques Canaques de Nouvelle-Calédonie [33rpm])❶.

Among recent dance festivals of significance the following are noted here :

- On 31st July and 1st August 1992 the A.D.C.K. organised at Nouméa a 'rencontre préparatoire au VIième festival des Arts du Pacifique' (Preparatory Meeting for the VIth South Pacific Arts Festival) in order to select, from 12 invited groups, the two or three which would represent New Caledonia at the 6th Pacific Arts Festival in Rarotonga, Cook Islands (see Ammann 1993 and 1994).
- In September 1993 the Association 'Akapik' organised a huge festival to celebrate the Year of Indigenous People (UNESCO). The whole event lasted a week, with a finale of two days (24th and 25th) of dances at Poindimié. More than 15 Kanak dance groups were assembled, and some other Pacific dances were performed by Tahitian, Wallisian and ni-Vanuatu communities.
- From 11th to 13th November 1994 the first provincial dance festival took place at Touho-Mission, bringing together more than 600 dancers in 17 groups, mainly from the North Province. This festival named 'Pwolu Jenaa' (meaning 'dance today' in the Cèmuhî language), was organised by several organisations and administrative services

(David Becker/A.D.C.K.1992, Nouville)

In some theatrical dances, the dancers become actors ; this dancer from the Touaourou *tribu* (Yaté) plays a turtle that is being captured.

❶ 'Mélanésie 2000' was taken to Rotorua, New Zealand, in March 1976 as the New Caledonian contribution to the Second South Pacific Festival of the Arts.

- In 1995 a second provincial dance festival, that of the Loyalty Island Province was held, at Luecila, Lifou. It was called 'Iahnithekeun' ('transmission and diffusion of knowledge'). Some 11 dance groups, from Maré and Lifou (none from Ouvéa because of political problems) together with two invited groups, from the Isle of Pines and Belep, gave performances.
- A dance festival of the South Province was scheduled for December 1996, but did not take place.

Modern dance festivals, successors to the *pilou-pilou*

The functions of the dance festivals of today differ from those of the ancient *pilou-pilou*. One of the most important functions of the dance festivals of today is to keep the Kanak dances alive. But they are also organised to satisfy the demand for the presentation of Kanak culture for inter-ethnic meetings. It has to be asked if the change in environment during the presentation of dances has influenced the dances themselves.

The huge *pilou-pilou* described by Leenhardt (1930/1980:143-178) consisted of a number of stages or periods over several days. The modern festival does not last more than two and a half days, over a weekend, because many people now hold Monday-to-Friday jobs (which would have been inconceivable to most Kanaks before the mid-20th century).

There is a period of preparation in which a representative of the festival organisers makes formal visits to each dance group. He asks the leader, in a traditional customary way (*faire la coutume*), for his group's participation. The group leader will, in turn, ask the members for their agreement before accepting. The actions and the order in which for the *coutume* (custom) has to be done and especially the person who has to be asked, must be respected. It can be complicated and susceptible to different interpretations but if all is not done as it should be, there may be tensions and some potential participants may withdraw or simply refuse to participate. All negotiations are carried out orally; there is never a written agreement or a written contract for a dance perfomance.

On a Friday evening or very early on a Saturday morning dancers and their entourages board coaches and travel to the place where the festival is being held. Groups from other islands will arrive by aeroplane or ferry. Each festival, whatever its importance or size must open with the *coutume*, and all participants have to be present. If a coach or other means of transport breaks down en route, everyone waits. The *coutume* begins with speeches of welcome from the organisers and the *chef* of the *tribu* on whose land the events are to be held❶. This is followed by speeches of thanks for the invitation to participate from a representative of each visiting group. Speeches are made in a Kanak language, if there is mutual comprehension in it between hosts and guests,

❶ Starting a big event with speeches of welcome is common in the Pacific. For example, the welcome protocols on Maori *maraes,* where the *tangata whenua* 'people of the land' welcome visitors with an exchange of oratory, either in alternation or by a suite of speeches from the hosts, followed by a suite of speeches from the visitors. After that, visitors are incorporated as *tangata whenua* for the duration of their stay (Peter Crowe pers. comm.).

a)

b)

c)

Three scenes from a contemporary Kanak dance festival :
a) chartered buses to transport the dancers
b) amateurs filming dances with their video cameras
c) customary speech given over a microphone.

and if not French is used as the lingua franca. These welcoming speeches are a reminder of the presentation speeches during the the *pilou-pilou* as reported by Leenhardt and others.

Dance festivals are for preference held on a sports field (for example, football or cricket) or other large, level tract of ground. Women's groups set up stalls along the perimeter, where they sell handicrafts such as baskets and mats, home-sewn clothes, or foodstuffs. There will be stalls selling tea and coffee, fruit drinks, and barbecues. Alcohol is almost always strictly forbidden at such festivals. Public address systems are ubiquitous, frequently excessively loud and often badly manipulated giving rise to feedback and distortion. All announcements and speeches are made over the microphone. Also along the perimeter are rented French army tents, inside which the dancers prepare for performance, putting on their costumes and painting their bodies. Such large tents are also used as dormitories.

The dances are presented one after the other on the one dance-ground. The dancers direct their performances towards a dais with a raised floor and a canopy for protection from sun and rain, where the principal guests and organisers are seated. The general audience is sitting around the dance-ground on mats which they have brought with them. When a new dance group takes the arena, a *coutume* may be offered to the host with a request for forgiveness that this dance on 'foreign' soil may raise the dust and break the grass. Before and during the dance a member of the performing group may explain over the microphone the subject and the sections of the dance. If the dance narrates a myth choreographically, the story may be read by a dancer, usually in French, for the benefit of the whole public. During performances, members of the audience may go onto the dance-ground with banknotes to attach to the costumes of family members or friends or in admiration of a dancer's skills[1]. There are plenty of cameras clicking, and amateur video recorders at work.

Lunch is usually taken between 11am and 2pm, and the stalls of foods and crafts are busy. Dances continue until dusk, and if the dance-ground has flood-lighting installed (for example, for night-time football), they may continue until late into the night, perhaps with a short break for dinner. When festivals continue over a weekend, an ecumenical service is invariably held on the Sunday morning before dancing is resumed. On the last night, the long awaited round-dance is held, and on the final morning the *coutume* to close the festival takes place during which the organisers thank the owners of the land and all the people who helped to organise the festival.

Dance creation and ownership

Inheritance of dances is normally patrilineal. This inheritance consists of ownership and supervision of the choreography, keeping the taboos or mythology of the dance, the costumery and decoration (including body painting), and in general a dance's 'total theatre' as a recognised local 'copyright'. It may happen that an inheriting son is not particularly interested, fails to support further performances, and gradually the dance for which he is responsible may be forgotten. If the father notes such lack of interest, he may seek the next closest male relative of his natural son, to maintain the tradition. A dance-leader (inheritor) may extend the right to perform 'his' dance to another group, but there are a number of opinions about dance ownership, and where differences are strong, a dance may not be performed at all. There can also be something of a generation gap apparent in the transmission of dances. Older men may be encountered who remember dances or parts of dances which are no longer performed, and which are often their titular inheritances. They say that the youth of the *tribu* is not willing to learn traditional dances, while the youngsters reply that the elders are not willing to teach them.

[1] This practice is also known on Samoa (Richard Moyle pers. comm.). It may have been observed at various Pacific festivals and adopted by Kanaks.

(David Becker/A.D.C.K.1994, Touho).

The dance tassel accentuates and adds grace to the synchronised motions of mimetic dances.

There is much creativity associated with the mimetic dances that are being performed. New dances or parts of dances can be 'dreamed' by a dance creator. Those who have received dances in dreams say that when they awaken every step is clear in their heads, and that they can teach them right away to the dance group (see also Yayii [1983]). Dances do not have to be received in dreams but can be invented when fully conscious. On Lifou the Wetr group has a reputation for dynamic dances which are composed collectively (see p. 232).

The dance group

In a *tribu* where dances are regularly performed, there may be two generations of dancers : a senior group of men, and a junior group of boys. For a particular dance, the performance details are identical. The person responsible for the dance will decide which group and what dancers may participate at a performance or festival. The same person often hands over the teaching of young dancers to a deputy, although he will supervise the group rehearsals.

The junior group usually has the less important events, or those given midweek (while their fathers are working). The senior group may include a child dancer positioned in the front line, who is likely to be much appreciated by audiences, but this must be regarded as a recently established custom.

Members of a dance group do not necessarily belong to one *tribu,* although it frequently is so. Some groups have dancers from several *tribus,* without any particular kinship relations among them. The positioning of a dancer within the corps is not decided by social status, as a rule, but this might have been the case in the 19th century. The Ti.Ga. group near Poindimié does not permit natural brothers to stand one behind the other in a dance where one line feints an attack against the other; a sham attack between brothers, whether choreogaphed or in a free style, appears to offend traditional Kanak morality.

Synchronisation as an ideal

Most mimetic dances employ synchronised movements, and early witnesses were often surprised at the perfection of synchronisation. Laville and Berkowitz (1944 :108) went so far as to say imperfections would only be detectable by slow-motion cinematography. Several decades ago dance rehearsals were tough experiences different from those of today. When elder informants were young dancers, they were supervised by dancers in the background holding long bamboo sticks. If a dancer made the slightest mistake or if he was not perfectly synchronised with the rest of the group, he received a smash on his back with the bamboo stick. This may seem rude to outsiders, but as shown above, this kind of dancing was originally a training for tribal war and there, a mistaken movement might be paid for with someone's life. In dance rehearsals today the dancers are no longer corrected by beating but the ideal of exact synchronisation has been maintained.

(David Becker/A.D.C.K. 1992, Nouville)

The *seï* dance from Pothé, one of the few mimetic dances on the *Grande Terre* with synchronised motions that is accompanied by the *rythme du pilou.*

CLASSIFICATION OF DANCES

No serious efforts to classify mimetic dances have yet been undertaken, although some writers have put forward a few generic terms to refer to dances with common characteristics. Little of this has been based on systematic choreographic analysis.

In *Langues et dialects de l'Austro-Mélanésie* (1946:450-2), Leenhardt gives a list of dances in 36 languages. He divided New Caledonian dances into five general classes : "dance of the dead" ("danse des morts"), "dance of the gods" ("danse des dieux"), "mimetic dances" ("danses imitatives"), "dances of the women of the maternal clan" ("danses des femmes du clan maternel"), and "theatrical scene" ("scène théâtrale"). The basis of Leenhardt's classification lacks specific examples but it is known from his other writings that the "dance of the dead" is the round-dance, and that "dance of the gods" was called in Ajië *pijeva* (1947/1985:115), which had already been discontinued by the time Leenhardt arrived in New Caledonia. Mimetic dances continue today, and certain of them include theatrical pieces or interludes. In the "dances of the women of the maternal clan" Leenhardt is referring to the *cèto* dances, which may be different today (see p. 163).

Sarasin (1929:221) makes a preliminary distinction between "feinted attacks" ("Scheingefechte"), which he does not consider to be actual dancing, and the mimetic dances which he calls "artistic dances" ("Kunsttaenze"). He does not pursue any definition of these two categories, but quotes Leenhardt as saying, at the time, that mimetic dances were more developed in the Loyalties.

(David Becker/A.D.C.K. 1995, Lifou)

Dancers from Wetr (Lifou) singing as they enter the dance-ground.

Eliane Métais (1979:30) makes a classification of three types : "dance of display" ("danse d'ostentation"), "war dance" ("danse de guerre") and "popular dance" ("danse populaire"). Once again, there are no supporting definitions. The borders of these types are too fluid for systematic use, for example, a dance dramatising local historical events may at the same time be a war dance for the encouragement of young warriors.

In this study the names of dances are those which the Kanaks use. Some confusion exists, for example, in the central part of the *Grande Terre* there are three similar men's dances known as *nêêkiipâ, ôdobwia* and *bèèmä*. On consulting elder people on the origins of these terms, and how they might be distinguished, information was scant and perhaps merely speculative. The reasons, why there are confusing statements among informants about the origin of these dances is discussed in the chapter on mimetic dances of the *Grande Terre* (see p. 143). A similar situation is found in the Loyalty Islands where, for example, the formal difference between the *pehua* and the *wahieko* is not really defined. It seems too late to re-establish former Kanak categories for mimetic dances. In view of this, the dance names and terms used by dancers today have been adopted, without trying to erect a classification.

Two major kinds of mimetic dances can be distinguished according to their form. Those which resemble theatrical plays (here they will be called theatrical dances) are mainly found on the Loyalty Islands and in the south of the *Grande Terre*. Those characterised by the synchronisation of the motions are found throughout the *Grande Terre* and in many places on the Loyalty Islands. However in the centre and north of the *Grande Terre* synchronised mimetic dances can include theatrical sections.

Dances with synchronised motions

For most dances employing synchronised movements, the dancers form a square grid with a distance of 150cm between each other, all looking in the same direction. The dance is made up of a suite of sections, each of which is a stylised imitation. The subjects may be the gestures of inter-tribal war (such as attack or defence with traditional weapons), or details of domestic life. The sections are marked by pauses. Some dances of this kind include a short theatrical section such as a comedy pantomime, in which synchronisation is abandoned[1].

Following Leenhardt, the term "theatrical scenes" ("scènes théâtrales") is retained for dances which present, or represent, myths and legends of the dance-owning group. In these performances dancers appear to be actors playing the protagonists of the story, and using individualised movements according to the character. Frequently there are dance-accessories in the hands of the dancer/actors, appropriate to the scene being evoked. In the Loyalties, theatrical dances are usually accompanied by a song referring to the legend, but such a song does not always tell a story chronologically and it may be in a difficult or archaic language understood by very few of those present.

[1] Like many other elements in Kanak dances there are also similarities with other places in Melanesia in the presentation of theatrical scenes. In the *na lenga* dances of central Vanuatu, synchronised dancing is interrupted for the performance of short theatrical scenes.

Dance costumes and body painting

A dancer from Wapan (Isle of Pines) with fish drawn on his body. Fish are the main subject of the *yaace* dance.

Costume for mimetic dances varies a great deal. The members of one group may retain their ordinary daily clothing, for example, T-shirts and shorts. They add a green liana as a crown, and small ad hoc decorations made from coconut leaflets. Other dance groups may invent highly elaborate costumes from natural materials, putting calico aside, and take off their wrist-watches. In traditional times Kanaks do not appear to have made special dance costumes, so that their creation and use today is a 20th century innovation. When dancing, a Kanak assumes the persona of an ancient tribal warrior, as explained above. In most of Melanesia, it appears that warriors did not wear special dress or armour[1] for combat (as for example on some Polynesian and Micronesian islands), but painted their bodies (Keitsch 1967:28). The principal colour of the Kanak warrior was black, and in tribal war reports it is said that the warriors painted their faces and upper bodies to act as camouflage and as a partial mask for body odours (Keitsch 1967:53). It may be assumed that, before commercial tobacco was introduced (and spoiled the sense of smell), it was possible for a Kanak warrior to scent a person hidden close by or even to detect whether someone had been present recently, at least on windless days in the forest.

The Kanaks not only used black paint for their faces and torsos in both fighting and dancing, but also during the whole of the *pilou-pilou* ceremony, and even for the journey there (Courtis 1984:114). Besides the general use of black, the use of other colours is only occasionally mentioned. Captain Kanappe (cit. in Courtis 1984:115) saw in 1880 one dancer painted red and black in a *pilou-pilou* at Hienghène, and La Hautière (1869/1980:223) described the paint of one dancer as black, red and green. On the Loyalty Islands and in the south of the *Grande Terre*, women dancers or women singers in the dance choir often employ white, in order to represent ancestral spirits. Examples are the *mwaxrenu* dance performed by the *tribu* of Touaourou and the *yace* dance of Wapan, Isle of Pines, where the women are wearing white paint on faces and feet, the rest of the body being covered by the *robe mission* (mother

[1] In the Highlands of Papua New Guinea, warriors are elaborately decorated and painted (the human body as an art-work) for the dance or the *singsing*, but in all the available reports of actual battle or skirmish, some of it filmed, the warriors are in ordinary or daily garb.

13. - NOUVELLE-CALÉDONIE
Indigènes de Koumac avec les décorations - Usages Canaques
W. H. C., éditeur, Nouméa

An old postcard, showing people from Koumac with writing on their bodies. Line decoration including writing on dancers' bodies is popular today and may have begun as soon as writing was taught. It was not used during tribal warfare.

hubbard). From Nece (Maré) Sarasin (1929:224), too reports a dance where two women had whitened faces.

In some cases these days, dancers do not paint themselves in solid black areas, but instead make black or white stripes on their bodies. It appears this is not at all to produce "a most hideous effect" as Laville and Berkowitz (1944:197) thought, but is a representation of a mimetic dance's subject. When members of the Wapan *tribu* (Isle of Pines) perform the dance of the *yaace,* which presents a legend of how the people received the technique of fishing with a net from the *yace,* they paint a net in white lines on their backs, and a fish on one arm. At Pothé, in the mimetic dance *seï* (shovel) about court-enforced obligatory labour for road construction, one may see shovels painted on the dancer's arms[1].

It is possible for dancers to express their individuality by means of black or white line designs. One sees, for example, fish depicted on dancers from coastal areas. Others may have KNKY, as an abbreviation for Kanaky. Many dancers have white or black lines, just as decoration and without a particular significance. Painting white lines on the body may have come about in the 19th century. It is possible that in the second half of the 19th century, the 'new' possibility of writing

Women dancers with spears and 'clubs with long points'. An illustration in Leenhardt (1930/1980:166).

[1] For petty cases, courts in New Caledonia and in many parts of Melanesia will sentence offenders to a period of labour for the public good as in road maintenance or construction, rather than jail. If not closely supervised, some men have been known to put more effort into composing songs or 'dreaming' dances than into the employment of their shovels.

was so exciting, that people had their names written on the body in the reservations and for the occasion in the studio❶. However there is no evidence that body paint or painted lines indicated the social status of the dancer.

Contemporary practice is to prepare paints or pigments from natural products in the old way and to carry them to the dance venue in plastic bottles. Preparation is done domestically and principally in liquid forms.

Preparing the colours

These days, there are two main ways to obtain the black pigments in common use. One is from the burned nuts of the candlenut tree or *bancoulier* (*Aleurites moluccana*), which are pounded and ground into powder and mixed with coconut oil, as already described by Patouillet (1873:182). A variation was observed at Poindimié during the present study. Nuts were roasted on a fire grated and then boiled in water. However, the use of coconut oil produces a more reliable product, sticking better to the skin. The second way is to use charcoal powdered and mixed with coconut oil (or even cooking oil from the store), but the result is a much less brilliant or shiny black than that obtained from the nuts of the candlenut tree.

A natural red pigment is obtained from the outer layer of the seeds of a bush called *mâta* in Paicî (*Bixa orellana*)❷. When the interior of the seeds are drawn directly over the skin they act like crayons or chalk, leaving red traces. These traces wash off easily with water; which is fine for cleaning oneself up after a dance, but not so good if rain falls during a performance. A modern technique to obtain red colour is found on the Loyalty Islands, where women dancers use red lipstick to paint huge circles on their cheeks.

White pigments are usually obtained from natural chalk found in the ground or near the sea as shell or coral. The material is, once again, ground to powder, often dried in the sun and boiled up in water. However, the preparations have a tendency to flake off rapidly and some dancers have resorted to modern white shoe-cream. This is less laborious to obtain, lasts longer and the result is perhaps more brilliant, but washing it off after a dance is considerably more difficult than with the traditional products.

Dance accessories

Traditional weapons

For the major part of the mimetic dances, the dancers carry traditional weapons, often a club, less frequently a spear, and sometimes an imitation of a sling or a propelling string.

There are several commonly found forms of Kanak club. They are usually between a half to one metre in length, the handle being plain or sometimes carved with a pattern to aid the grip. The head is often in the form of a phallus or in the shape of a bird's head where the branch, or the trunk with a lateral root, used to make the club, has been chosen for its natural L-shape. Some

❶ On early photographs one sees only the 'little name' (corresponding to the first name), the 'big name' (the name of the family line) which indicates the person's origin is only rarely pronounced and it is not written on the body.
❷ *Bixa orellana* is an American tropical bush widely cultivated for its red dye. The date of its introduction into New Caledonia is unknown. It was in cultivation in a garden of acclimatisation in 1883 (MacKee1985:24).

(David Becker/A.D.C.K. 1992, Tioumidou)

Members of the Ti.Ga. Association (Poindimié) showing dance tassels being made.

clubs today are coloured brightly with commercial paint.

In the past women dancers sometimes carried a special sort of club which Leenhardt (1930/1980:166 fig.41 and 167 fig.42) referred to as a "club with long points" ("casse-tête à longues pointes"). These clubs are still used in the women's *cèto* dance (see p. 163).

Kanak spears are light, flexible, straight sticks pointed at both ends. Spears for battle had a small knob in the centre, onto which a propelling string could be hooked. Spears for use in dances today do not have such a knob. Some groups paint their spears with a spiral line. Spears are mainly used in theatrical dances; in dances with synchronised movements they are to be seen only rarely. For example, in the *drui* dance, only the first few figures are danced with spears, which are then collected up and put aside.

The dance tassel

For most mimetic dances, the performers hold dance tassels in their hands. In the past the tassels alone were a symbol of war and of dance ; today they are considered to be the strongest symbol of a war dance, especially in the centre and north of the *Grande Terre*. The dance tassel may be just a tuft of dried grass, but many of them have been carefully made with a handle and binding. To make a standard tassel, aerial roots of a screw-pine (*Pandanus* sp.) are cut into lengths of 110-120 cm, and beaten against a tree trunk until they split into fine longitudinal fibres. The fibres are bent and twisted until they become flexible. A bundle of fibres 2-3 cm thick is bound in the middle section for some 15 to 20 cms with other fibres. The device is then bent in the middle and more fibre used to bind the two halves together, forming a loop. At the bound end a string is attached which goes around the dancer's wrist, so that the tassel will not be lost or dropped during performance. In the language of Paicî, the dance tassel is called *pwêêti,* this term is used in some other regions as well. In the Nemi and Fwâi languages the dance tassel is called *thit.*

Leenhardt (1937/1986:166) considered the dance tassel in the centre and north of the *Grande Terre,* to be a symbol of mimetic dances as a genre. In his description of the *pilou-pilou,* at the end of a performance, the dancers would throw their dance tassels at the feet of their cross-cousins in the hosting group. The meaning of this was that those who received the dance tassel had the responsibility of preparing a dance for the next *pilou-pilou,* to be hosted by the presently invited group. A messenger who goes to invite a group to a *pilou-pilou* hands over a dance tassel, which means that the group who receives the dance tassel is expected to present a mimetic dance at the *pilou-pilou* (Leenhardt 1930/1980:174). Throwing dance tassels at the feet of the hosts is no longer common, because the overall structure of the *pilou-pilou,* which required the continuity of reciprocity, no longer exists. Nowadays, some groups in the centre and north of the *Grande Terre* toss their dance tassels one after the other into the air, but whether or not this is a substitute for older practices is not clear.

Dance costumes

In the 19th century the Kanaks did not wear special dance costumes. "The actors [dancers], ordinarily dressed…"[1] says Lambert (1900/1985:160). In illustrations of a dance scene in the 19th century, the dancers are outfitted like warriors. In other drawings of dance scenes from the 19th century, and in some of the earliest photos, dancers may wear shell decorations, perhaps containing magical herbs, some strings, *bagayous* (penis sheaths) and turbans with feathers attached or *xiti* (cylindrical head dress). Sarasin (1917:124-125) gives two photographs of the dancers he saw in 1911 in Bopope which he had been told was a very traditional settlement. The dancers are wearing short *manous* and penis sheaths; some of them are also wearing huge turbans.

In three films, *Terre Missionaire* (Rouel, 1931[film]), anonymous (1954[film]), and *Remember New Caledonia* (Dagneau 1996[film]) which includes scenes filmed by the U.S.Army while it was stationed in New Caledonia in the 1942-1945 Pacific War, valuable evidence of costumes of the periods is shown. The women in the film of 1954 perform the *cèto* dance, dressed in 'mother hubbards'. In all three films the men are seen wearing *manous* (a piece of fabric wrapped around the waist and reaching to below the knees) and *xiti* on their heads. Their bodies are only partly painted, and there is little decoration. The same kind of costume is to be found in photographs of the time. From the same period, Dubois (1984:96) reports from Maré the wearing of *manous* for dancing.

Wearing a *manou* for dancing would be consistent with the older idea of not dressing up specially for dancing, because the *manou* was widely worn by men between the 1930s (or even earlier) and the 1950s. By the 1960s things had changed. A picture in Larsen (1961:183) shows a male dancer wearing a floral Hawai'ian shirt, a satin scarf around his neck, and hibiscus flowers in his

[1] "Les acteurs, vêtus comme à l'ordinaire…".

(David Becker/A.D.C.K.1994, Touho)

Women wear lianas with green leaves or just a scarf, or both, around the head at dance festivals or celebrations of any kind.

hair. This kind of dressing up is part of what is called in this study the 'pan-Pacific' influence. Today contemporary clothing is used and special dance costumes are created for major events.

Head dress

The habit of wearing turbans may have been abandoned with the disappearance of the *pilou-pilou* at the end of the mourning period, but there is no information about this in the ethnographical literature available. The turban was worn by men in mourning, to cover their hair, which they were not allowed to cut. Mourning was entered into on the death of a relative and lasted until the *pilou-pilou* held to mark its end, one or two years later.

Although the turban is no longer to be seen, it is notable that Kanaks like to wear something around the head. In the north of the *Grande Terre* some dancers wear the bark of the banyan (*Ficus* sp.), which is a substitute for the ancient *xiti*. Others make bands from coconut spathes, into which it is easy to attach feathers obtained from wild birds, especially the big Notu Pigeon (*Ducula goliath*). This head dress is principally found in the region of Hienghène. On Lifou particular feathers were once used to signal prestige earned in wars (Hadfield 1920:169; O'Reilly/Poirrier 1953:168), and today leaflets make up part of the male dance costumes of the Wetr group.

Many dancers wrap lianas with their green leaves still attached, or chains of flowers around the head. Green lianas are worn by both men and women all over New Caledonia. Chains of the creamy-yellow flowers of the frangipani (*Plumeria rubra*) are worn more commonly in the Loyalties, by both men and women. *Plumeria rubra* is introduced in New Caledonia and it is not reported in the 19th or early 20th century literature❶, but other flowers, as well as shells or stones, were commonplace (La Hautière 1869/1980:233).

The mother hubbard or *robe mission*

Women dancers almost always wear mother hubbards and on their heads a crown of green liana, as well as simple decorations made from coconut leaflets. The mother hubbard probably came via the L.M.S. from Tahiti first to the Loyalties and then to the *Grande Terre*. In Sarasin's Kanak photographic

❶ The genus *Plumeria* (Frangipani) is native to America. The first herbarium collection of *Plumeria rubra* dates from 1947 (MacKee 1985:17) but it could have been widely cultivated before then. Another species, *Plumeria alba,* rarely planted, is known from apparently only one herbarium collection made in about 1874 (Boiteau 1981:210 ; MacKee 1985:17).

portraits of 1911-12 all the Loyalty Islands women are dressed in mother hubbards, while the women of the *Grande Terre* are bare-breasted. The women in Lennier's photo of the north of the *Grande Terre* wear mainly traditional skirts (see p. 12). Today, the mother hubbard is the basis of everyday clothing as well as a typical dance costume. However, there are some exceptions of specially created dance costume beginning to appear. The women of the Wetr dance group are covered entirely in coconut leaflets, as are the women of Maré for some dances. The use of special costumes reflecting tradition or the natural environment is a measure of the importance attached to a dance event.

(David Becker/A.D.C.K.1994, Touho)

For important dance presentations, some dance groups invest much time and effort in making their costumes.

Dancing in everyday clothes obviates the need of special preparations, and is considered sufficient for occasions of lesser importance. However, the making of costumes for both men and women is invariably a long and complicated process. Some details of manufacture as observed among the Wetr dance group and the Ti.Ga. Cultural Association from Poindimié will be given below.

Male dance-skirts

The dance-skirt called *coo* in Paicî is made from small branches of the coastal hibiscus known popularly as *bourao* (*Hibiscus tiliaceus*). Fibres of about a metre and a half in length are taken from the bast inside the bark. Each is attached at its centre to a liana which goes around a dancers waist, so that the skirt is about 70 cm long. The same procedure is used for bracelets about 30 cms long, which are worn on the upper arms and also just below the knees (the latter is known as *pwiâ* in Paicî).

In the Hienghène region the use of grass leaves of some 50 cm in length was observed. They were first sun-dried, and then gathered in bunches about 2 cm in diameter at the point where they were attached to the liana to go around the waist. The grass thus inverted fans out below. Also in the Hienghène region some groups make their skirts with fibres from the aerial roots of a screw-pine *(Pandanus* sp.).

(David Becker/A.D.C.K.1992, Lifou)

A member of the Wetr group demonstrating how a dance belt is made from a piece of flexible liana.

Screw-pine leaves are also used to make dance skirts (*iut* in Drehu), as is done by members of the Wetr group. After being gathered, the leaves are boiled in water to soften them. The thorny edges are stripped off, and the leaves left to dry and bleach in the sun for several days. One end of the leaves is tied to the string that goes around the waist as a belt, letting the other end hang down loosely. Some leaf bunches are long enough to allow folding, to give them a curly shape.

There is a choice of having the skirts made of vegetable materials left in their natural colours (including bleaching), or of dyeing them. The Ti.Ga. use a red pigment made from the substance occuring in the layer beneath the bark of mangrove trees (known as *nyîbwe* in Paicî, cf. *Rhizophora* or *Bruguiera*). It is scraped off, ground into fine particles, then dissolved in water. The resulting dye is brought to boiling point and a costume immersed in the vat for ten

(David Becker/A.D.C.K.1992, Nouville)

Dancers from Canala wearing dance belts with long projections at the back.

minutes will become dyed with the colour.

Those who lack access to natural materials or have insufficient time may resort to synthetic products such as flour sacks, where the horizontal fibres are stripped away, and the skirt left is spray-painted.

The belt

The belt, known in Drehu as *epa* and in Paicî as *karapuu* is a dance accessory associated with war. Belts are commonly made from a length of flexible liana, its bark stripped away. This is wrapped several times around the waist of the dancer, and bound together with smaller pieces of liana, with the ends of the encircling liana projecting behind for up to a metre. These projecting ends may have been useful in pulling away a wounded body quickly during a skirmish, and they may be idealised today in the dance-belt. Other kinds of belts without liana projections were also used in war. Sarasin collected such belts made not from a liana but of woven dried grass.

Non-traditional contemporary use of tradition inspired costumes

The wearing of costumes conceived specifically for dancing is a relatively new development. It manifests a separation of traditional dancing from modern daily living, and at the same time expresses a historical awareness. The older idea of wearing one's daily clothes (or lack of them) persisted until the 1960s, including dancing with the *manou*. The design and fabrication of special dancing skirts may have come about through 'pan-Pacific' influences, such as contact with people from Fiji, Tahiti, or Wallis and Futuna.

CHAPTER 5

TRADITIONAL MUSIC OF THE CENTRE AND NORTH OF THE *GRANDE TERRE*

The Kanak rhythm

In contrast to the great variety of languages on the *Grande Terre*, music and dance, while far from invariable, have many common features, especially evident in the centre and the north. One of these is what Kanaks themselves call the *rythme kanak* (Kanak rhythm), usually referring to the music that accompanies *ae-ae* songs and many dances. The French word *rythme* (rhythm) is used in daily language in a more general, indeed metaphorical, sense than it is in European musical theory. The sense extends to that of the total musical background, as created by all persons present, whether singing, dancing, playing instruments, or actively watching and listening. In a few rhythms that accompany singing and dancing on the Loyalty Islands, some features similar to the rhythms of the *Grande Terre* exist. For most dances the musical conception is different and they will be considered later on. Inland Kanaks of the *Grande Terre* say the origin of their usage is that of the sound of running water, in rivers and creeks. Some referential sounds can only be heard in particular places, such as behind rocks, where water is splashing in regular rhythmical patterns. Coastal Kanaks refer to the roaring of the sea and the rhythm of waves breaking on the beach. Whether inland or coastal there are two major elements in the sense and sound of the continuous movement of river and sea as a constant background and secondly, that of discrete rhythms such as splashes of water or waves. Both these elements are incorporated in the overall metaphor of the *rythme kanak*.

Discrete components of the *rythme kanak*

The discrete acoustic elements of the *rythme kanak* on the *Grande Terre* may be divided into two sound sources : instruments and voices. Typical Kanak instruments are bark-clappers, stamping-tubes, sounding boards, slit-drums, body percussion and foot stamping, together with idiophones which make up part of the dance costumes. Additional modern instruments include boxes of various materials such as tin and cardboard, metal whistles and occasionally harmonicas (for example : track 6, on Ammann 1997 [CD], there is an *ae-ae* song accompanied by bark-clappers, stamping-bamboos, friction leaves and a harmonica). Voice sounds, which are not melodic singing, include hissing, whistling, chanted phrases and cries. Many such discrete sounds come from dancers and onlookers as well as the percussionists. The percussion part is a discrete acoustic component of the overall rhythm, a part which is ordered by its regularity while the additional voice sounds are improvised.

The percussion part

Usually, an indefinite number of repetitions of the same short rhythmic pattern is heard. On the *Grande Terre* two patterns predominate, one of two beats and the other of four. The two-beat rhythm is omnipresent, and is generally called the *rythme du pilou* (the *pilou* rhythm). The four-beat rhythm accompanies mimetic dances in some regions, but only in the Hienghène region does it have a name : *whaî.*

The *rythme du pilou*

Besides the *ae-ae* songs, the *rythme du pilou* also accompanies the round-dance when performed without singing and the mimetic dances of certain regions, including some dances from the Loyalties which probably have a *Grande Terre* origin or influence. It accompanies all sorts of spontaneous and joyful dancing, and is a kind of acoustic symbol for Kanak traditional music in general. On local radio stations and New Caledonian television (R.F.O.) recordings of the *rythme du pilou* are played to introduce an item on Kanak culture. In *kaneka* the *rythme du pilou* can act as a link between Kanak traditional and contemporary styles of popular music.

The percussion ensemble is often divided into two groups. One group takes the downbeats and the other the upbeats. Downbeat players are called *vëdi* in Paicî and *ceen bwan-jep* in Fwâi. The upbeat players are known as *temôôrî* in Paicî, and *thedua* in Fwâi. The division into these two groups appears ad hoc, working as follows : the ensemble leader begins striking, to be joined by others, establishing the downbeats, then another player begins to strike between the beats creating offbeats. He is shortly joined by some others. The number of downbeat players is normally greater than the number of upbeat players, so that an alternation of 'heavy-light' pulsation is established. There is no spatial division between the two groups, whose members are intermingled.

The use of sectional pauses is structured. In the *ae-ae* songs, there are breaks made to give rests for the singers to regain their breath. The leading singer gives a sign to the lead percussionist who stops the music with a particular shout.

When the *rythme du pilou* accompanies the entrance of a dance group onto the dance-ground, typically the group advances for about ten metres, pauses for 30 to 60 seconds, and then advances again for another ten metres to the rhythm, and so on. While this is sectionally structured there seems to be an element of suspense, for dramatic effect, before the actual dance begins. The pattern of the *rythme du pilou* is of only two beats and it is often said to be binary. However, there are regional differences in how it is played.

Roughly speaking, while some of the variations could be classed as binary, most would be classed as ternary and as will be shown below, it is best to avoid such terms. The percussion part of none of the various interpretations of the *rythme du pilou* is a simple and regular 'one-two/one-two' or 'one-two-three/one-two-three' metre. All contain peculiarities of synchronisation of the beats which render absurd attemps to define them as binary or ternary. A similar rhythm of a 'double beat pair' from Central Australia was analysed by Moyle (1995:57)[1].

An example showing the emic notion of the *rythme du pilou*, occurs when a singer, perhaps sitting at a table, sings an *ae-ae* song while accompanying himself with a specific way of interpreting the *rythme du pilou* on a palm spathe. He marks the downbeat by tapping the finger-tips of one hand on the table or on the spathe, and for the upbeat drags the fingernails of the other hand across the surface, making a sound 'tap-shhhh/tap-shhhh'. The precise beat is made by tapping the finger tips (tap) and the more open beat by dragging the fingernails on the surface (shhhh) in just the same way as the downbeats of the percussionists are quite clear, but the upbeats may be out of synchronisation as to the moment of attack.

Tempo, defined as the number of patterns per minute, varies according to the genre and region. To accompany the dancers coming onto the dance-ground in the Paicî region, the *rythme du pilou* is played at 140 patterns per minute. The *seï* dance of Poté in the centre of the *Grande Terre* is accompanied with the *rythme du pilou* at 97 patterns per minute, while the *ae-ae* songs of the Paicî region are accompanied at 120 to 130 patterns per minute.

The following notation shows some ways in which to notate the *rythme du*

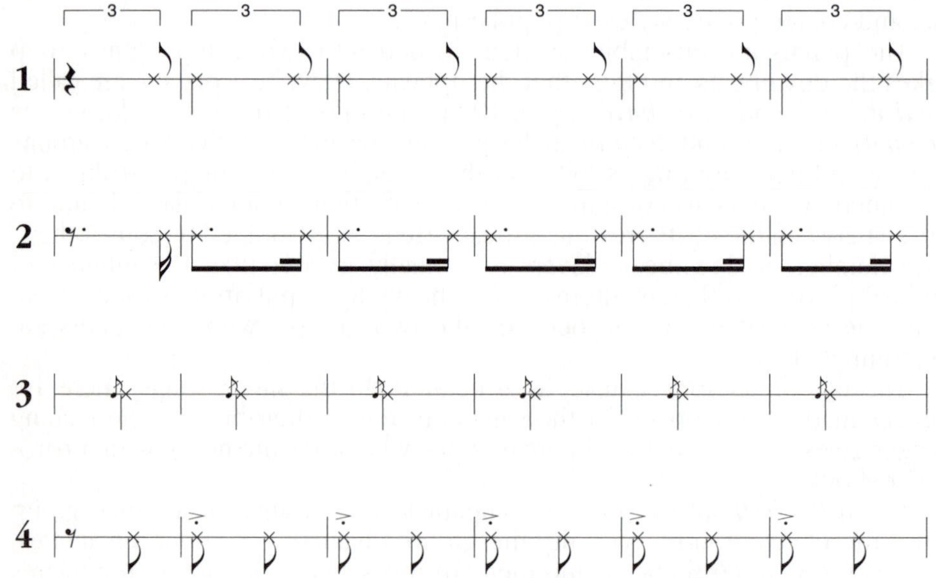

[1] Moyle found out that the proportion of the rhythmic value of the two beats is close to that found in human heart beats.

pilou. Examples 1 and 2 are from the northern half of the *Grande Terre* : one of the two beats is clearly longer than the other beat. Examples 3 and 4 are from the south of the *Grande Terre* : the difference between the two beats in example 4 lies in their dynamic.

It seems, taking into account the diversity given above, that individual perception of the dynamic level (loudness, force) of each beat, is as important as its durational value. Variations of dynamic and tempo by different players during a performance can produce a kind of swaying effect, incorporating individual liberties of expression, such as a percussionist limiting himself to striking on every fourth beat, or even striking on all beats. A *rythme du pilou* is equally characterised by the number of percussionists and how they are divided between the two groups. The *rythme du pilou* is undefined by metronome but it consists of the total acoustic background which has no precise temporal grid.

THE FOUR-BEAT RHYTHM

The four-beat rhythm distinguished by the Kanaks as an indefinitely long repetition of a pattern of four beats is less frequently encountered than the *rythme du pilou.* It is found in accompaniments for the mimetic dances in the north of the *Grande Terre* and again in some Loyalty Islands dances. It is called *whaî* in the Hienghène region, but, confusingly, some people call it *rythme du nord* (rhythm of the north) even though it is is not exclusively found there. The four-beat rhythm is played by one percussionist on a slit-drum or a struck-bamboo and if a second player joins in, the two will be in synchronisation. The first beat of the pattern may be struck on a louder part of the instrument, perhaps slightly prolonged before beats two and three are played, and the last beat of the pattern is generally delayed, forming a kind of anacrusis for the following pattern. Thus the simplest version would read :

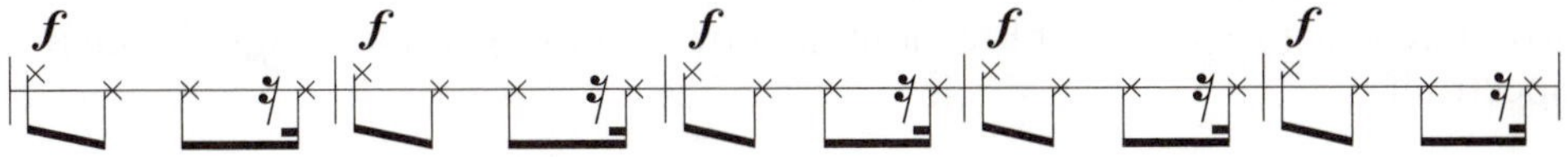

As the whole of the four-beat rhythm is left to slit-drums and/or struck-bamboos, there will usually be complementary rhythms from stamping-tubes in the manner of the *rythme du pilou,* which play on beats one and three of a the four beat rhythm.

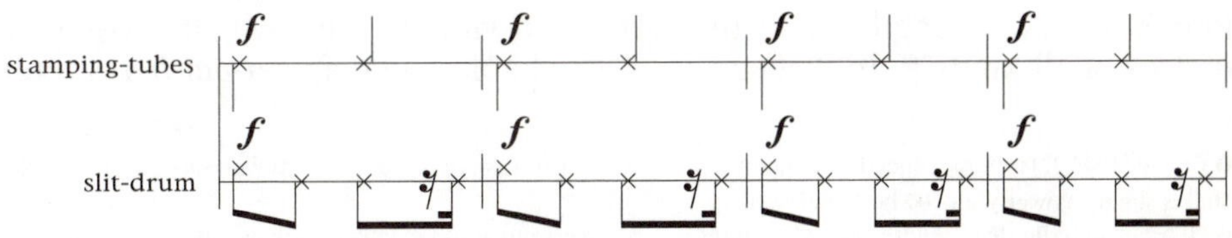

(David Becker/A.D.C.K.1992, Nouville)

The percussion ensemble of the dance group from the Isle of Belep consisting of two stamping-bamboos and two small slit-drums.

The tempo of a four-beat rhythm is ordinarily faster than the *rythme du pilou*, in any case too fast for stamping-tubes and bark-clappers to strike on all four beats. These instruments require a double arm-action per beat. To accompany the dance *hneen* from the region of Hienghène the four-beat rhythm is interpreted at 100 patterns per minute. To accompany the *faimanu* dance from Muli on Ouvéa it is interpreted at some 125 patterns per minute❶.

Impressions in the field of the sound-character of the four-beat rhythm ensembles may explain some of the enigmas that arise in discussing the Kanak rhythm. On Belep Island the ensemble is normally made up of two wooden slit-drums and two large stamping-bamboos, and in this case the four-beat rhythm is clearly audible. Now in the ensembles for mimetic dances at Ouaré near Hienghène there are many more stamping-tubes than slit-drums, so that the *rythme du pilou* tends to overpower the four-beat rhythm. Timbre thus plays an important role and a percussion ensemble is characterised by the combination of instruments and by the material used to make the slit-drum, wood having a spectrum of low dominant overtones, bamboo a high dominant spectrum.

THE VOICE ROLE :
ACOUSTIC ELEMENTS ADDED TO THE PERCUSSION PART

A number of elements are added to the formal percussion instrumental parts, to complete the overall sound picture of the *rythme du pilou*. They come from the dancers, the spectators and from the percussionists themselves. The participation of the spectators is an important and characteristic factor in Kanak dance music. Such acoustic elements are not formally defined, but follow typical patterns, where everyone is free to improvise as he wishes. One generally hears hissing, whistling, warbling, trilling, ejaculated syllables and even reiterated sentences. Lambert (1900/1985:155) notes, "It would be superfluous to talk at length about the songs and various cries which accompany dances of all kinds"❷. In Paicî a series of syllables such as *hei-hei-hei* is refer-

❶ Crowe (1995:27) reports a speed of 10 notes per second (= 600 stokes per minute) in Ambae slit-drum ensembles, Muli is slighty slower with 500 beats per minute.

❷ "Il serait superflu de s'étendre sur les chants et les cris divers qui accompagnent les danses de toute nature".

red to as *töii,* while whistles and hisses of variable length are called *uängi.* Some syllables, words or sentences as shouted out have a humorous or secret content. For example, two musicians may have shared an adventure, and one of them may make reference to it, but obliquely so that only his partner will understand. There are also a number of standardised words or sentences. Sentences called out, as well as whistled motifs, are rhythmical : sometimes reduplicating the percussion rhythms, sometimes in counter-rhythm. The following is an example of a sentence rhythmically recited to reduplicate the rhythm, the words in Paicî have a humorous content :

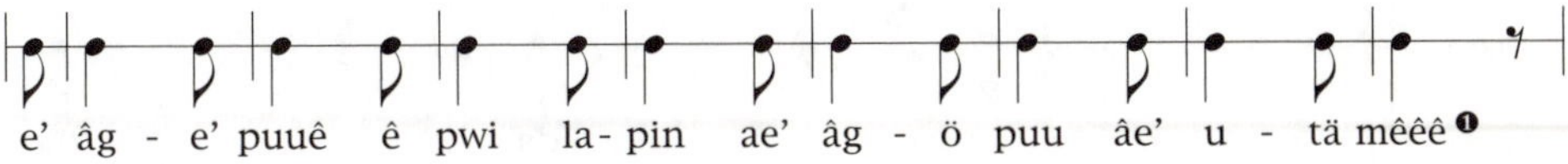
e' âg - e' puuê ê pwi la- pin ae' âg - ö puu âe' u - tä mêêê [1]

An example with anticipation at the end of the sentence

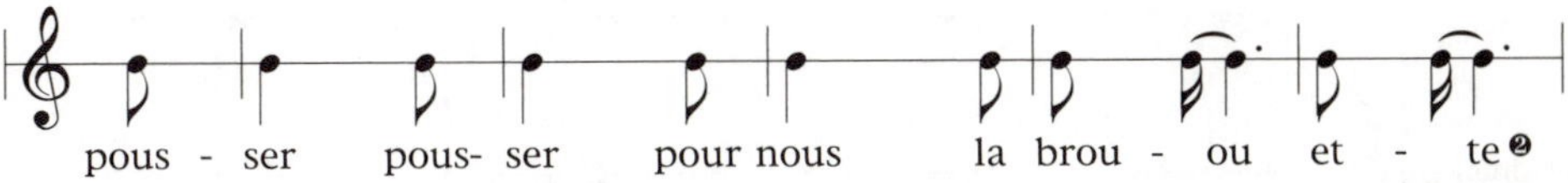
pous - ser pous- ser pour nous la brou - ou et - te [2]

The following example is in French. The first part reduplicates the rhythm of the percussion. At the end of the sentence it changes to a counter-rhythm and is a word-play with the word *militaires. Militaires* when pronounced in French is accentuated on the third syllable. Here it is the first syllable of the word that is in synchronisation with the downbeat of the rhythm. The result is a funny pronunciation of the word and an accentuation on the upbeat of the pattern ; the syllable *-taires* forms an anticipation to the following pattern.

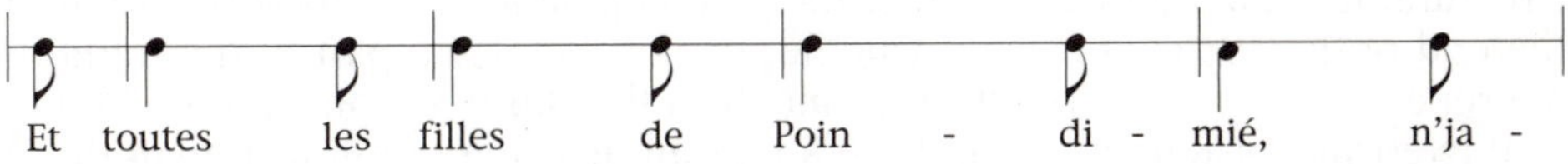
Et toutes les filles de Poin - di - mié, n'ja -

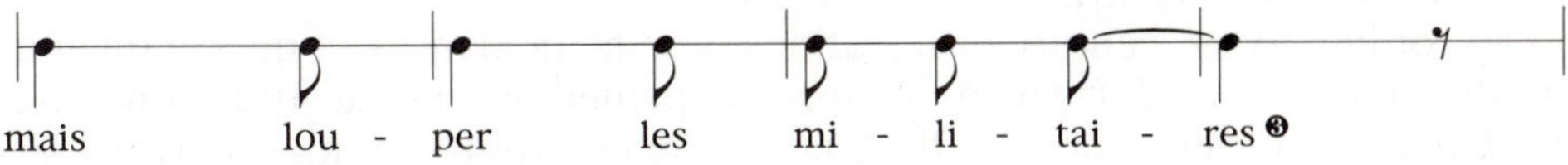
mais lou - per les mi - li - tai - res [3]

[1] "The hare mounts the female, and when he dismounts he has a blackout".

[2] "push, push, for us the wheelbarrow".

[3] "And all the girls of Poindimié, never miss [a chance] with the [French] soldiers".

The signal given by the dance-leader to interrupt the rhythm, is a special whistling motif, distinguishable from all other forms of mouth-whistling and hissing. In Paicî it is known as *uh-uh,* and it is given in time with the beats of the percussion instruments, defining the precise moment for an interruption or a change. The following is an extract from a idealised and fully-notated four-beat rhythm :

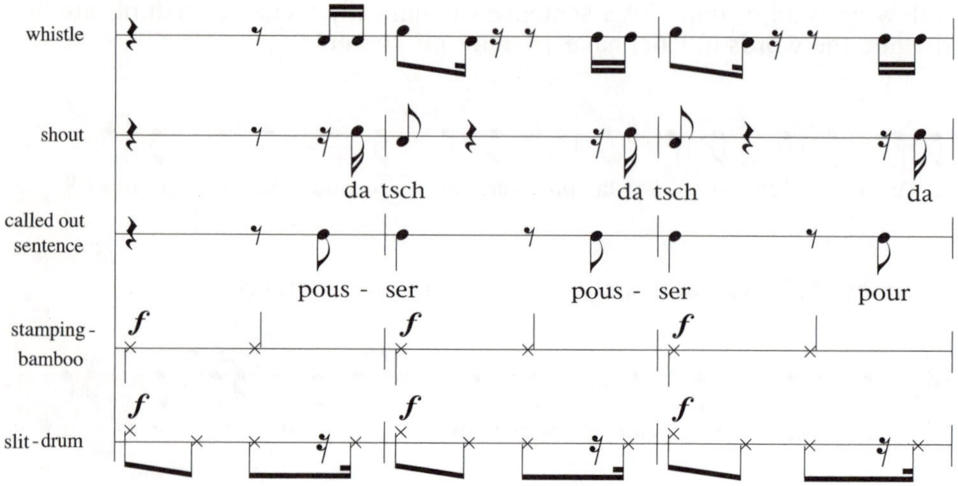

Traditional songs of the centre and north of the *Grande Terre*

Today most of the songs of the centre and north of the *Grande Terre* are composed entirely or principally of elements from the European musical system : major - minor tonal system (Siron 1992-1994:197) with a metrical time structure. It is thought that the first Kanak compositions of this sort date from the end of the 19th century and whether or not they form part of the traditional repertoire is a moot point. In as much as this study is concerned with the characteristics of Kanak music these songs are less important to it than those which show no or very little European musical influence. However it has to be taken into account that such songs are very rare today. The repertoire of Kanak songs seems likely to have once been larger and more diversified than it is now but there is little evidence to go on.

According to 19th century observations of mimetic dances of the centre and north of the *Grande Terre* were often accompanied by singing. Today only the *nêêkiipâ* dance performed by the Tiaoué dance group includes a particular song. As well as mimetic dances, exchange dances were also performed with singing but neither the dances nor the songs are performed nowadays. Something of the form of these songs, which were performed as evening attractions, is known, thanks to Vieillard and Deplanche (1862:208) "...they often meet in a case and a singer improvises a song in a monotonous tone which, according to its subject, gives rise to laughter, anger or joy on the part of the listeners..."❶. This sort of singing could last until late into the night.

Singing also took place in the *cases* to encourage warriors before battle. Lambert (1900/1985:176) says that the singer sat at the central post of the *case* and sang all through the night. Another kind of war song was sung on the battlefield immediately before fighting began (Rozier 1990:123).

A person familiar with traditional magic must have known a great many songs for all the occasions on which one was required, for example a song for rainmaking or for a safe sea voyage. Old people today are sure that these sorts of songs once existed but they no longer know them.

One of the first missionaries believed he heard a sort of love song❷ in 1843 or 1844. "Frankly speaking, I doubt that a musician could find a more infinitely harmonious duet than the kind which King Pakili-Pouma himself deigned to sing with one of his courtesans. This song, at first monotonous, became livelier little by little and had by the end quite a fast and very expressive rhythm, which was accompanied by clapping in time to the beat by most of the audience. With its ever increasing speed and seeing the expressions on the singers' faces, I guessed that the song expressed some sort of love scene"❸ (cit. in Rozier 1990:65).

Mrs. Mary Wallis described a kind of song or acoustic expression during the 1850s. "Occasionally, we have songs in the night. Mrs Blake is home sick, at times, and the Caledonians sing out their grief. They make a peculiar wailing sound, and call it crying" (Wallis 1994:134).

A mysterious report of a 'song of the spirits of Touaourou' recounts that every fifth month a "grand concert of spirits" is performed. In the afternoon people meet at the entry to a cave. As night falls someone gets up and announces : "You spirits within, may it please you to sing a song, that all the ladies and gentlemen out here may listen to your sweet voices". Immediately an "unearthly concert of voices" can be heard from the cave and that is the beginning of singing and dancing (Turner 1861/1984:429).

There may have been songs sung during particular tasks, taking up the rhythm of monotonous work movements (for example pounding taro, which is no longer done). However there are no reports of such songs in the literature and none of the old people encountered in the course of the study remember any.

Besides public singing there are songs for people to sing in private, as are found all over the world. Sarasin (1929:233) says about these songs : "The Caledonian [the Kanak] is able to sing to himself in a nasal and monotonous way for hours on end, sitting on a crag or beside the sea or when wandering about his garden; in sinister places, as around cemeteries, such singing gives

❶ "...souvent ils se réunissent dans une case, et un improvisateur entonne sur on ton monotone un chant qui, suivant le sujet, excite le rire, la colère ou la joie chez les auditeurs...".

❷ This is in contrast to the contemporary *kaneka* songs of the *Grande Terre* in which there are no love songs. Singers say that they are singing first for political independence and that other songs can be left until later.

❸ "Je ne doute pas, à franchement parler, qu'un musicien n'eût trouvé infiniment plus harmonieux l'espèce de duo que le roi Pakili-Pouma lui-même daigna chanter avec un de ses courtisans. Ce chant, d'abord assez monotone, s'anima peu à peu et prit, à la fin, un rythme assez vif et très expressif, qui fut accompagné des battements de mains en cadence de la plupart des assistants. À la mesure de plus en plus rapide et au jeu de la physionomie des chanteurs, je crus deviner que leur chant exprimait quelques scènes d'amour".

him courage"❶. Songs that Kanaks sing as solos in private today belong to the European music system. It seems that only a few cradle-songs have survived in their original form (see the song "Ololoi, Ololoa" on Ammann 1997:track 8b[CD]).

The form of traditional songs

For almost all writers the songs are "monotonous" (Vermast 1902:53; Sarasin 1929:233; Baudoux 1952:31; Patouillet 1873:204 ; Vieillard/Deplanche 1862:208; Moncelon 1886:22 etc.). In this context monotonous should perhaps not be interpreted in a pejorative sense. It indicates that the writers of the period heard part-repetition in the Kanak songs. However there are some observers who heard more than a monotonous voice. Garnier (1867/1991:190) said that the songs were full of "... sadness, joy, pain, rage..."❷. Marthe Lion found the songs that she heard during a *pilou-pilou* in the 1870s were "..., well cadenced... emanating from the depths of the forest, like the far away wings of a theatre"❸ (Lovreglio 1989:149).

Montague who made a number of important observations about Kanak music said in 1913 that all the songs are "duets" performed either by men or by women, and that solo or choral songs do not exist. It seems that Montague did not know about private songs, sung for personal amusement or solace, as recounted by Sarasin whose visit to the *Grande Terre* was undertaken only a year or two before that of Montague. Montague spent most of his time in the Houaïlou area and often it is not clear whether he is speaking of that region or of the whole of the *Grande Terre.* On the other hand his remark that there is no choral music on the *Grande Terre* appears to be exact for there are no reports of it in the literature, and today the only choral music is that of the *taperas.*

Metais (1979:30) says that old songs were polyphonic, sung with a falsetto voice and emphasised by a choir. She may be referring to the *ae-ae* songs which can be considered to be polyphonic and the backup choir as the hissing and whistling which accompanies them. In any case Metais does not think much of them saying "the tonality of these songs produces a dissonance and a discomfort which can be felt physically"❹.

The *ae-ae* songs

These days, apart from a few lullabies, the only songs belonging to the traditional repertoire which show no or very little influence from the European musical system are the two-part songs called *ae-ae,* found in the centre and north of the *Grande Terre.*

The origin of the word *ae-ae* is not clear. Some informants from the Paicî region say that it is derived from the Paicî words *jawé* and *èa* : 'the smile of the water'❺ and makes allusion to the legends of the origin of these songs.

❶ "Der Caledonier kann stundenlang näselnd und monoton vor sich hinsingen, auf einem Felsen oder am Meeresstrand sitzend oder in seinen Pflanzungen wandelnd; an unheimlichen Orten, wie in der Nähe einer Begräbnisstätte, stärkt er seinen Mut durch solches Singen".

❷ "... de tristesse, de joie, de douleur, de rage...".

❸ "..., bien cadencé... émanant des profondeurs de la forêt, comme les lointaines coulisses d'un théâtre".

❹ "la tonalité de ces chants produit une disharmonie et un malaise physiquement ressenti".

❺ "le sourire de l'eau".

Although it is possible that *ae-ae* is a Paicî word and that the songs originated in this linguistic area, it seems equally possible that the word *ae-ae* was created by French settlers. The repetition of the syllables *ae-ae-ae-* is very frequent in these songs and could have led to the name. The word is not found in the literature of the 19th and early 20th centuries although it is used nowadays by the Kanaks, possibly because of the loss of more precise terms. In the Hienghène region where the term *ae-ae* is not used, people distinguish two kinds of two-part songs : the *ayoii* and the *cada*.

Nowadays all the *tribus* to which *ae-ae* singers belong are to be found north of the line Bourail - Canala and there are only a few places where elderly singers who have a varied enough repertoire to accompany a round-dance, or make an evening of singing, live. Besides these there are a number of old people who have been able to maintain a song belonging to their family and during an evening they can be seen waiting for the right moment to perform the song. Sometimes, too, an old person in a *tribu* knows several songs but lacks a second singer to make performance possible (see, for example, Travant 1994[film]). The places where a sufficient number of singers can be found are well known ; they are situated in the areas of Koné, Gohapin, Hienghène, Poindimié and Canala.

The origin of the *ae-ae* songs

All the stories which are told in the different regions about the origins of the *ae-ae* songs have in common the idea that they originate in water. From the Poindimié area the *Vieux* Baptiste of Tiéti tells a story in which water, running over a rock in a stream, cracked the rock open and out came the *ae-ae* songs.

There is a story from the Pouébo region where an old man, on returning from fishing went to wash in a stream and suddenly heard a voice. On turning round he saw a *mwake* (a spiritual being) sitting on a rock striking two stones together and singing. Thus the old man was able to learn the archetype of the *ae-ae* songs. The *Vieux* Marcel of Tioumidou (Poindimié) has told how his father learned a song. He says that one day his father was sitting beside a stream, having a rest and smoking a cigarette, when he heard a song coming from the water. In a similar way the *Vieux* Ataba from the Bourail region pointed out the place in a stream from which the archetype of his song arose ; it is at the corner of a rock where the water is turbulent (Travant 1994 [film]).

It has to be borne in mind that rhythms also originate in the sounds made by water and it is not clear whether the expression *ae-ae* song in the stories of origin refers to the melody, the rhythm or both. If this last is the case the melody and the rhythm would share the same origin. However it appears that as far as the rhythms are concerned most of them are said to be heard in several places, including even in the waves of the sea, but the *ae-ae* songs themselves have only one place of origin for each region in which they are found. Thus it seems that rhythm is a musical phenomenon which has much the same kind of origin throughout the *Grande Terre*, while the *ae-ae* songs have an origin which is quite particular in each area.

The round-dance, the original sphere of the *ae-ae* songs

In their original state the *ae-ae* songs are accompanied by bark-clappers, bamboo stamping-tubes and palm spathes. The audience and dancers adding hisses, whistles and other rhythmic verbal expressions.

One informant and singer, the *Vieux* Ataba from the Bourail region said in a filmed interview (Travant 1994 [film]) that the *ae-ae* songs were performed only at night. This is surely related to the fact that the round-dance is also performed only at night.

An *ae-ae* singer who has been asked to accompany a round-dance spends the whole night singing and organising singers, both those whom he had chosen to replace him from time to time and those whom he has chosen to sing the second part. The singers stay in the centre of the dance all night and are able to refresh and relieve themselves in the surrounding forest only very quickly. They cannot leave the place where the dance is held before sunrise. Some well known singers can be asked to perform in places far outside their linguistic region❶.

In Kanak society there is a particular kind of plant associated with each traditional activity, usually called 'medicine' ('*médicament*') by Kanaks today. In earlier times, when there were many *ae-ae* singers, singing competitions were held. It was important to take 'medicines' in order to succeed and, conversely, other 'medicines' were known which had the power to make an opponent's voice tremble. The main adverseries in these competitions were singers from the west coast competing against those from the east coast.

Teaching *ae-ae* songs

A young singer was initiated into the *ae-ae* songs by his father or his uncles so that the gift and the right to sing remained, as far as possible, in the family line. The apprentice had to be in good health because all night singing demanded a great deal of energy, and he had to have an untroubled and open spirit. Becoming a singer also implied becoming a composer, as *ae-ae* songs required a sound knowlege of the language and a talent for composing new melodies.

Young singers were taught about the plants which give the power to sing and the confidence to sing well. There are several ways in which the plants can be taken and this can vary according to the region. Some plants, for example, have to be taken every three months, others once a year, and then there are those which are taken on the actual day of the performance. Exactly how the 'medicine' is to be taken is well defined traditionally and all things concerning the administration of plant 'medicine' are highly respected and kept secret.

Taking the appropriate plant 'medicine' is not enough to become a singer. The physical apprenticeship demands much effort. A singer from Hienghène described how he learned to sing when he was 21 years old. Two elderly singers from his family were his tutors. Lessons took place at night in a *case*. The two tutors were sitting down facing each other with the apprentice in the middle. In this way the young man learned both parts of the song. The two elders sang each strophe slowly and the apprentice had to repeat each strophe after them.

A singer from the Bourail area said that during his apprenticeship lessons were carried on at night. The songs were sung very slowly at first and after

❶ Inviting singers from distant parts is still practised today. At a festival in Témala (north of the *Grande Terre*) in 1992, for example, the group of singers from Gohapin were invited to lead the round-dance with their *ae-ae* songs.

having listened carefully he had the right to hum softly with the singers. Once the apprentice had learned the melody by heart, he had the right to learn the words and after that the song was sung increasingly quickly until normal tempo was reached. This singer said that after the singing lessons he had to go to sleep immediately which helped him to memorise the words.

In face of the danger of losing these songs a school headmaster from Koné, who is also a well known singer, teaches the *ae-ae* songs to boys between 12 and 14 who are interested in them, in the cultural classes at the school. This method of learning breaks with the traditional way of teaching *ae-ae* songs but in the present situation it may help to preserve them.

In the majority of cases a singer learns both parts of a song but he can have a preference for one or other of the parts. During a song performance he depends on a second singer who knows the second complementary voice part.

THE *AE-AE* SONGS OF THE HOUAÏLOU REGION

There is a recording made in the 1980s from Houaïlou but it seems that now there are no more *ae-ae* singers there. It is quite possible that several singers know some songs but no longer perform them. Only a few elderly singers from the Gohapin *tribu* now perform *ae-ae* songs in the Ajië language.

Leenhardt makes few remarks about singing in Houaïlou, and then only of a very general kind. The Montague manuscript contains much more detailed information❶. Montague says that there are two sorts of songs from the Houaïlou region: the *ururua,* house songs, and the *daro* dance songs. (Montague ms.V:12). Linguists who have studied the Houaïlou language have not heard of these terms and, at least today, there are no terms in the Houaïlou language for traditional songs apart from the word *ae-ae*.

Montague says "The *ururua,* or house songs, are sung to some extent by anybody, but there were proper choral singers [❷] who travelled long distances and were paid large sums to sing on festive occasions. The two singers sit down side by side, and sing to the accompaniment of soft tapping upon the coconut leaf-bases❸, and the sh-sh sound made by the whole audience. They seem to find it difficult to sing without this". Montague continues "The *ururua* are the most melodious; they are sung with great emotion, and singers and audience are often reduced to tears. They usually begin in a soft falsetto and gradually work up".

In referring to the song's content Montague says "The themes of these songs are excessively simple, though to translate them word for word and keep the sense and atmosphere seems to be almost impossible, and I have found nobody who could do it, - even those well acquainted with the language. Some idea of one of these songs (Gramophone Records 4 - 5) may be gleaned from the following. It calls to mind all the localities in the district where wood, leaves, and creepers for various purposes may be gathered. In the actual words the men are wandering about from place to place, gathering

❶ Montague's cylinder recordings (which are probably the earliest recordings of Kanak voices and music) are housed in the British Library in London.

❷ 'Choral singers' must refer to 'duet singers' because elsewhere Montague says that on the *Grande Terre* all songs were performed as duets.

❸ This is the only reference to coconut palm leaf bases used as an idiophone.

specimens for no apparent reasons, until arriving at the sea shore, they throw the whole bunch into the water, and the song thus ends. It begins 'We are sitting down breaking wood. I divide a creeper with my feet, and break a branch across the soles of my feet. Now we gather some leaves to wrap up shells, and another kind, which we tear into strips to mend a basket. At *Aou* we find a certain tree, of which we cut branches, and we now go to *Mé Wa* for the trees that grow there. We find fine wood at *Ne da Bourra* and we gather the growing creepers at *Newaira*... etc. The song thus continues for the minutes or so, until they came to the beach and throw the bunch they have collected into the sea".

The content of this song is typical of the *ae-ae* songs. It can be taken that the meaning of the song is not limited to a story about collecting wood and leaves, but that there is a secondary meaning which is not apparent today when the owner of the song is unknown. The fact that the song mentions several places could be an indication that it is recounting the ancient migration of a group, but that is only a hypothesis.

Montague describes the second kind of song from the Houaïlou region as follows : "The *Daro,* or dance songs, are archaic, and the words not generally understood. I am informed by M. Leenhardt that they are in a language approximating to the Poya dialect, and that there is a great similarity in these songs from all over the island, the language being almost the same in all". On this basis Montague concludes : "This is a possible indication that the language approaching that of Poya or Houaïlou was formerly very widely spread, and has since disappeared from the extremities of the island owing to immigrations of other races". The musicological interest in Montague's remarks is to see that it is possible that the two-part songs from Houaïlou could have come from Poya and would then be sung in the Paicî language. As will be shown later, songs from the Paicî region went to Hienghène where they are still sung in the Paicî language. Today there are two-part songs in the Gohapin *tribu* which are sung in Ajië which suggest a reverse movement. In any case it is quite possible that the *ae-ae* songs originated in the Paicî language area and later diffused from there.

Still on the *daro* Montague says "These songs were sung only by professional singers, of whom there were few, and they were well paid. These were both men and women who sang in the various dances. Like the *ururua* they were duets, but the airs are much more rugged and less melodious and of a wilder nature. They are thought, never-the-less, to be superior to the house-songs. The singers sit down, and the dancers form a circle about them, and follow each other round and round with the usual step". This description is close to the way in which the *ae-ae* songs are sung to accompany the round-dance, except that nowadays the singers are not seated. There is no other report from Houaïlou of the time describing similar singing.

The *ae-ae* songs of the Canala region

Unfortunately it has not been possible to research this region in any great detail. The only early analysis of the *ae-ae* songs from the area was made by

❶ Paul Vois (1895-1959) arrived in New Caledonia in 1921 as a qualified engineer for the nickel company (Société Le Nickel). He became director of the company but fell into German hands as a result of a boat accident in 1940 and was made a prisoner of war.

Paul Vois❶ (1939:10-13). His viewpoint, rather eurocentric and evolutionist, owes much to the anthropological ideas of the time but his article includes data that is of interest to the present study. For example Vois does not use the expression *ae-ae* to refer to the songs but calls them "the music of the Old Ones" ("la musique des Vieux"). This may mean that the term *ae-ae* was not used to designate two-part songs throughout the *Grande Terre* until after his report, and perhaps only from the 1960s onwards.

Vois says that there is "no harmony in these songs but there is certainly a melody"❶. He then gives two short transcriptions of the melodies. The first song, "the song of the valley" ("le chant de la vallée") is, according to Vois, in C-minor which he says is like a funeral dirge. Vois did not understand that to associate a minor key with sadness is a European idea and that other ethnic groups do not necessarily find the minor mode at all sad.

The second song, described as a song from beside the sea, is quicker (♩= 180) than the first song and is in a major key.

The *ae-ae* songs of the Paicî region

Most of the *ae-ae* songs still extant are in the Paicî language. Besides the narrative *ae-ae* songs, the Paicî tradition also contains other kinds of narratives. They can be divided into three classes : *popai, jèkutä* and *nyäbi* (D. Gorode 1994:10-11 ; Bensa/Rivierre 1976:31-65).

Popai can generally be translated as speech. As a generic term *popai* covers several kinds of speeches, each of them reserved for a specific occasion. For example, the speech *popai o picijü*, a speech given when saying goodbye to a group of people at a ceremonial meeting. The *popai görö upwârâ*, 'speech given from a tree' (*le discours sur le bois*) differs from and is more important than the *popai nâpuu*, 'speech on the ground' (*discours à terre*).

Jèkutä, has its etymological origin in the expression 'we stay to murmur together' (*nous restons à marmonner ensemble*). *Jèkutä* is the generic term for all kinds of recitation including mythological stories, fictitious stories, historical stories or present events and stories in a conversation. The term *jèkutä* can sometimes be replaced by its synonym *jèmâä*. But *jèmâä* is also a

❶ "pas d'harmonie dans ces chants mais qu'il y a certainement une mélodie".

generic term for a group of specific recitations about events which were important in the creation of the world and those concerning the mythological world of the clans (*wââo*).

Nyäbi means chant and song in general. For example the Christian song book is called *tii goro nyäbi* (book of song). *Pwa nyäbi*, means 'to sing', or translated by the precise meanings of these two words, 'make a song/a chant'. As a generic term *nyäbi* includes all sorts of vocal singing expression : from venerated epic songs, presented in the form of an *ae-ae,* to children's songs, *nyäbi kârâ èpo*, or lullabies *ololo*. To refer to traditional singing such as the *ae-ae,* the term 'real song', *âju nyäbi*, is often used.

Ténô is a poem that can be performed in either rhythmical recitation or in a song. When singing a *ténô,* the lyric differs from the recitation form. The language of the *ténô* does not use direct approaches, but instead a language of symbolism.

Pwärä-pwa, is a poem in which the lyrics refer to the history of the group and it is reserved for the group's internal information. The content of a *pwärä-pwa* can be modified and it can then be used as the poetry for an *ae-ae* song. *Pwärä-pwa* can also be sung as children songs, *nyäbi kârâ èpo*, and lullabies, *ololo*. *Pwärä* is the name for an acoustic manifestation, for example *pwärä-tùra* is 'the voice', 'sound of the voice' (*voix, bruit de voix*) *pwärä-èa* is 'the sound of laughter' (*rire*).

There is a corpus of lyrics, taken from the narratives suitable for recitation as *ae-ae,* which can be referred to as epic songs. There are also a number of *ae-ae* in which the contents deal with less important subjects, such as an expression of joy or an invitation to dance (track 1 on Ammann 1997 [CD]). A corpus of melodies exists to which the lyrics can be sung. Any of the lyrics can be performed with any of the melodies and more than one melody can be sung to the same lyric within one performance.

The stories told in a song's lyric can be very long and a song can consist of more than 30 strophes. Several breaks will be made during the performance of the same song and the melody of the *ae-ae* can change after a break but the lyric of the story continues. However, a number of lyrics are in general performed with the same music, because the individual singer prefers this particular choice of music and lyric. The way in which melodies are interchangeable may indicate that the most important element in the *ae-ae* songs is the story told in the song. Singing an *ae-ae* song is the same, from an emic approach, as telling a story.

The singers say it can be difficult to sing with a person who speaks a different kind of Paicî dialect, for example people from the east coast with people from the west coast. Singers say the difficulty lies in the differences in pronunciation. It is not impossible they say, but they do not feel at ease when singing. On the other hand singers speaking the same dialect can sing together without rehearsals❶.

The *ae-ae* songs with epic-like content of the Paicî region recount legends of the group's history. Most of the lyrics of the *ae-ae* songs are in the possession of certain families and the recitation is restricted to relatives of one family.

❶ For example the song on track 7 on Ammann (1997[CD]) is performed by an ad hoc group of singers from different *tribus* around Koné : Tiaoué, Néami, Oundjo, Paouta.

In general one *ae-ae* is referred to by the name of the composer and owner, for example, *nyäbi* Goromeatu (Goromeatu's song), and the songs may refer to the history of the composer's lineage. Much of Kanak history is concerned with the migrations of historical and mythical times (sometimes the border between the two is vague). Many groups from the region around Koné were obliged to migrate to other places because their land had been occupied by French settlers (*colons*) or as part of reprisals after insurrections such as that of 1917. A large number of the *ae-ae* songs of this region are in relation to the migrations of the period. The poetry includes much symbolism and information is coded at several levels. From the region of Poindimié, there is a song which refers obliquely, and in only a few words, to an ancient migration, by naming toponyms in the order that the migration took place. The song refers to the journey of the mythological founder of the *Dui* and *Bai* moieties northwards along the east coast. The journey starts at Tchamba and ends at Poyes. On this mythological journey, some of the protagonists stay at certain places and so name the region's geographical features such as valleys, mountains, rivers etc. The song divides the journey into several legs. Each part is represented by one strophe and its repetition. The first strophe and the strophe after each break consist entirely of neutral syllables, as in all the *ae-ae* songs. At the beginning of the other strophe the name of the place where the leg of the journey begins is recited followed by the neutral syllables a-e-a-e. The first strophe begins with Tchamba, followed by Wiindö, Tié, Wagap and finally Poyes, in the order from south to north, in which a traveller would encounter the places. This song identifies a region and at the same time is a reminder of historical events on which present land claims are based (see track 6 on Ammann 1997 [CD]).

The structure of the *ae-ae* songs of the Paicî region

The *ae-ae* songs in the Paicî region are two-part songs structured in strophes. The text words of the *ae-ae* songs are recited at the begining of each strophe, followed by a longer part in which only neutral syllables are performed. The melodies of the *ae-ae* song of the Paicî region, are called *wééggè-ré nyäbi*, meaning lliterally 'nutrition' or 'meat' of the song❶, *wééggè-ré nyäbi* also refers to the one melodic theme which corresponds to a strophe of a song which last between approximately 20 and 40 seconds.

There are only two singers singing at the time, but there are other singers standing by, who will continue the song when a singer wants to make a break and gives a sign with his head. In such a strongly hierarchical system as that of the Kanak society, it is obvious that in each group, and also between two singers, there is a *chef*. The first singer of an *ae-ae* song is called in respectful terms *eru ukai kärä nyäbi* (intoning-*chef* [or husband]-of-the-song) and the second singer, *eru wâdërë nyäbi* (intoning-wife-of-the-song). These are formal terms, in less formal speech the principal singer is called *eru* and the second singer *täbwi* (to break). The first pair (*eru ukai kärä nyäbi* and *eru wâdërë nyäbi*) sing a few strophes and then they pass the song on to another pair of singers. After singing a few strophes the second pair either gives the

❶ In many Kanak languages the word used to refer to the text of the song signifies nutrition or meat in contrast to the Paicî language where it signifies melody.

song back to the first pair or passes it to another pair. If, for example, *eru ukai kärä nyäbi* has given his part to somebody else, but there is no other singer present who knows how to sing *eru wâdërë nyäbi*, only *eru ukai kärä nyäbi* changes.

The *eru ukai kärä nyäbi* starts the song and the *eru wâdërë nyäbi* enters together with the first *jepa* (concussion bark-clapper), just a few seconds later. For the first strophe, *bërë nyäbi* (literally 'a piece of a song'), only neutral syllables, most often in the form of a-e-a-e, are recited. The second *bërë nyäbi* follows immediately and begins the recitation of the legend. When the *eru ukai kärä nyäbi* wants to interrupt the song, to give all the singers and musicians a short rest, he starts singing the following *bërë nyäbi* with the neutral syllables a-e-a-e. This will indicate to the singers and the percussionists that after this *bërë nyäbi* the singing will stop[1]. After a short break the song starts again with a *bërë nyäbi* of neutral syllables. If there are enough singers among whom the sharing of the song works well, the singers do not like to interrupt the legend with a pause, but continue until the whole legend has been told.

The music of the ae-ae songs of the Paicî region

The singing of the old or, at best, middle aged men is not very loud, and it has become impossible to achieve the same sound today as that of the *ae-ae* some 50 years ago when they were performed with the rich strong voices of young men. In all the songs heard in the field and in recordings, a falsetto voice has been used (see p. 122, for the use of the falsetto voice for *ae-ae* songs).

Melody

There is a certain liberty in the way an *ae-ae* melody is interpreted. The melodic line can be slightly changed, the term *köcö* (to play) referring to such improvisation. But the following features are common to all the songs heard.

In general an *ae-ae* melody is tetraphonic with one or two 'added notes', (notes that are rarely and briefly intoned and which do not affect the melodic line). The *ae-ae* have in general a range of a perfect fourth (P4), with the possible extension of the 'added notes', giving a range of an augmented fourth (Aug4) or for certain songs even P5. The singers very frequently use ornamentations on long notes, where the difference between ornamentation and melodic line movement can be fluid. The melodic intervals most often used are whole and half tones. The melodic lines are undulating around one or two tonal centres, rarely they are descendant.

The singers of today say that their fathers sang *ae-ae* songs with intervals which sound strange to the singers of today. This means that in earlier times the intervals were not of the tempered scale and were more strongly ornamented than they are today. In contrast some songs today may consist exclusively of notes of the tempered scale.

A singer has the freedom to improvise melodically, 'playing' with the song, and he can create several variants of one melody.

[1] To stop the singing in such a manner the word *taciö* (to cut) is used.

Polyphony

The two-part *ae-ae* songs are from the musical point of view neither responsorials nor canons as often found in Melanesia. Most of the time the two men sing together but sometimes they alternate. The principal characteristic of the alternating two-part system is that the second singer fills in the breaks of the first singer. The alternation is comparable with that of the *rythme du pilou*, and is confirmed by the use of the word *täbwi,* that indicates the 'second singer' as well as the 'offbeat' in the *rythme du pilou.*

The entering of neither the *eru ukai kärä nyäbi* nor of the *eru wâdërë nyäbi* is fixed. One singer continues to play (*köcö*) with the melody while awaiting the entrance of the other singer. Usually this period does not extend beyond a few seconds but it can vary from one *bërë nyäbi* repetition to the next, resulting in different lengths of time for each *bërë nyäbi* so that, for example, a *bërë nyäbi* may last longer than the one which follows it. Both singers of an *ae-ae* song sing in the same register (there is no bass-tenor relation), parallel singing can occur for some moments, interrupted bourdon sometimes occurs and sometimes the second part creates, possibly within an improvisation, a kind of counterpoint, where the two parts are rhythmically and harmonically independent.

The rhythmic relationship between percussion and singing

There is a general correlation between the tempo of the singing and the tempo of the percussion part with the two agreeing on the tempo beforehand. However, two independent rhythmical levels are apparent because the strophes of a song do not always have the same length, while the *rythme du pilou* never changes. A strong beat of the *rythme du pilou* does not fall on the accentuated note of the melodic line except by chance. The rhythmic relation between the singing and the *rythme du pilou* can be considered as a superposition of two different rhythmic levels; the *rythme du pilou* as a periodic repetition of the same rhythmic pattern as one level and the principally nonmetrical singing as the second level. The correction between the tempo of the singer and the tempo of the percussion is, however, preserved. No *ae-ae* song of the Paicî region was heard where the accompaniment was an extraordinarily fast or slow interpretation of the *rythme du pilou,* as is developed in the *ayoii-cada* of the Hienghène region.

Mikael Néa

The song called Mikael Néa tells about the activities of this respected man during and after the events of 1917. The people of the Koné region refer to Mikael Néa as a warrior, perhaps in the sense of his being an important man and not particularly as a fighter. The story of Mikael Néa is preferentially sung with the *wéëggè-ré nyäbi* (it was never heard with another melody, although that would be possible). The transcription represents one *bërë nyäbi.* It is based on a tetratonic scale with a range of P4 (e, f♯, g, a) and the added note g♯ with the tonal centre of f♯.

♩. ≃150
ja he- e da- wa u dne e da dna e
e e a
e a ja ja ja ja a oh oh- oh
e a ja ja ja ja a oh oh oh a e
ja ho a e- e ja ho a e
a e e a e a e e e a
a a la e e e a o - o a e
e a e e e e
jo o o o o o o a e
jo o o o o o o o o o o

Näbë cäbu

The *ae-ae* song *näbë cäbu* is an invitation to the round-dance. It is based on a tetratonic scale with two added notes (slightly higher than f and c). The song has a range of a little less than a fifth.

TRADITIONAL TWO-PART SINGING FROM THE HOOT MA WHAAP REGION

The language zone Hoot ma Whaap includes some 11 languages (Haudricourt/Ozanne-Rivierre 1982:7). Many terms of the music and dance vocabulary are similar throughout the languages, others vary greatly. In many of these languages (as well as in other Kanak languages) there is no word other than that for bamboo to cover the idea of music in the European sense. The word *hyavic* (in Nemi, Fwâi, Pije and Jawe) or *ga* (in Nenema) refers to bamboo and as many Kanak musical instruments are made of bamboo, this term has been extended to music and musical instrument in general. Older people from this region also refer to the record-player and the radio by the word *hyavic*.

In the Hienghène region where Fwâi is spoken, a number of old and middle-aged men still perform two-part singing and the particular vocabulary in relation to this kind of traditional singing still exists. In other regions of Hoot ma Whaap, traditional two-part songs may still be known to some degree but, during the period in which this study was carried out, the only performances seen were by people from the Hienghène region.

In the Fwâi language the word *kot* means 'to sing' or 'song' and refers to traditional singing and to modern and Christian singing. Two kinds of traditional two-part songs are known : *ayoii* and *cada*. Besides being the name of a class of traditional songs, the Fwâi word *ayoii* also means 'to tell a tale'. When a traveller comes back from a voyage and tells his family and friends what he saw during his journey, the recounting is refered to as *ayoii*. The word *cada* refers to something that is stranded, or something that was found on the beach, indicating that the *cada* songs have come to this region from somewhere else.

For both *ayoii* and *cada* the melodic singing is called *geen kot* and the song's lyric is called *pae-kot*. The word, *geen* means melody or timbre; for example *geen-vhali-n* means the colour or timbre of the human voice. *Pae* is the name for an edible root or tuber. Therefore *pae-kot* means the tuber of the song meaning that this is that part which nourishes the song. The possessive form of *pae* is *pain*, this form is sometimes used when referring to 'my ' or 'his' song words. A general difference between the lyrics of the *ayoii* and *cada* lies in the way a story is told. The people from Hienghène say that the *ayoii* recount events in a chronological way, whereas the *cada* describe only pictures or scenes in poetic and symbolic language. *Ayoii* and *cada* differ in structure and melody, but both are accompanied by the *rythme du pilou* of the bark-clapper (*bwan-jep*) and bamboo stamping-tubes (*hyavic*) but at different tempi; the striking of the instruments is slower for the *ayoii* than for the *cada*. *Cada* and *ayoii* are both used to accompany dances, but they can also be recited on their own.

The *ayoii*

The origin of the *ayoii* probably lies in the valley of the Tanghène. In an interview with M. Bealo Wedoye the late Paul Bwerou from Haut Coulna, said that the *ayoii* were created by some men of his *tribu* six generations ago, which would give a date of the mid-19th century (Bealo Wedoye pers. comm.).

The *pae-kot* of the *ayoii*

There is one basic melody for the *ayoii* and all the *pae-kot* of the *ayoii* are sung with the same melodic contour. The *pae-kot* of the *ayoii* have various subjects. They can refer to the composer's private life or his personal ideas and they can equally well be concerned with historical events important to the group. The two examples of *ayoii* on Ammann (1997[CD]) demonstrate this wide variety of *ayoii* lyric. The first example (track 3) tells about traditional customary life and the second example (track 4) has a popular theme❶. Two singers, Benoît Boulet and Salomon Mayat, for example, composed an *ayoii* on the occasion of their visit to Nouméa to sing their songs in a concert at the museum. The text of an *ayoii* is in the ordinary language of everyday life

veda ven mala yé tamé ru Hoot ma Whaap	**Here the day which arrive those (from) Hoot and Whaap**
Yélu tamé vha nynyami ngen aman pé nethuugi	**These two arrive to recall the things which (are) forgotten**
Ai Wéga dani ngen naii men paguui	**For this will be way of our children and grand children**
Thui ai wé nei téna	**Explain that we will hear**
Yélu tamé thui ven hun mooé ven nga	**These two arrive explain the way of being of the house**
Ngê ngen jinu ngen duu kahok né ven kaémoo Kalédoni	**House of ancestor spirit of the real men of the land Caledonia**
Thui na néi maan daahma maan daahma Drubéa ma Kapuné	**Explain to you those two big chief those two big chief Drubéa and Kaponé**
Ai wéga jinu men mwii	**For this will be the ancestor spirit and the power**
ai wéa balei wéga thôôwéragi ven Kanaky	**of the strength to go around the island of Kanaky**
wéga thôôwéragi ven Pacifik	**To go around the islands of the Pacific**

(For the direct French translation see p. 260.)

For the composition of an *ayoii,* the composer needs to adjust the lyric (*pae-kot*), to the melody (*geen kot*) so that the rhythmical form of the lyric can be recited with the given melody, in order that the words are understandable. This is a difficult task and there is only a handful of singers who can compose new *ayoii*. A new *ayoii* will be accepted by other musicians and so have a chance to be performed publicly only if the words are well suited to the music and the text is interesting. Today composers write down the *pae-kot*; in earlier years it all needed to be memorised.

Normally people who sing together are from related families which does not mean that they necessarily speak the same language. A singer whose mother tongue is Fwâi may well sing with people whose mother tongue is Nemi or Jawe. When two singers of different languages sing together, a difference in accentuation and pronunciation of the words can be heard which is referred to as a difference in the *hwerise* (turn, accent, pronunciation).

❶ The translation of this *ayoii* with a very popular content is given in the booklet of the Ammann (1997[CD]).

(David Becker/A.D.C.K.1994, Nouméa)

A group of singers from the Hienghène region during a performance of *ayoii* songs in front of the *case* of the museum ('musée territorial de Nouvelle-Calédonie') in Nouméa.

The *geen kot* of the *ayoii*

The *geen kot* (melodic contour) of all the *ayoii* consists of one musical theme that is repeated in a complex pattern during the whole song (see below).

The musical theme *geen kot* can be divided in two parts A and B. Each part, A or B, ends with the exclamation *a-ii* always intoned on the same pitch. Each of the two parts, A and B, consists of a descending melodic line.

Each part A and B consists of two tonal centres. In part A they are separated by the interval of a minor third (m3) and in part B by a major third (M3). The tonal centres of part A are c - a, the tonal centre of part B are b - g. Forming a total scale of g-a-b-c (with a c slightly higher for the reciting of the vocal *a* [-*ii*], between each part. Sometimes the tones can be replaced by others of the scale; mainly at the beginning of the A part. For example a instead of c. In both parts the melodic line is descendant. The pitches are not always purely intoned, often sliding up and down a little. The rhythmical form of the musical theme can be changed slighty in order to pronounce the words of the text.

The *bwan-jep* of the *ayoii*

Each rhythm group which accompanies *ayoii* singing, is led by the first percussionist called *ceen bwan-jep*. He is responsible for the relationship between the singers and the rhythm group. The singers start an *ayoii,* with long notes sliding up and down as if searching for the right sound (timbre and

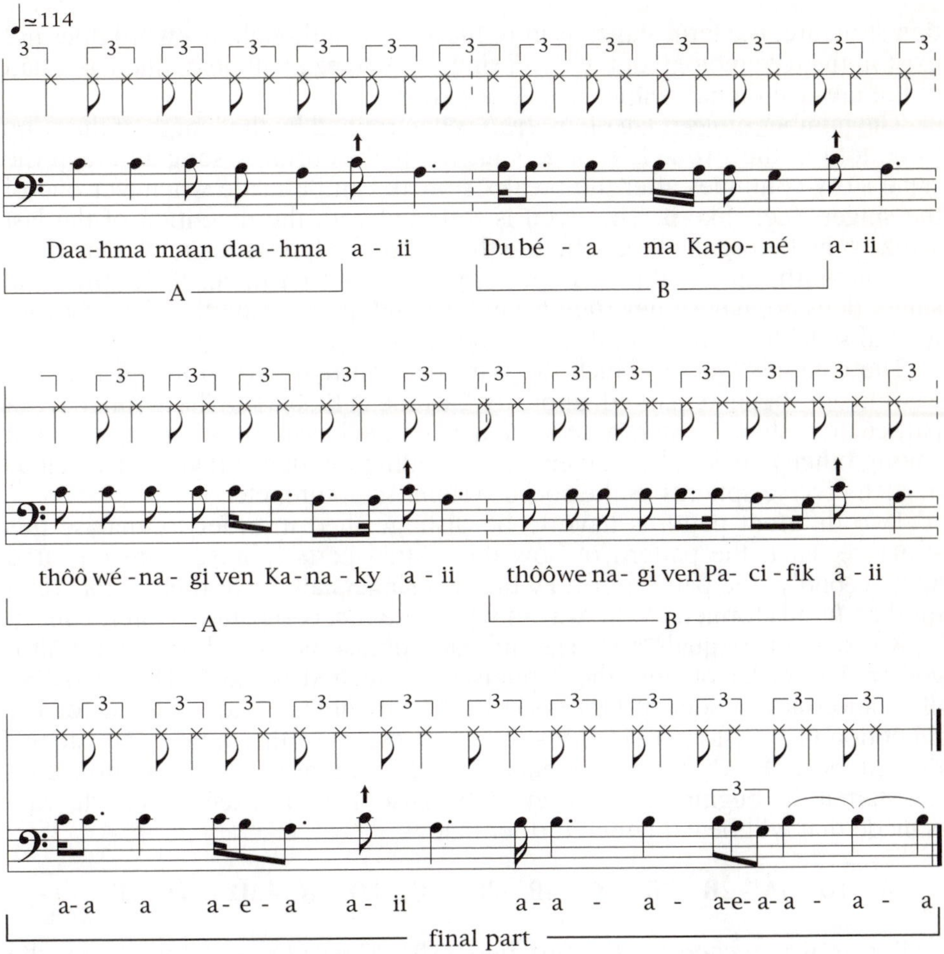

pitch). Before the actual melody starts, the *ceen bwan-jep* begins and the *thedua bwan-jep* (*thedua* refers to the complementary part of the *ceen bwan-jep* : to the offbeats) strikes in between the beats, thus making the *rythme du pilou*. The *ceen bwan-jep* directs the percussionists with specific standard commands. For example, he may shout *thedua, thedua*, to tell the musicians to strike precisely. In the course of the song the *ceen bwan-jep* may call *tabi, tabi, tabi,* (to listen) in order to indicate to the other percussionists to accelerate the tempo. The words *thai, thai, thai* signal that the strokes need to be more dynamic and *colli hyuu* (*hyuu* - to break) tells the other percussionists to make a break (as can be heard on track 3 on Ammann 1997[CD]).

There is a stronger correlation between the '*rythme*' and the singing than for the *ae-ae* in general. *Ayoii* are metrical songs (although the accentuation of the downbeat is not always obvious) and their parts are always equally long. Particular notes of the singing are always in synchronisation with the corresponding stroke of the *rythme du pilou*.

The repetition system of the *ayoii*

The two parts, A and B, of the *geen kot* of the *ayoii* are repeated in a complex pattern during the whole song. To facilitate the analysis of the repetition structure, the term stanza is introduced here, although this word does not exist in the terminology of the *ayoii* singers. A stanza will be defined as a half of the musical theme : either part A or part B.

The number of *geen kot* of an *ayoii* is determined by the length of the story to be told in the *ayoii*. The singers make breaks during a song although the same story continues after the break. A break can be made whenever one of the singers feels like it. The *ayoii* is restarted with the repetition of the last stanza sung before the break, before the rest of the lyric is recited❶. One *ayoii* can follow the next without a special pause between them. If the principal singer does not have a new *pae-kot* in his mind, he can sing the *geen kot* with neutral syllables until he finds a new *pae-kot*.

The complex way in which the stanzas of an *ayoii* are arranged together has already been remarked upon by Beaudet (1986:54). The *ayoii* have a particular system of stanza repetition and the basic pattern is also found among other Kanak cultural elements including the dance rhythm, as well as in such diverse spheres as the social system, sculpture, etc.

Two different patterns have to be distinguished in order to analyse this structure. First, the pattern of how the textual parts (phrases) are repeated and, secondly, the pattern of how the two singers alternate their parts. Yet a third pattern is formed by the way in which the first two patterns interconnect.

A text phrase equals a stanza and each phrase is recited four times altogether. The order of how these phrases are recited is fixed. The following illustration is a model of this system : The numbers (1 to 4) stand for the repetition (1 = first recitation, 4 = third repetition) of the phrase and each of the letters **A**; **B**; **C**;..etc. represents a different phrase. The illustration does not start at the beginning of the *ayoii,* because there an exception to the rule is made that will be explained further below.

3**A** - 1**B** - 4**A** - 2**B** - 3**B** - 1**C** - 4**B** - 2**C** - 3**C** - 1**D** - 4**C** - 2**D** - 3**D** - 1**E** -

Phrase B is recited for the first time (1**B**). Then phrase **A** follows for the fourth time (4**A**). Two recitations of the phrase **B** follow (2**B** and 3**B**) and then the new phrase **C** appears for the first time (1**C**). The phrase **B** is recited for the fourth and last time (4**B**).

The beginning of an *ayoii* varies slightly because there is no phrase preceding phrase **A** which is therefore recited three times followed by phrase **B** (1**B**) where the system shown above is taken up.

There are two singers and therefore three possibilities of how a phrase is performed : - solo of singer I; - solo of singer II; - duet of singers I + II. The pattern of how these three possibilities are used is illustrated below. SI stands for the first or principal singer and the second singer is indicated as SII (using the roman numbers avoids a confusion with the pattern of the phrase repetition). SI sings a phrase in solo, the same phrase is sung twice by the two singers together and finally the phrase is sung as a solo by SII.

(SI) - (SI + SII) - (SI + SI) - (SII) - (SI) - (SI + SII) - (SI + SII) - (SII) - (SI) -

❶ To restart after a break, the *ceen bwan-jep* begins quietly, soon getting louder in his strokes and advising the other percussionists to enter by calling *thedua,* and finally the singer begins. The breaks are called *hmuet* and the part at the beginning of an *ayoii* is called *thaun*.

The two patterns, one of phrase repetition, the other of singer combination, are already complex in themselves. The two patterns are connected in a way which creates yet another pattern. The new phrase (1**B**) is always introduced by SI. The following phrase, the last repetition of the preceding phrase (in this case 4**A**), is recited by both singers (SI + SII). The phrase (2**B**) is recited by both singers (SI + SII) and finally (SII) sings phrase (3**B**) as a solo. After (SI) has introduced the new phrase (1**C**), the phrase (4**B**) is recited for the last time by the two singers (SI + SII).

(SI : 1**B**) - (SI + SII : 4**A**) - (SI + SII : 2**B**) - (SII : 3**B**) - (SI : 1**C**) - (SI + SII : 4**B**) -

To perform an *ayoii* the singers need to concentrate all the time in order to keep track of this system. Sometimes in *ayoii* performances a singer makes an error and the system collapses but after a few repetitions out of pattern the two singers find their way back into the system.

As mentioned above, from time to time the singers take a break. In this case, the system begins with a repetition of the combination which was sung immediately before the break. For example :

(SI : 1**B**) - (SI + SII : 4**A**) - break - (SI + SII : 4**A**) - (SI + SII : 2**B**) - (SII : 3**B**)

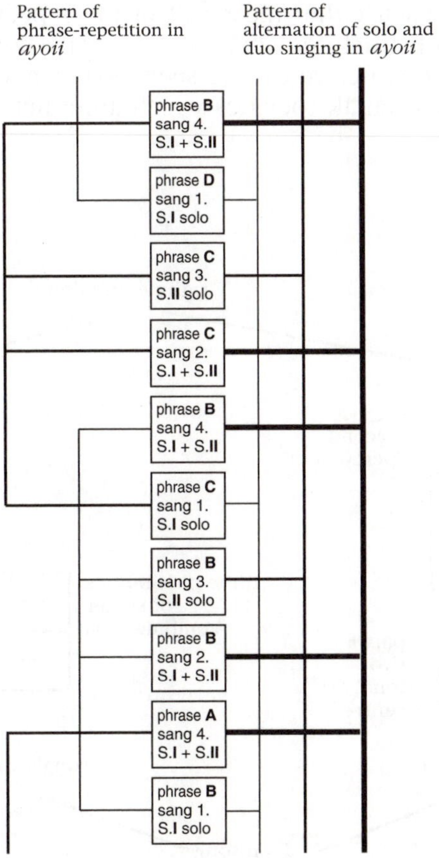

Symbolism in the *ayoii*

As described above the structure (of phrase repetition and singer combination) of an *ayoii,* brings together two different factors, each of which is already structured in an alternating system, into a third complex alternating system.

The phrase repetition structure is based on a period of four (this is an aesthetic selection not a mathematical restraint because it could just as easily consist of a period based on three or five) while the voice diffusion pattern is based on three elements (SI, SII and SI + SII). Thus the overall structure of the *ayoii* is based on an intermingling of periods of four and periods of three. Furthermore these two systems are in addition to the other alternating systems present, the percussion group with the *rythme du pilou* and the melody itself. Each part A and B has two tonal centres. The pitches of the tonal centres themselves are actually interlocking (c-a/b-g). As noted earlier, the essential element in traditional Kanak life is exchange : exchange of wives, goods, ideas and wars. This idea is present in the overall form of *ayoii*-songs in a very concentrated and complex form. Allusions to the exchange system are found in other areas of traditional Kanak cultural expression, for example in the arrangement of alleys and counter-alleys, and also in the sculpture of door posts etc. But what is essential in the *ayoii* structure, is that it is much more complex than merely a simple interlocking system that could represent the two lineages, maternal and paternal. The *ayoii's* structure is a play of action and interaction on several levels : melody, structure, rhythm group. Each of these elements is itself either the result of the repeated interaction of other elements or it is not structured at all, like the voice components in the *rythme du pilou.* The *ayoii* structure can be seen as a symbol resembling closly the reality of traditional Kanak societies which are a net of complex interactions on several levels.

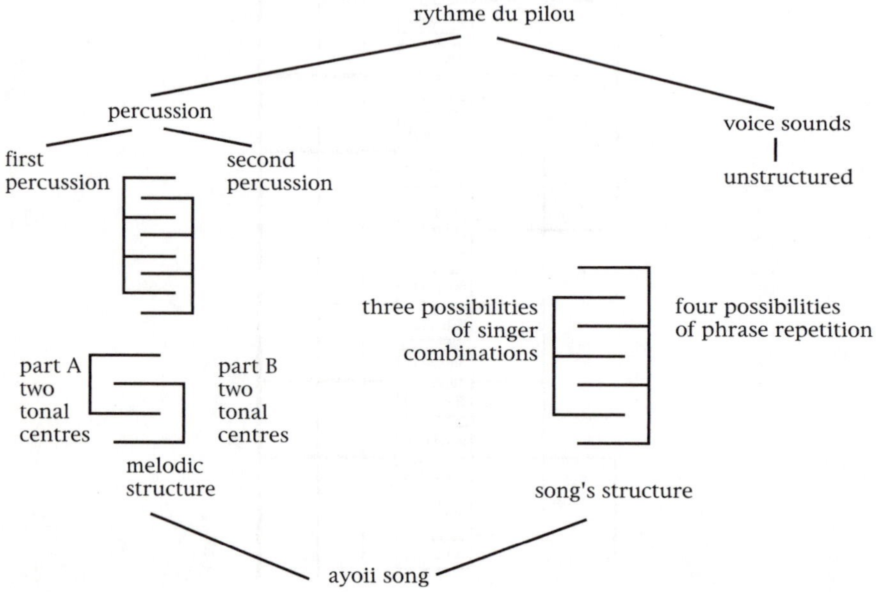

The *cada*

The word *cada* makes allusion to the origin of the songs outside the region. Although there exists a *cada* with a text in Fwâi, it is no longer clear who composed the Fwâi words for this *cada.* Beaudet (1990:track3[CD]) recorded a song that came to Hienghène from the Couli *tribu* around 1945. However, most of the *cada* have their text words in the Paicî language which indicates the region where the *cada* came from.

Most of the *cada* performed in Hienghène were originally *ae-ae* songs from the Koné region. Singers from Koné were asked to listen to recordings of the *cada* from Hienghène and they immediately recognised the melodies and said that these were old songs from the Koné region which have almost been forgotten. The words of the *cada* are in the Koné dialect of Paicî. The singers from the Koné region were surprised how well the Hienghène singers pronounced the Paicî words. The Hienghène singers did not, however, sing all the poetry of the song, but only several strophes which were repeated several times. Beaudet and Tein (1985:19) see the period of the 1917 rebellion as the years when the *ae-ae* moved from Koné to Hienghène. Informants say that it is also possible that the *ae-ae* songs reached Hienghène earlier via Vamalé and Tipindjé, where people originally from Koné had already settled, and from where some moved north to Hienghène. Thus families from Koné who were forced by the events of 1917 and 1918 to leave the Koné area moved to places where they had relatives. Movement from Koné to the Hienghène area continued after 1918 and some of the *cada* tell about the 1917 rebellion and could be compositions of Paicî speakers who had settled in the region of Hienghène after the rebellion.

The music of the *cada* in Paicî corresponds to that of the *ae-ae* of the Koné region. To avoid repetition, the music of the *cada* will not be analysed here except to describe a few structural differences from the Koné *ae-ae* songs.

The structure of the *cada* differs from that of the *ayoii* and also from that of the Koné *ae-ae* songs. Whereas in the Koné region breaks will be made whenever a singer gives a sign, the *cada* are regularily interrupted after three stanzas. After a break, SI recites the strophe sung just before the break. Then SI + SII sing the following strophe together and repeat it, before the next break follows.

SI recitates stanza n ; SI + SII sing stanza n +1 plus its repetition ; break ; SI recitates stanza n +1 ; SI + SII sing stanza n +2 plus its repetition, etc.

If irregularities in this structure occur, the singers find their way back after a few repetitions.

It seems reasonable to think that the *ayoii* were created around the mid-19th century, and that the *cada* arrived later in the region. The structure of the *cada* has more similarities to the structure of the *ayoii* than to the *ae-ae* of Koné which could mean that the people of Hiengène created their own structure for the *cada.* There is a change between solo and two-part singing as in the *ayoii,* which is unknown in the *ae-ae* on the other hand in a *cada,* the second singer is allowed to make improvisations, called *mween* in Fwâi, as is permitted in the *ae-ae,* whereas in *ayoii* no improvisations are possible.

The *ayoii-cada*

The people of the Hienghène region say it was the people from the *tribu* of Tanghène who were the first to make a fusion of *ayoii* and *cada* : the *ayoii-*

cada. These songs were already known before the childhood of the older people today, so it must have happened quite soon after the *cada* arrived or were first created in this region, perhaps in the 1920s.

For the *ayoii-cada* the singers from Tanghène took over the percussion part of the newly arrived *ae-ae* (*cada*) and adapted it to the singing of the *ayoii*. One of the creators of the *ayoii-cada* still known is the late Boulawat.

People say that at first it is difficult to sing the *ayoii* with a different percussion accompaniment, because the singers are not used to it and are still connected with the 'traditional' slow striking of the instruments. To make it easier, one of the percussionists may fill his stamping-bamboo with water. This tube, with a sound clearly distinguished from the others, is the leading bamboo for the other percussionists and the singers can then orientate their song on the particular sound of this beat. The *ayoii* are metrically structured and the strokes of the instruments are coordinated with the singing. For the *ayoii-cada*, the singers have to learn new temporal fixed points given by the percussion instruments. This is like singing a song in a 2/4 metre; accompanied by a drum that plays once by ♩=80 and once by ♩=100, without changing the tempo of the singing. The singers can perform the same *ayoii*, once with a slow percussion accompaniment and once with a fast accompaniment.

CHAPTER 6

MIMETIC DANCES OF THE CENTRE AND NORTH OF THE *GRANDE TERRE*

Men's mimetic dances from the centre and north of the *Grande Terre* are all performed with synchronised movements and may include a theatrical play. In most of them the dancers form a square keeping a distance of 150 cm between one dancer and the next and with all the dancers looking in the same direction. A dance consists of a number of parts and sections as will be explained below.

Mimetic dances were originally part of the various activities of a group attending a *pilou-pilou.* Today all these different activities can be correlated with particular dance-parts of a mimetic dance performance. Presentations of mimetic dances can be divided into four parts :

part A - the entry of the dance group
part B - customary speeches
part C - mimetic sections
part D - the round-dance

The number and order of these parts can vary. For example, the round-dance (Part D) may be left out, especially at dance festivals, where groups follow each other in presenting dances. Sometimes a round-dance gets started after a mimetic dance presentation and it may continue for a few minutes before it stops and gives place to the next mimetic dance presentation.

Part C, which in this model includes the actual mimetic dances, is further divided into several sections[1]. Each section has one or several specific

[1] The Kanaks often use the French word *figure* (figure) to refer to a section with a mimetic character where specific subjects are imitated. As indicated by the Study Group for Folk Dance Terminology of the ICTM (earlier : I.F.M.C.) the term 'figure' should be excluded from the terminology of dance analysis because "it has been fixed in language usage in various national dance traditions, describing, however, very different form units within a dance" (Report of the I.F.M.C. Study Group for Folk Dance Terminology 1972:119).

subjects that are mimed in the dance motions. These mimed subjects are often related to tribal warfare, for example an attack or a defence using traditional weapons may be imitated; actions from daily life are also mimed, for example the construction of a traditional house; the subject can also be simply the imitation of an animal. Between each of the sections there is a short pause.

A dance presentation can include a section where the dancers perform a real play - always with a humorous content. For example, a dancer may fall down and pretend to be ill. The corps of dancers will call and search for a doctor, and one of their number, hiding to the side and previously disguised in a white coat, with a stethoscope and carrying a doctor's bag in a comic fashion, will run on stage in pretended panic to 'treat' the 'injured' dancer, whereupon a miracle cure will occur with the dancer suddenly springing up and the next synchronous section will take place❶.

There is a difference between arm and leg movements. The most significant motions of Kanak dances are carried out with the feet when stamping on the ground. There is no jumping and most of the time the dancers remain on the spot although there are a few sections in which they advance a few steps to imitate an attack with the club, afterwards retreating to the original spot. Stamping the feet very probably originates in warfare, expressing the warriors' anger and fury. The same kind of accelerating stamping was performed before a battle. Stamping as a medium to express fury is not limited to the *Grande Terre*, it is, for example, clearly an important element of the *bua* dance from

(David Becker/A.D.C.K.1994, Touho)

The Ti.Ga. dance group entering the dance-ground. The front dancer jumps and moves quickly, like a warrior in order to escape the thrown spears (see p.83).

❶ Comic doctors and nurses are a popular theme for such pantomimes in Melanesia for doctors arrived with colonisation. Many people owe their health and indeed their lives to the colonial network of dispensaries, so that the subject is worthy of the Melanesian capacity for irony. The dichotomy between the approaches of European medicine and traditional healing is also expressed.

Lifou (see p. 217) and in other places in southern Melanesia, for example on Tanna (Vanuatu) (Humphreys 1926:86), or from the Melpa in the Highlands of Papua New Guinea (Strathern 1985:120).

In contrast to the heavy leg movements, arms are moved quickly and gracefully. Besides its war symbolism, the dance tassel adds grace to the motions of the arms (as mentioned by Leenhardt 1930/1980:174) and may even add some minor acoustic effects. It certainly underlines the synchronisation of the motions clearly and smoothly.

The strong relationship between these dances and tribal warfare is apparent in the aesthetic of the dances. The criteria used for judging a fine performance are those necessary for a victorious fight : discipline, fast and powerful movements, motionless waiting or hiding between one section and the next. When kneeling and camouflaged with leaves dancers, like warriors, can hardly be detected. The dance leader goes from one dancer to another, whispering instructions, criticism and the name of the next section in his ear. A pause can last even longer then a section. Some sections are carried out so rapidly that a section of a mimetic dance can seem like a wild storm coming up quickly followed by silence immediately afterwards.

In the Hoot ma Whaap region mimetic dances are accompanied by the four-beat rhythm and the dance from Pothé (centre of the *Grande Terre*) is accompanied by the *rythme du pilou*. Although mimetic dances were once accompanied by singing, today most dances are performed without a singing accompaniment, because of the lack of singers and because the songs are no longer known. In the Paicî-Cèmuhî region, where there is no percussion music to give a temporal grid, the dancers hiss in a specific rhythmic pattern for each section, which helps to keep them synchronised. The leader of a dance may shout commands to the dancers in words.

(David Becker/A.D.C.K. 1994, Touho)

At local festivals people are happy to meet and to socialise, the atmosphere is relaxed and there is much laughing and joking.

A mimetic dance leader in the centre and north of the *Grande Terre*, will know a number of sections. From this repertoire he decides which and in what order the sections are to be performed. This means that not all performances of the same mimetic dance by the same group are identical. In general, a mimetic dance can last between 10 and 20 minutes, consisting of between five and ten sections. Although in this time only a small part of the dance leader's sectional repertoire can be presented, performances should not last longer or the dancers will get too tired due to the physical effort involved. Each section has a name which refers to its subject or to its overall function.

Each section consists of a number of motifs. A few sections, usually those at the beginning of the mimetic part (C) of the dance, are in a homogeneous chain form, but most sections are divided into a heterogeneous chain form of motifs, including repetitions of a motif. All the motifs in one section can be classified according to their mimed messages, either being part of the imitation of the section's subject, for example an attack with a club, or having no relation to the subject. Motifs which imitate the subject of the section will be called : subject motifs (S.M.) and the motifs with no relation to the subject of the section : neutral motifs (N.M.). The neutral motifs are the same in each section of the dance. A section can be composed of either one S.M., that may be repeated in alternation with the N.M., or it can be composed of several S.M. where the subjects are thematically related : for example rowing a boat (S.M.1), fishing with a spear (S.M.2), and distribution of the catch (S.M.3). A few sections, often at the beginning of the mimetic dance part, do not refer to a specific subject and so present a homogeneous chain of repetitions of the neutral motif. The diagram below, shows the form of an idealised dance part (C) where the mimed sections are performed. It is not based on any existing dance:

Part C :

I.	section :	- motifs : N.M./N.M./N.M./N.M.
II.	section : fight	- motifs : N.M./S.M.1/part of N.M./S.M.2/N.M.
III.	section : yam	- motifs : N.M./S.M./N.M.

In the centre and in the north of the *Grande Terre*, mimetic dances with the same name are performed by different *tribus*. After the complex population movements and the long period without dancing, the present dance distribution must be far from what it was at the end of the 19th century. A dance with the same name performed by different groups will usually have some common forms and structures, but the various versions are certainly not indentical. Similarities are mainly to be found in the dance motions of the neutral motif. Subject motifs are individual from group to group, although it is possible that two groups perform some subject motifs in exactly the same way. When a dancer says he dreamed a new dance of 'cutting wood', this means that he dreamed the subject motif 'imitating cutting wood'. The subject motif will be added in the dreamer's own way to the neutral motif to form a new section, or to add a new element to an existing section.

Dances of the Paicî region

In the Paicî region a large number of *tribus* are still actively engaged in maintaining traditional cultural life and especially mimetic dancing. During the period in which this study was made all the dances that will be mentioned have been seen and often filmed. Knowledge of the dances has been complemented by discussions with the people responsible for the dances. There have also been discussions with elderly people in the Paicî region who can remember dances which have not been performed for many years. In this chapter the

Paicî terminology for dances will be given and the *nêêkiipâ* dance, as performed by a dance group from the west coast, will be analysed. A comparison with other dances from the north of the *Grande Terre* will complete the chapter.

Dance classification in the Paicî region

All the dance classifications established earlier in this study were once present in the region. The name of the trade-dances performed inside houses, can no longer be recalled even by elderly people ; when they were children the dances had already died out. A sort of exchange system is remembered, where objects were hung on a horizontal rope and everybody could go and make exchanges with his own object. There was no music or dance accompaniment, in contrast to the region around Hienghène.

The 'speech given from a tree', *popai görö upwârâ*, (i.e. speaking from an elevated position either on a tree itself or on a wooden perch) that used to be associated with a particular dance (*cäbu têê*), is very rare today when there is no-one left who can recite one of the very old speeches in its entirety. It is one of the cultural components most threatened with extinction.

The round-dance, *cäbu tabéa* 'dance in a round', in its present form (see p. 64) is performed quite often. Mimetic dances in Paicî are called *cäbu tütin. Tü* means 'to throw' as in, for example, *tü boo i pwé kêê* 'to throw a fishing line'. In Paicî the verb for performing a round-dance is *cäbu* (to dance), while the verb for dancing a mimetic dance is *tü* (to throw) : *tü i cäbu*. The generic term *cäbu tütin* can be translated as 'dance to be thrown'. A *cäbu tütin* is exclusively a men's dance and it is described as a war dance by the population. Of the large number of *cäbu tütin* which presumably once existed only three forms have survived to the present day : *bèèmä, ôdobwia* and *nêêkiipâ*.

All three *cäbu tütin* are structured in a way typical of the northern half of the *Grande Terre*, as already described. The principal part where the mimetic sections are presented, is performed without any percussion music in contrast to those of Hoot ma Whaap.

There is also a women's dance, called *cèto,* that is performed by a group from the Paicî region as well as in parts of the Cèmuhî region. As *cèto* is a women's dance it cannot properly be counted among the *cäbu tütin.* Nevertheless it is interesting to find that the mimetic part of this dance is accompanied by percussion music.

Results of investigations into the origin, structural differences and forms of these dance sub-classes, were somewhat confused. Some people who are responsible for dances were unable to identify their dance as belonging to one of the three groups. In the 19th century each of the three sub-classes was in the possession of a particular social group but after the bans (effectively in place from 1900 to 1950) on performance were lifted and dances were taken up again, the demographic and socio-geographic situations were very different. People learned mimetic dances which were not necessarily the ones danced by their grandfathers and by this time only a few old men remembered the choreography of the *cäbu tütin.* A dance teacher, in remembering how a dance was performed some 50 years earlier, might easily confuse the motions of two dances, thus inadvertantly creating a 'new' dance (Antoine Goromido pers. comm.). Today there is no claim to ownership of a dance by one of the moieties of the Paicî region, the *Dui* or the *Bai*.

In dictionaries of vernacular languages some helpful information is given :

- ***Bèèmä*** is translated as "war dance" ("dance guerrière") (Rivierre 1983:44) belonging to the lineage named Baraotâ. There is no indication of the origin nor of any distinguishing features of the dance. Here it can be added that the formal particularity of this dance is that in the neutral motif the dancer swings his hanging arms back and forth while holding a dance tassel, in Paicî called *pwêêti,* in each hand.

- ***Ôdobwia*** or ***wâdobwia*** is translated in the Paicî-French dictionary as "name of a dance" ("nom d'une danse") (Rivierre 1983:259). In the Cèmuhî-French dictionary (Rivierre 1994:273 and 383 resp.) *ôdèbwia* or *udèbwia* is translated as "dance holding club and dance tassel" ("dance - en tenant casse-tête et bouquet"). This does not distinguish it from the *nêêkiipâ* dance where the dancers hold the same objects in their hands. A feature of the *ôdobwia* dance as performed today by the Néami, Poindah, Tchamba and Tiwaka is its particular movements during the neutral motif.

- ***Nêêkiipâ*** is translated as "name of a war dance" ("nom d'une dance de guerre") (Rivierre 1983:162). The *nêêkiipâ* dance is probably the most widespread dance in the Paicî region at the moment. It will be studied in detail so that it can be compared with the other dances of the Paicî region and with other dances from the northern half of the *Grande Terre.*

THE *NÊÊKIIPÂ* DANCE PERFORMED BY THE DANCERS OF TIAOUÉ

Many dance groups in the Paicî region perform the *nêêkiipâ* dance, and each group performs the dance in a particular way. Differences can occur in the dance movements, in the hissing rhythmic patterns that acccompany the dances and in the costumes worn.

For a detailed study of the *nêêkiipâ* dance, the version performed by the dance group of the Tiaoué *tribu,* situated about 15 km inwards from Koné on the west coast, has been chosen. This group can retrace the origin of the dance within their lineage quite exactly and they respect the obligations that are inherent in the ownership and performance of the dance.

The origin of the *nêêkiipâ* dance is to be found in a valley situated close to Gohapin, near Poya, whose name is written as "Neguipin" on the IGN[1] map. The valley is uninhabited, but traces of Melanesian settlement can easily be detected. It is said that at the time when the valley was still inhabited, a man who was working in his garden, was attracted by the movements of the bird *nyäti-nä-môtö* also called *dörönäri* (*Rhipidura spilodera verreauxi,* the Speckled Fantail). This bird is said, when walking, to move from side to side in a particular manner[2]. The following night the man dreamed of the undulating movement of the bird and realised that it was showing him dance steps. The man then taught these steps to the other men in his lineage and that was

[1] Cartes IGN (Institut Géographique National) Nouvelle-Calédonie (3) Nr. 514, 1991.

[2] "It [the Speckled Fantail] is often seen in undergrowth and thickets, flitting from branch to branch, spreading out its tail and wagging it from side to side, quite fearlessly following the observer around". ("On le voit frequemment dans les sous-bois et les buissons, voletant de branche en branche, deployant et remuant lateralement la queue, suivant l'observateur sans aucune crainte".) (Delacour 1966:136-138).

the origin of the *nêêkiipâ* dance. The movements of the bird are those which are expressed by the dancers in the neutral motif. The parts where subjects are imitated are then added by the dancers.

On a date which may be guessed at as about 1870, a huge *pilou-pilou* ceremony was held in the Neguipin valley during which the families Mendupowé and Mereâtu, by presenting an *âdi duu* (*monnaie Kanak*), received the *pwêêti* of the *nêêkiipâ,* meaning that they were given the right from the people of the valley to perform the *nêêkiipâ* dance. Later on the Mereâtu family went to the Koné area and settled on the Tiaoué reservation where they still live. Today the person responsible for the dance is the *chef* of the lineage, Seraphin Mereâtu of Tiaoué.

The dance group from Gohapin is the only other group on the west coast of the Paicî region which performs the *nêêkiipâ* dance. On the east coast however, there are several dance groups performing the *nêêkiipâ* dance as will be shown later on in this account.

The Tiaoué group performed the dance at the cultural festival Melanesia 2000 (Mélanésie 2000) held in Nouméa in 1975 and they also performed it in 1994 at Touho for the 'Pwolu Jenaa' dance festival.

The dance group maintains the obligations or *tabous* (taboos) which accompany this dance. The area where rehearsals are held is highly respected : eating there is not allowed and neither is spitting nor breaking wind. One is not allowed to cross the area diagonally : only forward, backward and sideward movements are allowed. At the front of the area where, during a performance, the *chef* of the host group and other notables are placed, stands a little tree with 'medicine' attached to it. The 'medicine' is covered with straw. Rehearsals take place before performances of the dance.

Before the dance particular medicinal substances have to be taken. Physical contact with women during a specific time period before the dance is prohibited. For very important events the dancers live for a certain period, which can last several days, in complete isolation from the rest of the *tribu.* Before going to the place, where the dance is to be performed, the dance is shown to the population of the *tribu,* especially to the elder men who will not be accompanying the dancers. The expression *wailu,* 'twice', is used, meaning that the dance is performed at the actual place for the second time. This double performance is quite usual, even though some other taboos concerning the dance may be neglected. Its origin is probably to be found in the fact that the dance was performed before warriors went on a war party, and that it was actually a form of warrior training and demonstration before the elders of the *tribu* so that the best warriors could be chosen.

The following analysis is based on the performance given at the 'Pwolu Jenaa' dance festival where the dance was performed as it would have been at a *pilou-pilou*. The dance is remarkable in that it is treated as something that is given away to the host as an exchange object. First the dance is performed and then, with a speech, it is given, or 'thrown', to the host. In earlier times a 'speech given from a tree' would be made after the performance with the 'throwing' of the dance. Sadly, there is nobody left in the region who can remember the speech.

In part A of the dance, the entering dancers are hidden behind branches held by accompanying persons, two singers within the group sing the *ae-ae* songs and several people beat percussion instruments. The dancers wear *manous* and have decorations made from the central yellow unopened frond of a coconut palm crown. They wear coconut leaflets around their ankles and a band around the head with feathers stuck into it. The club is carried in the right hand, a *pwêêti* is attached to each wrist and held in the hand on the right side together with the club.

The dancers form a square at the back of the dance area, at the place where the mimetic part will take place. Several people stand about 20 m in front of the dancers. One of them holds a dry tree to whose branches ribbons have been fixed. This tree will serve after the dance is over as the customary gift ('*la coutume*'). There are two singers who intone a special song at the beginning of the dance. One person holds a big club over his right shoulder with a special *manou* fixed to it which contains the specific *nêêkiipâ* 'medicine', called *pwö*. This club with the *pwö* normally stays in the possesion of the *apooro cäbu* (the owner and *chef* of the dance). In this case the *apooro cäbu* was taking part in the dancing himself, so he gave the duty of holding the *pwö* during the dance to one of the singers, who was thus in a prestigious position. It is important that the *pwö* is in front of the dancing, so that the dancers face the *pwö* during the whole dance.

As the dance was given with a speech after the presentation there was no part B.

Part C of the dance was then composed of the following sections :

I. *acëu cäbu* (to pull the dance)
II. *apooro cäbu* (the owner/*chef* of the dance)
III. *kupwa* (gun)
IV. *paaci* (cattle)
V. *nâni* (goat)
VI. *pwa wêêë* (to fish)
VII. *gö* (club)
VIII. *pi waaté* (to pass by)
IX. *pwändi* (to call for someone, give a sign)
X. *pädi pwêêti* (divide the dance tassel)
XI. *märüdù* (bird, sort of buzzard [*Accipitridae*])
XII. *wâri mâniô* (skinning manioc)❶

Part D

XIII. *dooté* (doctor, theatrical play)
XIV. *cäbu tabéâ* (round-dance).
XV. *cia jawé* (to fetch water)
XVI. *tü pwêêti* (to throw the dance tassel)

In this performance 16 sections were presented without repetitions. This is very long when compared with *nêêkiipâ* dance performances given by other groups. From the list above it can be seen that sections I, II, X, XIV, XVI express typical *nêêkiipâ* dance subjects. The sections VII, VIII, IX, XI, XII, XV have a direct relation to war even though the titles may not always indicate this. For example the section 'fetching water' involves a certain movement used in traditional warfare. Today, where tribal wars are history, the actual

❶ There is a specific vocabulary for the different sorts and parts of the manioc. *Mâniô* seems to be a word used only recently.

meaning of these movements may no longer be known to every dancer. It is also possible that, under pressure, in order to make the dance conform to missionary ideals at the restart of the dances in the 1950s, name changes were made in certain sections. As already mentioned in relation to other Kanak dances and songs, there can be different levels of information available to different sections of the population. Perhaps only initiated warriors knew, for example, that the gestures for 'fetching water' are in fact those for killing the enemy in a certain way. In the same way sequence XII, supposed to be concerned with peeling manioc, has actually nothing to do with manioc as a vegetable food. In this case the long bulky manioc tuber stands for the male sex organ and this section plays on the abstinence from sex before going to war or before the dance performance. Sections IV, V, VI and XIII are concerned with daily life. The sections representing cattle and the scene with the doctor are about subjects from the white man's world which in general are ridiculed. When the dancers imitate the cattle's horns by holding the fingers on the side of the head, they also imitate the sound of the cow or goat, which makes the audience laugh. Section III, the gun, can be interpreted as a scene from the white man's world, or as a scene concerned with tribal warfare.

In order to avoid repetition not all sections of the dance have been referred to in the following notation and analysis. Only the most informative sections are dealt with.

I. *Acëu cäbu*

In the first section, *acëu cäbu*, the dancers come forward to the *pwö* which is held in front by a person facing them. This sequence is accompanied by a specific song, which can be sung only on this occasion. The song is performed by two people and is of the *ae-ae* genre. It starts slowly and accelerates with the motions of the dancers. The words of the song refer to the motions which the dancers now have to carry out and encourage the dancers by calling on the chief dancer to advance. The song stops with the sound *ititi,* which is a sign for the mimetic section to start. The song is very strongly associated with a taboo and although it is recorded, it will not be given here.

All the sections start as follows : the dancers have their upper bodies slightly bent which is a particular feature of the *nêêkiipâ* dance. One of the dancers in the front row starts to stamp with his left foot. Both arms move inwards and outwards together. The motions start slowly but then accelerate. All the dancers watch the feet of the man in front and then start to stamp in the same way. Thus each dancer gets into the frequency of the steps in turn from front to back. A dancer in the front row gives a hissing signal called *tëpö duru.* The sound is made by pronouncing tsch-tsch-tsch…, one sound on every left foot, accelerating with the frequency of the steps. The *tëpö duru* has the function of giving an acoustic signal for the frequency of the steps. Thus the dancers at the back are able not only to watch the steps of the men in front, but can also hear the frequency of the steps. Once the necessary frequency is reached the sound *ititi* indicates the actual start of the section. The sound *ititi* is made by tsch-tsch sounds, as in *tëpö duru*, but here the sounds, and the time intervals between them, are shorter. It is given by the dancer in the last row, once he sees that the steps of all the dancers are synchronised. The neutral motif of the *nêêkiipâ* dance, performed by the Tiaoué group, is accompanied by a specific hissing pattern called *mäbu ûgé* (short hissing).

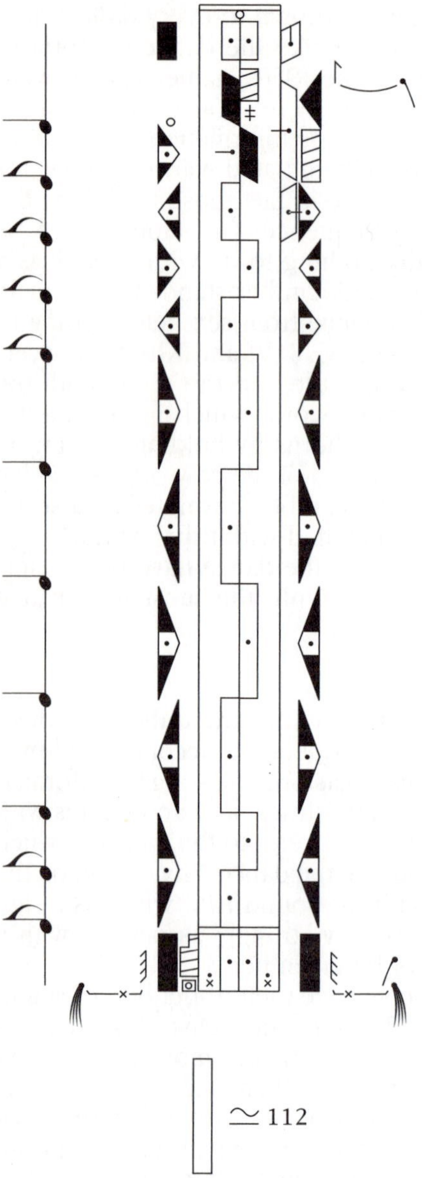

Neutral motif of the *nêêkiipâ* as performed by the dancers from Tiaoué. The arms are moved alternately inwards and outwards.

The neutral motif which is carried out at the beginning of each section is called *apooro cäbu*. This name can be translated as the owner of the dance and also, on a more symbolic level, *apooro cäbu* refers to the bird *yäti-nä-môtö*, who is the original owner of the dance and whose gestures are now imitated. If the neutral motif is repeated after a subject motif, it is not called *apooro cäbu* but *bërë,* yet it should be noted that one of the first sections of the dance that consists entirely of a repetition of the neutral motif is itself called *apooro cäbu*.

The neutral motif starts with the left foot and the first part is a kind of walking on the spot with the feet stamping heavily on the ground and moving the arms inwards and outwards. Still with the feet stamping on the ground, the dancer turns 90° to the right and then quickly turns 180° to the left bending deeply so that the right knee touches the ground at the same time as the dancer moves the right arm quickly downwards, as if striking. The dancer then stands up and this is the end of the neutral motif or *apooro cäbu*. The subject motif follows without any interruption.

Both the neutral motif and the subject motif are accompanied by specific hissing, whistling or trilling patterns. Each type of sound is given by a different dancer. The sound needs to be loud enough for everybody to hear. Some dancers have a reputation for being exceptionally good at producing a particular sound.

For the section *acëu cäbu* the dancers use a special walking style to approach the *pwö* in a demonstration of respect. The name of the section, *acëu cäbu*, can be translated as 'pulling' the dance. The dancers 'pull' the dance to the actual spot where the dance will take place. At the same time the dancers are pulled by the *pwö* to perform the dance.

For the subject motif of section *acëu cäbu*, each dancer puts his left arm akimbo and holds the club in his right hand over his right shoulder. After three steps on the spot with the left arm swaying each advances with special skipping steps. The steps of the right foot are on a straight line whereas the left foot touches the ground to the left - to the right - left - right... of the line of the right foot. The dancers stop two metres from the *pwö* and then retire backwards for three steps and carry out the neutral motif once again. Then they take two long steps forward to finish the section. The approach of the dancers is accompanied with a long hiss, one hiss (*mäbu göri*) for each time the left foot touches the ground.

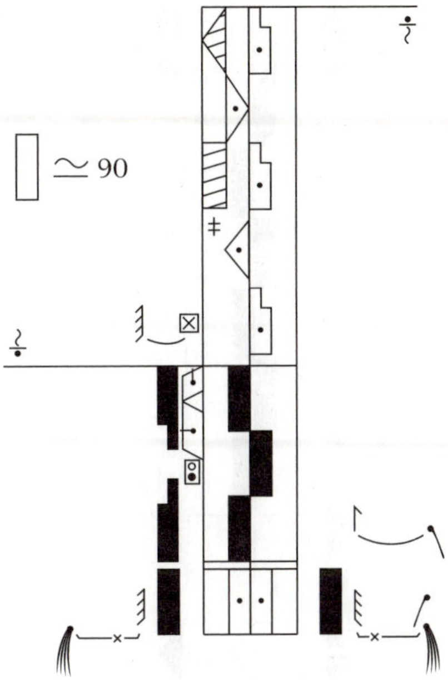

The part where the dancers come forward during the *acëu cäbu* section.

The movement of the setting of the left foot forms a sort of hocketting or alternating pattern. This pattern can be found in many other components of Kanak culture and is symbolic, standing for the exchange of women between moieties, exchange of material during *pilous-pilous* and much more. The section *acëu cäbu* is the most important section of the *nêêkiipâ* dance for this is where the *pwö* is honored. It is a perfect place to present this pattern, demonstrating one of the fundamental bases of Kanak culture.

II. *Apooro cäbu*

The second mimetic section *apooro cäbu* starts with the neutral motif (*apooro cäbu* not to be confused with the name of this section) the subject motif follows, again the neutral motif (*bërë*) and finally the repetition of the subject motif. The structure of this section can be noted as follows : N.M. - S.M.1 - N.M. - S.M.2.

For the subject motif the dancer goes three steps sidewards left, then sidewards right. Back on the spot he holds the club with both hands on the level of his breast and then the dancer turns 180° to the right and back again

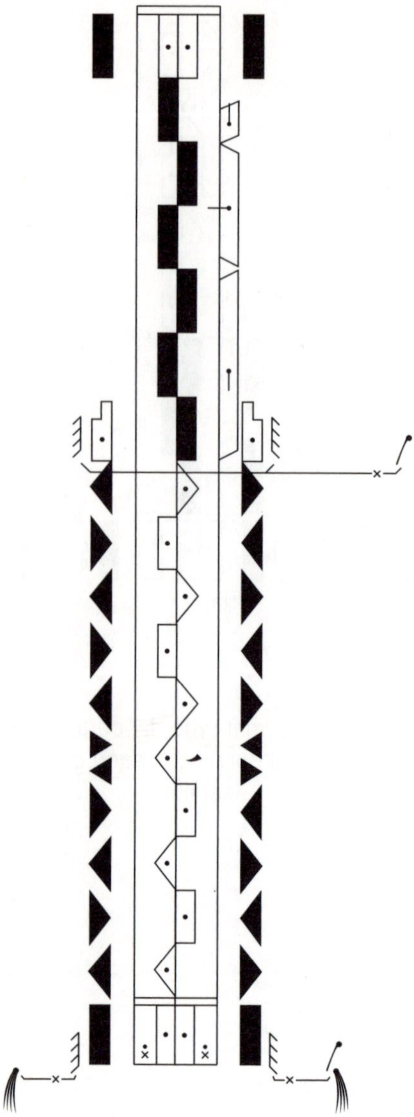

Subject motif 1 of the section *apooro cäbu.*

270° and then turning back to the original direction. After the second neutral motif the dancer imitates a hit with the club and again with the club in front, he turns 360° to the right kneeling on the right knee to end this section.

III. *Kupwa*

• contents : carrying the gun, shooting in kneeling position.

• structure : N.M. - S.M.1 - N.M. - S.M.2.

For the first subject motif the dancer holds his club, which represents the gun, behind his neck carried on the shoulders and with the hands resting on the club (James Dean's way of carrying a gun). The dancer turns 90° to the left carries out two light hops on the spot with the left foot, while the right foot is in the air. This is repeated at 180°, 270° and finally back in position. In the S.M.2 the dancer walks four steps forwards and pushes the pointed club diagonally downwards in front of him, once left, once right with each step. The dancer then goes down on the left knee and imitates shooting with the gun.

VI. Pwa wêêë

• contents : rowing the boat, driving a spear into the fish and handing it behind, killing the fish by striking it.

• structure : N.M. - S.M.1 - N.M. - S.M.2 - N.M. - S.M.3.

The three subject motifs of this section represent the actions of a fisherman. In the first the club is held with one hand at each end. The dancer skips, imitating with every skip a push-like motion. The dancer then goes backwards to his place while with his arms he imitates rowing the boat. The second subject motif represents how the fisherman drives a spear into the fish. He leans forward and with the right hand he imitates the strike with the spear and with the left hand he takes the fish from the spear and hands it backwards to an imaginary assistant in the boat. This motion is repeated twice and each time, the dancer hands the fish backwards over his shoulder he says 'this is for you', showing that he fishes not for himself but for his entire clan, and each fish is for each nuclear family in the clan. This small detail demonstrates yet again that in Kanak culture food gathering is carried out for the benefit of the social group and not for the individual. In the third subject motif the dancer skip/walks two steps, has the right knee on the ground and kills the fish by striking it with his club.

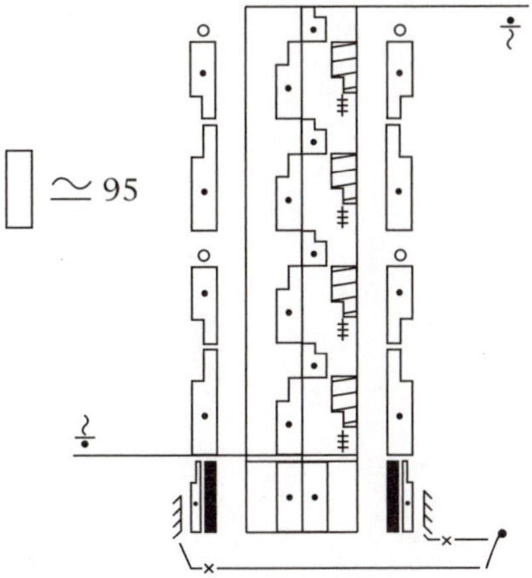

Extracts of subject motif 1 of the section *pwa wêêë.*

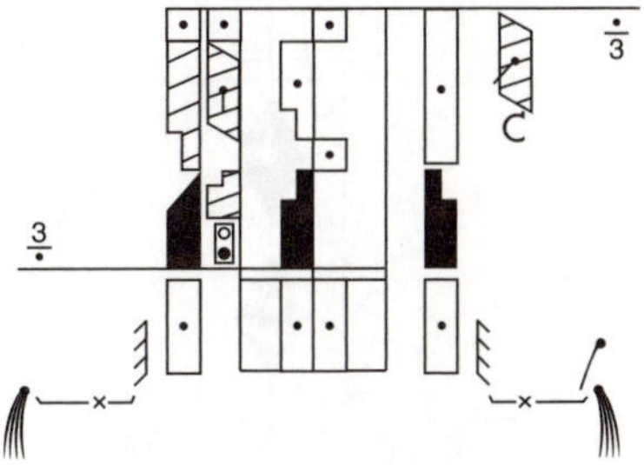

Extracts of subject motif 2 of the section *pwa wêêë.*

VII. *Gö*

- contents : exercise with the club.
- structure : N.M. - S.M.1 - N.M.

At the beginning of the section *gö,* the dancers make two lines facing each other. The dancers carry out the neutral motif in this formation. The action of striking with the club is carried out by the dancers of one line attacking the dancers of the facing line, who hold their clubs vertically over their heads as a protection. The action is repeated in reversing the roles of attacker and defender. The section of attacking with the club occurs in *nêêkiipâ* dances of all the other groups.

XII.*Wâri mâniô*

- contents : provocative movements with the haunches.
- structure : N.M. - S.M.

In the subject motif of this section the dancer carries the club behind his neck and jumps forward with both feet together. With each jump he thrusts his haunches forward, imitating the movement of copulation. After having carried out 14 jumps, in the last movement the dancer brings his haunches backwards and so bends his upper body. This last action, which is the contra-movement to the copulatory one, refers to the sexual abstinence that is demanded before going to war.

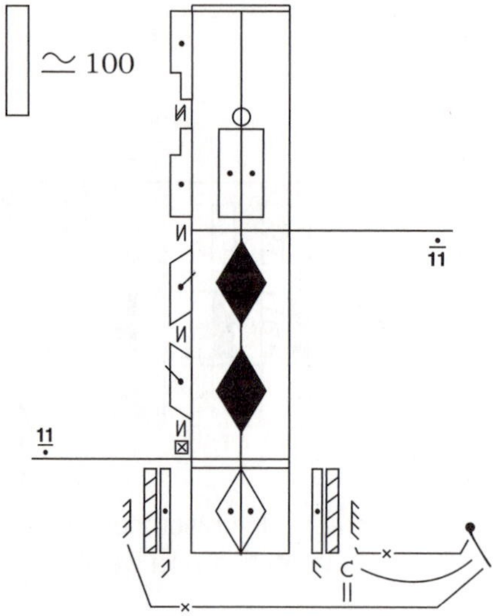

Subject motif of the section *wâri mâniô.*

XIII. *Dooté*

It was explained above that the short scenic play forms an intermezzo before the 'speech given from a tree'. In this scenic play one dancer lies on the ground playing the person who is ill. All the other dancers kneel in a circle around him and he cannot be seen by the audience. Sometimes he lifts a leg, or an arm, that can be seen by the audience which reacts with laughter. A dancer shouts in French 'we need a doctor, is there a doctor?' then, suddenly, the dancers all get up and perform the dance that originally accompanied the 'speech given from a tree'.

The performance of this dance is very short. Nobody in the region of Tiaoué can recall the traditional 'speech given from a tree' and therefore the dancers only perform the dance part of it. After the last mimetic section, carried out by the dancers forming a circle, the closing section is performed.

XVI. *Tü pwêêti*

- contents : throwing the *pwêêtis*
- structure : N.M.-S.M.

The dancers perform the neutral motif in a circle about 20 m in diameter. In the subject motif the dancers walk to the centre in the same manner as in *acëu cäbu*, putting the left foot to the left, to the right , to the left, over the straight steps of the right foot. Once the dancers stand crowded together in the centre, they throw the *pwêêtis* in the air. It should be remembered that the *pwêêti* is actually the symbol of the mimetic dance and that performing the mimetic dance in Paicî can be translated as 'throwing' the dance. Leenhardt says that during the *pilou-pilou,* at the end of the mimetic dance, the *pwêêti* was thrown at the feet of the maternal cousins, in order to finally 'give' the dance which has just been performed. It also lets them know that for the next *pilou-pilou,* it is they who have to prepare a mimetic dance. The throwing of the *pwêêti* in the air is what is left of this ritual.

At the 'Pwolu Jenaa' dance festival, the Tiaoué group, after the performance of the mimetic dance, in a speech made by the *apooro cäbu* did indeed 'give' the dance to the organiser of the festival. The *apooro cäbu* also gave a little tree with the bark taken off to which ribbons were attached, to the organizers. It had been held in front of the dancers during the performance and is comparable with the tree that is given to the maternal hosts at the end of the *cäbu tabéâ.*

NÊÊKIIPÂ PERFORMED BY THE DANCERS FROM GOHAPIN

Gohapin is the *tribu* closest to the Neguipin valley, where the *nêêkiipâ* dance obtained its name. Dancers of this *tribu* perform the *nêêkiipâ* dance and the dance-owning family received the right to perform the dance at the same *pilou-pilou* ceremony in the Neguipin valley as the group who now live in Tiaoué. The performance of the *nêêkiipâ* dance by the dancers of Gohapin is formally very close to the performance by the Tiaoué group. Dancers from Gohapin performed the dance in 1984 at a 'Mini-festival' at Poya, and then, only ten years later, the dance was taken up again and performed at a regional cultural festival that took place at Ometteux in 1994. It was possible to film the dance during its performance in the Gohapin *tribu* in preparation for the regional festival. A comparison of the performance in 1994 with that filmed in 1984 at Poya, showed no significant differences.

The Gohapin dancers wore *manous* and decorations made from coconut leaflets as well as rattles made from coconut leaflets on their ankles. They hold the club in the right hand and a dance tassel in each hand. When the dancers came out of the place of preparation and walked to the dance ground, two men were singing *ae-ae* songs (Gohapin is, like Tiaoué, one of the rare *tribus* where a number of older men still know how to sing *ae-ae* songs [see Ammann 1997:track1[CD]). The first section *acëu cäbu*, is performed in the same way as it is by the dancers from Tiaoué but it is not accompanied by the specific *nêêkiipâ* song. The motions of this section differ slightly from the Tiaoué performance. The difference is mainly in the foot movements. The Gohapin dancers advance with less pronounced foot movements than those of the Tiaoué dancers. The legs are not lifted as high and the skipping part is more like a kind of springy walking.

In general, the Gohapin dancers express the motions less vigorously than

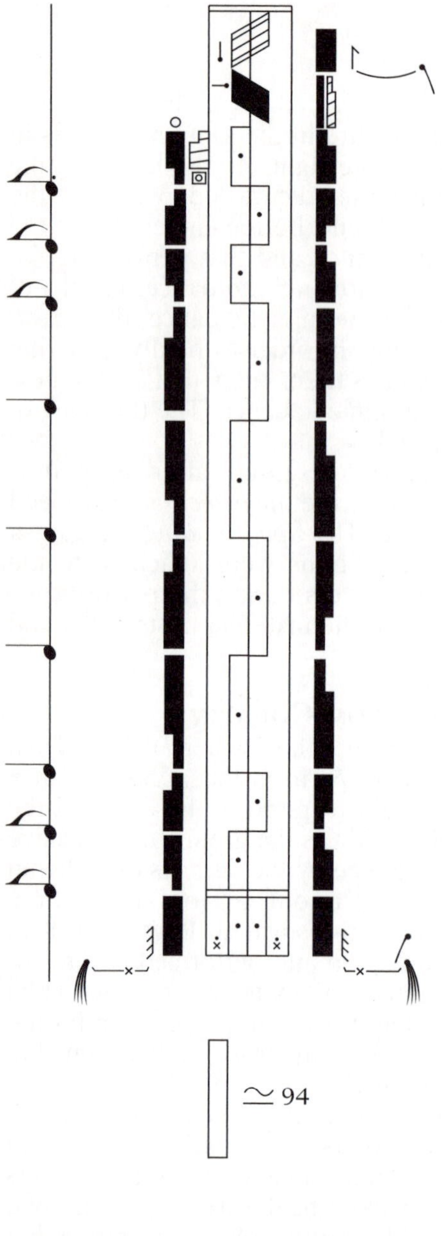

Neutral motif of the *nêêkiipâ* as performed by the dancers of Gohapin
Dancers are upright and swing their arms in front and behind to accentuate their steps.

the dancers from Tiaoué. A comparision of the neutral motif shows the difference : where the Tiaoué dancers turn to the left and bend as the right knee touches the ground, the Gohapin dancers perform a simple turn with a slight bend. There is also a slight difference at the end of the *mäbu ûgé*.

Most of the sections of the *nêêkiipâ* are performed in the same way by the dancers of both Tiaoué and Gohapin. While a few sections performed by the Gohapin group were not danced at the Tiaoué performance, this does not mean that they are not in the repertoire of the Tiaoué dancers. However, there are some differences in the form especially at the end of the dance. Whereas the Tiaoué dancers perform the section called *cia jawé* 'fetching water' while walking on the periphery of a circle, the Gohapin dancers perform it while standing in a square.

The dance that accompanies the 'speech given from a tree' is also performed differently. The Gohapin group performs this section while in a square formation. The dancers carry out the neutral motif and remain a few seconds in a bent position, then they stand up and perform the sliding backward steps typical of the dance. The very last section where the dancers come together in a circle and throw the *pwêêti* in the air corresponds to that of the Tiaoué dance performance.

It can be seen that there are some minor differences in the way the *nêêkiipâ* dance is performed by these two *tribus* but that the basic motions and the order of the sections are identical. A comparison with the *nêêkiipâ* dance as it is performed by some dance groups from the east coast shows that the same dance can be performed in quite different ways, even though it is always referred to as *nêêkiipâ*.

NÊÊKIIPÂ PERFORMED BY THE DANCERS OF THE GROUP TI.GA.

The dance group of the Association Ti.Ga. perform a *nêêkiipâ* dance. The motions of the neutral motif are different from those performed by Tiaoué or Gohapin, and so is the *mäbu ûgé*.

The Ti.Ga. *nêêkiipâ* includes different sections from those of the other two groups and sections with the same name, but in which the subject is interpreted differently. The Ti.Ga. dancers perform, for example, the attack with the club not between two neighbouring lines, but in rows. The first row turns back and carries out the attack against the second row, and the third row against the fourth.

Two subject motifs of the Ti.Ga. group's performance are, however, specific to the group. Nicaise Amo, responsible for the dance of the Ti.Ga. group, dreamed three new sections to perform. He had taught two of them when Marcel Koaté, the second dance-leader, recognised them as being from an old dance that had not been performed for decades.

The dreaming of new mimetic dance sections may be seen as a parallel to the myths which explain the origin of certain dances (see the *nêêkiipâ* dance [p. 148] or the *hneen* dance [p. 166]). These two sections which are called *gi* 'cut a tree with a hachet' and *otëpwe* 'to pull/transport the trunk with a liana' are now included in every dance performance.

NÊÊKIIPÂ PERFORMED BY THE DANCERS OF THE *TRIBUS* OF THE UPPER AMOA VALLEY

The men of the *tribus* further up the Amoa river than Ti.Ga. form a second dance group. This group's dance is also called *nêêkiipâ*. The group performed the dance in its present form for the first time in 1953 (Emille Ngaroad pers. comm.). In these *tribus* some

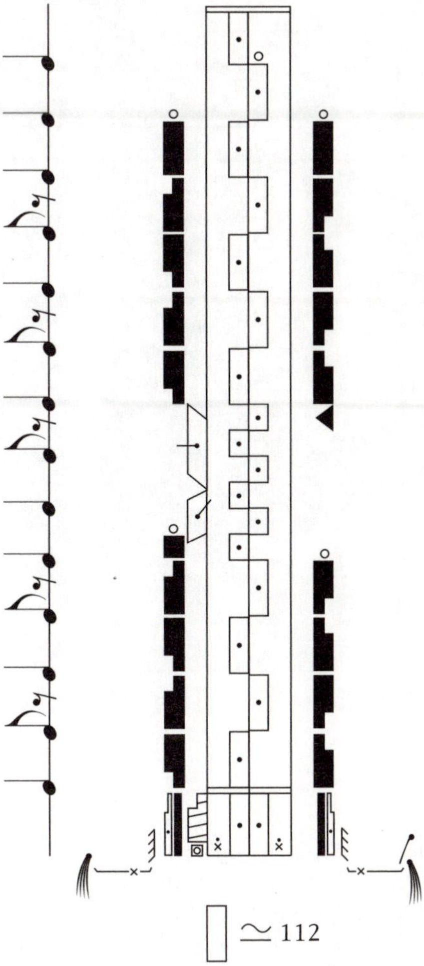

Neutral motif of the *nêêkiipâ* dance as it is performed by the Ti.Ga. dancers.

For some sections of the *nëëkiipâ* the dancers move very fast, making the synchronisation of movements difficult.

older men can still sing *ae-ae* songs and they are performed as the group comes forward onto the dance-ground. The group performs the neutral motif in a way similar to that of the Ti.Ga. group, with the exception of the *mäbu ûgé*, which differs slightly. In sections with the same subject and the same name the dance motions are the same as those of the Ti.Ga. interpretation. Other sections are particular to the group, for example the buzzard presentation. One of the sections is called *bèèmä,* and here the dancers carry out a *bèèmä* section within the *nêêkiipâ* dance.

The *bèèmä* dance

The *bèèmä* dance has its origin in the lineage called Baraotâ in Paicî or Beleot in Cèmuhî. As a result of the 1917 rebellion, some of the Baraotâ lineage were forced to leave their original home locality and today they are dispersed through the Paicî-Cèmuhî region. Today the *bèèmä* dance is performed by several dance groups in the northeastern part of the *Grande Terre,* and each group performs it in a slightly different way. The characteristic of the *bèèmä* dance is that the dancers hold a dance tassel in each hand and do not carry clubs.

The *bèèmä* dance has been seen several times and the performance by the group from Poyes at the festival of 'Indigenous People' at Poindimie in 1993 is given below. In the *bèèmä* dance structure the different sections are separated by short pauses, as are almost all the interpretations of mimetic dances from the northern half of the *Grande Terre.* However, during the pause the dancers crouch and move their arms back and forth, sweeping the ground with the dance tassel in synchronised motions. The dancers stand up while continuing to move their arms, and they begin to perform steps on the spot searching for the step frequency, until all the dancers are moving their legs simultaneously. Once all the dancers move their legs in synchronisation, they swing their arms at chest level left, right, left. This motif is in fact the neutral motif.

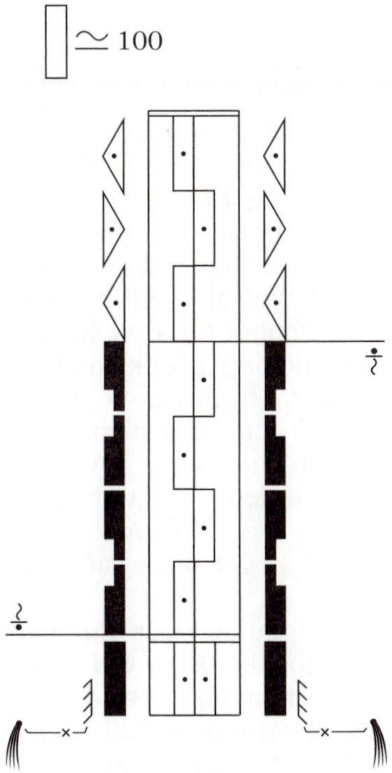

Extract from the neutral motif of the *béémä* as performed by a group from Poyes dancers at the festival for 'Indigenous People' at Poindimié.

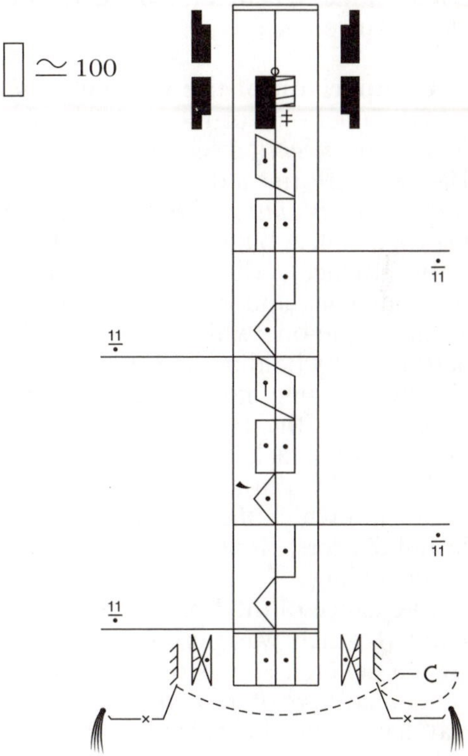

Section cattle (*bétail*) of the *béémä*.

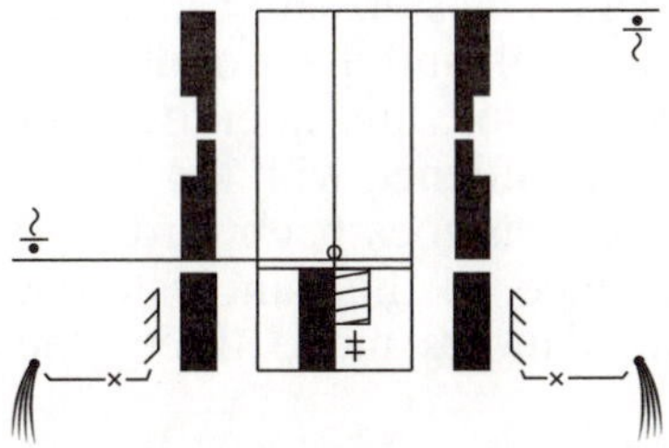

During the pauses the dancers rest on one knee and swing their hanging arms back and forth.

The *bèèmä* dance differs from the *nêêkiipâ* not only in the absence of the club but in many other ways. The arms of the *bèèmä* dancer hang down and swing back and forth and the leg motions are lighter than in the *nêêkiipâ.* The dancers move their arms during the pause and the neutral motif is limited to the indication of the step frequency with swaying arms. During the subject motif the dancers leave the spot but come back to it at the end of the section. Finally, the motions which imitate the subject are much more abstract than those of the *nêêkiipâ,* for example, the subject of searching for a particular shell is imitated by walking to the left side and then back to the original place. But as in the *nêêkiipâ* the dancers throw the dance tassel in the air at the end of the dance.

Comparison of the various *nêêkiipâ* performances

The repertoire of the dance group of the upper Amoa valley consists of *bèèmä* and *nêêkiipâ* sections. The dance group of Néami (a *tribu* not far from Tiaoué), performs a dance which seems to have been made up from the same two dances *bèèmä* and *nêêkiipâ,* not in the way of adding a *bèèmä* section to *nêêkiipâ* dance, but in such a way that each section seems to contain elements of both dances. The sections begin, as in the *bèèmä* dance, with the arms swinging back and forth, while the subject motifs are typical of *nêêkiipâ,* for example, the one which the Néami dancers say is a symbol for a wedding, is performed by holding one arm upright in the air and moving it back and forth. Exactly the same motions are carried out by the dancers from Tiaoué in their *nêêkiipâ,* but the Tiaoué dancers say that it is *pwändi* 'calling' or 'giving the sign for an attack'. The subject motif, *cia jawé* 'fetching water', which is performed by Tiaoué at the end of the dance with the dancers standing in a circle, and which the Gohapin perform in a square, is also performed by the Néami dancers. However, the Néami do not refer to it as 'fetching water', but as 'shovelling'.

The dance of the Bopope *tribu* (in the mountain range between Koné and Tiwaka) which was performed for the first time in the 1960s to welcome a French general, shows only very basic similarities in its motions to those of either *nêêkiipâ* or *bèèmä*. According to Sarasin's description (1929:221) he may have seen the *bèèmä* dance in Bopope in 1911. The dance performed today does not correspond to the old and apparently forgotten dance.

ÔDOBWIA PERFORMED BY THE DANCERS FROM TCHAMBA

The entering dancers are hidden behind branches held by assistants and are accompanied by the *rythme du pilou.* The dancers then go in formation of four lines, each with five dancers, and with one dancer dancing in front of the group.

As in the *nêêkiipâ* dance the dancers of the *ôdobwia* hold two dance tassels and, in the right hand, a club. One of the dancers in the front row indicates the frequency of the steps to the rest of the dancers. The steps are carried out in a special stamping way. The knees are held very high and the foot does not hang but is flexed parallel to the ground, before the sole and heel touch the ground at the same time. The arms move in correspondence with the legs so that when the right foot is on the ground, the left arm goes backwards. The right hand holds the club over the shoulders. Once all the dancers are in synchronisation, the neutral motif follows. The dancers move three steps forwards and then retreat backwards. They turn to the right and put one knee on the ground. This is repeated three times to make up the whole neutral motif.

THE WOMEN'S *CÈTO* DANCE

In the north of the *Grande Terre* there is a women's dance called *cèto*❶, which is performed fairly frequently on special occasions. Given the number of times the name of this dance occurs in the literature, a dance with that name must have been widespread in the 19th century. Leenhardt (1946:452) refers to a *jeto* dance, saying that during the *pilou-pilou* the dance is performed by the women of the hosts' maternal lineages, but he does not describe it. Without a description it is impossible to make comparisons and to decide whether or not the choreography is the same as that of today's dance.

There are confusing statements about the actual *cèto* dance. Beaudet and Tein (1985:15) says that the dance was performed up to the end of the 19th century only in the north of the *Grande Terre*. In the Paicî-French dictionary the *céto* dance is described as "women's dance" ("danse des femmes") (Rivierre 1983:66) and in the 1994 Cèmuhî-French dictionary (Rivierre 1994:139) the women's *cèto* dance is said to be a "women's dance of the maternal clans [performed during a ceremony] for the end of a mourning period [sitting dance]" ("danse des femmes des clans maternels lors d'une fin de deuil [danse assise]"). This corresponds to Leenhardt's statements about the *jeto* dance. In his dictionary the dance is said to be a "sitting dance" ("danse assise"). Today the women's dance referred to as *cèto* is not performed sitting, nor is it performed only by women of the same maternal clan.

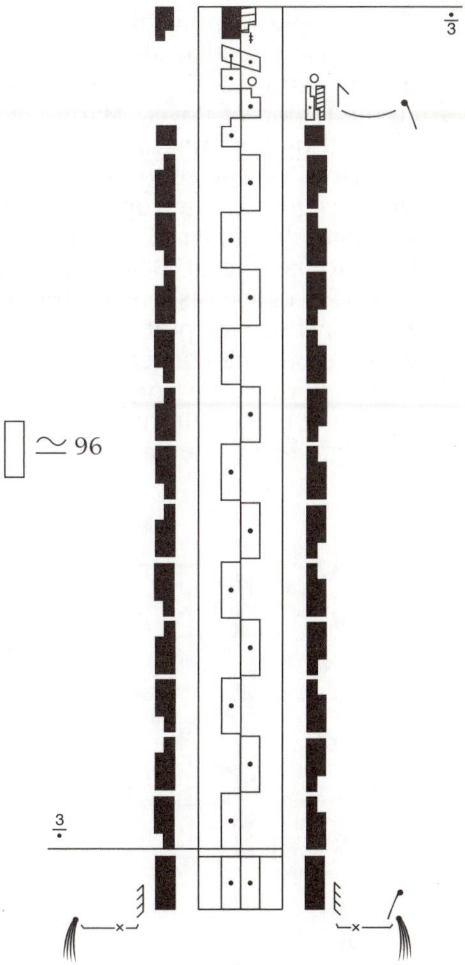

Extract from the neutral motif of the *ôdobwia* as performed by a group from Tchamba dancers.

❶ In this study the Cèmuhî spelling *cèto* is used. In Fwâi it is *cerbo*; in Nemi, *cero*; in Paicî, *céto*.

The people responsible for the dance in its present form and status are Marie-Louise Ouindia, also called Mani, and her sister Boie Ouindia. In an interview Marie-Louise said that the dance as she learned it, was originally from the region of Poyes. Marie-Louise saw the dance when she was a child performed by her aunt, and her father gave her some information about the dance. However the continuity of performances and the traditional passing on of knowledge was interrupted so that the dance as it is performed today may not be entirely similar to the ancient form of the dance. Marie-Louise's father belongs to the lineage Béléot/Baraotâ.

The *cèto* dance, as it is performed today, mimes how the Béléot women chase away the bad spirit *duéé* (a specific spiritual being) during the construction of a *case.* The dancers arrive at the dance place in several lines walking in a specific way. The front woman of each line beats bark-clappers. The bark-clappers are beaten alternately : once on the left hand side of the dancer then on the right hand side and so on.

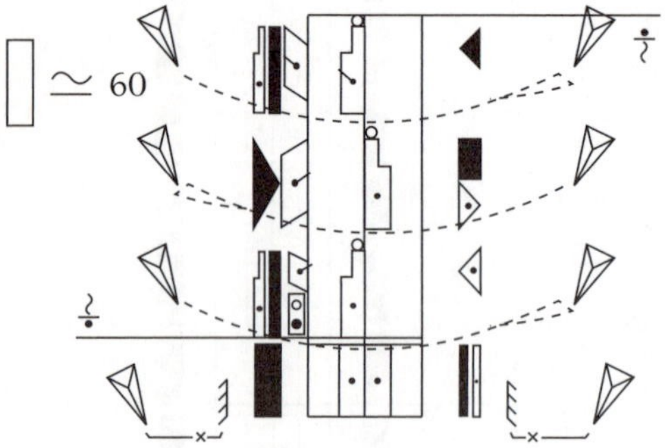

Extract from the *céto* dance : the front women beat bark-clappers when arriving at the dance ground.

The other women hold an object in their hands that today is specific to this dance. It is a small stick (40 to 60 cm long) with 5 or 6 branches (ca. 20 cm long) at the upper end. Leenhardt (1930/1980: 166, fig.41 and 167, fig.42) names this object "club with long points" ("casse-tête à longues pointes") and in illustrations these objects held by dancing women, can be clearly identified. Sarasin collected one of these objects, calling it a "dance whorl" ("Tanzwirtel"). Today the women call it simply 'casse-tête' (club) and any original name for it has been forgotten. On an incised bamboo in Geneva (Musée d'Ethnographie [Ethnographical museum]) analysed by Dellenbach (1936:268-272) a *pilou-pilou* is shown. A few women participtating in a round-dance hold the same club in their hands (see p. 69). This suggests that the club may have been used in various dances in the 19th century.

For the *cèto* dance the object is said to represent the central post of the traditional Kanak *case.* With the club in the right hand, the women move their right arms forward with every step, symbolising the transport of the central post in the construction of a *case* . In the left hand they hold a dance tassel, moving it back and forth. This motion symbolises the sweeping of the ground before the construction of a *case.* The movement of swinging the dance tassel back and forth with hanging arms is a typical motion of the *bèèmä* dance, the men's dance of the Béléot/Baraotâ. Besides the sweeping function, the swinging of the dance tassel may be a basic movement allowing identification of this group.

Behind the group of dancers walk two women, one of them holding a spear in her hand, moving it back and forth with every step. Once the group has reached the dance ground, they make a circle looking to the centre, holding up their arms to the centre, thus forming a traditional Kanak *case*. A woman who has been dancing at the side, is playing the bad spirit, *duéé*, which will try to settle down in the new *case*. The spirit dancer moves between the dancers into the centre of the circle, into the *case*. The woman with the spear follows the spirit dancer and tries to chase it away. The spirit dances in and out of the *case*, followed by the woman with the spear. Finally the woman with the spear manages to chase away the bad spirit or to kill it, so ending the dance. The dance can be performed with small variations, for example there can be two women with spears chasing the *duéé*.

This is the *cèto* dance as it is performed today. The short sequence in the film of 1954 (anonymous[film]) has a similar form. The present *cèto* dance is one of the very few exclusively female dances of the north of the *Grande Terre*. There is another women's dance known from the Mou *tribu* (and possibly other *tribus*). The women form two parallel lines and stamp with long bamboos diagonally and in alternation between the dancers of the opposite parallel line. The dance was not seen in the field; the people of the Mou *tribu* said that it has not been performed for a long time but that the choreography is still known.

THE *HNEEN* DANCE FROM HOOT MA WHAAP

The mimetic dances in the region Hoot ma Whaap, neighbouring the Paicî-Cèmuhî area, share general features. A dance widely known and performed by

(David Becker/A.D.C.K.1992, Nouville)

A group of young dancers from Ouaré giving a very fine performance of the *hneen* dance.

several groups is called *hneen*. The *hneen* dance is performed by dance groups from the *tribus* : Ouaré, Tchambouène, Pouébo, Yambé, Oubatche. The dance is accompanied by the four-beat rhythm. The basic choreographical features show some similarities with the *bèèmä* dance. However the *hneen* dance is accompanied by music and none of the dances of the region Paicî-Cèmuhî have a rhythm group accompaniment. Like the *nêêkiipâ* dance the *hneen* is said to have been given to the people by a bird, in the *hneen*'s case from the large notou pigeon (*Ducula Goliath*)❶.

The sections performed today imitate activities from daily life in a *tribu*. Several subject motifs are performed during the same section, for example, the section *walek* consists of *tabigu* (to stamp the earth), *vala* (to build a fence), *thowan* (to carry something on the back), *thiibu* (to massage 'medicine' on the inguinal region), *colai* (to carry something in the arms in front). The leg movements of the *hneen* dance do not consist of the heavy stamping found in the *nêêkiipâ* and *ôdobwia* dances, but are rather fine and dynamic. The arm motions for the *hneen* dance are quick and graceful.

(David Becker/A.D.C.K. 1992, Nouville)

The dance group from the Isle of Belep performing the *sodi* dance which has fecundity as its subject.

❶ There is a second legend about the origin of the *hneen* dance. In a dream an old man called Koihin from the *tribu* of Pwé-Radam saw the dance performed by the spiritual beings called *mwakheny*. They performed it on a rock in the middle of the creek that divides the *tribu* into two parts (Whaap 1992 [film]).

The dances from Belep

The dances from the island of Belep to the north of the *Grande Terre* have a reputation for their dynamism. The motions of the dancers are synchronised, but the dances differ formally from the dances of Hoot ma Whaap. However, they use the four-beat rhythm for the percussion accompaniment, as is used for the *hneen* dance. The group of dancers, divided into two or three rows, move in a circle during the whole performance, carrying out the neutral motif in a walking movement.

Often the dancers perform a synthesis of several dances, one dance is added to the next after the neutral motif : *sodi* has the fecundity of men as a subject, *arawi* and *kaolea* are exercises for the warriors, while *konvac* the white faced heron (*Ardea novaehollandiae nana*) and *galawitch* the osprey (*Pandion haliaetus melvillensis*) are imitations of birds. The dances of Belep owe their particularity among Kanak dances to a certain drive which is apparent. The dancers move constantly, there are no breaks between sections and the beating of the percussion goes on without interruption during the whole dance. The percussion instruments which accompany the dance are one or two wooden or bamboo slit-drums, and two stamping-bamboos. The four-beat rhythm of the Belep dance accompaniment has a more accelerated tempo than is used for the *hneen* dance. The dance motions are perfectly coordinated with the beats of the rhythm.

The relation of past and present

Changes of domicile, often arbitrary and makeshift, together with the period when dancing was forbidden, have weighed very heavily on the people in the north of the *Grande Terre* making reconstruction of the 19th century situation next to impossible.

Questions referring to 19th century ownership and to particularities of the still-existing dances are difficult to answer, not only because a large number of dances have been lost and informants lack knowlege, but also because of the demographic changes that took place after the 1917 insurrection in the north. The present situation of the dances, the question of origin, and characteristic features can be traced back only to the 1940s, using choreological data and methods. An idea of the period before 1940 and of the 19th century can be obtained by consulting the few references in the literature, as is done in the first part of this study.

CHAPTER 7

DANCE AND MUSIC OF THE LOYALTY ISLANDS

The four populated Loyalty Islands lie on a line running northwest-southeast, with Ouvéa the most northerly, then Lifou, small Tiga, and Maré the most southerly and the closest to southern Vanuatu. They run parallel to the east coast of the *Grande Terre*, some 100 km distant. All these islands, plus the uninhabited islets, are of raised coral and covered with bush. Ouvéa is not much above sea level, but has an extensive lagoon. Lifou was raised in four successive geological phases, and Maré in five, by tectonic plate movements. The higher cliffs of Maré reach 100 m, and it is the only one of the Loyalties to have, in a few places, outcrops of basalt.

Archaeologists estimate that the *Grande Terre* and the Loyalties were first inhabited about 3200 and 3000 BP (Sand 1994:248-258)[1]. There were many later immigrations from various Pacific islands, so that the present Loyalty Islanders can be thought of as a mixture of Melanesian and Polynesian peoples. It appears that the Melanesian immigrations were from Vanuatu and the *Grande Terre*, while Polynesians arrived later from Wallis and Futuna, from Samoa and Tonga[2] and eventually from Fiji.

Two environmental factors have had a definitve influence on the Loyalty Islands. The first factor is the proximity of the sea with its potential harvests, and pervading maritime climate. Outrigger and large double-hulled canoes made possible trading voyages among the islands and with the *Grande Terre* and possibly Vanuatu. The second factor is the lack of running water, due to the permeable coral. There are a few underground waterholes, and some sunken water-shafts (wells), otherwise rainwater has to be collected in whatever containers are available[3]. This situation lead to an important exchange

❶ Irwin (1992:65) cites a date from Green of 3470±210 BP from New Caledonia.

❷ Some families on Maré recall their origin as far as the Marquesas.

❸ A modern solution to the problem is the desalination plant that treats sea water chemically to make it drinkable, good enough to use in soup. The first of these desalination plants is already in use on Ouvéa.

system in which, for example, large tree trunks of the *Grande Terre* forests for making the canoes were exchanged for Loyalty Island women.

The culture of the Loyalty Islands shows similarities to the *Grande Terre* as well as to Polynesia. Social structures in the Loyalties resemble those of the *Grande Terre*, with a pyramidal hierarchical system. At the apex is a *grand chef*, then a number of *chefs*, each with specific duties and responsible to the *grand chef*. Cultural elements of the Loyalties which reveal influences from Polynesian visitors and immigrants, can be found, for example, in the design and construction of large canoes and, notably, in dances and music.

General remarks on dance and music of the Loyalties

Each of the islands has its distinctive dance and music repertoire, but there are also some dance and song genres that are common to the whole group. The common genres will be discussed below, before dealing with the particularities of each island in turn.

Early writers frequently said that Loyalty Islanders were good choral singers (as has been remarked about many Polynesian peoples), compared with the populations of the *Grande Terre*. "The women of the Loyalty Islands have a natural sense of harmony, and they sang in perfect unison and quite effortlessly. Their voices were full and rather low. They seemed to enjoy their singing, and we were told that they would continue right through the day" (Larsen 1961:181). Early missionaries may have taken advantage of the people's gift, and perhaps the women were able to adapt easily to Christian choruses, in a mutually satisfying manner, so that a reputation was established. Christian hymns of the Loyalty Islands consist of two types : the *doh* and the *taperas*.

DOH AND *TAPERAS*

Mission songs and hymns are now a principal category of contemporary music. They have been known for some 150 years, but as such they are not part of a study of traditional Kanak dance and music. However, today the *taperas* and other Christian songs, such as *dohs* or *cantiques* make up most of the active song repertoire of the Kanaks. The major-minor tonal system has influenced musical creativity based in traditional forms of Kanak culture, so that the *doh* and *taperas* do need to be taken into consideration. A short presentation is given below.

Doh and *taperas* are not exclusively Loyalty Islands songs. They originate in the Protestant church and as the L.M.S. set up the first churches in the Loyalties these songs are more widespread on the Loyalty Islands than on the *Grande Terre* where the Catholic Marist Brothers established mission stations and and the Protestant church has fewer members. *Doh* and *taperas* on the *Grande Terre* are mainly sung in one of the Loyalty Islands languages (excluding Fagauvea ; whose speakers are mostly Catholics). There is a song book in the Ajië language (Aramiou/Euritien, undated). The Catholics sing their canticles in French or Latin, but, some members of the Catholic church also sing *taperas* in one the vernacular.

Some Kanaks see the origin of the word *taperas* in the French word 'tempérance' in the sense of modesty. At the beginning of the 19th century, the French Evangelist church and especially Pastor Maurice Leenhardt, fought vigorously against alcohol abuse and for a life of moderation. However, these songs were known first in the Loyalty Islands and at a time when the population had started to speak English or Bislama but not French❶. It is not known if the songs were named differently at that time and if the word *taperas* derives from French 'tempérée' or English 'tempered' both with the meaning of tempered scale. An argument that speaks for an English origin of the *taperas* and *doh* lies in the terms with which the Loyalty Islanders refer to the different parts of these songs. The bass is called *bas* in all the Loyalty Islands languages, *treno* (Iaai) or *trena* (Drehu) stands for tenor, *otro* (Iaai) and *oregio* (Drehu) for alto, and *trebol* (from the English treble and not the French word *soprano*) refers to the high women's voices. In the *taperas* however women often sing a voice above, or at least in addition to, the *trebol,* this voice is called *ela* in Iaai, a word deriving from *ölö,* meaning 'to climb', in everyday language it is also called *alto.*

The *doh*

In the first strophe of a *doh,* for each pitch the corresponding solfège-syllables are recited, in the way they are pronounced by the Kanak (do = *doh*; re = *ray*; mi = *me*; fa = *fah*; so = *soh*; la = *lah*; ti = *te*). The actual text starts only with the first repetition. A second feature of the *doh* is its polyphony. A *doh* consists of four parts and the composer of a *doh* writes down (with a special notation system as will be explained below) each note of each part. Improvisations are generally not allowed in a *doh*. At first sight it seems that the people and children are at ease in reading the *doh* notation, which would mean that they know the intervals of the diatonic system by heart. However, when listening to the song and verifying it with the notation, differences can be detected. Notes may be replaced by others of the same chord, which shows that although the song is notated, people are really singing by ear.

The *doh*-notation system was introduced to the Loyalties by the L.M.S. A variant of the *doh*-notation system is found on Tonga, where it was introduced by a British missionary in the early 20th century (Moyle 1991:10)❷.

In New Caledonia the first letter of the *solfège*-syllable is used, where d = *doh*, r = *ray*, etc., and de = d♯. In general one stays within the octave. But, for example, in a step from the tonic to the dominant (*doh -soh*), *soh* can be interpreted as the dominant below or above the tonic. In this case, a little vertical hyphen (either at the top or at the bottom) after the letter may indicate the octave (but often the hyphen is missing and the singer may choose according to his ability).

The rhythm is indicated as follows. A measure in 2/4 metre is shown as | : | ; a measure in 3/4 metre as | : : |; and a measure in 4/4 is | : ı : |. Many *doh* consist of measures of different metres and it seems that there is no regularity in the structure of how the various measures are ordered. As a general remark it may be added that the *doh* have their principal expression

❶ There are still many English words in the languages Drehu, Nengone and Iaai.
❷ On Tonga instead of the solfège-syllables numerals are used : 1/2 is a semitone up, do is 3, re is 4, thus e♭ (d♯) would be written as 4 ½.

in polyphony, creating songs with worked out metrical or rhythmical structures seems to be of lesser importance. The copy of a *doh*-notation gives an idea what they look. The relative pitch of *doh* is indicated by writing 'key doh'❶ at the beginning of the notation. The *doh* are four-part songs respecting the rules of harmonisation (although crossing of parts and parallel fifth movements were heard in the field). Chords are either in root position or in inversion, dominant seventh chords and secondary dominants may occur.

Key C

:m	f	:l	s	:f	m	:—	—	m'	r'	:d'	d'	:t	d'	:—	—
:d	d	:d	d	:t,	d	:—	—	s	s	:m	s	:s	m	:—	—
:s	l	:f	s	:s	s	:—	—	d'	t	:d'	r'	:r'	d'	:—	—
:d	f	:f	m	:r	d	:—	—	d'	s	:l	s	:s	d	:—	—

:s	l	:fe	s	:t	r'	:—.r'	d'	l	s	:m	r	:m.f	m	:—	—
:m	m	:r	r	:s	s	:—.s	s	d	d	:d	d	:t,	d	:—	—
:t	d'	:l	t	:r'	t	:—.t	d'	f	s	:s	s	:s	s	:—	—
:m	d	:r	s	:s	f	:—.f	m	f	m	:d	s,	:s,	d	:—	—

The following musical transcription shows the same *doh* with standard music transcription.

❶ That the English word 'key' is used, instead of the French equivalent 'clef', is yet another indication of an English origin of the *doh* songs.

The singing of *doh* is very popular among Protestant church members, but only a very limited number of old *doh*-notations and song books (some from the Presbyterian church in Vanuatu) exist and these are kept in great security by the owners who do not lend them, nor allow them to be photocopied. The system is no longer taught in the Protestant schools but there are still some elderly Kanaks who were well-drilled in the system and can notate songs with it.

The *taperas*

The Christian songs, *taperas,* can be interpreted with more liberty in their polyphony than the *dohs*. For a *taperas* only the principal voice is composed and presented to the choir. The choir members themselves then harmonise the melody in general using the same kind of harmonisation as the *doh*. A *taperas* can consist of more than four parts or of fewer, depending on the people who perform the song. In the interpretation of *taperas* improvisation is allowed. A popular *doh* can become a *taperas* but a *taperas* cannot (unless it is rewritten by a composer) become a *doh*. The composition of *taperas* is very popular and many new *taperas* are performed on each Christian feast. As for the *doh,* the major importance lies in its polyphony and not in its metrical and rhythmical structure. Besides the *doh*-harmonisation typical *taperas* polyphony can be defined as heterophony. Sometimes the bass sings a bourdon or it may intone the fundamental or the dominant of the chord and alter with each chord-change.

(David Becker/A.D.C.K.1994, Nouméa)

A group from the Loyalty Islands singing *taperas* and *doh* at a performance in Nouméa. They are dressed in the same way as for other celebrations : liana-crowns and *manous* over long trousers for the men and mother hubbard dresses for the women.

THE *CAP* DANCE

The *cap* dance is performed by all the youth of the Loyalty Islands, but not of the *Grande Terre.* It is most commonly seen on Maré and Lifou (where it probably originated), while it is rare on Ouvéa. Sam (1980:35) translates the name *cap* as "a very rhythmic mixed dance"❶, the reduplication *cap-cap* means stamping of the feet on the ground in Drehu, which is the principal choreographical element of the dance. It is a joyous dance offering a chance for young men and women to perform together. There is no ownership of the *cap,* and performances are open to everybody. There is no singing, but people standing or sitting around will clap their hands or leaf parcels in the *cap* rhythm which is a variation of the *rythme du pilou.*

To the rhythm are added whistles, hissing, warbling, trilling and laughter, and those who have metal whistles (dancers and audience) blow ostinato rhythmic patterns. Onlookers may shout encouragement or satirical comments at particular dancers, and everyone is in high spirits.

A pair of dancers face each other, not touching. Movements are freely improvised and no rules are expressed about how to dance the *cap,* but there is some kind of formalisation in the constant repetition of certain movement sequences, which normally differ between the boys and the girls. The girl will dance with soft and graceful movements, while the boy will seek to demonstrate his power and endurance to attract the admiration of his partner and of the onlookers. A boy's motif may be of sideways steps while bending the upper body in the opposite direction to the steps, then vice versa. If a male dancer becomes tired and his movements become slower and less 'stylish' there may be jokes from the onlookers about his lack of stamina or fitness. A brother or a friend present could make a kindly gesture in replacing the dancer, to avoid humiliation in front of people, and after a rest the boy can return to his girl.

The *cap* can be performed on any joyful or festive occasion, such as weddings or school feasts. There may be several couples dancing at the same time, and some couples may retire and have their place taken by another couple who have been watching. In this way, a *cap* can go on for a whole night. At some festivities today, the *cap* may be danced to foreign music such as reggae or rock or to *kaneka.*

There is a question as to the origin of the *cap* dance. It is performed on the Loyalty Islands, but the accompanying sounds seem to have been adapted from the *Grande Terre.* It is a relatively modern dance, probably early 20th century. It could have begun on Lifou; it did not reach Maré until the1950s (Dubois 1969/1980). Its origin may be related to the game of cricket which came to the Loyalties with the L.M.S. missionaries, and Samoan teachers. The L.M.S. station established at Mou on Lifou was called Kirikitr, the Drehu word for cricket which is itself derived from the Samoan word *kirikiti,* and the name still refers to the *tribu* of Mou. One of the strongest New Caledonian cricket teams comes from this region.

Frequently, supporters of a cricket team perform dances with movements that recall the *cap,* notably when their side makes some runs. At times a small slit-drum is used as an accompaniment (see Bironneau 1990 [film]) and the metal whistle is used, as in the *cap.* The whistle is a cricket umpire's device, and is used in the version of cricket now played in New Caledonia. Metal whistles, held in the mouths of the dancers, which are blown in short rhythmic patterns, are used today in many dances and frequently so in the *cap* dance.

❶ "danse mixte très rythmée".

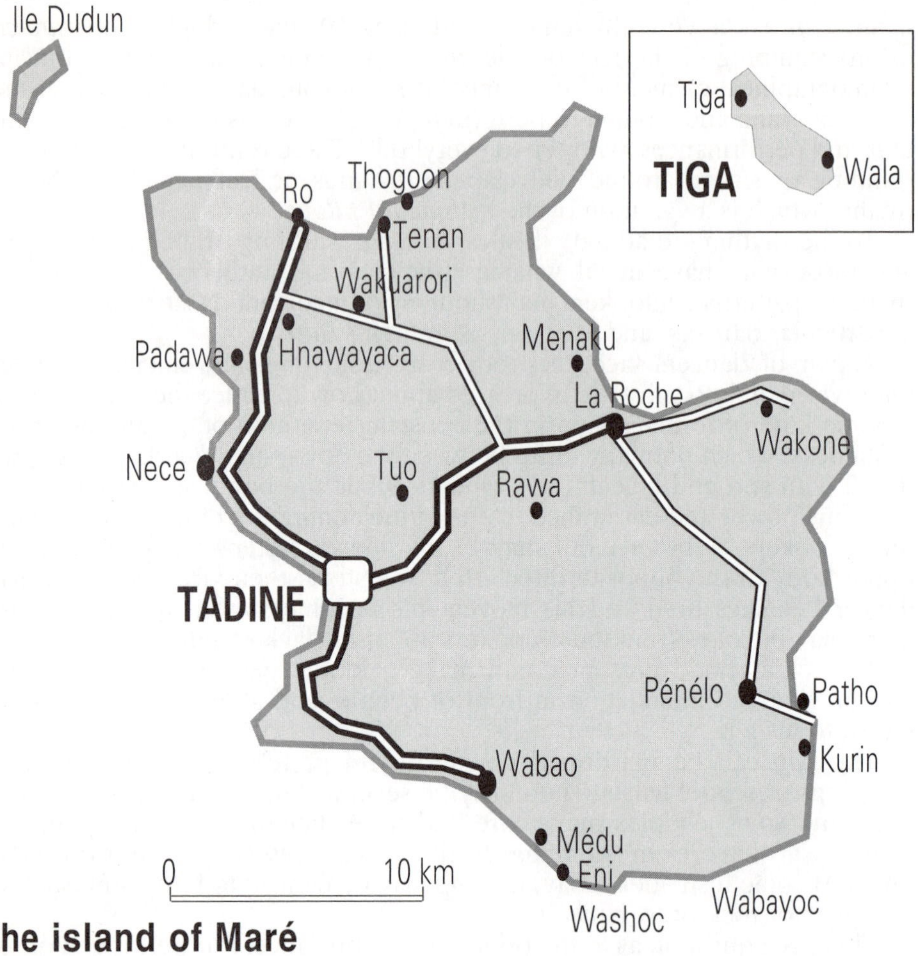

The island of Maré

Maré was the name used by the people of the Isle of Pines for their northeastern neighbour and it was used as such in 1803 in the logs and charts of the sailing vessel *Britannia*. The Island's inhabitants called it *Nengone* from the Drehu word *mengöni*.

Each *tribu* on Maré belongs to one or other of the eight *chefferies* called *padoku* : Hnaisiline, Sinewami, Etoroi, Jalo, Waetheane, Jewine, Wanaro, Waikedre. Each *padoku* corresponds to an administrative district.

Historical events in relation to dance and music

Anthropologically, Maré is the most thoroughly researched and documented island of the Loyalties, mostly thanks to Father Marie-Joseph Dubois❶. The works of Dubois on language, legends and history are voluminous. Dance and music are treated only in a very general way which is sometimes confusing. He

❶ Marie-Joseph Dubois (b.1913) came as a Marist Brothers missionary to New Caledonia in 1938. He stayed, with few interruptions, between 1943 and 1967 on Maré, where he studied the language and the oral history of the island. Back in France, Dubois resumed an academic career and in 1970 returned to New Caledonia as a linguist for the CNRS to study the language of the Isle of Pines.

was interested in the texts of Maré dance songs which contain important information about mythological and historical events, and transcribed many of them. Many historical events of Maré in the 19th and 20th centuries are known because of the information contained in dance songs. Furthermore, the dates of composition of some dance songs may have been established by reference to the Marist documents to which he had access, but also, more interestingly, on the basis of internal textual data, such as counting back the age of a coconut plantation referred to in a song as being planted then. Nonetheless to understand the significance of certain songs, and to investigate the way in which Maré identity is expressed in its dance and music, a study of myth and prehistory as well as history, is required. According to oral tradition, the first population of Maré emerged from a hole in the ground called *rawa*. At that time, extensive parts of the present Maré were under water. The first people possessed a type of boomerang and, as a musical instrument, the bull-roarer (Dubois 1987:5)❶. Later there were several migrations to Maré. It is thought that people came from Anatom in southern Vanuatu (also called Kiamu), and also from the small island of Héo (Beautemps-Beaupré), north of Ouvéa. A place called Ma is referred to from whence the 'real' yam is said to have been introduced. Dubois sees Fiji as a possible place for Ma (Dubois 1984:14); Guiart (1953b:93) mentions Ma, but makes no comment on its possible whereabouts. The first population which emerged from the *rawa* together with the first migrations are called Eletok in Nengone, where *elene* means 'head' or 'peak', and *toke* means 'elder'.

There are stories in the oral tradition about immigrants coming on huge outrigger boats whereas earlier vessels were smaller, possibly even rafts. These immigrants were "singer-dancers" ("chanteurs-danseurs"), according to Dubois (1981:7), now called in Nengone the si-Talegukaw. Dubois' informant was Jon Drikon of Ukan, and in his book *Les Eletok* (Dubois 1975:36-37) the interview is transcribed (a copy of the interview is in the Archives of the A.D.C.K., classified as Dubois BM 1) :

70/ The si-Talegukaw were a people. They were blacks.
71/ They had no chiefs. They arrived in giant canoes.
72/ They disembarked at Cerethi. They had no witchcraft❷.
73/ Their talents were singing and dancing the thuruket
74/ All the Eletok chefs asked them to sing very beautiful songs, to feel the beat in their feet, until they [the chefs] fell asleep.
75/ After the si-Talegukaw had sung, the Eletok chefs gave them girls to be their wives, and land to be their land.
76/ That is how they obtained land on Maré. They settled and then dispersed throughout Maré❸.

❶ The existence of bull-roarers on Maré has not been reported in any other text.

❷ The word used by Drikon could also mean "thing" : they had no "things".

❸ 70/Les si-Talegukaw étaient un peuple. C'étaient des noirs.
71/Ils n'avaient pas de chefs. Ils sont venus dans des pirogues géantes.
72/Ils ont débarqué à Cerethi. Ils n'avaient pas de sorcellerie
73/ Leur spécialité était le chant et la danse thuruket
74/Tous les chefs Eletok leur demandaient de chanter, des chants très beaux, de sentir la cadence de leurs pieds, jusqu'à ce que les chefs s'endorment.
75/Lorsqu'ils [les si-Talegukaw] avaient chanté, ils [les chefs Eletok] leur donnaient des filles pour être leurs femmes, et de la terre pour être leur terre.
76/C'est ainsi qu'ils ont eu de la terre à Maré. Et ils se sont installés en se dispersant à Maré.

In a text on Maré's history, Dubois (1981:7-9 and 1990:3) refers to the si-Talegukaw as being Polynesian, having "clear" ("claire") skin, concluding that, "the style of the songs and dances of Maré recall those of Tonga"[1]. He does not explain how the si-Talegukaw can be both Polynesian and yet in Jon Drikon's word "blacks". But then, in his book *Géographie mythique et traditionnelle de l'île de Maré* (1968:630-631) Dubois finds Jon Drikon's narrative barely credible, seeing the origin of Maré's music and dance as being on Lifou : "Whatever the exactitude of this tradition, Maré dances appear to be influenced by Lifou. There are relations in words, phrases, melodies, indeed of whole songs. The Maré people even sing of their deeds in songs composed entirely in a more or less correct Drehu" [2].

(David Becker/A.D.C.K.1995, Lifou)

Men and women dancers from Médu wearing costumes made entirely of leaves.

[1] "Le déroulement des chants et dances de Maré rappelle celui de Tonga".

[2] "Quoiqu'il en soit de l'exactidute de cette tradition, les danses maréennes paraissent être sous l'influence de Lifou. Il y a des rapport de mots, de phrases, de mélodie, voire de chants entiers. Les Maréens chantent même leurs hauts faits dans les chants composés uniquement en un drehu plus ou moins correcte".

Dubois documents Lifou influence on Maré from the 16th century, when he describes a migration from Lifou to Maré. Yet economic and social exchanges certainly existed well before this. The main islands are separated by only 50 km, with a few smaller stepping stone islands such as Thuthun and Toka in the strait.

The Lifou immigrants of the 16th century became known as the si-Xacace. They are said to have imported the magic stone known as *kaze* to Maré, of which Dubois (1981:11) remarks : "This stone produced a real religious revolution and strengthened the warlike tendencies on Maré"❶.

The Eletok are said to have established themselves as the superior class, holding control of all land❷. Cané (1948:16) speculates that the Eletok were in fact from Vanuatu, and probably Melanesians, while the later arrivals were certainly from what is now called Polynesia. Oral history is clear that towards the end of the 18th century the subject classes revolted against the Eletok. The revolution lasted until about 1820, with many inter-tribal wars, to the detriment of the Eletok. Dubois (1977:191-254) writes of "the massacre of the Eletok" ("*le massacre des Eletok*"). There were further wars provoked by the arrival of Christianity, which may be seen as a continuation of the wars with the Eletok. It is clear that there was vast destruction in the first half the 19th century, and that when the wars had abated, a new hierarchical system has been established, with land and power divided anew.

The turmoil must surely have affected Maré's dance and music, and there are a host of questions it would be useful to be able to answer. Were dance and music until the 18th century exclusively in Eletok possession or control? After the massacre of the Eletok, had dance and music to be redefined? Would that have meant Lifou styles being imported, as Dubois thinks? Are the si-Talegukaw, (the singer-dancers who came direct to Maré), or the si-Xacace (who came from Lifou), the source of the dances and music known today? How much time was there after 'the massacre of the Eletok' to reform an indigenous musical culture on Maré, before the Christians (first the Protestant L.M.S., then the Marists) came and put their stamp on Maré life and culture? The evidence that has been gathered is given in the following account.

The dance and music repertoires of Maré

Dubois' dictionary (1969/1980) lists names of some dances that are no longer performed; most of these names are no longer familiar and neither are the dances, an example being the *thuruket,* which according to the narrative of Jon Drikon (see p.175) was brought to Maré by the si-Talegukaw.

Thuruket

The name of this dance comes from two Nengone words : *thuru,* to tie something, and *kete,* the poule de sultan❸, a metaphor for the woman in an adulterous liaison. The dance began at night, inside a house. The texts were of risqué recollections. During the dance men would seek their sexual

❶ "Cette pierre produisait une véritable révolution religieuse et enforça les penchants guerriers des Maréens".

❷ Maré is noted for the largest pre-European stone building in the region : a fortress made of huge coral rocks (some of them estimated at several tonnes) dating from about 2250 BP (Sand 1993:50). A Nengone legend recounts that the construction was achieved in one night in a competition between two *tribus.* It is said that this fortress was built by Eletoks.

❸ Swamp hen (*Porphyrio porphyrio caledonicus*)

The dance position called *waxejeon* in Nengone is typical of the *fehoa* dances. In tribal warfare this position, which offers only a narrow target for spears or stones, was taken to face the enemy (see p. 181).

partners for later in the night. Dubois' informants said that couples could stay in the house itself, or go out into the surrounding bush.

Pia

In Nengone today *pia* is a generic term for dances of all kinds, including modern ones. Dubois (1969/1980:706) writes that the *pia* was an erotic Maré dance, for a man and a woman together. Some current Nengone expressions contain allusions to the former overt eroticism, such as *pia ne ic*, meaning 'to dance with the one I call my sister'. Behind the idea of dancing with a sister-lies the hint of incest and attendant potential shame.

Pia sadram

Dubois mentions a second *pia* dance, the *pia sadram* (or *sadran*), sometimes *pia-cahmen*. It is thought to have been introduced to Maré from the Isle of Pines prior to the arrival of the missionaries. There were two rows of male dancers facing each other, one row of bachelors and the other row of married men. The bachelors would offer gifts, while dancing, to their married opposites. It took place during a ceremony called *noke,* where food was exchanged or offered. The name *pia* makes allusion to a Polynesian relationship, whereas the name *thuruket,* a dance said to be introduced by Polynesians, is a Nengone name.

Genu

Both women and men took part in the *genu*. This dance accompanied the yam to be offered to the *grand chef* for the meal called *kodraru*. It also accompanied the special yam being brought to the piled up food, *xeroen*.

The *genu* was a dance of joy or celebration, with much individual improvisation and little apparent coordination (according to reports), although there is mention of dancers running backwards and forwards, then making sudden backward jumps. Today, when dancers advance onto the dance ground, *hna era* (*hna* : place ; *era* : song/to sing), to perform a *kutera* dance (see below), they may be accompanied by people dancing in this way. Such informal dancing has now become known as the *genu,* and its recent counterpart may also be seen today on the *Grande Terre.*

Besides the ancient Maré dances mentioned by Dubois, Sarasin (1929:224) also witnessed a dance during his stay at Nece. "Men, boys and women, stood in a circle, all well dressed, the last in long robes. Two women with their faces painted white came forth, made some motions with arms and legs, touched each other and danced a European round-dance, as did the men and boys after them. The music was made by a harmonica, clapping of the hands and hisses, the light was given by burning coconut leaves and a petrol lamp"❶. Sarasin was astonished to see a dance on Maré so strongly reminiscent of what he calls the European round-dance. Today a dance in the form described by Sarasin is unknown on Maré.

The *drui* dance is today owned by the people of Drueulu, on Lifou (see p. 222), but it has been performed on Maré at times during the last few decades by members of the *tribu* at Hnawayaca (Davel Cawa pers. comm.).

DANCES ACCOMPANIED BY SINGING : THE *KUTERA*

Today the most important and oldest dances of Maré are accompanied by singing. The generic term for them is *kutera,* although Dubois (1990:3) writes *kurutera.* The term incorporates *kuru-(ti),* meaning 'to come out (of something)', and *era,* meaning either 'song' or 'to sing'. As far as the language of the songs is concerned not a great deal is understood today although it is known that the texts refer to historical events on Maré.

The *kutera* dances are reserved for performance at special events, for example, the birthday celebration of a *grand chef.* There is a person responsible for the continuity of each *kutera* dance (this person is called *aca-era*), a duty and honour usually passed on from father to son (or close relative), who will give permission for a performance, but who has to consult his dancers. Sometimes permission to perform a particular *kutera* can be extended to another group, but this is rare. Dubois (1990:3) distinguishes three classes of *kutera,* known as *pehua, nyineuatro* and *wahiek(o).* These three are all men's dances, and Dubois excludes the *wayai* women's dances from the *kutera,* but some of the informants encountered during the present study disagree with this. One of Dubois' informants states that the *nyineuatro* and the *pehua* are one and the same❷.

It is unfortunate that Dubois fails to give the formal definitions of the bases

❶ "Im Kreise standen Männer, Knaben und Frauen, alle wohlbekleidet, die letzteren in langen Röcken. Zwei Frauen mit weiss beschmiertem Gesicht traten vor, machten einige Bewegungen mit Armen und Beinen, fassten sich dann an und tanzten einen europäischen Rundtanz, ebenso nach ihnen Männer und Knaben. Die Musik bildeten Mundharmonika, Händeklatschen und Zischen, die Beleuchtung Kokosblattbrände und eine Petrol lampe".

❷ Hadfield (1920:132) notes for Lifou a dance called *nyineu a tro* under the heading of *fehoa* (*fehoa* is the corresponding Drehu name for *pehua*).

of in his classifications. Confusion is also caused by Dubois' reclassification, for example, he classes the dance *be be nod* (see p.183) as a *wahieko* (1989:21), and then a year later (1990:3) as a *pehua* without any explanation for the change. Dubois says that the *wahieko* came to Maré from Lifou with the si-Acakaze, arriving before the *pehua* and the *nyineuatro* which also have a Lifou origin. In his classification Dubois appears to have seen Maré dances as variations of those from Lifou with the same name and has thus imposed a Lifou origin on nearly all old Maré dances. It is certainly possible that the internal struggles on Maré concerning the Eletok allowed cultural importations to gain ground easily and it is true that dances with the same name on Maré and Lifou share similarities in their structures, movements and themes. However what one actually observes today on Maré and Lifou are variations of what may well be the same, or at least related, dances and it needs to be stressed that the relationship may be one of independently mixing elements of diverse origins and forms.

Now, on a first level, all *kutera* dances are classed on Maré as war dances, and their poetry refers to Maré's history or mythology. They share a basic choreography, with some differences in the women's *wayai*. Each *kutera* consists of the same kinds of parts and sections and are referred to with the same names. The participants, dancers and singers, march to the dance ground, *hna-era*, singing, as they arrive, a song that may have no relation to the dance which is to follow (sometimes a *taperas* is chosen). On arrival at the *hna-era*, the participants kneel or sit close together on the ground, the singers form a circle facing inwards to where the conductor, the *naca-era*, stands, holding an *ae-be* (leaf parcel) or a stamping-tube in his hand. Most of the singers also hold an *ae-be* in the hand. The chorus of singers can see little of the dancing, so it is the *naca-era* who is responsible for the coordination between singing and dancing. He gives a sign, and the singers begin very quietly and slowly, so that it is difficult for the audience to hear. There is a pause after the *naca-era* signals the end of the first sequence. A few moments later the same song-part is repeated, only a little louder. There is another pause, another repeat, again louder and also a little faster, and so on until the *naca-era* considers that the singing is at normal volume. For the first few repetitions the singers do not strike the *ae-be*. This opening part is called the *hneumalan* (Dubois 1969/1980:627 writes *neumalan* as well). During the second or third repetition the dancers walk slowly away from the outer rim at the back of the circle. They move in a particular style with a distance of about two metres between them (moving either clockwise or anticlockwise) and finally form a straight line between the chorus and the audience. The textual content of what is sung in the *hneumalan* is the repetition of a combination of words related to the song's title, such as 'be-e, be-e, no-od-ea' for *be be nod* or 'pe-e, ru-e, cakui-ia' for *pe rue cakui*. Once the dancers have formed their line, or even while they are still forming it, the next part may be begun by the chorus.

This second part is called *gukaden*, a word which may also mean 'chorus'; *kaden* means 'to tie two things together', as for example, in *thurukaden* 'to tie two things together for prolongation', *thakaden* 'to prolong'. In the *gukaden* part of the *kutera*, there is another repetition of the same words, but usually with a slightly different melodic line and certainly at a faster tempo than in the *hneumalan*. Then the singers continue in normal volume and strike the *ae-be* on the strong metre pulses of the songs. This part contains the histories found in the dance song texts, and is called *ia-ilen* (Dubois 1990:3 gives *iail*), which means 'meat', and this is where mimetic choreography and symbolic gesture underline or comment on the texts. At the end of each song segment, either the audience or the singers can call *wa-yaw(e)*, (literally : 'small one again') for an 'encore' of the last *gukaden*. Then at the end of the *gukaden* or the last *ia-ilen* part, a special formulaic succession of words is recited and it is actually these words that decide the classification of the dance (see p. 192). Similar formulas called at the end of songs in northern Vanuatu can be heard on Crowe (1994:track8[CD]).

During the *gukaden,* and also during the *bneumalan* when the dancers are moving away from the chorus, use is made of the classical fighting posture of Maré (also known on Lifou) in the face of an enemy. The right knee is bent to 90°, and the left leg is held straight to the rear. The shoulders are on a line with the legs, and the right shoulder forward. The right elbow is bent upwards to 90°, the club in hand, while the left arm is straight back and downwards, in the position to throw a spear with a spear thrower normally called a *waced*, which is replaced for the dance by the *buru*[1]. The *buru* is a short rope of vegetable fibres which a dancer constantly rotates, to show his alertness, but some dancers add that this helps them to keep in the rhythm of the song. The shoulders are turned to present the narrowest profile towards the enemy, the head then angled to look over the right shoulder. This reduces the warrior's size as a target for stones and spears[2], yet he is in position to use a sling or to throw his spear, and in his tensed posture he can move easily and quickly sideways or forwards and backwards, for attack and retreat. The dancer shakes his forward (right) shoulder from side to side, as if in mockery of the shower of spears. This complex postures is called *waxejeon,* the 'lesser frigate bird' (*Fregata ariel ariel*). The description given here follows the instructions as taught by older dancers, and may be an ideal form. At some dances performers have been seen who do not follow all these points. The frigate-posture may be tiring for those who now are not as fit as the former real warriors had to be.

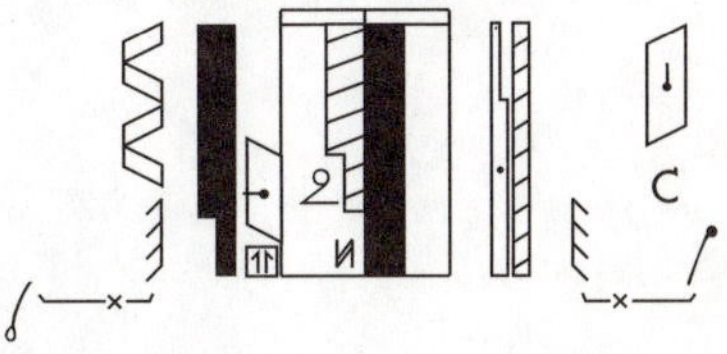

The ideal *waxejeon* position.

It is during the *ia-ilen* that the dancers make the mimetic movements referring to the events related in the songs. These motions are carried out only with the upper body and the arms, while the legs do not move. They should be

[1] Dubois (1990:5) gives the following information about the *buru* : "the *buru* is used as a message when proposing or reversing an alliance." ("Le *buru* servait de message pour proposer une alliance ou son renversement.") (see pp. 109 and 157 for the use of the war/dance tassel on the *Grande Terre*).

[2] Today some of the dancers have voluminous bellies, in which case the war position becomes meaningless, because a belly can furnish a wide target.

carried out in synchronisation. The dancers placed at either end of the row, the *necem* at the head (closest to the audience) and the *aden* at the rear, are in their positions because they know the choreography best. The main corps of dancers watches them for cues to movements. The *necem* and *aden* have the right to move to other parts of the *hna-era* to dance, and even to move close to selected persons in the audience and improvise 'offensive' gestures in front of them. Such improvisation is called *wayeac*. Additionally, older men and former dancers may go onto the *hna-era* to dance beside an inexperienced performer, with redoubled energy and precision. This may amuse the crowd, but at the risk of humiliating the dancer who is thus taught a lesson in full public view.

The *pehua* dances

Two *pehua* dances from Maré which are part of the active dance repertoire are *be be nod* and *be ko be*. Both poems have been transcribed by Dubois

(David Becker/A.D.C.K.1995, Lifou)

Dancer from Maré, in the *waxejeon* position (except for his left hand which is not holding a club in an upright position) swinging the *buru* with his right hand.

(1975:285-290 and 1989:15-25) who has also transcribed the text of the *pehua* dance *dua i wadrorim(a)* (1968:126-128). No performance of this last dance has been seen in the course of the present study nor has it been possible to hear the song.

Be be nod

The name of this dance, *be be nod*, means 'struck - struck - land [or] people'. The dance *be be nod* is in the possession of the Wamedjo family. The dancers are mainly the younger men of the Cerethi *tribu* of Pénélo. The choir consists of older people from the same *tribus* and also from neighbouring *tribus*. (The recording of this song for Ammann [1997:track9 [CD] was made at Kurin, a small *tribu* in this region.) Several people are responsible for a performance of the dance *be be nod*. The owner of the dance, *aca era*, the leader of the dance and the song (the 'conductor'), *naca era*, and a person who is called *polis*, derived from the French word 'police', whose role is to supervise the behaviour of dancers and singers during a performance.

Text

The poetry of the song is not entirely understood today by the population. Oral tradition and an understanding of some words indicate that the song recites parts of a legend, and that in the telling specific places in a region of Maré are recalled. Dubois notated the song's text and with the information he received from Laurent Acakaze si-Lehmi *retok* de Hnaenedr in 1945, he was able to write down the words told in the song and has proposed a possible translation (Dubois 1989:15-25). A shortened version of the story (Dubois 1951:145-146) is given below. The principal hero of the legend is the well known mythological figure Wamirat. Wamirat is a *yaac,* and the *chef* of all the other *yaac*. A *yaac* is a being who can assume a human appearance and yet be part of nature, for example he can be present in the wind.There are many stories about the deeds of Wamirat, see for example Dubois (1975:250-255). The extract from the legend which is told in *be be nod* deals with the way in which Wamirat gets a wife.

Wamirat wants to marry the *yaac* woman Adreajune but two men arrive from Lifou with the intention of taking Adreajune and a girl-friend of hers to Lifou. At first, the two *yaac* women manage to resist the courtship of the two Lifou men, but in the end they give in and return with the two men to Lifou. Wamirat is angry and wants to free his fiancée Adreajune and her friend, and to do so, he calls on all the *yaac* of Maré to help him. Some of the *yaac* do not want to help Wamirat and a fight breaks out among them. While they are fighting, Adreajune and her friend manage, with the help of a *yaac* from the western side of Maré, to escape the two Lifou men. The two *yaac* women are on their way swimming back to Maré pursued by the two Lifou men. Siwene, a powerful *yaac* from the island of Tiga (between Maré and Lifou), who has power over the winds and the seas, brings forth a current so strong that the two Lifou men have to give up their pursuit. The two *yaac* women return to Maré and, finally, Wamirat has Adreajune back[❶].

❶ The fights among the yaac of Maré recounted in the story took place in the southeast of the island, from Watheo to Wabayoc. No-one lives in this area of the island, which was a battlefield during the 'massacre of the Eletok'. Particular places in this region have names of mythological figures which indicates its importance in Maré mythology.

The text words of *be be nod*, as it was transcribed by Dubois in 1945. The same text is still used today.

Bee bee nood ea	**strike, strike, the people ea**
rue haicahan ea	**two young folk ea**
rue haerow ea	**two young women**
'ngee komeej ? ea	**"why are we here ea**
xeyu a ngai (e) ea	**decorated with ngai (branches of a certain tree ea)"**
theitheicoon ea	**they pull back ea (by jerky shakes [dodging the spears])**
iaa theicoon ea	**they pull still [the dancers imitate the dodging]**
ha cara ti ri hnawe	**they fall with the girls from Hnawe**
hna-nue-rune wedr	**at the place where screwpine leaves are thrown**
ha sere lo hula	**they are standing upright in the east**
hnaee lo huli	**they fly towards the west**
cahane biengo dridri	**the men black butterflies**
hnaee lo huli	**they fly towards the west**
rue waxeje drera ea	**two small, red frigate birds**
hnaee lo huli	**fly towards the west**
ca lenec a rue beti ea	**between the two islands**
ha ruu lu so hulu ea	**they dive into the deep**
ha sei thea ni koko	**there where the yams landed**
bee bee nood ea	**strike strike the people ea**

- 2. strophe -

bee bee nood ea	**strike strike the people ea**
wamiiratene	**Wamirat**
si o re adra - are	**breaks a branch of the are tree, to give a sign**
areona hadri ea	**give a sign to the south**
rue sia i ore	**the two girls of the morning**
areone hadri ea	**give a sign to the south**
karenin ni shokaw	**Shokaw's elbow**
e so hna karenin	**for ever his elbow (is raised)**
wanaacashuba	**wanaacashuba**
e so hna karenin	**is still raising his elbow**
tiri-uc-i-yaac	**the spear of the octopuses of the yaac**
e so hna karenin	**still the elbow is raised**
sei kediudrone	**with kediudrone**
dede wano ti lo	**jump while turning (the dancers turn in round)**
ima re thothobene	**the twilight of the red dust**
inoo gurewene ea	**like a rainbow, ea**
ci tho tho jo huni	**make the dust fly in the north**
gua ta idraro ea	**to the little place of the Idraro ea**
ci tho tho jo huni	**make the dust fly in the north**
gua ta idraro ea	**to the little place of the Idraro**
ci tho tho jo huni	**make the dust fly in the north**
o waimadrane	**waimadrane**
de lu ko re nood	**destroys the people**
hnakuyadrone	**hnakuyadrone**
rue cahan i po	**two men from Po**
theicoone yawe	**pull up again [dodging the spears]**
hna-be ni yaac	**at the dance place of the yaac**
theicoone yawe	**pull up again [dodging the spears]**

waete i gec	**at the stone wall of Gec**
ha ru luso hulu ea	**dive into the deep**
sei thea ni koko	**there, where the yam landed**
bee bee nood ea	**strike strike people ea**

- 3. strophe -

bee bee nood ea	**strike strike the people ea**
loi Adraejuni	**it is all right for Adreajune**
lew o hna egoon	**to have said "yes" (to the wedding)**
loa sicoone lo	**she mounts on a wave and escapes**
ile ci seroo lene	**getting in my way**
Wajaea ne Numanum	**Wajaea and Numanuma (a)**
theicoone yawe	**pull back again (dodging the spears)**
sei rabatetone	**by Rabatetone**
loa sicoone lo	**she mounts on a wave and escapes**
cacane tadrane	**the man Tardane (tells her)**
zikozikone lo	**"hurry up, hurry"**
ca ienece ca reu beti	**she passes between the two island**
hna ru lu so hulu	**dives into the deep**
sei thea ni koko	**there where the yams landed**
bee bee nood ea	**strike strike the people ea**
a bee bee nood	**strike strike the people ea**
cahane Megenine	**the man Megenine**
se loo i nie	**is standing upright at Nie**
theede kaaduo	**gliding (on the wave) to the west**
Nacawa keludre	**at Nacawakeluedr**
theede kaaduo	**goes down towards the west**
coocoo ri rue gunin	**he goes to 'two beaches'**
ri ta re-te wanod	**to the reefs**
namaea i siwene	**the current of Siwen**
ha hna ro renood ea	**it is there where the people were sunk**
rue biengo dridri	**the two black butterflies**
tica-dedone lo	**pull up and fly**
ha sasa dodon	**the sasa dance sasa is performed (in front of) Dodon**
bee bee nood ea	**strike strike the people ea**

(For the direct French translation see p. 260.)

In the song the story of *Wamirat* and *Adreajune* is not told in a chronological way. There are only a few references to specific toponyms and allusions to events of the story. A person familiar with the story will on this basis understand the meaning. Dubois (1989:21) says "the text proceeds by allusion. In earlier times one knew what it was about. Now memories have become blurred"❶. Most of the dancers themselves do not know the exact story. Many of them carry out the dance motions without knowing what they are imitating.

❶ "le texte procède par allusion. Autrefois on savait de quoi il s'agissait. Maintenant les souvenirs s'estompent".

Structure

The following description of the dance's structure was taken from the way in which it was performed at the 'Iahnithekeun' dance festival, on Lifou in November 1995. In other performances the number of repetitions of the *hneumalan* part varied and parts of the *ia-ilen* were sometimes left out❶. Such decisions are made by the *naca-era*. Each part ends with the words *hanga,* shouted by the *naca-era* and the answer *ngai,* shouted by the choir. A pause, where the dancers kneel down and the choir is quiet, may follow before the next part begins.

Part A *hneumalan* very slowly and quietly without the *ae-be*.
Part B *gukaden* sung with normal volume and striking of the *ae-be*. Once the dancers enter, the tempo becomes suddenly faster.
Part C *ia-ilen*
Part D *ia-ilen*
Part E *ia-ilen* (All the *ia-ilen* parts consist of part-repetiton)
Part F *gukaden*

Music

The composer of this song and dance is Wabuaka si-Cohmu si-Ruetin, subject of the *padoku* si-Medu who died during the 1890s. According to Dubois (1989:15) the composition probably dates between 1855 and 1866, several years after the arrival of the first missionaries on Maré. Wabuaka found the melody of this song while striking the *aloth* (see p. 12) and the words were given to him by a *yaac*.

According to Dubois' date of composition, the dance *be be nod* could be a Nengone creation without any influence from Christian music. And so the study of the song brings up a problem that is of great importance for all musicological research on the Loyalties. Did the musical system, especially the new kind of polyphony that was introduced to Maré by the L.M.S., change the way of singing this traditional song? Is the way *be be nod* is sung today exactly the same as the way it was sung 130 years ago? Although it is one of the oldest observed songs in this study, the possibility of influence of the major minor tonal system cannot be excluded in this traditional Loyalty song, especially in its polyphony.

The two parts *hneumalan* and *gukaden* have separate melodies and metres. The *ia-ilen* part follows the melodic line of the *gukaden* and its basic rhythmical form varies from that of the *gukaden* only in order to pronounce the words of the text.

The present transcription of the *hneumalan* part shows the complete musical theme, which is infinitely repeated. *Hneumalan* starts very slowly (♩. = 50). Tonal centre is c and the range of the melodic line is a perfect fourth (P4), except for the g at the beginning of the second half of the melodic line. This note is rarely intoned and only by some of the singers when the others intone the tonal centre. A question of authenticity immediately arises for to replace a note in liberal occurrence with its subfifth seems very likely to have

❶ The version recorded on Ammann (1997:track 10[CD]) was not recorded during a dance performance and does not correspond to the form above.

been taken over from the *taperas,* where such replacements are part of polyphonic improvisation.

After several repetitions of the *hneumalan* theme in a heterophonic way, the bass changes to a distinct accompaniment as notated here. The bass sings the word *be be nod* more slowly and does not follow the melodic line exactly nor the rhythm, thus forming a kind of interrupted bourdon. The same sort of bass accompaniment is often heard in the *taperas.* For the *hneumalan* there is no percussion accompaniment in the slow part. When the tempo suddenly accelerates the *ae-be* are struck on the downbeats.

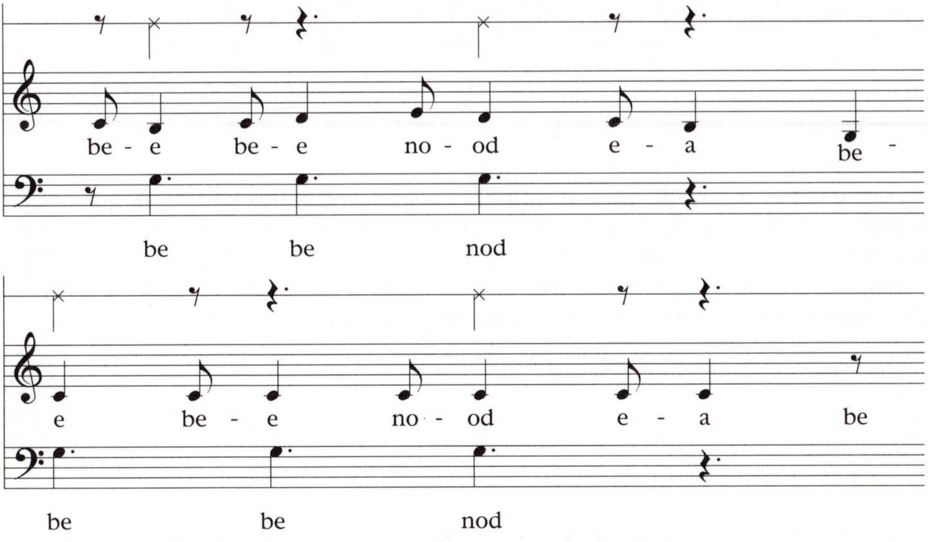
be - e be - e no - od e - a be -
be be nod
e be - e no - od e - a be
be be nod

Extract from the *hneumalan* of *be be nod.*

The *gukaden* is much faster than the *hneumalan.* The range of the melodic line is narrower (m3) than in the *hneumalan.* The melodic line of the *gukaden* consists of an alternation in leaps from the tonal centre a♯ to either c♯ or b. The bass forms an interrupted bourdon.

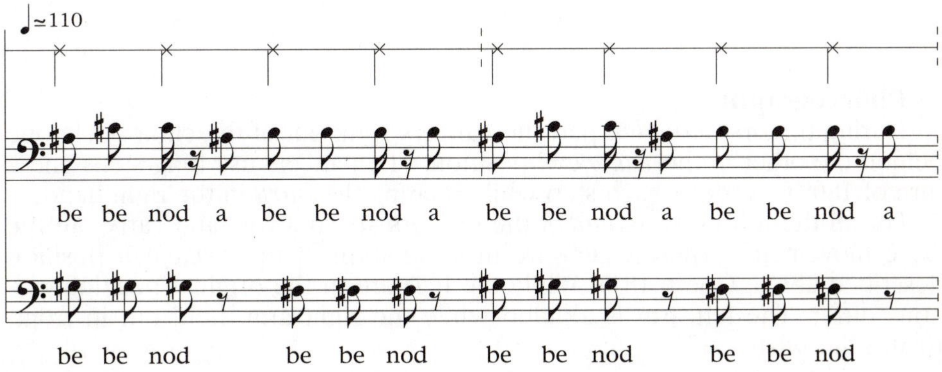
♩≃110
be be nod a be be nod a be be nod a be be nod a
be be nod be be nod be be nod be be nod

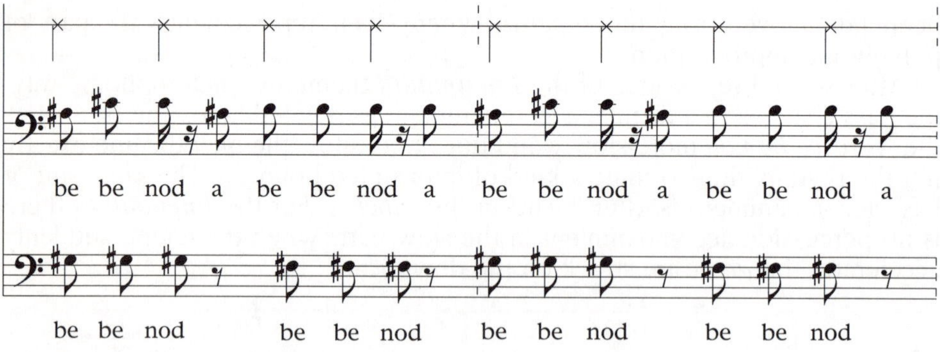
be be nod a be be nod a be be nod a be be nod a
be be nod be be nod be be nod be be nod

The ia-ilen has basically the same rythmical form and the same tempo as the *gukaden*. The *ia-ilen* part is compressed with text words and to be able to pronounce them, the eighth notes of the *gukaden* are divided into sixteenths in order to recite all the necessary vowels. Due to the fast tempo, in places, only some of the words of the text can be pronounced.

≃110
be be nod a ru- e hai-canan ea rue hae-row ea 'ngee ko mej ea xe -
ju a ngaiea thei-theicoon ea iaa thei coon ea ha ca- ra ti ri hna(we) ea

Choreography

During the first *gukaden* part the dancers walk out of the choir circle one behind the other in the *waxejeon* position. The dancers use long steps and a turn of 180° is made at each step while rotating the *buru* in the right hand.

For all the following *gukaden* the dancers are in a row and carry out the same movements. The dancers are in a variation of the *waxejeon* position described above (see p.181). While the legs are in the original position, the arms differ. The left arm is akimbo while the right arm, held out in front, rotates the *buru*.

Specific motions in relation to the text are performed only in the *ia-ilen*. In the song's poem some indications for the dancers are recited (for example lines 6 and 7 *theitheicoon ea,* 'pull back or dodge the spear' and strophe 2, line 14 *dede wano ti lo*, 'jump while turning'). As far as they can be understood these words describe events told in the poem as well as giving instructions to the dancers.

BE KO BE

The text of the song *be ko be* was transcribed by Dubois (1975:285-290) as it was recited to him in 1944 by Ferdinand Wathodrawa of the si-Thuahmijoc. At that time the dance was performed by the si-Medu and the person responsible for the dance was Alfred Kaiwhatr. The song was recorded in November 1994 and a performance of the dance by the people of La Roche was observed both at the 'Iahnithekeun' festival and during the TA.PE.NE cultural days in December (1995), when it was performed by the youth of La Roche.

The words have hardly changed from the version of 1944, except that strophes 2 and 5 were not sung when it was recorded in November 1994. Dubois' notation (1975:285-286) of the text is used today as an aid in remembering the text words, but they are not read during a dance performance. The text includes *Drehu* and *Nengone* words together with words that are not understood. Dubois' informants said that this song tells about female spirits *kaze ri woc* that live in the caves in a swamp area in the region of Wabao (*era ni mo-yaac wene ri malu*). Dubois guesses that the song tells about how the *kaze* arrived on Maré from Lifou and about the first events concerning the *kaze* on Maré. Dubois sets the date of this dance song in the late 18th century and says that there is a relationship between the ancient *chefferie* of Xetiwan and the *kaze*.

be ko be ae	**strike thus, strike, ae**
be ko ba	**strike thus, strike**

- 1. strophe -

be i kaze ri woc	**strike the kaze from the bush**
itranine lu ko	**[hold back] bind him well the kaze**
yengu ri hnawawa	**the wind is in the battlefield**
wawane ruecil	**one goes to Ruecil**
wawane lu Pakad(a)	**one goes down to Pakad(a)**
theitheicoon	**one pulls up again, and then again**
ci hai pawaroi	**one watches Pawaroi**
theitheicoon	**one pulls up again**
ci hai padewia	**one watches Padewia**

- 2. strophe -

watyaluma	**watyaluma**
raba, raba, raba	**watches, watches, watches**
raba makalua	**watches makalua**
trotro nineko	**"where must I go?"**
hwako nineko	**"I went up there"**
gurewoe parac(a)	**Gurewoc and Parac(a)**
nue lu parapeu	**leave Parapeu**
tha te lui loi ya	**untranslatable**

- 3. strophe -

kukuama celam	(untranslatable)
noda yeco	in the land of the yeco
ukesinane lu	light the torch
ne sineunamaea	and burn the house
uke lu ri mayo	untie over there
lo na ithithir	(?) who is honest for heritage
doku ni Ketiwan	the chefferie of Ketiwan
ha iru iru kom	has fought, has fought here
sia i wayaw	sent to Wayaw
ha i-sia ko dreudreu	has sent to Dreudreu (?)
me lue padaw(a)	and the two Padaw(a)
ke cie hna wedreng	(untranslatable)
ru lu i Adong(o)	disappeared at Adong(o)

- 4. strophe -

wewe lu anga yo	they go down there
eraba eonin	looking out together
there no linen	searching
hnei sa i wayaw	by one of the Wayaw
there no linen	searching
hnei sa i wayaw	by one of the Wayaw
rue Malanyim	the two Malanyim (?)
i kaze ri woc	the kaze from the bush
i wawa ri eng (o)	go (or fight) on the wind
there la anuma	look for the track
tha numa numa ko	search, go, go
ea wahmirat	wamirat

- 5. strophe -

Wewe lu Lolong(o)	go to Lolong(o)
thede lu yewe	come back (surfing) on the wave
ale ale ri woc	swim swim in the forest
gurepedibaroi	piece of a small eel
kome uni tronem(u)	here is tronem(u)
hna uni weliehme	one found Weliehme
Di re hne dra era	feather, stays song of blood
tice naca-xeje	the big frigatebird bird goes away

- Finale -

he a e ie ie o	he ae, he says the one who
be i kaze ri woc	strikes the *kaze* of the bush
hanga ? Ngai !	

(For the direct French translation see p. 262.)

The following transcription shows the end of a *gukaden* part of *be ko be,* including the particular and, for *kutera* dances typical, recitated formula at the end.

Final part of *be ko be, gukaden.*

The *wahieko* dances❶

Dubois (1969/1980:946) defines the *wahieko* as a "kind of men's dance with songs, telling of clan wars"❷. The textual content of the *wahieko* is concerned with *Nengone* history, especially with the 'massacre of the Eletok'. The words are partly in *Nengone* and partly in *Drehu,* a language which Dubois calls "burlesque Lifou" ("lifou macaronique"). The population of Maré call it, more respectfully, *shede.*

Dubois analysed the text words of two *wahieko* dances, *wahieku ni Rabadridr(i)* and *wahieku ni Kedititi(i)*. The text of the former *wahieku ni Rabadridr(i)* has been analysed precisely (Dubois 1977:206-227). It tells of the events that took place from 1802 to 1825, the period during which the

❶ Dubois gives also *wahieku.*

❷ "sorte de danse d'hommes avec chants, raconte les guerres des clans".

(David Becker/A.D.C.K.1995, Lifou)

For the *hneumalan* part the dancers use a particular way of advancing, partly walking and partly dancing, to get in a line between the audience and the choir.

massacre of the Eletok occurred. According to Dubois the latter, *wahieku ni Keditit(i)*, was composed between 1860 and 1866 (1977:274).

In the music and choreology of the *wahieko* there are no formal characteristics which distinguish them from the *pehua*. The distinction lies rather in the contents : the *wahieko* tell about the massacre of the Eletok and the *pehua* recount myths, so that the border between them may be fluid. However there is also a small formal difference in their endings.

The parts of a *wahieko* do not end with the exclamation *i hanga? - ngai!* as do those of the *pehua*, but they end with the exclamation : *Kacahmi or Jewine ha tako* (*Kacahmi* and *Jewine* stand as examples of the names of the heroes of the poem) '*Kacahmi/Jewine* is gone'. Then all the singers shout *hi*, an exclamation to express their pain. The formal end of the song parts is also used in the song *era ni Wahnara* (Dubois 1990:5). The song tells about the events of the second world war in the same manner as the ancient Maré wars were recounted. The final shouts of the song are : *Hitler, ha tako? - hi!*

The *nyineuatro* dances

In Drehu the name of this dance can be traced back to the expression *nyine au a tro* 'why should you go'. In his dictionary, Dubois (1969/1980:659) explains the word *nyineuatro* as "A Lifou word used at the beginning of certain songs which are therefore called : *nyineuatro*"[1].

The *nyineuatro* dances of Maré have the heroic actions of the *padoku (chefferie)* as their subjects. In the *gukaden* of these dance songs the word *nyineuatro* is recited and the songs' parts end with the word *hanga? - hai!* There are several *nynieuatro* on Maré : *nyineuatro oni ange hmae*, tells about the fights between the si-Gurewoc and the si-Ruemec, the si-Hnadidi and the si-Gureshaba. This dance song was composed around 1866, when the Catholics began their mission work on Maré (Dubois 1975:15). The *nyineuatro guli Simako*, (Dubois 1977:376-381) tells about the war of the si-Gureshaba.

Many *kutera* dance songs contain Drehu words but that does not necessarily mean that these songs were originally in Drehu. The strong relationship between the populations of the two islands of Lifou and Maré, in which Maré seems the more often to have been in a receiving position, gave the Maré population a general understanding of Drehu and some people spoke it, too. The use of some Drehu words by Maré composers may have been a technique to camouflage the content, one which is common in the Loyalty Islands and in Polynesia. The content of a dance song is available on several levels. Putting some Drehu words in a Maré song text makes a preliminary selection : people who do not understand the Drehu words, are immediately excluded. A simpler explanation was given to Dubois (1977:371) from one informant who said that *shede* (the language consisting of *Nengone* and *Drehu* words) is used because it is a very graceful language for the songs ("très élégante pour les chants").

THE *WAYAI* DANCES

The Maré women's dances that have a choreological structure and a content similar to those of the *kutera*, are called *wayai*. In his dictionary Dubois (1969/1980:943) writes *waiai* or *wayai* : "Women's dances. They are accompanied by some men;..."[2]. It is possible that a relationship exists with the Ouvéan women's dances, which in the Fagauvea language are called *waiai* and in Iaai *wahaihai*. The word *wayai*, can also be related to the word *wasai*. Leenhardt (1935:348 and 1930/1980:174) uses this word to refer to the theatrical scenes in the dances from the *Grande Terre*. He says : "Mimed scenes and performances in the pilous. Mimicking life ridiculous antics... "[3]. According to Leenhardt, these plays originated on the Loyalty Islands. Leenhardt does not say that there it is a female dance.

The performances today show that the male accompaniment part of a Maré *wayai* is limited to the mixed choir and sometimes a performance by a *wayeac*[4]. The content of the *wayai* dance songs recounts myths and historical events. The contents of the *wayai* are of the same historical importance as those of the men's *kutera* dance.

Besides the *wayai* dance *washongoshongone*, that will be studied below, Dubois (1968:129) transcribed the text of the *wayai*, *gubune ne podraw(a)*, composed between 1880 and 1890 by Ngazo Wani(a) of the si-Hnadid. Dubois uses its content for his geographic-mythic studies of the island. The *wayai*, *wareda* of the si-Gureshaba transcribed by Dubois (1977:382-386) tells about

[1] "Mot lifou commençant certains chants appelés pour cela : *nyineuatro*".

[2] "Danse de femmes. Elles sont accompagnées par des hommes;...".

[3] "Scènes mimées et spectacles dans les pilous. Imitation de la vie grotesque bouffonnerie...".

[4] A male dancer who dances freely among the women dancers.

(David Becker/A.D.C.K.1995, Lifou)

In the women's *wayai* dances the principal movements are carried out with the arms. Dancers bend their knees only a little or some dancers may lift one foot slightly to the rhythm of the song.

war, cannibalism and important historical events that took place before 1862. The date of compostition of this second *wayai* is unknown. A *wayai* was also recorded in the Institute de Phonétique at Paris in 1931 (O'Reilly 1946:103).

The structure and form of a *wayai* is similar to that of a *kutera*. From the mixed choir the dancers come out, one behind the other and take up a position in a row between the choir and the audience. The passage is carried out with special dance/walking motions. It starts with the left foot, then the right foot and the following step brings the left leg beside the right leg. After a short pause the same procedure is repeated. The dancers, holding dance tassels in their hands, swing both arms to the left side of the body, and then both arms go to the right side. When the legs come together for the second time the hands touch the dancers' breasts. The whole motif is repeated until each dancer reaches her place on the *hna-era*. The same motions are carried out after the dance when the women rejoin the choir.

Dubois (1975:69) refers to the song of the dance *washongoshongone*, which describes the migration of the owner group of this dance, the si-Thuun. *Washongoshongone* describes the arrival of the people from Kiamu to Maré (Dubois 1975:15).

Washongoshongone was performed by the group from Medu in 1992 at the 'rencontre préparatoire' and at the inauguration of the 'centre culturel Yeweine Yeweine' (May, 1994). Both performances were filmed in the course of the present study. The text used today corresponds exactly to that given in Dubois (1975:69).

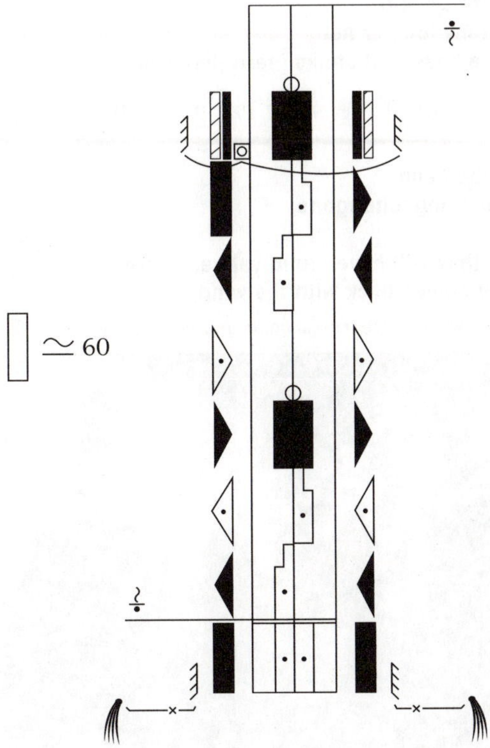

Entry of the dancers in the *washongoshongone* dance.

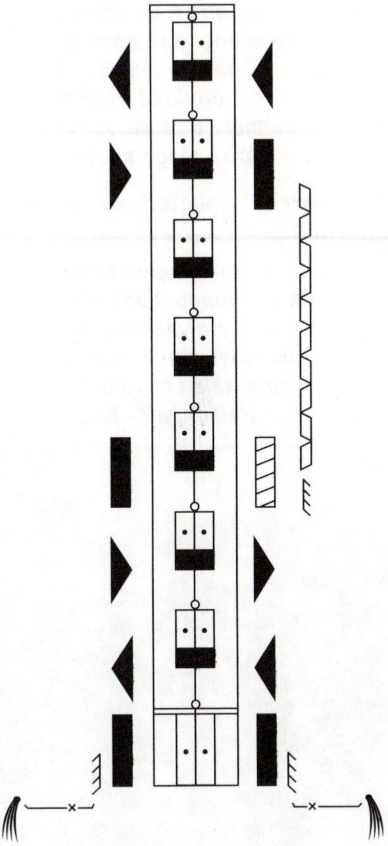

Extract from the *washongoshongone* dance.

Dubois interprets the story in relation to the arrival of the 'real' yam from the mythical place Ma, which for Dubois (1975:111) is Fiji although when coming to Maré the 'real' yam passed by Kiamu. There are some allusions in the poem which suggest that the mythical place Ma might be Kiamu (Anatom) but in most of the references it is Tanna, which is relatively close to Anatom and where a migrating party could make a visit before going on to Maré. Dubois (1975:69) says : "The story of Washongoshongone must certainly be understood as that of yams coming from Ma which fled from the fire. It is about muffled rumbling. The goddess is heating up her stomach by means of the fire"❶.

❶ "L'histoire de Washongoshongone doit être certainement comprise comme celle des ignames venant de Ma qui fuyaient le feu. Il s'agit ici de grondements sourds. La déesse se chauffe le ventre par le feu" (Dubois 1975:69). Dubois (1996:83) says that perhaps a volcanic eruption caused a migration to Maré and the song may be alluding to this event.

Hoiyee hoiyee...	
Ca washongoshongone	**Eh washongoshongone**
sere o ? Kio ehme ?	**Where do you come from ? where are you from ?**
Inu serei Kiam (u)	**I come from Kiam (u)**
Mama da kaio nu,	**big brother call me**
da hna ti lu o re iei,	**bring me fire**
co shengi o re oreg (o)	**to heat up my stomach**
Inu ha leulebu(e)	**I am cold**
co hue i Deceiri	**to go to Deceiri**
co there o re warog (o)	**to get my lobster net**
We ! cenge shukeli	**He, the basket of shukeli fern (fish trap)**

This part is repeated a number of times until the *naca era* gives the sign for the final :

ome ci sere te ole	**hold the helm**
Ca washongoshongone !	**Eh washongoshongone**
Hoiyee hoiyee...	
ma ona yahu(e) wayaw	**when they will have found yahue, wayaw**
nine wala i re yeng (o)	**the fly comes back with the wind**
Ha ahnga ? - Ngai !	

(For the direct French translation see p. 263.)

(David Becker/A.D.C.K.1995, Lifou)

The women's dance group from Maré walking out from the choir and taking up there position in a row for dancing. This walk is carried out with special motions between walking and dancing.

Dubois finds the last few words of the song are obscure. Perhaps it is "...an allusion to the mosquitoes at Kiam(u), while on Maré there is almost no problem with them, and to the Yahoue volcano on Tanna"❶. The name of the volcano, Yahoue (Yasur), is recited in the last line of the song. A somewhat different interpretation of the content of the *washongoshongone* song comes

❶ "...une allusion aux moustiques de Kiam(u), alors qu'à Maré on n'en souffre pratiquement pas, et au volcan Yahoue de Tanna".

from the people who perform the dance today. They say that *washongoshongone* is a *yaac* who went to Tanna (Vanuatu) to fetch fire from the island's volcano, Yahue (Yasur).

The *washongoshongone* dance consists of two principal parts, *gukaden* and *ia-ilen*. Each part and each repetition of a part is separated from the following by a short pause. In part A, *gukaden,* the word *hoyie* is recited. In part B, *ia-ilen,* the words of the text are recited and the dancers carry out particular motions. Part C, *ia-ilen,* consists of several sections, and each one is repeated. The whole *ia-ilen* part (B and C) is repeated three times. The dancers come out of the circle during the *gukaden* part. When they have reached their positions the *gukaden* part stops with the words : *hanga? - hai !.* The *ia-ilen* parts begin and each one ends with the repetition of the word *hoyie.*

Beginning of *Washongoshongone* dance song.

Music

The melodic line of the *gukaden* part goes from the b upwards to f♯ and back to the b. In the *gukaden* the syllable *-ye* starts slightly before the strong metre pulse, thus creating a kind of anticipation. This effect occurs sometimes in the *kutera* music repertoire and is a feature of Maré's music. During the fieldwork a similar effect was not encountered amongst the dance songs of Lifou or Ouvéa. The *ia-ilen* part consists of a melodic theme which is repeated 4 times to recite the text. The same tonal material is used as for the gukaden part but notes with less rhythmical value can be used in order to pronounce the words. The metre is symmetrical (2/4) with the strike of the *ae-be* on the downbeat of each measure. Each part ends with the same finale, making reference to Yahoue and the mosquitoes. Finally the *naca era* shouts "*hanga, hanga*", which is answered by the choir with "*ngai*". Then the *naca era* makes a sound "*brrrrrrrr*" and the choir answers with "*y*".

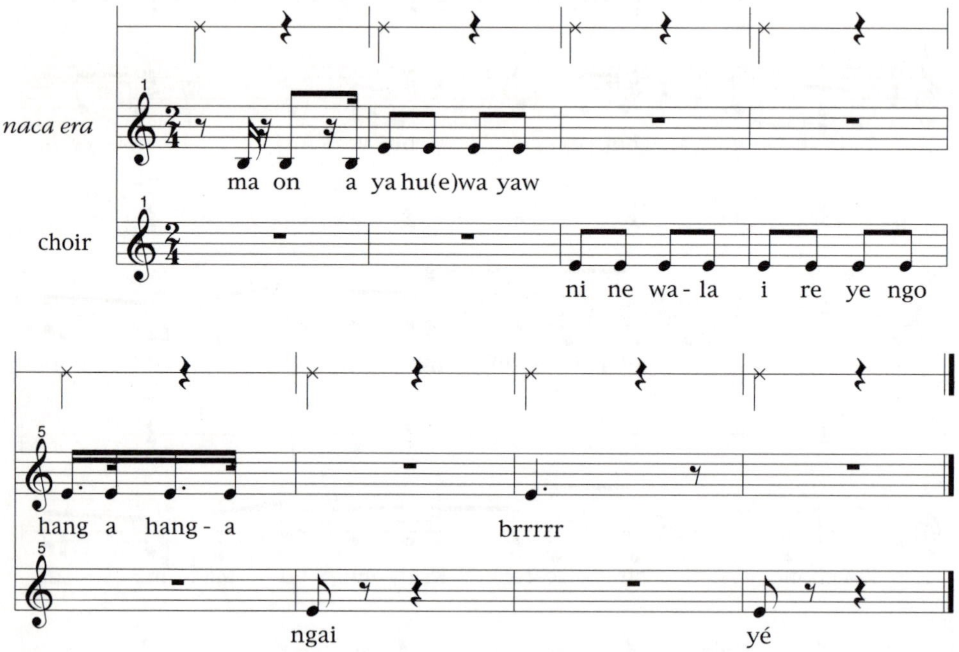

Ending formulas of *Washongoshongone* dance song

Choreology

Once the women are standing in a row, the specific movements to accompany the story are carried out exclusively with the arms. The legs are only very slightly bent on each downbeat of the song or the right foot can be slightly lifted up. The motions start on a downbeat and for most of the motions both arms move together. One or two women, who know the dance best, may stand a little aside so that other dancers can watch and copy them when they are uncertain. There are no indications in the text words to direct the dancers' motions, as is the case, for example, in the dance *be be nod*.

(David Becker/A.D.C.K.1995, Lifou)

A *wayai* dance performed by a group from the island of Tiga. The principal movements are carried out with the arms. The long dance tassels make the movements soft and graceful.

Pe rue cakui[1]

This *wayai* tells the story of two women who search during the dry season for waterholes at Wapete. On their search they pass through the coastal region between Thoon and La Roche (Dubois 1975:15). The text refers to the names of places in this region in the northeast of Maré, *pe rue cakui* being itself the name of a place there. Besides the recitation of place names, some words indicate to the dancers what movements need to be carried out (Ammann 1997: track10 [CD]).

The *hneumalan* part of the *pe rue cakui* has the same melodic line as the *hneumalan* of *be be nod.*

The heterophonic *gukaden* and *ia-ilen* parts of *pe rue cakui* are different from those of *be be nod. Be be nod* has a separate melodic line and a separate metre for the *gukaden* and *ia-ilen* parts, whereas in *pe rue cakui* the same melodic lines continue in the *gukaden* and *ia-ilen* parts but accelerated in tempo. This modification in energy is indicated by striking on the leaf parcel on the downbeats of the 6/8 metre. The sort of interrupted bourdon present in the *hneumalan* of *be be nod* (see p. 187) does not occur in the *hneumalan* of the *pe rue cakui.*

[1] Dubois also uses the orthograph *pe rue cakoe* (Dubois 1975:15).

Pe rue cakoe	**On the two red mullets of the nights**
watini hidra i Thoon ea	**The fresh water of Thoon**
Pe rue cakoe	**On the two red mullets of the nights**
Walalu i Hnakingen(i) ea dai	**The descent of Hnakingen(i)**
hnide lo te	**come back a bit**
ice n'garangara lo	**climb up steeply**
la hne tha waw	**to the track where one throws the ball**
karenione lo	**lift your elbow**
si Gi ne Si Puan	**the si-Gi and the si-Puan**
Wadrarepien	**Wadrarepien**
token ore Yaac	**Chef of the yaac**
rue Waithorone	**the two Waithorone**
Wabubu re Waitru	**the extremity of Waitru**
ice lo i Ngarangara	**ascend steeply at Ngarangara**
Gurewala ni Yaac	**the small track of the yaac**
Dukewi ne Wadusa	**Dukewi and Wadusa**
ceceni Hnawanyo	**the father of Hnawanyo**
Pe rue cakoe	**On the red mullets of the nights**
Oiaa he i waiyawe	**(Exclamation)**
Ha pe rue cakoe	**It's on the red mullets of the nights**
Hanga ? - Hai !	(For the direct French translation see p. 265.)

Melodic theme from the *hneumalan* part of the dance song *pe rue cakui.*

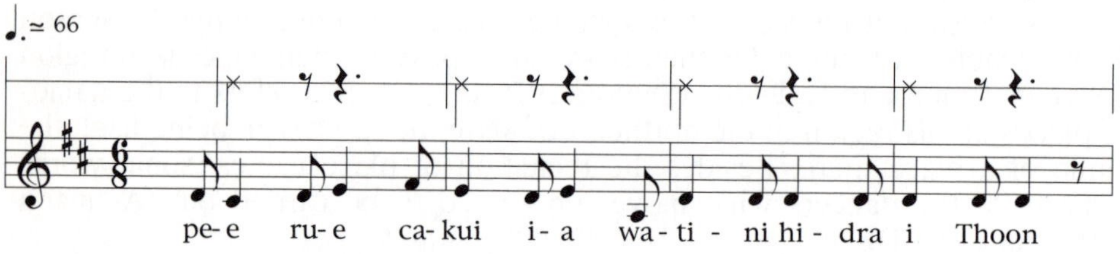

The *ia-ilen* part is sung one tone higher than the *hneumalan* part.

That the music of the *hneumalan* of *pe rue cakui* is the same as that used for the *hneumalan* part of *be be nod* could be a coincidence. In discussions with a few singers it transpired that they were surprised to hear of it and had never themselves made the comparison. *Be be nod* belongs to the people at Cerethi in the southeast of Maré and *pe rue cakui* belongs to the people at La Roche and the song tells about their home places❶. The song's lyrics given here are qotations from Dubois (1968) and the same words are used today.

❶ According to Dubois (1989:21), in the 1880s the people of La Roche bought permission to perform the dance *be be nod*. They do not perform this dance any longer, but it could have influenced the *pe rue cakui*.

Wa-biengo

Another class of women's dances is the *wabiengo.* Dubois (1975:15) refers to them as *wa-bieng(o)* a class of songs which "cheerfully mock the world alluding to funny forgotten things. As these songs accompany women's dances they were not considered important enough for the mockery to lead to serious consequences"❶.

DANCES WITHOUT MUSIC

Only a few dances on Maré are performed without singing accompaniment : the *cap* dance, already described in the introduction to the Loyalty Islands, and the dance called *sasa.*

The *sasa* dance

The term *sasa,* translated by Dubois (1969/1980: 749-750) as "war dance" ("danse guerrière"), is a specific Maré dance. The *sasa* is performed mainly before the performance of a *kutera* dance, but not all *kutera* dances are preceded by a *sasa*. The *sasa* dancers, exclusively men, have the whole body painted black and are so heavily camouflaged with green lianas and leaves that the person is hardly recognisable. The *sasa* dancer carries spears and clubs and demonstrates the furious behaviour of a warrior.

The audience is sitting on the ground waiting for the *kutera* dance to be performed. Suddenly, out of a hidden place or out of the dark, the *sasa* dancers appear. Shouting loudly, they run and jump, carrying out sham attacks with club or spear against certain people in the audience. The performance of *sasa* lasts for a few minutes and the number of dancers varies. There is no coordination among the dancers and there is no music. If, during a *kutera* performance, some dancers break out of their positions and behave in the same way then that part of the *kutera* is also called *sasa.*

The *sasa* performed before the *kutera* prepares the audience for the following dance and chases the spirits off the *hna-era* (dance-ground), in order to prepare the ground for the *kutera*. The form of the *sasa* dance at the end of the 19th and beginning of 20th century was different from what is seen today. Dubois (1975:160) describes this warrior dance : "It [the dance] consists of running in front of a chef to honour him. One advances in profile, left foot first and then bringing the right foot near to the left foot as if going to throw a spear held in the right hand"❷. This is the way in which each group of warriors marched past the pile of food during exchange ceremonies. At the end of the dance the dancer stopped immediately and raised his knee (the account does not say which one) in front of the person to honour. Dubois says further that *sasa* means 'to present oneself in front of the enemy for battle' and also 'to hurry up'.

The name *sasa,* in relation to dance and music, is also known on Samoa. However on Samoa it was the name of the introductory part of the *ma'ulu'ulu* dance. In the 19th century the *sasa* part was separated off and performed as a

❶ "se moquent allégrement du monde, et font allusion à des faits comiques oubliés. Comme ces chants accompagnaient des danses de femmes, la moquerie était estimée comme ne prêtant pas à conséquence".

❷ "Elle [la danse] consiste à courir devant un chef pour l'honorer. On avance le profil, le pied gauche en avant, et en ramenant le pied droit près du pied gauche, comme si on allait lancer la sagaie que l'on tient dans la main droite".

dance in its own right (Richard Moyle pers. comm.). The choreography of the Samoan *sasa* differs greatly from that of the Maréan *sasa* and they do not seem to be directly linked. The name *sasa* is also found on Bellona Island in the Solomon Islands, where it indicates singing and beating the rhythm of *tangi* (laments) or *huaa mako* (song dances) (Rossen 1987:129). On Bellona Island the name *sasa* can mean 'to be crazy, lunatic' (Rossen 1987:113).

Music on Maré apart from dance accompaniment

Most of the traditional songs that are known on Maré now accompany dances. The songs that do not accompany dances are in the following groups :

- *doh* and *taperas*
- Songs of the 20th century in the European musical system
- *hae hae* - children's and game-accompanying songs
- *waueng* - boys' songs

Era, as already explained, means 'to sing' or 'song' in Nengone. On Maré the people distinguish between two components of the song : *hnathuthur* and *lan. Hnathuthur* refers to the textual content of the song. The word *lan* generally means 'juice' but in a song *lan,* signifies on one hand the melody and on the other hand the principal voice part. Dubois (1969/1980:474) translates the word *lan* as 'singing a duet', the two singers accompanying themselves with musical instruments❶. Dubois does not say if this song accompanied any dancing. His description suggests a relationship with the accompaniment of the *bua* dance from Lifou (see p. 214), although such songs are not known on Maré today. *Era, hnathuthur* and *lan* are generally used when referring to traditional songs and singing. They are not used for *taperas.*

Song-compositions in the european music-style

There are no clues as to when the first person on Maré composed a song in the European system and it is possible that compositions in a major-minor tonal system were already created in the late 19th century.

The songs are formally close to *taperas,* with a structure in strophe and refrain, and the use of the typical *taperas* heterophony. The content of these songs can include myths of the island, in such cases the myths are told in a chronological way, which is not apparent in *kutera* dance songs. A reference to Christianity is made in the content of many of the songs. In telling about a local historical event such as a legend, one strophe, usually the last one, has a biblical subject that is may be unrelated to the rest of the song's story or may make a comparison with it. This can be seen, for example, in the song *sine i wacoco,* telling of how the yam came to Maré but with a Christian subject for its final strophe.

Ya nore nodei ia - The voyage of the animals

This song was composed by the *nata*❷ Shene, probably in the 1960s. It is based on the legend of how the animals crossed over from Maré to the island of Tiga at a time of famine. The performance transcribed below was recorded on the 26.10.1994 at Tenan where it was performed by the mixed choir of Kaloi Cawidrone.

❶ "chanter en duo, les deux chanteurs s'accompanient d'un instrument donnant la cadence".

❷ A *nata* was a person educated as a *pasteur* (pastor) by the French Evangelical church. The *natas* from the Loyalties went as missonaries to the *Grande Terre.*

- 1. strophe -

Se yeretiti co laenatan'ore
ya nore nodei ia
hna ekote ha thu co ya, ha
thu co ya jew'ose nod
pakone kore toka koe, meni
hna ie inu paelatre
inu ha ul'ore pathe, hne
pathe ri bet'omelei

A legend tells of the passage of the animals
They arranged to travel together to a land.
The buzzard will be the commander, I will be the pilot
says the owl
Because I know where the pass is, the pass to this
island.

- chorus -

paelatre i meni, ha paekoc,
wala ya i mene ha kaleka
ha rewerewe kei toka koe,
ha te ri peda kore koe.

Mene the pilot was was suddenly silent,
Mene the guide is overcome by sobbing
The commander regrets, the ship is on the reef.

- 2. strophe -

Ma hna nuebot'ore nod, hna
ya ri ridin' ore ridri
hna ethedone co paelatre,
ca sererekane koi meni
meni ci kaie : nue icelu,
nuelu ome, ha ci kwu te
kore ceku
ri naca koe, paelatre ha
adreadre

They leave the island to travel during the night
but they quarrel over the piloting the ship. Mene was
finally chosen.
He shouts then, 'this way', 'that way'! while at the
same time the moon rises
and dazzles the pilot at the front of the boat

- 3. strophe -

Ta hnatale, yan'ore koe, sio
ne hamu ne drera
hna hmutilu ri hne pathe,
hmen'ore hna walaya i meni
cengeni me hmare thuben,
ha hna luzion ha gupako
kore hna ruace, koe ha
kapa, ka matelot ha etha sic.

The merchandise stuffed into the boat,`
the riches were engulfed
at the bottom of the pass
because of the fault of Mene
Precious stones lost for ever
Vain efforts, the ship is broken and the sailors have
fled.

- 4. strophe -

Numu se ya inomelei, ya
nore rekokonien
hna loaze i Gethesemani,
hna pareu ne newrew
Ca ha hna ' ore ci une, hna
wakewi ne hna cacere
ale hna sice, ka Yesu di,
odene ri satauro.

Do you remember
that other journey: that of the apostles
Strayed at Gethesemani, taken by fear and regret
treachery and lying
they fled,
abandoning Jesus, alone on the cross.

(For the direct French translation see p. 264.)

First strophe of the principal part of *Ya nore nodei ia*

Children's songs and games

The songs called *hae hae* are performed for small children either as lullabies or just to play. The *era bane ci athaethini buic* are songs that are performed by the children themselves, often to accompany a game. Maré as well as the island of Tiga are places where many lullabies and children's games or songs are still known, although they rarely fulfil their traditional function now that television sets and videos are available on the islands.

A song reported by Larsen (1961:181) is probably an exception "One tune, a rather sad one, will remain in our memory. It was sung by the girls of Maré. and was a kind of cradle song which seemed to echo the murmur of the waves stealing softly on to the beach, and the whisper of the wind in the palms". The text words of the *hae hae* may allude to mythological figures or events, but most of them are games with words or have a humorous content.

Waene - Caterpillar

This *hae hae* consists partly of real words and partly of made up words (see Ammann 1997:track13[CD]).

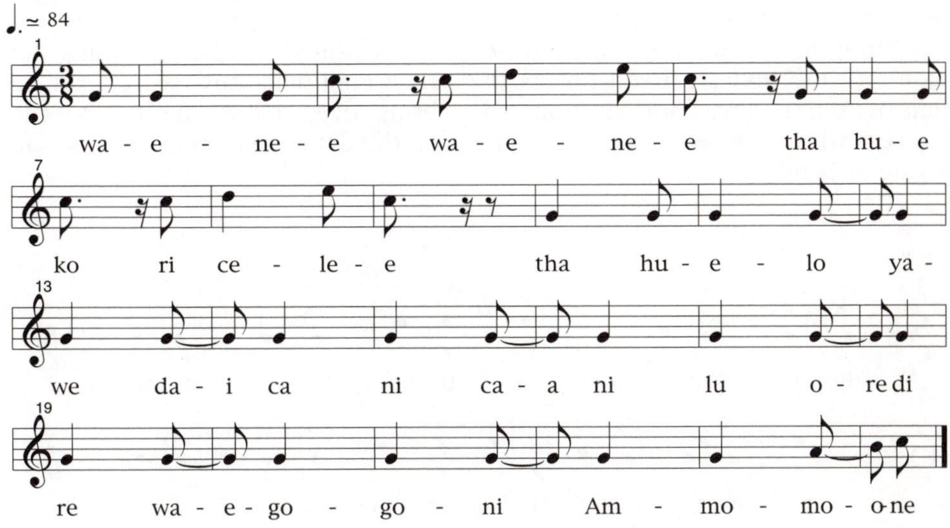

Another *hae hae,* very popular on Maré, is called *wakede.*

Era bane ci aopodoneni ore ta wamorowe

Very few traditional games are played by children today. Older people remember these games and on occasions, for example at the cultural day organised by TA.PE.NE in December 1994 on Maré, they are presented and taught to children, in the hope that the games will be played again. Some of the games for children over eight years old are accompanied by singing, others, especially when they have a more sportslike character are without singing. The following description of two games accompanied by singing describes the performance observed during the TA.PE.NE cultural days.

Hielo

This game is a children's dance which can also be performed by a mixed group of adults and children. The participants stand in a row, holding hands. The dancer at the beginning of the row walks while bending his head to pass between the second and the third dancers under the arch made by their arms. All the other dancers in the row follow him. The row then passes under the arms of the third and fourth dancers, then between the fourth and fifth and so on, until finally all the dancers walk in a spiral. There is much fun and laughter over these dance motions.

During this dance the following song is performed. At the beginning the words of the text are fixed but as the dance continues new words can be improvised. Funny improvisations may bring even more laughter to the dancers who are already full of laughter and the dance generally collapses in a gale of laughter.

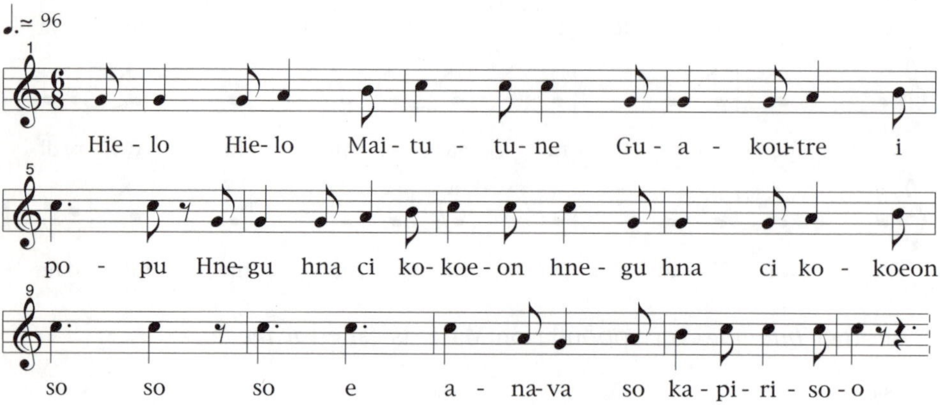

Beginning of the song *hielo.*

Hielo, Hielo, Hielo, Hielo, Hielo, maitutune	**Let us give our hands let us give our hands**
Guakoutre i Popu	**Popu's little coat**
Hnegu hna ci kokoen	**that I was wearing**
So so so e anavaso kapiriso	**(untranslatable neutral words)**
Wa kumala, wa kumala	**small sweet potato, small sweet potato**
Wa kamarade ne suri	**little friend of the mouse**

(For the direct French translation see p. 263.)

Therelo re waco

This game is only performed by girls or women, because wearing a 'mother hubbard' dress is necessary. The game is played by at least ten women. All the women - except one - sit very close in a circle facing the centre. The legs are stretched to the centre, with the knees slightly lifted up and hands under the lifted knees. One woman stands in the centre. One of the seated women hides a small ball-like object, called a *waco,* usually made of a rolled up coconut leaflet, in one hand under her knees. The woman in the middle has to find out who has the *waco.* She may pull the arm and open the hand of the woman whom she guesses has the *waco* and this woman has to open her hand for verification. Because all knees are covered by the skirts of the 'mother hubbard' the woman in the centre can only find out who has the *waco* when it is passed from one woman to another either under the knees to a neighbour or, more risky, but much appreciated by the audience and the players, by throwing the *waco* to another seated player behind the back of the the standing woman. When the woman in the middle finds out who has the *waco* she changes places with her.

During this game the seated women sing the song *therelo re waco* (Find the *waco*). These words are the only text of the song and they are repeated indefinitely with the same music theme.

♩≃ 98
The - re - lo-re wa-co re - lo-re wa-co re- lo-re wa-co re - lo-re waco

The *waueng* songs

The generic term *waueng* refers to a specific class of songs which are particular to Maré. The word *waueng* consists of the the morpheme '*wa-*' meaning 'small' and the word '*-ueng*', which is the name of a tree (*Dodonea viscosa*) or of the plain where it is the only tree. Young men go to clear a space for their plantations there and sing the *waueng* songs during the work on the plantations and on other occasions when they are together and there is an ambience as, for example, at weddings. There, the young men sing a certain distance away from the other people. The boys joke and laugh, perhaps they drink a beer, and finally they start singing the *waueng*.

For the people of Maré there is a strong difference between the *taperas* or the *kutera* and the *waueng*. The *waueng* are seen as being of less importance and they are taken less seriously than other songs. There exist an infinite number of *hnathuthur* (lyrics) for *waueng* (a few *waueng hnathuthur* are in Drehu), but only a small number of *waueng lan* (melodies). The *hnathuthur* of the *waueng* have a romantic-poetical content, often with some 'risqué' reflections. This is the reason why the *waueng* are performed only in the bush or, during festivities such as weddings, away from the other guests.

Some examples of the textual contents of the *waueng* :

Yesu keriso kabanulo ri node om	**Jesus Christ, take me away from this earth**
Ma ci nia du nu kei wa thu hulo lia	**this ungrateful person has done me so much harm**

Kolo ci ranelo re cekole ci kurulo	**What a beautiful memory, this lovely moonrise**
Ci nerenonelo re parowo ni wacanor	**Which iluminates the sweet face of my darling.**

Ie du cecene ni bo me ci ane dunene ni inu	**Say to your father who harbours resentment against me**
Ko inu co hue ne bo ke dekote ma hmani bo	**Tell him, that I will go out with you, but certainly not with your mother.**

Kinikinibot' ore gunine i Asicen	**Dig, dig the sand at Ascien [beach at Nece]**
Bane ci iedi oiru ko guhnegu ne wanacor	**in remembering my darling**

Nuelo ore yelego ri pon'ore yele ni bo	**Write my name close to your name**
Efase cileboto yele ni hna marie ne bo	**and banish for ever that of your husband.**

(For the direct French translation see p. 263.)

There is only a small number of *lan* for the *waueng,* with which all the *hnathuthur* can be sung. During an evening of *waueng* singing, the singers often sing the same *hnathuthur* with different *lan,* before starting with the next *hnathuthur,* and proceeding in the same way. As in the case of new *hnathuthur,* new *lan* can be invented but it is rather rare. To adjust a *hnathuthur* to the *lan* either certain syllables are repeated or the neutral syllable *lo* is used as a filler.

All the *lan* are responsorial, the main voice, also called *lan,* always begins with a short solo. In some *lans* a very short solo by the second singer follows and finally the heterophonic choir starts. There is no fixed distribution of parts and improvisations are allowed, as in the *taperas.* In general the voices are led in parallels and partially a bourdon may appear. Sometimes rather dissonant sounds can be heard without a resolution according to the rules of music theory. Quite often there is one young man who sings in parallels but on a very high pitch❶. All the *waueng* finish with a long chord and a downward glissando at the end. The quality of a *waueng* performance is judged by this chord. It has to be as long as possible and the glissando must end in perfect synchronisation.

During an evening of *waueng* singing, the young men try to pitch the next *waueng* a bit higher than the one before, eventually reaching a point where they are shouting rather than singing. At such a moment all the singers start laughing, then the next *waueng* will be sung at normal pitch and the game starts again. Sometimes the *waueng* texts are sung with a different melody and guitar accompaniment. It is even possible for women to sing with the young men but it is rather exceptional.

The musicality of the *waueng* seems to be a persiflage of the music of *taperas* songs. In the *waueng* the boys can shout and laugh; there is a liberty

❶ This raises the question, of a relationship between singing *waueng* songs and the breaking of the boys' voices.

that contrasts with the severity of the Christian songs. The basic music of the *waueng* is the same as that of the *taperas* : polyphony with tempered intervals and improvisations, but often without following the rules of how to proceed from tension to resolution. It appears as if the boys took the music of the hymns and modified them for their own ends. This idea is confirmed by the songs' poems, which deal with subjects of great interest to adolescent young men but which are strictly not for the ears of a pastor or priest.

The *waueng* song *yesu keriso* (Ammann 1997:track 13[CD]).

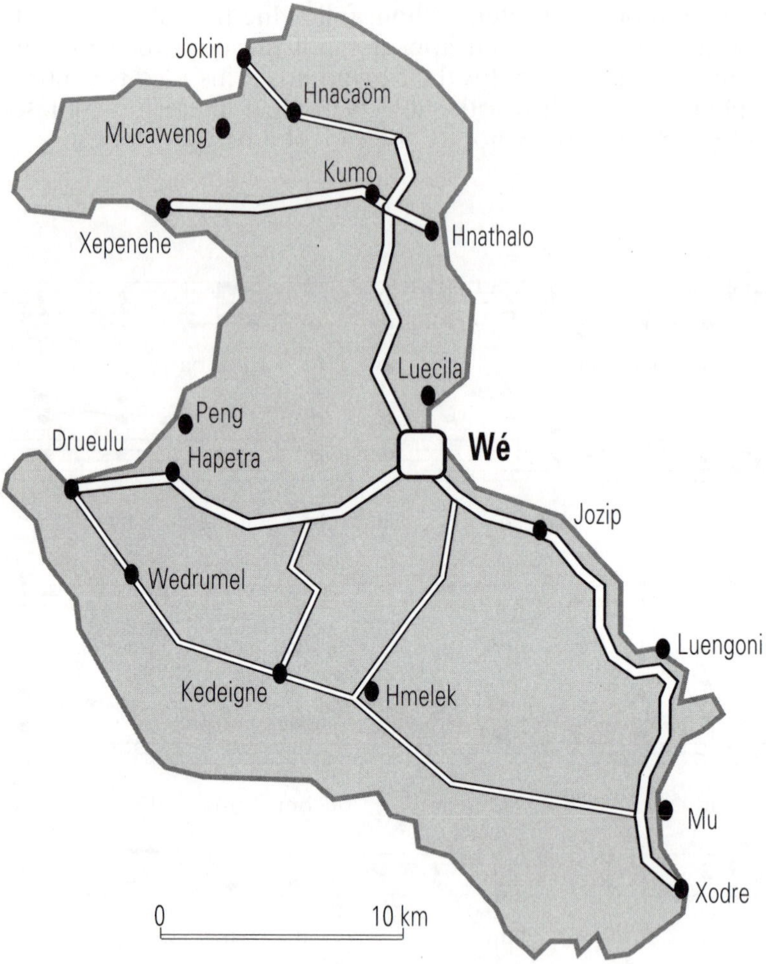

The island of Lifou

Lifou, the biggest island of the Loyalties, is called Drehu by the indigenous people. Lifou is divided into three administrative districts, each corresponding to a *chefferie* (*angajoxu*) : Wetr, Gaïca, Losi. The Sihaze *chefferie* of Wetr is situated at Hnathalo, the Zehoula *chefferie* of Gaïca at Drueulu, and the Boula *chefferie* of Losi at Mu.

HISTORICAL EVENTS IN RELATION TO DANCE AND MUSIC

Research into the archaeology of Lifou has yielded interesting information in diverse fields although as yet no musicological data have been found. The tracing of history chronologically as in the archaeological approach is not the only source of insight into the past. Myths and legends tell of times long ago,

only source of insight into the past. Myths and legends tell of times long ago, before European contact and the arrival of missionaries. One myth about the origin of the island was collected and written down by Lenormand and Sam (1993:19). According to this myth, at the beginning the island was without vegetation and its surface was very dry. Then just a few plants appeared. People lived in the north, in the south and in the east of the island. Each of the three groups divided its land in three separate parts. At this time the *haze*❶ already existed and each one was related to a specific place on the island. As the plant cover increased, new *haze* appeared. The first population named a *chef* but he ruled badly so that the *chefferie* was abandoned and the *chefferies* of today were created. Today each *tribu* has a *chef* (*petit chef*), who is subject to the *grand chef*.

During the 19th century, the *chefferies* of Wetr and Losi were dominant. The populations of these *chefferies* were in constant war with each other. But neither of the two groups was able to subdue the other and there was a balance of war power between these two populations. The district of Gaïca, which geographically forms a wedge between the *chefferies* of Wetr and Losi, frequently had a function of arbitrator during these wars.

Tribal warfare on Lifou hindered business with sandalwood traders who arrived in the waters of the island at the beginning of the 19th century. Still, of the few European or American mariners and traders who settled on Lifou, a fair number married into high ranking and *chef* families. English family names from this period are common today on Lifou.

Besides the European arrivals there were also Pacific islanders for example from Tonga and Samoa (Guiart 1953c:94) who reached Lifou as shipwrecked mariners and were made welcome. There is a legend telling about a group of emigrants from Kiamu (Anatom) who arrived on Lifou. They were called the *Angetre onatr* and they had the gift of being able to fly back to Kiamu. To do so, they formed a circle, held each other's hands and closed their eyes. They sang a certain song in the language of Kiamu (there is no further information about the song) and then they were there. It is said that the power was lost when a woman opened her eyes during the voyage.

The dance and music repertoires of Lifou

The only reports from Lifou during the 19th century from a person who actually lived for several years on the islands are from a missionary's wife Emma Hadfield❷. Concerning the song repertoire she writes "There are songs for men and songs for women; action songs; duets and solos; there are fighting songs, love songs, and songs to soothe to sleep, but no comic songs

❶ A *haze* is a supernatural being, living in the bush on Lifou. A *haze* can be a god which protects a family. These beings are useful for negative power, *haze* refers also to stones or other objects. Inside these objects is a powerful man; without him the *haze* is just an ordinary stone. The origin of the power of the *haze* lies in a being and its medium such as shark, lizard, tree etc. The *haze* of Lifou were introduced to Maré where they are called *kaze*. Guiart places the origin of the *haze* at Hulup on the island of Ouvéa.

❷ Emma Hadfield, the wife of the L.M.S. missionary James Hadfield, came to Lifou in 1879 with her husband when he took over the position of the Rev. Greagh. The Hadfields travelled extensively on all the Loyalty Islands. On Ouvéa they had a house where they spent several weeks each year. In 1920, after the death of her husband, Emma Hadfield published *Among the natives of the Loyalty Group*, a biography containing ethnological data.

that I ever heard of"❶ (Hadfield 1920:133).

A particular dance scene of the 19th century is described by Rivière (1881:86). "Like all primitives, she [the Lifou woman] is a mimic artist of the sensational. On a slow and measured rhythm, arms dangling, feet fixed to the floor, the dancer moves only her hips which undulate and roll with extreme flexibility. And from time to time there are a few jolts of the supple and powerful back. Then the rhythm of the dance accelerates, stops suddenly, and the woman with a bestial laugh and a sort of confusion of her person, flees and disappears among her companions. Animal lust, too, has these brutal explosions and this instinctive shame"❷.

According to this description the dance shows some basic similarities with the way women's dances are still performed on Lifou. Rivière's account is however influenced by a strange kind of exotism. The missionary MacFarlane on the other hand described a woman's dance that is quite unknown today.

During a ceremony in which food was distributed, two men ran up against those present and began to feign attacks against them. The men arrived in formation, singing for a while, to present their gifts. A square of people arrived at the place, guided by two persons. On arrival they stood still and the two guides called the names of the ancestors. Some dancers attacked the square and the people opened the square and inside there was another square made up of women dancers. The women dancers had blackened faces, and were decorated with flowers; they held dance tassels in their hands. The women did not move but only moved the dance tassels, and a woman in the middle began a deep sound which rose higher and higher. Then there was silence. The first line danced to the stamping feet of the second line, and vice versa. The women then performed several sequences, each followed by a pause. A second dance group, surrounded by accompanying persons arrived. These were men dancers who sat on the ground, each striking a "drum". The dance was accompanied by drumming and singing. (MacFarlane cit. in Sarasin 1929:225).

There are some astonishing details in MacFarlane's description, such as the way in which the dance group made its entrance on to the dance-ground. Unfortunately there are no details given about either the drum or the sitting dance. A sitting men's dance from Lifou is not mentioned in any other text and informants had never heard of such a dance.

La Hautière also describes a dance from the Loyalty Islands, very probably Lifou, which is not performed any more and about which no information is available from informants on the Loyalty Islands. "In one of the most frequently performed figures young people, painted black and decorated with tawdry finery, come forward in tight formation; then their lines suddenly open revealing the sight of young girls, chosen among the most beautiful, wearing white egret plumes and dancing a sort of ballet while unwinding garlands of

❶ It is quite possible that the action songs and, perhaps, the fighting songs that Hadfield mentions were to accompany dancing.

❷ "Comme celle de tous les primitifs, elle est la mimique de la sensation : Sur un rythme lent et cadencé, les bras ballants, les pieds fixés au sol. La danseuse n'a qu'un mouvement les hanches qui ondulent et roulent sur elles-mêmes, avec une flexibilité extrême, et, par moments, quelques soubresauts des reins souples et puissants. Puis, le rythme et la danse s'accélèrent, s'arrêtent net, et la femme, avec un rire bestial et une sorte de confusion de sa personne, s'enfuit et disparaît parmi ses compagnes. La luxure animale a de ces explosions brutales et de ces hontes d'instinct."

greenery"❶ (La Hautière 1869/1980:240ff). Although there seems to be some similarity with MacFarlane's description it is impossible to say if the two saw performances of the same dance.

Today on Lifou each *chefferie* has a special dance repertoire of venerated traditional dances. Among the most revered dances can be counted the *fehoa, bua* and *drui*. The *fehoa* dances can be performed by groups from all three *chefferies*. The *drui* dance is keenly guarded by the people of Gaïca whereas the *bua* dance is in the possession of the *chefferie* Boula of Losi. A particular situation exists in the Wetr district. Traditional dances have not been transmitted but the 'Wetr Cultural Association' (Association Culturelle de Wetr) has very recently begun to create dances and to perform them with much appreciation from audiences.

There is no class of purely women's dances, as exists on Ouvéa (*wahaihai/waiai*) or on Maré (*wayai*). Although the noun *waiai* exists in Drehu and is translated in Tryon (1967/1971:124) as "a dance (ritual)", the term was not recognised by any informants and it cannot be said to be a women's dance. In the revered dances women participate in the choir of the *fehoa* dances and they may today dance in special parts of the *drui* dance. Before the performance of a revered dance such as *bua, drui* or *fehoa,* the people on Lifou sing a special kind of song called *uke hajin.*

THE *UKE HAJIN* SONGS

The difference between the songs *uke hajin* and *wejein* (see p. 237) is not very clear. *Uke hajin* texts may be sung to *wejein* melodies and there are many similarities in structure and music within these two song classes. However, older people and those cognisant of Drehu culture make a distinction between the two.

The main difference lies in the textual content. *Uke* as the first part of the term *uke hajin*, is a prefix meaning 'a collection of something', for example, *ukemac* is 'a matchbox'. *Hajin* means 'reminding, giving good advice or to correct somebody'. *Uke hajin* can therefore be translated as 'a number of good counsels'. The textual content of the *uke hajin* has an advisory meaning although the advice is sometimes hard to understand outside the immediate context. Many of the *uke hajin*'s texts are reminiscent of proverbs.

Before one of the traditional dances is performed, one or several *uke hajin* are sung, either the dancers walk onto the dance-ground, *hnë fia*, singing an *uke hajin* or they are already in position on the dance-ground. In a break in the dance performance or at the end of the dance, when it is time to leave the dance-ground, a *uke hajin* may again be sung. *Uke hajin* are very short songs and the text of the *uke hajin* is not related to the dance. The *Chef* Wahnyamalla from the *tribu* of Kedeigne says, that in times of tribal warfare, the *uke hajin* were sung individually by the warriors before going off to war, in order to calm down and concentrate for their efforts in war. A *uke hajin* can also be sung as a lullaby and in this function its 'good advice' is transmitted to the child.

❶ "Dans l'une des figures le plus souvent reproduites, des jeunes gens, peints en noir, ornés d'oripeaux, s'avancent en lignes serrées, compactes; puis leurs rangs, s'ouvrent subitement, laissant apercevoir des jeunes filles, choisies parmi les plus belles, ornées d'une aigrette blanche, qui exécutent une sorte de ballet, en déroulant des guirlandes de verdure".

Some examples of texts of *uke bajin* :

Kölö eneila hi,	**I think now**
eneila hi kölö	**I think now**
ngo tha	**and never**
loi ngo tha	**certainly never**
ngo tha elanyi, elanyi macak	**never tomorrow**

The following lyrics can also be sung as *wejein*

hnimi modeti pi hë ni,	**I think of you my love**
pi hë ni, lo e hna	**for ever and ever**
e hnafego,	**You are I do not know where**
ne hnagejë	**on the sea**

kölö itre mama,	**I think of you my older brothers**
itre mama koloi nyiné	**older brothers, what does it serve,**
lo nyiné,	**what does it serve,**
nyiné ouela,	**what does this serve**
ouela uke jia	**the cudgel**

(For the direct French translation see p. 264.)

The *uke bajin* are heterophonic and responsorial. The first singer begins with a short solo, then a second singer sings in solo before the choir enters. The following solos of the first singer are covered with a bourdon by the choir. The heterophony shows typical Loyalty Island features that may have been derived from a particular interpretation of the polyphony introduced by the missionaries. The number of voices for the *uke bajin* is not determined. Most frequently the main melody (first singer) is followed in parallels generally fifiths and fourths, either throughout the song or only in parts. At places where the parallel movement is abandoned a bourdon is intoned.

Uke hajin song (see Ammann 1997:track14[CD]).

The *bua* dance

The *bua* dance of the Losi district belongs to the *Grand Chef* Boula. All the *tribus* of the *chefferie,* both those on the coast and those from the interior, have the right to perform this dance. Also the *tribu* of Wedrumel which belongs to the Zehoula *chefferie* (Gaïca) has the right to perform the *bua,* because there are kinship ties between the population of this *tribu* and the population of the Boula *chefferie.* However, today the *bua* dance is almost always performed by the Kedeigne *tribu* from the interior of the district of Losi. The *chef* of this *tribu,* Wahnyamalla, is also the person who is responsible for the dance. The *bua* is a war dance, in which young men and boys are taught how to fight and it is exclusively a man's dance.

There is a description of a Lifou dance from the late 19th century by Rivière (1881:85-86). It does not give all the information required to confirm its identity as the *bua* dance, but it does seem to be formally close to the *bua* dance as it is performed today.

"In the light of the flames which they sometimes pass through, Canaques dressed for war, painted black here and there on both the face and body, axe or spear in the hand, shell at the knee and a feather on the head, hold a sham fight. With repeated hoarse growls they stamp the ground where they stand, waving their spears, brandishing their axes, gnashing their teeth and grimacing. They separate into two enemy camps. Each group turns in a circle for a long time giving out increasingly guttural cries reminiscent of tigers, stamping faster and faster, more furiously. In the end they meet and rush, screaming, at each other, striking in front of them with the axes and stopping only at the precise moment when someone would be struck. The whole of the savages' way of fighting is here. Patience and cunning are rendered more acute by the movement of the nervous fluid and excitement increases until courage sure of its aim is generated"❶.

The *bua* dance has some very special features which make it unique in the Loyalty Islands : it is a round-dance and, if Rivière saw the *bua* dance, it was already a round-dance in the 19th century although other details might have changed since, and the music is provided by two singers. Lenormand and Sam (1993:22) describe the movement of the *bua* dancers : "They draw up in two columns while two among them sing. This dance is called the *bua*"❷.

Legend of the origin of the *bua* dance

Chef Wahnyamalla of the Kedeigne *tribu* recounted this legend about the origin of the *bua* dance. The place in the legend is in the area of his *tribu*.

Two *sine lapa* (a special kind of servant of the *chef*) of the *chefferie* of Kedeigne, went to fetch wood for the *chef* in the forest behind the *hmelöm*❸ at Pim, a place within the *tribu*. One of the two *sine lapa* accidently struck a tree trunk when passing by. The sound of this wood was so special, that it sent a shiver through the *sine lapa*. He demonstrated this sound to the other *sine lapa* and he too began to shake throughout his body. The two *sine lapa* decided to bring the wood to the people of the *tribu* and let them listen to the sound. When the people of the *tribu* heard it they began to dance around the wood and after a while they began to dance daily❹.

Description of a performance of the *bua* dance

At the time when today's older informants were young men the *bua* dance was performed at every feast or celebration. The dance was observed several times and films of the dance were used to help transcribe and analyse it. It was always performed by people from the Kedeigne *tribu*.

The *bua* is a war dance and the dancers appear as ancient warriors. They have their upper bodies blackened and carry clubs as weapons. However they wear costumes that were not worn during warfare. There is no particular costume associated with the dance and the kind of outfit worn is decided by the dance leader. For example in 1995 at the 'Iahnithekeun' dance festival, dancers' bodies were painted black with white spots.

The basic form of the dance is a circle. A group of musicians stands in the

❶ "A la lueur des flammes qu'ils traversent parfois, les Canaques, en tenue de guerre, peints en noir ça et là sur le visage et sur le corps, la hache ou la sagaie à la main, le coquillage au genou, et une plume sur la tête, font le simulacre d'un combat. Avec des grognements rauques et répétés, ils piétinent sur place, agitant leur sagaie, brandissant leur hache, grinçant les dents, grimaçant des traits. Ils se séparent en deux bandes ennemies. Chaque bande tourne longtemps en cercle avec des rauquements plus gutturaux, des piétinements plus précipités, plus furieux. Enfin elles se retrouvent en présence et s'élancent avec un cri l'une sur l'autre, frappant devant elles de la hache et ne l'arrêtant qu'à la limite précise où le coup va porter. Toute la façon de combattre des sauvages est là. La patience et la ruse s'exaspèrent par la fluide nerveux en mouvement et s'exaltent jusqu'au courage sûr de son coup."

❷ "Ils se mettent an deux colonnes, tandis que deux d'entre eux chantent, cette danse s'appelle le *bua.*"

❸ *Hmelöm* is the house where the young men lived and were educated in the traditional life style of Lifou.

❹ The legend of the *bua* dance is told in Whaap/Ravel (1994b[film]).

(David Becker/A.D.C.K.1995, Lifou)

Dancers from Kedeigne (Lifou) are divided into two groups, each representing a war-party. The two groups walk or dance on a line against each other on the periphery of a circle.

centre of the circle and the dancers progress around the periphery. The group of musicians usually consists of two singers who simultaneously strike a hollow piece of wood or, frequently, a wooden box. There may be a third man standing close by to replace a tired singer. The dancers form two groups, each of from 4 to 10 people, the number of dancers not being fixed. In each of the two groups the dancers are positioned one behind the other, forming a line with a principal dancer at the front. Each group represents a war party with the front dancer as its war chief.

The two lines walk or dance against each other on the periphery of the circle, beginning behind the musicians, from the audience's view point. The two front dancers carry out the motions more energetically than the other dancers. These two dancers are used as models for the rest of the troupe.

The first time the two groups meet (in front of the musicians) they just walk by each other. When they meet for the second time, the front dancers stop at a distance of 2 - 3 metres from each other. An acoustic signal is given by a musician in the centre and all the dancers begin to stamp their feet heavily on the ground, becoming faster and faster. When there is a large number of dancers the audience actually feels the ground shaking. A second signal is given and the subject motions begin.

The two principal dancers shout the name of the subject motif that is about to be performed by all the dancers. The names are divided into three morphemes or a group of morphemes each separated by a little break. The word gives the sign for a specific dance motion.

In actions such as attacking or defending the two front dancers perform against each other although without any harm being done. The other dancers perform against a invisible enemy. For example in the attack, one of the two front dancers jumps up in the air, bending one knee and holding the club as

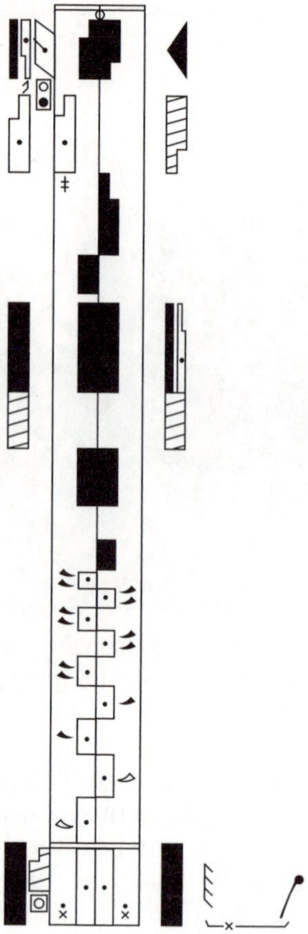

Section *isi* of the *bua* dance. This notation shows the movements of the attacker.

high as possible. On coming down he strikes out against his adversary, who at that moment is on his knees, protecting himself with his club.

After this action there is silence for a moment while the dancers kneel down and there is a short break in the music. It is the music that restarts the dance. The dancers get up and the front men change places. Now the section is repeated from the moment of stamping with the feet. Not all the sections are danced at any given performance. The dance leader decides the number and order of the sections.

Each dance performance begins with the section called *wëtresij hne iaï* which is the name of the morning star (the planet Venus that appears early in the morning). At first sight this seems to be unconnected with war. But in tribal war, this was the time for attacking the enemy. When most people are still asleep and a few come out of the houses to urinate, warriors hidden around the settlement start the attack. In this dance section the dancers look towards the rising morning star.

The following sequence imitates an attacker sneaking into the enemy's *hmelön*. The dancer/warrior stands over the sleeping enemy, shouts some words at him so that he wakes up and then drives a spear into the enemy's chest. The words that are shouted when carrying out this dance action can be translated as 'here, this one is in honour of you', where 'you' is refering to the attacker's own *grand chef*.

The third section is called *isi*, meaning war and here the actual fight is mimed. The enemies in the *hmelön* who are not killed, defend themselves and it is in this sequence that the techniques of attack and defence are imitated.

A final section is called *aköni atë*,

meaning 'laying down (something) three times'. The dancers jump slightly in the air three times, holding their arms up and lowering them slowly on landing. This movement can be interpreted as putting straw on the roof during the building of a *case*. It can also represent the honouring of the *grand chef* which could refer to the way in which a *grand chef* who has waged a war is honoured at its end. Finally, the gesture of the arms can be seen as a Christian sign of benediction. On the Loyalty Islands songs composed in the 20th century concerning local subjects, often have a last strophe added which has a Christian subject and the same idea could be behind this dance section. While it is true that such a section would make the war dance more aceptable to the missionaries it could also be a way for the dancers to indicate that despite all the ancient wars, they are now Christian.

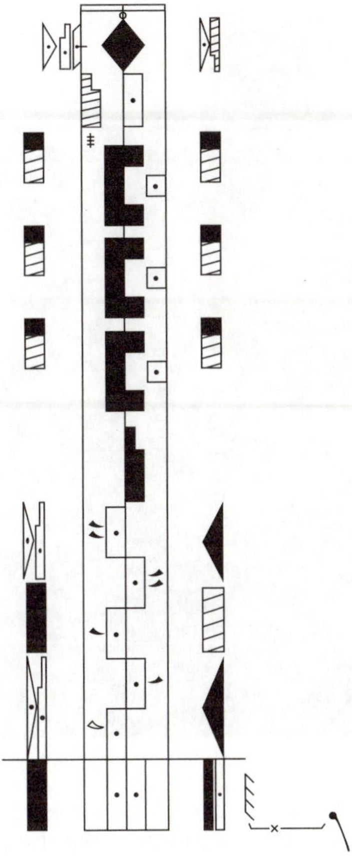

Extract from the *aköni atë* section of the *bua* dance.

Music of the *bua* dance

The music made by the two singer/musicians who accompany this dance is very specific and most unusual for the Loyalty Islands. Several musicians are able to perform the singing part of the dance, but mostly it is sung by the same two singers.

The musical instrument used for this dance was originally, as described in the legend, a hollow piece of wood. For the 'Iahnithekeun' dance festival at Luecila in 1995 a hollow trunk was used although the group performs most of the time with a wooden percussion box. The percussion box or the hollow tree trunk are set on the ground and the two musicians stand behind the box. Each holds a beater, about 40 cm in length, in one hand to strike the idiophone. The musicians are slightly bent in order to reach the box or the

(David Becker/A.D.C.K.1995, Lifou)

A 'war-party' from the *bua* dance.
For the 'lahnithekeun' dance festival the dancers had their blackened upper body painted with white spots.

trunk. The two men strike the box and sing at the same time, because of their bent position they sing directly onto the percussion instrument so that the volume of the singing is reduced and not very audible (The extract of the *bua* dance music, track 15 on Ammann 1997[CD] was not recorded during a dance but was especially arranged in a traditional Lifou house).

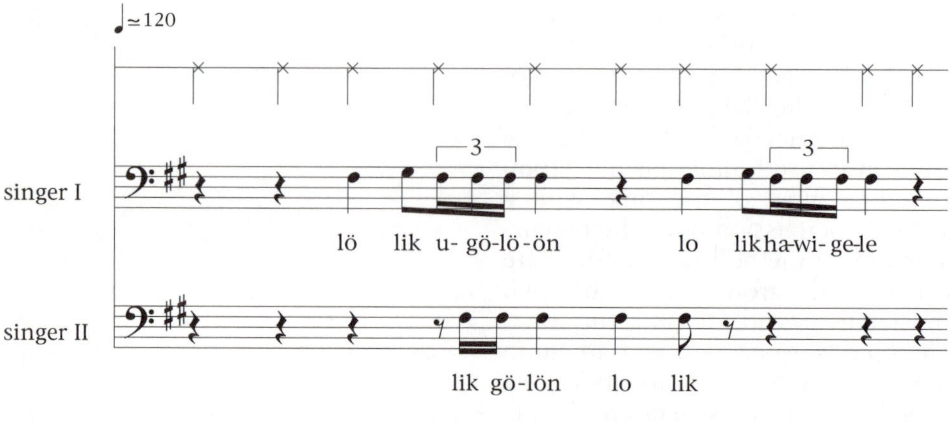

Extract from a fast part of the *bua* dance song.

In the *bua* dance the musicians sing and at the same time strike on a section of a hollow tree trunk.

At the beginning of the dance and for each new section an introductory part is played by the idiophone only. At first the percussion plays with about 120 pulsations per minute, then accelerates towards the middle of the singing while at the same time the stroke frequency is doubled so that it is playing with 300 pulsations per minute.

The song which accompanies the dance is of interest mainly because of its textual content. The words of the text are no longer understood, and some informants have said that they are ancient words. However, it seems that the text of the song is unimportant or, at least, no longer important, for the singers may change the syllables of the song if they want to do so.

The singers use word combinations that work well with the melody and the intonation. They say that when they were young men, other syllables were used for the song. In the field it was observed that when, during a performance of the dance, one singer was replaced by another, the new singer recited new syllables. The singer who was not replaced then simply changed and recited the same syllables as the new singer, although slight differences in pronunciation might occur.

The *bua* dance has its own characteristics but also shows some formal similarities to the *fehoa* dance, while its music shows similarities with the *Grande Terre* rather than with other Loyalty Island dances. These similarities are for example the percussion rhythm which is close to the *rythme du pilou* and the accompanying song is performed by two men, as are the *ae-ae* songs, instead of the usual Loyalty Island mixed choir.

The *drui* dance

The people of the Zeoula *chefferie* (Gaïca district) know various dances but the most typical and the one with which they most closely identify themselves is the *drui* dance. For the people of Drueulu the word *drui* refers not only to one single dance but to several dances which can be performed together.

The *drui* dance is the property of the Nyikeine family. A late member of the family had a sister called Qalune (born around 1900). She married a man of the Bolo family on Ouvéa. When Qalune's younger brother, Simane, married on Lifou, the Bolo family (which has its origins on Wallis Island) 'gave' the bases of the *drui* dance as a customary wedding present (*tro*). Simane passed on the responsibility for the dance to his son (born around 1930) and he passed it on to his son Roland. The Nyikeine family have kept the basic form of the dance as it was given to them, but they have added several new sections including a play where a masked figure appears.

In the silent black and white film (Rouel 1931[film]) a short sequence (10 seconds) of the *drui* dance is shown. There is no commentary with the film, but there is no doubt that it is the *drui* dance as performed in Gaïca. The mask resembles the mask used today.

The *drui* is one of the rare Loyalty Island dances which is accompanied not by singing but by a percussion ensemble consisting of stamping-tubes and handclapping. The dance consists of several parts, each one treating a different subject. Part A consists of a particular introductory section, where two dancers 'search' the dance. Part B and C are performed with synchronised motions and are divided into several sections, representing scenes of warfare and house construction. Finally in part D, the masked figure appears. A performance does not necessarily present all the parts or sections.

Appearance of the dancers

If they dance for an important event, the dancers wear screw pine (*Pandanus*) skirts, garlands around their necks and green liana crowns and have their upper bodies blackened. In each hand they carry a dance tassel. They march onto the dance-ground with spears in their hands and get into a square formation with a distance of 1,5 m between dancers. In the first part, the dancers are kneeling in a square and two dancers walk in a dance-like manner around the group, thus showing that they are 'searching for the dance'.

The first few sections of part B include the use of the spears. After these sections the spears are collected up and for the rest of the dance only the dance tassels are held in their hands. The dancers carry metal whistles in their mouths and let out improvised rhythmic patterns during the performance. Neither in the film of 1931 nor on old photographs do the dancers have metal whistles, so they may have been added to the dance only a few decades ago. However, at the performance on Lifou in 1995 ('Iahnithekeun') the dancers did not use metal whistles but were hissing and whistling with the mouth. Another difference between the old pictures and today is that the masked dancer does not wear European clothes any more.

Unlike the situation shown in the old photographs and films, women dance with the men in some presentations❶. One member of the Nyikeine family

❶ At performances where women dance together with men, the sections directly related to war are not performed.

(David Becker/A.D.C.K.1995, Lifou)

At the beginning of the *drui* dance two dancers walk in a dance-like manner around the other dancers who wait in a kneeling position.

teaches the basic *drui* dance every Wednesday afternoon to children of both sexes. The occasions to present the *drui* dance are few and regular repetion helps the children to memorise the dance.

The music ensemble stands apart from the dancers. It consists of bamboo stamping-tubes which are imported from the *Grande Terre*. The *drui* dance is accompanied by the *rythme du pilou* which suggests that the dance was created under influence from the *Grande Terre* or that the dance's roots lie on the *Grande Terre*.

(David Becker/A.D.C.K.1995, Lifou)

The *drui* dance performed by the Dancers from Drueulu at the 'Iahnithekeun' dance festival on Lifou in 1995.

Description of a presentation

The following description is based on the way the dance was performed in 1992 at the 'rencontre préparatoire' at Nouville (Nouméa) because this seems to be the most complete of all the observed presentations. As explained above other presentations may differ by leaving out some sections or even parts. Once the two dancers who 'search the dance' have finished their tour around the dance group, the two join the other dancers in the formation and part B begins.

B - war :
1. training with the spear, *koiê, kolopi* (east - west) The dancers advance in each direction with a few steps.

C - construction of a house : 1. *a caa jumé la pulu* (swing the dance tassel once); 2. *Jidro* (pick); 3. *Sa Pel* (shovel); 4. *Buruet* (wheelbarrow) 5. *Hané jez* (placing the straw); 6. *kiré jez* (distributing the straw); 7. *Cili,* (the huge wooden needle that is used to bind the straw to the wooden construction); 8. *wege hne lïma* (walking backwards, once the house is built to criticise the work); 9; *thilë* (The flying fox turns around above the house.) The name of this sequence derives from a proverb saying a flying fox circling above a house means that the house is completed.

D - Finale : 1. *memaligi* (introduction); 2. *até* (to place); 3. *jugé keu* (the dancer are facing each other).

Like the dances with synchronised motions of the *Grande Terre* each mimed section of the *drui* dance consists of neutral motifs (N.M.) and subject motifs (S.M.). For the neutral motif (N.M.) the dancers are upright while the arms are hanging and swing back and forth with each step.

The dancer has his left leg in front as in an ordinary step. The steps are carried out on the spot and the feet stamp alternately on the ground to each rhythmic pattern. The first beat of the rhythm pattern is so short, that the pad of the toe only slightly touches the ground before the foot is set down more strongly❶.

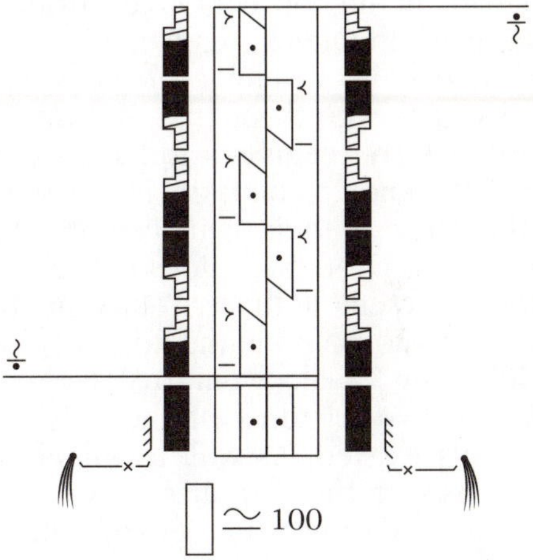

Neutral motif of the *drui* dance

The play with the mask

In the last part the dancers, still in a square formation, stand without moving. Three dancers are standing in front of the group. A masked figure appears and walks around the dancers, presenting himself to the audience. The masked figure touches the first man of a line and all the dancers in this line fall to the ground feigning death. The masked figure continues to touch the front dancers of each line, one after the other, until all the dancers are lying on the ground. The three dancers standing in front of the group represent the owner of the dance and two particular *chefs* in the customary system (*Keme i angajoxu* and *Keme i Gaïca*) whose subjects have been attacked. They turn their heads round and see the masked figure which represents evil, one of its names being *satana*. They hit the mask and make demands (mostly in French) to force it to bring the dancers, their subjects, back to life. The masked figure touches the front dancer of each row and the whole line behind the front dancer stands up again.

This scene can be interpreted in several ways. Most obviously the story refers to the power of the Gaïca *chefs* and their sovereignty over their subjects. The masked figure represents a stranger who came to poison the subjects and the two dancers represent *chefs* who were alert and could save their subjects' lives.

❶ In the *rythme du pilou* used for the *drui* dance the weaker of the two pattern beats is very short and can be notated as a 'grace note'.

Secondly, the scene refers to the arrival of Christianity, as mentioned in E. Kasarherou (1993:60). It may show that 'evil' represented by the masked figure followed the Samoans of the L.M.S. who arrived on Lifou (at Mu and came to Gaïca) in the 1840s. It is a way of saying that 'evil' (or a *haze*) can be hidden behind 'good' (Christianity)❶ and 'new' (E. Kasarherou 1993:61). On one of the old black and white pictures with *drui* dance scenes, the masked figure wears European clothes and it may well be that at this time the masked figure represented a European.

However the name of the mask is *momoa* (E. Kasarherou writes : *ihmoh-moa*). *Momoa* (Hollyman 1987:176) is the name for mask in the Fagauvea language in the north of Ouvéa, from where the dance came to Lifou, yet there is no mask in Ouvéa's dance.

There is no resemblance between the mask of the *drui* dance and the masks of the north of the *Grande Terre*. A direct link to the masks of the *Grande Terre* seems not to have existed although the people on Lifou might well have known about the masks of the *Grande Terre* and added a mask part to the dance of their own accord❷. This is very hypothetical, especially as the form of the Lifou mask does not resemble that of the *Grande Terre* but seems rather to resemble those from Vanuatu. E. Kasarherou (1993:62) points to the masks of Vao Island in the north of Malakula as a possible influence. Since the 1950s many Kanaks went to Malakula to teach at the Protestant mission there. Still the first pictures of the mask are from 1930, before the mission on Malakula existed. As well as this the *drui*-family, although Catholic, has no relations with the Catholics on Vao.

There are similarities between the *drui* dance and the dances with synchronised motions from the centre or north of the *Grande Terre*. These similarities are in the rhythm that accompanies the dance, in the formation of the dancers and in the dance motions. Although it is stated (Guiart 1953c:96) that there were migrations from Canala and Houaïlou to Ouvéa, from where the original dance came to Lifou, it is impossible to tell which parts were added or what was changed in the dance on Ouvéa or Lifou. Equally, it is impossible to find out who would have been the receiver and who the giver in such an exchange. During the study, no dance with this name has been found either at Canala or at any other place on the *Grande Terre*. It is also quite possible that the dance was created on the Loyalty Islands under strong influence from the *Grande Terre*. There are many unsolved questions about the nature and origin of the Lifou mask including the origin of the *drui* dance itself.

THE *FEHOA* DANCES

The *fehoa* dances are known on all the Loyalty Islands, on Maré pronounced *pehua* and on Ouvéa *fehuô*. The choreographies of the Lifou and the Maré *fehoa* and *pehua* respectively differ slightly. The Loyalty Islanders say that the *fehoa* dance was diffused from Lifou to Maré and to Ouvéa.

❶ Now as the owner family of the *drui* dance are Catholics the mask could represent Protestantism.

❷ Masks influenced from the *Grande Terre* existed on Maré. Dubois (1978:656) mentions the mask *kae-namaco, kae baru, baru-baru* which he says is "the Mareen mask is the degenerated final outcome of the mask of the North of the Grande Terre" ("le masque marén est l'aboutissant dégénéré de masque du Nord de la Grande Terre"). The mask is made of banana leaves and played with by children. Children's masks also existed in the region of Houaïlou, where they were made out of bamboo (E. Kasarherou 1993:16).

(David Becker/A.D.C.K.1995, Lifou)

In the *fehoa* dances a few experienced dancers perform slightly to the side of the group. The other dancers can watch them and follow their lead especially if they have any doubts about the choreography.

The origin of the word *fehoa* lies in the Samoan expression *fehoa'i,* meaning 'walking around'. The name seems to refer to the marching directions of the *fehoa* dancer. On Samoa there is actually no dance called *fehoa* (Richard Moyle pers. comm.). Direct or indirect voyages of Samoans to Lifou are confirmed by anthropologists and linguists, and the *fehoa* dance could have been brought by such a migration. Migrants could have used traditional Polynesian canoes or been on board a European vessel, such as a whaler, trader or blackbirder.

On Lifou, *fehoa* are known in all three *chefferies* or districts. In the district of Losi, the *tribus* Hmelek and Naeon have a reputation for performing these dances (comparable with the Kedeigne *tribu*'s reputation for the *bua* dance). In the Gaïca district, about seven *fehoa* are known, all of which date from the arrival of the missionaries according to informants. The dance group from the district of Wetr, has started to create new *fehoa,* along with their recent dance creations.

The *fehoa* dances today are held in great respect by the population of Lifou. The people say the *fehoa* are 'sacred dances' and 'war dances' ; their poetry tells about ancient wars. Lenormand and Sam (1993:31) say "their theme is always warlike"[1] and Hadfield (1920:135) designates the *fehoa* as the "real war dance" of Lifou. Hadfield says that the *fehoa* "... encouraged the men to fight, stirring their blood by suggesting the valiant deeds they would accomplish; and reminding them how they would drink the blood of their enemy, the opposing chief, and enjoy eating his liver". Hadfield also says, in

[1] "leur thème est toujours guerrier".

relation to the participation of women, "...it was their custom, however, to send forth their men to the fight with rousing war songs still ringing in their ears - the song 'Fehoa' being the favourite, because it extolled their great bravery and strength, and told with what pride and joy the men would return bringing with them the bodies of their enemies" (Hadfield 1920: 169).

Benjamin Goubin recites in a rather poetic language the dances he observed as a missionary on Lifou in the 1880s. The occasion was the inauguration of the *case* of the big *Chef* Okénéssés of Wetr, to which people from all over the island were invited.

"That's when the dances begin. Their music consists of making a sound with a packet of banana leaves having the form of a round, 1 kilo, loaf of bread[❶]. They tap it on top with the hand. Others tap on a piece of wood. The musicians sing while tapping. At first they go slowly. Then 4 or 5 dancers come out of the group and get into a line, following the cadence; soon the music quickens the march, the dancers follow the movement, become furious, run after the enemy, beat a retreat, return to the charge and all is finished. What suppleness! It needs to be said that not believing themselves black enough they daubed themselves to the waist. It is always much the same, each time it is done"❷.

The *fehoa* dance was taught to the young men and boys, *nekö-trahmany,* in the *hmelöm*, where they lived separated from the rest of the *tribu*. Here, the *fehoa* were practised every evening (Lenormand/Sam 1993:30) supervised by the elders *qatr.* "During the apprenticeship of the Fehoa at the qenehmelëm [❸] the *qatr* encouraged the boys to make the ground shake with their feet to show their fervour and their strength. These *Fehoa* evoked various war strategies allowing the *qatr* to choose their future warriors"❹ (Ihage 1992:17).

Preparing young men for war by means of the dance was carried out in two ways. The dance motions were the same as those used in war : attack, defence etc. and the words were "designed to excite the fervour and bravery of the future fighters"❺ (Lenormand/Sam 1993:31).

Choreography

A mixed choir is at the heart of the *fehoa*. The singers sit on the ground close together in a circle. The song starts slowly and the dancers emerge out of the choir. They walk in several lines imitating the war stories told in the

❶ Goudin refers here to the leaf parcel. He may be referring to an old form of the instrument; today this instrument is not made of banana leaves.

❷"C'est alors qu'ont commencé les danses. Leur musique consiste à faire du bruit avec un paquet de feuilles de bananier ayant la forme d'un pain rond d'un kilo. Ils frappent là-dessus avec la main. D'autres frappent sur un morceau de bois. Les musiciens chantent en frappant. Ils vont d'abord lentement. C'est alors que 4 - 5 danseurs sortent des rangs, se mettent en ligne, suivent la cadence; bientôt la musique accélère la marche, les danseurs suivent le mouvement, se mettent furieux, courent à l'ennemi, battent en retraite, reviennent à la charge et tout est fini. Quelle souplesse! Il faut bien vous dire que ne se croyant pas assez noirs ils se barbouillent jusqu'à la ceinture. Pour recommencer c'est à peu toujours la même chose" (Goubin 1985:89).

❸ Ihage (1992:15) writes *qenemelön* for *melöm* and *thöth* for *nekö-trahmany.*

❹ "Durant l'aprentissage des 'fehoa' au *qenehmelöm,* les *qatr* incitaient les jeunes à faire trembler le sol, avec leurs pieds pour montrer leur ardeur et leur force. Ces 'fehoa' évoquaient les différentes stratégies guerrières permettaient aux 'qatr' de sélectionner les futurs guerriers".

❺ "destinés à exciter l'ardeur et la bravoure des futurs combattants".

songs. The basic gesture of the dancer consists of the position of the warrior which is the same as on Maré (see p. 181). From this base position the dancer imitates some of the events and ideas contained in the song's text words. The dancer imitates these motions with the upper body but in general does not move his legs. The front dancer of each row dances more freely than the others, occupying little more than the width of the line.

The words of the *feboa*

The words in the *feboa* songs are understood only by insiders. Besides the general stock of words that are not understood by anybody, some words are often modified and they are recited so fast that even someone fluent in Drehu, but unfamiliar with the song, cannot understand the words. The techniques of camouflaging the words of songs so that only people of the group to whom the dance belongs know its content is widespread in the Loyalty dance songs. Lenormand and Sam (1993:32-33) transcribed two texts of *feboas* composed by two warriors. One of the songs is cited below.

Upine une	**entrails of the snake**
Upine une	**entrails of the snake**
Xelene une	**intestines of the snake**
Zöhuni jë la goe tro lue	**Zöhun looks at the two children**
Jö mina ha ciwë e Tama	**the sun is in the west at Tama**
Sasaqe tro ange hmaeë	**quick let's hurry up**
Drulima ha e hnine etë	**Drulima is in the pile of rocks**
Kapa pi hë Zike Ukewetr	**carry the Zike Ukewetr**
A wetrë ukeineqë jë	**he is our meat**
Qalikötre jë Kicima	**kicima wriggles**
Traqa i angetre atresi	**at the arrival of the atresi**
A nyinyapëne hë Ngazoeo	**ngazoeo runs to meet them**
Ea jë la ketre wene peiny	**takes a snake egg**
A thithingë hë la koi Wahel	**my offering to Wahel**
Hlegehlege hnameci	**he has stripped the body**
Hadredreu cia pi kö ni e catr	**bursting my strength has surpassed**
Aeng uthe Lösi	**Aeng the nephew of Lösi**
A nanë hë nyupë e Xumoz	**you guard the passage to Xumoz**
Kötrene ju pë hë	**you will be abandonned**
Kötre wa hë ge ca	**the man with the limp escapes through the bush**
Thaa hë e Huluialo	**Don't shout at Huluialo**
A koho e Huilati	**up there at Huilati**
A hmekë ni ju pë hë	**take care of me**
Wamitu me Sapotr	**Wamitu and Sapotr**
E kohië a Hnamek	**down there at Hnamek**
Ke matre gaa co jon	**because there are fewer spears**
Upine une	**entrails of the snake**
Upine une	**entrails of the snake**
Xelene une	**intestines of the snake**

(For the direct French translation see p. 265.)

The music of the *fehoas*

Lenormand and Sam (1993:31) said of the music of the *fehoa* songs "These epic songs are most often performed in a minor mode and the melodic theme can be resumed in a short musical phrase of a few notes which, repeated incessantly, takes on the character of a real incantation, galvanising the muscles and the heart of the future warriors"[1]. Leaving aside the remark on the minor mode, Sam's account explains the most important element in a *fehoa*'s music : the repetition of a short musical theme. The musical theme of a *fehoa* takes its melodic and rhythmic form from the words which are recited in the chorus part of the song. The words of the text will then be recited in the same rhythm. This means that sometimes words have to be modified in order to fit the rhythm and such modifications are one way of camouflaging textual

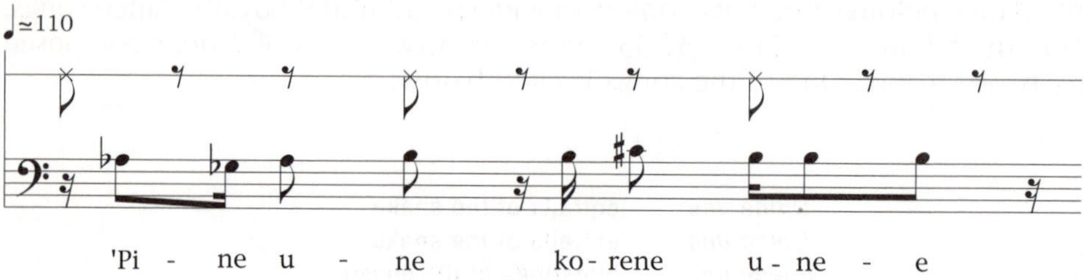

The melodic theme from the *fehoa upine une.*

content.

Halftone intervals in the *fehoa*'s music themes are frequent and the song's character lies more often in the play of the different timbres of vocals, for example, 'a' and 'e', than in the melodic line. In all the examined old Lifou *fehoa,* the range was never wider than a minor third. One tends to refer to the *fehoa* music as a fast 'recitative' (*Sprechgesang*).

Hadfield found some Lifuans who knew the *doh*-notation system and they transcribed a *fehoa* in this system. This *doh*-notation (Hadfield 1920:132) transferred in standard music transcription gives the following melody.

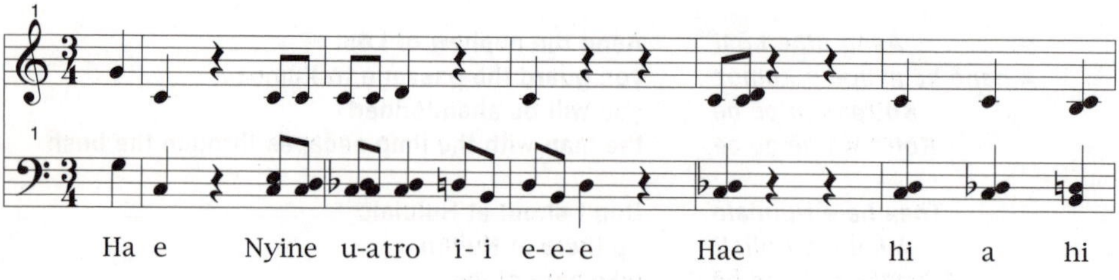

Hadfield (1920:132)

[1] "Ces chants épiques se déroulent le plus souvent sur un mode mineur et le thème mélodique se résume en une courte phrase musicale de quelques notes qui, répétées sans cesse, prennent l'allure d'une véritable incantation magique galvanisant les muscles et le coeur des futurs guerriers".

It seems that Hadfield's informants transferred the *fehoa* song into a polyphonic song that resembles a *doh*. None of the old *fehoa* heard on Lifou had a similar polyphony. And none of the *fehoa* songs that were heard in the field corresponds with the transcription published in Hadfield.

Quite different in function from the *fehoa* songs, which encourage warfare, are the songs called *nyineuatro* which have the function of calming down the warriors. Hadfield describes the "nyine eu a tro" as "... a song of persuasion, intended to calm the warriors and, if possible, persuade them to abandon the idea of war", and as a song of peace sung by women to express their "... pride and joy at the return of the warriors safe and well" Hadfield (1920:134). The dances referred to as *nyineuatro* today show no particular difference in their overall form to that of the *fehoa*.

Modern dance creations of Lifou

Besides the old dances *drui, fehoa* and *bua* there are dances on Lifou which were created and composed only a few decades ago. In general, there are mixed choirs singing in the major - minor tonal system and the dancers, men and women, stand in front of the audience and imitate with arm movements what is said in the dance song. The dancers stay more or less in the same place, perhaps advancing a few steps to retire again, women bending their knees slightly in correspondance with the downbeat of the song. The movements are relatively easy to recognize. For example, if the song words are invitations to dance, the dancer's arms which are held in front are slowly pulled against his breast, indicating 'come to me'. The words of these songs use ordinary language and there is no deliberate hiding of the sense. New dances may have a biblical content or a simple joyful theme such as an invitation to dance, as for example the dance *drengeju* of the Association Clanique Culturelle Ahmelewedr (A.C.C.A.) .

Beginning of the dance song *drengeju*.

Another very famous dance song is the *tutuaho* dance of Drueulu composed in the 1950s by Wasai Nyikeine. The dance presents the story of Saul and his brothers in the Old Testament. *Tutuaho* (*tutu* stands for the conch shell) is the sign of victory. The conch shell sound can be interpreted as a sign of the victory of Christianity over heathenism. This dance is often performed by children.

The creativity of the group from Wetr

In the last few years a dance group from the Wetr district (Wetr Cultural Association) has created several dances and performed them on various occasions in New Caledonia and abroad. The group tries to bring traditional and new elements together in dance performances with a theatrical character. Traditional dancing of the Wetr people was interrupted at the beginning of the 20th century and it was only in 1992, because of an invitation to the 'rencontre préparatoire', that they started to create new dances. There is no traditional choreographical base left on which new dances could be built and new choreography has had to be created[1]. There are however, old legends and songs which have been passed on within this group, and these songs and legends have served as a basis for the dances.

For example, there is a dance that recounts the legend of the two brothers Capenehe and Hlemusese. This version of the legend was kept by the late Wahiope Hmakanyi of the Hnathalo *tribu*[2]. The legend recounts the heroic actions of the two mythical brothers. It makes clear the moral respect and duty that in the traditional Lifou way of life a younger brother must have towards his elder brother. Hlemusese, the older of the two brothers, wanted to win the hand of a mystical woman Hna So Hnei Drë (Wind from the north) who lived as a rock in the waters north of Ouvéa close to the island called Héo (island of Beautemps-Beaupré). Hlemusese and his brother swam to Ouvéa where they met the mystical woman's grandmother. She told them that one needs to be tough to obtain the hand of her granddaughter. The two men, after putting on their magic belts, *uke epa,* and clothes made from fibres of the coconut inflorescence, *fezine zianou*, swam out to the rock. Capenehe, the younger brother, touched the rock first. The duty demanded was that the rock would be held onto until the sun came up, only then would the rock become the beautiful woman Hna So Hnei Drë. In the night a strong storm arose and it was Capenehe the younger of the two who managed to hold onto the rock, the elder was holding on to his brother. Finally the morning came and the rock changed into the mystical woman who now belonged to Capenehe. Following traditional obligations the younger brother then gave the woman to his elder brother, so that Hlemusese could marry her.

This legend is presented in a theatrical dance consisting of several parts (Boussat/Ammann 1993 [film]). The first part is a song performed by all the participants. The words of this song are not related to the theme of the dance but it is a eulogy for the *chefferie* of Wetr.

That the composer of this song was influenced by the musical form of the

[1] Except for one dance that had been given to the people of Gaïca. In 1996 the dancers of Wetr asked for it back in a customary way. The absence of a traditional base has allowed freedom of choreographical creation.
[2] A second version of the same legend was written down by Mangematin (1976).

hna ni Jo xu - i po-o- po le- e e ti ti xe - e - i
ang-e- tre wetr su - e su - e su - e je draje

taperas can be seen from the use of a D-major modus, parallel voices and the change in metre, which are typical elements of the *taperas*.

At some performances, a dancer reads the story that will be represented, so that the audience has no difficulty in following it. The dance is divided into three main parts, in which the story of the two brothers is told. A number of dancers represent bad spirits. They move uncoordinatedly and fast, to represent their difference from real human beings. The two dancers who represent the two heroes of the story carry a spear and their 'magic' belt. The part of Hna - So-Hne-Drë is taken by a woman dancer. She stands in the centre of the dance place with her face covered while the two heroes are trying to hold on to the 'rock'. When the 'rock' becomes a woman the dancer takes off the cover over her face. During the dance the two heroes recount in a dialogue some of their activities. The two songs which are sung during the sections when the bad spirit dancers representing the wild sea, are on scene, are particular. The first song, *uke nyine iahle*, the waking of the spirits, contains only neutral syllables, and is sung very slowly, with long chords moving in seconds.

(David Becker/A.D.C.K.1995, Lifou)

A dancer of the Wetr group during the performance of the legend of Capenehe and Hlemusese.

The second song, *meje i ange tepolo*, the murmur of the spirits, sung to accompany the movements of the bad spirit dancers, follows a quite different system and dynamic. This song, accompanied by the strokes of the *itra pë*, is a very fast recitation of words which are not understood today. The song's intervals are very narrow and include micro-intervals. The song consists of a short musical motif that is repeated indefinitely to express all the words of the text. With every repetition rhythmical modifications occur to enable the pronunciation of the text. A similar kind of musical structure is found in parts of the old *fehoa* songs of Lifou, although *meje i ange tepolo* is not classified as a *fehoa*. The origin of the song goes back to an old woman, Geihaze Wasalu, who learned the song from her grandmother. It was actually her grandfather who received the song in a dream and who taught it to his wife.

Next there is a *fehoa* song which tells in a chronological way, the adventure of the two heroes, Capenehe and Hlemusese. In each dance part, a part of the *fehoa* song is sung and the dancers act the history of the legend at the same time as it is being told in the *fehoa* song.

The old traditional *fehoa* songs of Lifou contain mainly words whose meaning is not understood and which are intoned very fast. These songs are composed of a short musical theme, generally consisting of a narrow range which is repeated during the whole song. This new *fehoa* song, also consists of a short musical motif, but the words are understandable, and the intervals are of the tempered scale. The song, as well as the choreography, was composed in 1992 by Tim Obao and Wata Kameo.

The *fehoa* song of the *caéé* dance is a composition with similar elements. The 'bass' is a mixture of interrupted bourdon and parallel movement. It intones the fundamental of the cord, alternating between b and e with passing notes, a typical *taperas*-bass.

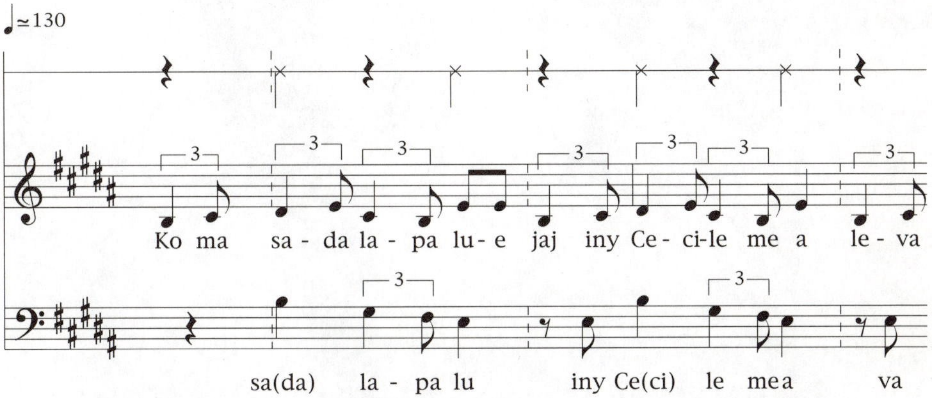

The dances *caéé* and 'Capenehe and Hlemusese', are new Kanak creations in which an ancient legend is presented within a dance in such a way that it can be followed by the whole audience. The story is read before the dance and the words of the *fehoa* are understandable for every Drehu speaker. This concept, surely much appreciated by foreign audiences (the dances have been performed in Australia and Vanuatu), is in contrast to the way in which the old dances' meaning was hidden.

(David Becker/A.D.C.K.1995, Lifou)

Dancers of the Wetr group performing a dance that they have newly created.

The *wejein* songs

On Lifou young people sing a particular class of songs called *wejein*. The word *wejein* is translated as 'to intone a song, to give the pitch' ('*entoner un chant, donner le ton*' [Sam 1995:18]). The word is made up of two words '*wej-*' and '*-in*'. The first part '*wej-*' means 'to follow' or 'to chase'. The second part '*-in*' means the non-edible part of a plant, for example the roots of the sugar cane. If '*wej-*' is translated as 'to follow' *wejein* means something like 'to follow the roots'. It can also mean 'to go or to follow into the garden' and it is there where the *wejein* are performed by the young men and women. The people of Lifou refer to the *wejein* in French as *les chants de la route* ('songs of the road or wayside'). Translating '*wej-*' as 'to chase', gives *wejein* the meaning of 'to chase the roots', roots in this sense standing for tradition.

The *wejein* are songs of young people and their poetry is described by older people as romantic or trivial, which demonstrates the separation of the *wejein* from both traditional dance songs and Christian songs, such as the *taperas*. *Wejein* are also performed during festivities by younger people to amuse themselves.

A huge number of poems, called *trenge ewekë* or only *ewekë*, exist for the *wejein* and new text can be created spontaneously. Subjects include historical events, romanticism, love, or the sorrow of the composer.

Ka jë hë pikok, ke ma, ke matré trona	**Where are you pikok❶ so that I can look for**
ngénu thel, e ciejë é Nouméa, the, thei mama, ketré loi.	**a job in Nouméa, with people, who are well off.**

(For the direct French translation see p. 268.)

Today the word 'melody' is usually used to refer to the music or melody of the song. However, the Drehu word *nin* refers to the melody of a song (Sam 1995:125). There is only a small number of *nin* for the *wejein*. To create a new *wejein* the words need to be set so that they can be sung to the *nin*. The *wejein* are heterophonic and responsorial. The first singer starts a *wejein* in solo and the choir enters a little later. The choir is composed of several parts depending on the number of the singers and improvisation is allowed in the accompanying voices, as is done in the *taperas*. A *wejein* consists of a musical theme that can be repeated indefinitely to present the *trenge ewekë*. At the end of a theme a long note is sung. The principal voice begins, the next theme on this note or holds on to it thus letting the other singers know that the end of the song has been reached.

The music of the *wejein* is influenced by the *taperas*. A singer is free to choose his part and to add improvisations, intervals are of the tempered scale although not always perfectly intoned. On the other hand the text words of the *wejein* run counter to Christian texts. This suggests that the *wejein* are sung as a youthful reaction to Christian behaviour making fun of it, which the *wejein* may have in common with the *waueng* of Maré.

❶ *pikok* - from the French term 'picoler' : to tipple.

The *wejein nomeredi.*
The melodies of the *wejein* are short.
They can be repeated several times during a performance.

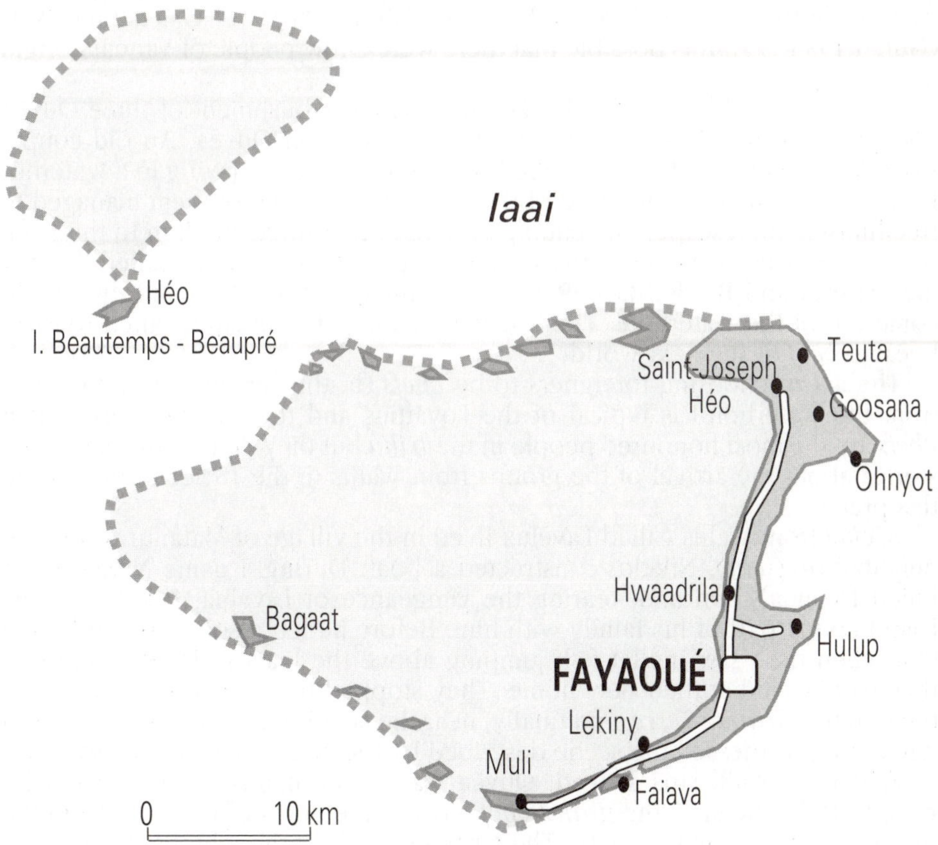

The island of Ouvéa

Ouvéa is the only island of the Loyalties where the population is divided into two language groups due to an immigration from Wallis in the 18th century. The Iaai language is spoken in the central part of the long island and Fagauvea in the two wider extremities. The present name for the island, Ouvéa, is the Fagauvea❶ name. The people in the centre call their island Iaai and Fagauvea speakers call the central part of the island Ate❷.

Ouvéa is divided into three *chefferies, taboony* in Iaai and *aliki* in Fagauvea. In the north of the island the *grand chef* is the *aliki* Bazit and the main village is St. Paul, in the centre is the *taboony* Ouenagay at Fayahoue and in the south the *aliki* Doumai at Mouli. Each *chefferie* corresponds to an administrative district.

❶ Fagauvea has retained its Polynesian morphology and syntax but has borrowed considerably from Melanesian languages (Howe 1977:9).

❷ Informants say that Cané is mistaken in saying that *ate* is the old name for the whole island (Cané 1948:15).

HISTORICAL EVENTS IN RELATION TO DANCE AND MUSIC

Until the middle of the 18th century Ouvéa was populated by people who came from the *Grande Terre* and the two Lifou districts of Gaïcha and Wetr (Guiart 1953c:95). It is possible that there were a few people of Vanuata origin too.

A legend cited by Laville (1949) tells of the establishment of three Ouvéa *chefferies.* In the old days only one *tribu* existed on Ouvéa. An old couple from this *tribu* found four boys aged between 12 and 16 playing in a waterhole. The old woman caught hold of the boys' hair but one of them managed to free himself and escape. The couple took the other three children to the *tribu* where they were welcomed and became *chefs.* The boys were called Wanyome, Wassau and Basile. Basile❶ was the youngest of the boys and the first to come out of the waterhole. The boy who managed to escape, called Nyioxu, became *chef* of the next world.

The act of choosing foreigners to be *chefs* (in this legend it was the boys from the waterhole) is typical of the Loyalties and the *Grande Terre.* Such *chefs* are the most honoured people in the *tribu* but they do not own land. The stories about the arrival of the groups from Wallis in the 18th century confirm this practice.

A *chef* from Wallis called Lavelua lived in the village of Matautu where the neighbouring *chef,* Nikelo, constructed a boat. During a game Nikelo's son killed Lavelua's son and, fearing the vengeance of Lavelua, Nikelo left the island taking part of his family with him. Before he left a soothsayer told him that when they saw mullet fish jumping above the leaves of the mangroves they had arrived at their new home. They stopped first at Futuna in Vanuatu, then on the *Grande Terre,* and finally, near the small island of Unies by Ouvéa where they witnessed the scene described by the soothsayer (Cané 1948:15).

When the Wallisians arrived, Ouvéa was in the hands of two *chefs* who were terrible enemies, the *grand chef* Bazit in the north of the island and the *grand chef* Taume in the south. The *Grand Chef* Bazit thought that the newcomers were good warriors and offered them land and women if they would fight on his side.

Of the newcomers, Beka and Nikelo, joined *Grand Chef* Bazit and settled in the north of the island while Dumai, and the Tongan, Pumali, (who came with the Wallisians) settled in the south of the island under the authority of *Grand Chef* Taume. The south of the island was given, after the death of Taume, to the Wallisian Dumai and his friend the Tongan Pumali. This is the story as told in Cané (1948).

After the arrival of the Polynesians on Ouvéa a group of warriors from Koné landed on Ouvéa and began a war against the south of the island. The warriors from Koné were beaten and their *chef,* Ouenegay, created a new *chefferie* (Guiart 1953c:95).

This myth appears to simplify the origin of the present-day people on Ouvéa. In fact, according to Guiart (1953c), there were several west Polynesian migrations, not just one. People from Samoa arrived on Ouvéa and some of them continued their voyage as far as Houaïlou on the *Grande Terre.* Migrations from the *Grande Terre* (Houaïlou, Canala, Hienghène among others) and

❶ The names Wanyome and Wassau occur on Ouvéa at the present day, the name Basile is unknown today on the island.

from other Loyalty Islands also came to Ouvéa to make up the present population. People from Ouvéa also settled on the *Grande Terre*, notably at Hienghène. Besides the migrations, commercial relations also existed between Ouvéa and the *Grande Terre*.

With the arrival of the L.M.S. missionaries and the Marist missionaries from the 1860s, tribal wars, far from dying down, became ever fiercer. The Catholics of the north and south were at war with the Protestants in the centre.

For the purposes of the present work it is not necessary to give details of all the battles and fights which the Ouvéans fought in the name of a church. This part of Ouvéa's history shows that Melanesians and Polynesians met on this small island. While Ouvéa is not the only Loyalty Island to have been subject to Polynesian influences, it is the one with a language defined as Polynesian by linguists (Hollyman 1966). This raises the question as to whether or not there are differences in the music and dance between the two groups.

The dance and music repertoires of Ouvéa

Ouvéa is the least ethnographically researched island in the Loyalties and there is no early ethnographical literature from which an idea of original traditional music and dance can be found. Thus the account given in this chapter concerns exclusively interviews with present-day informants and field observations made during the last five years.

Neither Fagauvea nor Iaai contain a word for 'music' which corresponds to the European word. In Iaai the term *walak* means 'to make music' ('faire de la musique') ; it also means 'to play' in a theatrical sense and in the sense of children's games. When referring to singing in Iaai the word *xumwong* is used. This word also refers to a voice, particularly in a polyphonic song as will be explained below. Words for 'dance' exist in both Ouvéan languages : *bia* in Iaai refers to a particular dance and in Fagauvea *pia* means 'dancing' in general. The Fagauvean word *mako* means 'to sing' or 'song'[1] although on Futuna (the island neighbouring Wallis Island) *mako* means today 'to dance' and on Wallis Island *me'e* means 'to dance'. This word is not found in Fagauvea despite the language's origin on Wallis Island.

Besides these generic terms for songs and dances several Ouvéan dances have individual names : *dru, fehuâ, seleweilewei, ofefetu* and others. Each of these dances is unique and is performed by only one group of dancers. On the other hand there are a number of womens' dances all designated by the term *wahaihai* in Iaai or *waiai* in Fagauvea. The Fagauvea term *kawische,* used on Ouvéa for the *rythme du pilou* is also used for the round-dance of the *Grande Terre.* The term *pia taua,* translated as a 'war dance' (Hollyman 1987:216), does not refer to a particular dance but to a class of dances. However people do not class their traditional dances as war dances. The *bibia* dance, translated by Ozanne-Rivierre (1984:33) as 'pilou' does not refer to a particular dance either, but rather to informal dances with singing, dancing and jumping. Thus on such occasions when people are at ease, for example during a party or while waiting for a boat or during a cricket match, women clap their hands, sing a few lines and above all, laugh and joke together. This is rerred to by the term *bibia*. Guiart (1952:33) refers to three dances *dru, fehuâ* and *wahaihai*

[1] In the protopolynesian language *mako* means 'dance' (Hollyman 1987:163).

saying "There are neither songs nor dances originating in Wallis"❶ and the fact that there is no Wallisian word for the verb 'to dance' reinforces this assertion. A comparison of the dance and music repertoires of the Fagauvea and the Iaai speakers will be attempted in the following account.

THE *WAHAIHAI* DANCES

Although there is a slight difference in the spelling and pronunciation of the words *wahaihai* in Iaai and *waiai* in Fagauvea, there is no corresponding difference in the basic choreography of these dances nor in the music that accompanies them. The term *wahaihai* is used in this book to refer to this dance throughout Ouvéa, in order to avoid confusion with the *waiai* dances of Maré.

The *wahaihai* dances are women's dances and are accompanied by singing. The dancers are arranged in two or more lines in front of the choir, which can include a few men to sing the bass (for the recording on Ammann [1997:track21[CD]] a man was spontaneously asked to sing the *bas*). Members of the choir are seated and tap their hands or the *bwinji-bet* (leaf parcel), or a choir member may be standing and stamping a tube in time to the song. The dancers, legs together, bend just their knees in time to the singing. Only the arms mime the events contained in the song. The dance tassels held in each hand correspond to those of the *Grande Terre*. They are called *wathuathap* in Iaai.

The subjects of the *wahaihai* songs are very varied. Guiart (1953:3-16) noted and translated several *wahaihai* texts. He says that they may be about historical events, especially those concerned with mourning or about public events such as the construction of a house for the *grand chef*. They may also be simply love songs describing the beloved. Guiart quotes a *wahaihai* song in which the words tell the dancers the movements which should be made :

"Sing Meijo / sing my song / it's my *wahaihai* / I turn my back / I face the song / I turn my back, hiding my dance tassel of the song / I turn again / I face the audience / I show the dance tassel of my song / the audience applauds me" (Guiart 1953:5).

The texts of the *wahaihai* songs often contain symbols, placenames and the names of plants. Most of this symbolism is no longer understood and it may even be that from its creation the symbolic message of a song was unknown outside a small circle of people.

The *wahaihai* given below as an example recounts the events of the building of the small church at Lekiny in the south of the island❷. The text describes the different stages with great precision of observation. Each verse begins with the same phrase *dénéa é missi hano* ('He who goes gently goes surely').

The song begins with a solo of the principal singer who recites the phrase *dénéa é missi hano*, then the choir enters for five repetitions of this phrase.

❶ "Il n'y a pas ni danses ni chansons provenant de Wallis".

❷ The *faimanu* dance, which is described later in the chapter, has as its subject the reconstruction of the church of Muli after it had been destroyed in a cyclone.

dénéa é missi hano	He who goes gently goes surely
ma mouna agé dé wésel	The first sound of the whistle is blown
godé wésel o Vito	It's the signal given by Victor
go Vito ma Kapua	By Victor and Kapua
é tapa fafiné	Gathering of all the women
o hano ni mako	For the rehearsal of singing and dancing
ni mako mai Tonga	Gathering in the Tonga tribu
idé poo madé Ao	Night and day
gidé Asso odé Sehnyün	For the day of the feast
dénéa é missi hano	He who goes gently goes surely
Lékiné mai dé Atua	Lekiny tribu, first subject for the construction
Faga tai dé Fofonu	All the tribu gathers together under the gaze of the Lord
Tou agé Waboula	Waboula, an important man in the tribu
O Mounéa daou Mouna	Makes a speech
tahina Mao Mai	You, the men of the *tribu*
gégou nago Mounéa	Take on the work
dé Bongon odé Huliwa	And you the women
Tangata faga tafa	You are going to contribute
Fafiné oukataué	You are going to help
Soli lima kéou oti	One devotes oneself.
dénéa é missi hano	He who goes gently goes surely
Go Thamoa dé Makéké	Thamoa is the *petit chef* of Lekiny
go dodadoü döhnu	He is the technical, physical and moral support
lima i a taou néi	Of the people on the job
Péna péna ina oti	Strength is considered to be as our tool
Amoa gé dé Fatou	To achieve the objective
Névéagé dé Belai	Five years of preparations/
Saon Saoua dé Oné	Today all is ready, stones, gravel and sand
Goa paré dé Koloa	All the building materials are ready.
dénéa é missi hano	He who goes gently goes surely
Kéliagé mala tranché	An order is given
Soukiagé mala Oumou	Dig the trenches,
Saounagé mala poteau	prepare the concrete or the mortar
Toukiagé dé kofrage	Drive the posts into the ground
Lingiagé dé béton	Prepare the formwork and pour the concrete
Goa siai ogou Ména	No more rest
Goa Malingi dé Kakava	The sweat flows
Goudé kai Madé Sasa	One is eating in the dust.
dénéa é missi hano	He who goes gently goes surely
Goa Toukia dé Kapa	I contemplate the sky,
ogou ngala gidé langi	the men nail the tin roof
Déma goia tou dé Kourousé	The cross is already in place on the belfry
idé clocher	Victora a person of importance by her respect of
Touagé à Victora	The appeal a bouquet is presented to her
Tapagé à Doumai dénéi dogu bouquet	The bell calls us
Goa fétapa dé Fao Godé aso Alleluia	Hallelujia, it's the day of the fete
dénéa é missi hano	He who goes gently goes surely
Godé 29 juin	The 29th of June
Lékiné toagué dé Foé	The day of the patron saint of Lekiny
Ouvéa, Lifou et Maré	Ouvéa, Lifou and Maré
Calédonie oti oti	And all New Caledonia
Ekétiagé de Vaka	Get into the boat
Saint-Pierre idé langi	St. Peter, think of the gagniere
Ihoagué a Gagnière	Who has worked very much for the chapel
Merci l'évêque Pierre Martin	Thank you, Bishop Pierre Martin.

(For the direct French translation see p. 266.)

Before the final repetition of the phrase a singer gives a signal by singing a held note with the syllables ya-a-a-a-a, which indicates a change to the text.

Music of the introductory and final part of each strophe.

The pattern for the repetition of the phrases is as follows :

A -B - A - B - B - C - B - C - C - D - C - D - D -...

After phrase A is sung for the first time phrase B is sung, also for the first time, followed by A and then B sung twice, after which phrase C is sung for the first time and then B for the last time. The repetetive structure of the phrases is like that of the *ayoii* songs of the Hienghène region where people originating in Ouvéa have settled and there may be a relationship in the structure of these two classes of song. Each strophe ends with a kind of formula of question and reply between the principal singer and the choir.

During the song each phrase is sung with the same basic melodic line, which is tritonic with a range of a minor third. The only intervals are minor descending and major seconds and a minor third ascending to the tonal centre. The minor third is the dominant interval which suggests a minor mode to European ears. However the minor third is not always exact, often approaching a neutral third. The song's metre is symmetric and the rhythmic structure changes slightly according to the pronunciation of the words. After the first stanza the tempo quickens slightly and the percussion enters. On Ammann (1997:track 21[CD]) the relative pitch descends during the performance about a halftone.

Short extract from the dance song *dénéaé missi*, showing the melodic theme.

The way in which the strophes end and the slow opening of the song indicate the song's relationship with the *wayai* and *kutera* dances of Maré.

These dances also have a similar choreography and their accompanying music, while showing some slight variations, has the same structural features. It seems more than likely that the *wahaihai* dances of Ouvéa and the *waiai* dances of Maré have a common origin. In the Pacific similar dance names generally indicate dances having the same origin (Moyle 1991:49), and this is above all true in the Loyalty Islands which are close neighbours and where inter-island migrations and exchanges have existed since they were first populated. However, although it is easy enough to establish the common origin of the *wahaihai* (Ouvéa) and *wayai* (Maré) dances it is not possible to say where the dances originated nor which of the two islands first had the dance.

Informants on Ouvéa think that the name of the dance comes from the Iaai word *wahai* which means 'pulling leaves off a branch' as, for example, pulling the leaflets off a coconut palm frond. This kind of work is exclusively women's. The word *wahai* is unknown on Maré, so if the name of the dance is indeed based on it then it would look as if the dance went from Ouvéa to Maré. However no further information is available at present.

Fehuâ

People from the Ohnyot *tribu* in the north of the island perform a dance called *fehuâ*. This is the same kind of dance that is known as *fehoa* on Lifou from where it has been introduced. The choregraphy is the same as that of the Lifou dance and the words, at least in so far as they can be understood, are in the Drehu language. The textual content speaks of the spirits of Lifou and tells of migrating from Lifou to Ouvéa. Some families from the Ohnyot *tribu* are of Lifou origin and the dance is linked to their arrival in Ouvéa.

Dru

People from Teuta, a *tribu* in the Fagauvea linguistic area in the north of the island, are the guardians of the *dru* dance. Hollyman (1987: 68) says of this dance "a men's dance from Teuta, carrying tao (spear) and crown, danced to the rhythm of the bamboos". He adds that the dance has an origin on the *Grande Terre.*

The rhythm of the *dru* dance is the *rythme du pilou*, played with stamping-tubes, and with whistles in the dancers' mouths. The dancers are drawn up in a square and perform synchronised movements. All these features indicate a *Grande Terre* origin, yet, strangely, the dance is in the possession of a group from Wallis and how they have got it from the *Grande Terre* is unknown.

Even if the *dru* dance did originate on the *Grande Terre* it is not known from which region it came. On the other hand migrations from Canala and Houaïlou are known about and it must be said that the way of dancing with spears in the hand strongly resembles that of dances known from these regions. Although a relationship has been established between the north of the *Grande Terre* and Ouvéa it seems that the *dru* dance does not come from the Hoot ma Whaap area.

The dance is properly respected on Ouvéa and it has a direct relationship with the north of the island where it is danced. When could it have arrived? It may be supposed that the latest time for the dance's arrival would be the beginning of the 20th century. It could then have been 'given' during the 1930s to Drueulu where it developed and acquired its present form. People from

Teuta revere it, above all, because it is danced in the 'next world' which is to be found in the sea near the island❶.

Seleweilewei

Seleweilewei is a dance from the Heo *tribu* (St. Joseph) in the north of Ouvéa. The song accompanying the dance is like that of the *fehoa* songs. At the beginning the name of the song, *seleweilewei,* is recited as a fast recitation.

The melody of the refrain follows the timbre of the word *seleweilewei* as it is normally pronounced with a clear timbre on the 'e' and a duller sound on the 'ei'. This is expressed by the 'ei' intoned a halftone lower than the 'e'. The 'ei' at the end is intoned in breathing out air thus adding a good deal of wind noise.

se - le - wei - le - wei - le - wei - le - wei - a

This way of singing a song's or a dance's title with accentuation of the timbre and the rhythm of the spoken word is also found in the *fehoa* dances from Lifou. The *seleweilewei* dance shows the relationship between language and song in the *fehoa* songs very clearly. The large number of repetitions of the word reminds one of a magic chant in which a word accumulates energy the more it is repeated. In the case of the *fehoa* the word used is the title of the song, like a refrain which is repeated periodically. The musical motif which is thus created by the word forms the basic melody of the whole song. This word, formula or title is thus the key word of the *fehoa* songs.

The *ofefetu,* the dragonfly, of the Ouassaudjeu *tribu* in the centre of the island is given in the literature as a sitting dance. Most unfortunately it has not been possible to see this dance performed but the *chef* of the *tribu* has described the positions of the dancers as having their legs apart and the knees bent. It therefore seems that the squatting position in this dance is quite different from the sitting dances known from Polynesia.

The *Vieux* Kas Poulawa remembers a dance, although not its name, which the people in the north and south of the island used to perform during marriages. A marriage was made between one partner from the south of the island and one from the north. The newly marrieds, with their families, lined up facing each other. The bride began to dance in the space between the two lines and the bridegroom followed suit. In the centre there was a pole and all the people present, the two parties to the marriage, moved forward dancing and left their presents for the married couple at the foot of the pole. No further information about this dance has been uncovered during the fieldwork. The likeness to the old exchange dances of the *Grande Terre* is worth noting.

❶ It may be remembered here that on the *Grande Terre* the ancestors in the 'next world' perform the round-dance. On Ouvéa the men and women of the 'next world' dance the *wahaihai* according to Guiart (1953: 19).

THE *FAIMANU* DANCE

In the *faimanu* dance, dancers approach the dance area holding spears in their hands, but the spears are collected up and put away before dancing begins. In the following sections where the dancers are arranged in a square and where the movements are synchronised, the dancers carry only dance tassels in their hands. Women may now participate in this dance. When the dance was performed at Nouville in 1992 there were two lines of women arranged alternately with two lines of men. The subject of the *faimanu* dance is such that it can be performed by both sexes.

The dance represents the reconstruction of the small church of Lekiny after its destruction by a cyclone in 1932. The dance shows the different stages of building : the dancers mime cutting wood, working with spades or with wheelbarrows etc.

In the final section when the dancers spread out their arms they are imitating both the flight and the sound of birds. A dancer separates from the group and runs around the group of dancers who mime hunting the bird with slings. Kas Poulawa says that this represents the situation after the cyclone when a large part of the island suffered dammage. The destruction of food crops was so serious that people had to hunt birds and live off them in order to survive. The dance was presented in this form for the first time after the second world war. It is possible that the *faimanu* dance has its roots in another dance and that the section about the birds has been kept intact and is now being explained in a way different from that in the original dance.

The *faimanu* dance resembles the *dru* dance from the north of the island or from Lifou and it is possible that the composer of this dance was inspired by the *dru* dance. However it differs in the rhythm of the accompaniment. The *dru* dance is accompanied by the *rythme du pilou* but the *faimanu* dance is

(David Becker/A.D.C.K.1992, Nouville)

The group of dancers from Mouli who performed the *faimanu* dance at the 'rencontre préparatoire' in 1992.

accompanied by the four-beat rhythm. During the dance the four-beat rhythm is played fast, at 145 motifs per minute, which is far more rapid than when it is performed in the north of the *Grande Terre.*

The *waneuname* dance

The *waneuname* dance belongs to the Poulawa family and the dance leader today is Kas Poulawa. The dance tells of the history of the family who has allowed it to be told in outline here. The family used to live on the small island of Bagaat to the north west of Ouvéa and moved to another small island nearer to Ouvéa. One day the ancestor of the family was attracted by some music and arrived at Mouli. The *grand chef* welcomed him and gave him a place on his right to settle on. The *waneuname* dance which mimes this story was dreamed by the *Vieux* Poulawa and transmitted to the family and was also given to the *grand chef.* Today it is necessary to have permission from two people for a performance : that of the *grand chef* and that of the family who are the owners. The message of the dance is so important that it can be performed only by men. Dancers are arranged in a square formation and carry out synchronised motions accompanied by the four-beat rhythm.

The *seloo* songs

The word *seloo* is used in Fagauvea, as in Iaai, to refer to specific songs. It probably comes from the bislama words *sail ho* used in the north of Vanuatu to mean 'sailor' (Joël Bonnemaison and Jean-Claude Rivierre, pers. comm.). The word has probably been in use in Vanuatu and Ouvéa to announce the arrival of a pirogue or a boat since the time of the first sandalwood traders. The first person to spot a boat cries out *sail ho*, or *seelo*, and all the rest of the people go down on the beach to welcome the boat which enables them to exchange goods thus obtaining metal objects and alcoholic drinks❶.

Today it is mostly old people, both men and women, who sing the *seloo* songs and, as in the case of the *ae-ae* songs of the *Grande Terre*, they may be lost for lack of young singers. The present singers say that they sang the *seloo* songs very frequently when they were young, despite the fact that they were much frowned upon by the Catholic Church. One singer said that she and other young people of the time were beaten by the priest for singing *seloo* songs, and that therefore they used to hide in the forest to sing them. The priest justified his conduct by saying that in singing *seloo* songs the young people spoilt their capacities for singing canticles. *Seloo* songs were sung by young people while they worked, while they were out walking and for general pleasure. The songs are not classified as sacred and can be sung whenever desired, alone or in a group. Today the songs are sung during festivities, especially at Christmas and New Year, but also whenever singers find themselves together. They sit down and one starts singing. The others join in and in an informal and ad hoc way a *seloo* singing session begins.

Seloo song texts exist in Fagauvea and in Iaai and it is normal for a *seloo* singer to know songs in both languages. The Iaai speakers distinguish two parts of a *seloo* song : *uuthofuuc,* the words, and *deeny,* the music. The subjects of the *uuthofuuc* are very varied. They may tell of events in the

❶ The *Vieux* Eloa of Ouvéa says that the word *ovi* originates in the French word 'eau-de-vie' and was used in the same way as the word *seloo.*

composer's private life or describe historical events of the area, they may be concerned with daily living experiences or with stories from the Bible.

The *seloo* are made up of parts which are the equivalent of strophes. In Iaai they are called *jee ut xumwong*, a 'piece of a song' (*un morceau de chant*). The number of *jee ut xumwong* varies according to the individual *seloo* song as does the *deeny* (melody) which is quite different from such songs as the *waueng, wejein*, or *ayoii,* etc. In all the *seloo* songs the last part of each *jee ut xumwong* is repeated. The responsorial structure of the *seloo* songs is limited to a short solo of the *hwiik xumwong* (the first voice part) at the beginning of each *jee ut xumwong* (verse).

It is the polyphony which is such a special feature of the *seloo* songs. The polyphony is made up of several voices depending on the number of singers who are available. The characterisic polyphony of the Loyalty Islands has already been discussed above. *Seloo* songs contain a peculiar polyphonic feature which can sometimes sound quite dissonant to unaccustomed ears. In *seloo* a particular voice called the *laasho* is sung. The *laasho* accompanies the principal voice in so-called dissonant intervals and has the function of creating an oscillating sound.Some parts of a *seloo* sound dissonant with the use of the tritone and minor seconds. Improvisation in the voices is possible but limited so that the special dissonant character is not modified. The intervals are not sung with absolute pitch but, as in the *waueng* or the *wejein,* a singer may modulate and play slightly with the pitch.

The *seloo* are defined by a regular pulsation. The entries of the voices are not quite precisely timed. However each *jee ut xumwong* of a *seloo* contains the same number of pulsations and, because the tempo does not change during a performance, each *jee ut xumwong* lasts for exactly the same time.

Walaang ötinaa löng ge bongon Jurop
Walee ke thaan hnyi Jomen jia Guillaume ien
Ame penapena tajee unyi hnâân ûâât
Baïonnette hele ûâât kuha ame cuha

Walaang anyin ke metâ ame penapena

Ame kunâ je sumara ka he eû hnyin köiö
Heka koû je hu walee jee mââniwââ
Eti gaan sangbetenge ge at ame na laus

Walaang hnen hnaûnykûme hnyi ûnykûmënen
Ame na weeny he ka ûâât me Paris
Hnyi anyin tang metâ me anyin tanghwege
Kene oo but ame na ûâât ge hele me kuha

Walaang jee thauzan aa hiaa but
Hnen anyidrin jee metâ a e na kong obiny
Ana bâ but at hwadeeny hnen je poizin
Aeropilan, hele, kuha ame cuha

Listen to the news coming from Europe
It's about a German king called William
He is preparing armaments for the war
The bayonet, war knife and firing gun.

Here is one of his inventions that he is planning

he sends submarines under water
to sink the ships that are man o' wars
Much sadness with regard to man who dies.

Here is what he envisages in his plan
he wants to enter into war against Paris
in his intelligence and his strength
Until he fighjts with knife and gun.

Thousands have gone because of
these inventions with a tragic goal
Many men have died because of his poisons,
aeroplanes, knives, and firing guns.

(For the direct French translation see p. 267.)

Seloo from the 1914-18 War.

Te(hi) o gos bong se - e - ven-trin k'a- mekhöp töci - ca
me Ko- pe k'e - ne hi - ö - u bi - ju Mo- re in(y)
ka - nyu- a a - u k'a - me na khu-
la- li de - kö iö- humn Mo - re in(y)-ka - nyu-
a a - u k'a - men - a khu- la- li de
kö iö hmu - - - u - - - u - un

Tehi ogos bong seventrin k'ame khöp tö cica me Kope, k'ena hiöu biju. More inykanyua auuuh ! k'amena khula, li dekö iöhmun

On the seventeenth of August Papa and Kope disembarked, but you were no longer there. More is in a foreign land, oooh ! how our tears flow.

E sangbetenge ânyâm mök, una mokcu hon gatin m'öhmun na hnyi delûöuju

Your death is moving, if only you could die at home with us so that we could carry you.

Ohmuna hnyi delûöuju me me na khula deköi iöhmun ka hnyi ûlâiâm

So long as you have been carried, so that our tears cover your breast.

Ohmune na he kana khaû hlitr, ae na hiö More biju hnyi anyihmun bunyen

We are going to dress ourselves in black, because More is absent from our group.

(For the direct French translation see p. 266.)

Seloo « Tehi ogos bong seventrin » (see Ammann 1997: plage 19[CD]).

A discussion of the origin of the *seloo* songs

It is difficult to estimate the age of *seloo* songs. Old people on Ouvéa say that their fathers used to sing *seloo* songs and it is possible that they existed at the beginning of the 20th century. They cannot be earlier than the 19th century because they have a Bislama name❶. On Ouvéa, Bislama was spoken before

❶ In the 18th or 19th centuries similar songs, perhaps with another name, may have existed which formed the base for the songs known as *seloo.*

Seloo « Tehi ogos bong seventrin » (choir).

French became the official language when the French Government took possession in 1865. However the polyphony found in *seloo* songs shows similarities to that of the religeous songs and it seems as if the *seloo* were composed in reaction to religeous singing. The *seloo* are not accompanied by instruments. They are structured in strophes following one after another with a sort of refrain between them. They are sung in polyphony of several parts, like the Christian polyphonic songs, in contrast to traditional songs which are monophonic or heterophonic. The intervals of a fifth and a third are often sung in the *seloo* while those in old dance songs are, in general, smaller. The conspicuous use of dissonance is interesting. It could be said that the difference between consonance and dissonance is not thought of in the same way as it is learned in European music theory.

Recent songs from Ouvéa

Almost all the songs composed in the 20th century use the major-minor tonal system which until the 1950s was known in Ouvéa only in religeous songs. With the arrival of radio after the second world war and television in the 1970s other singing styles were heard by people on Ouvéa, without counting those who visited the *Grande Terre*, or went further afield; and who were able to listen to the 'new music'. The song Masina, for example, is a composition from the 1940s, a lamentation of the people from Ouvéa who went to work in the nickel mines at Gomen on the west coast of the *Grande Terre.*

Masinaé oku ifo dou fai	**Moon, I would really like to have your eyes**
mataekité otina go mala fai	**In order to look at and to contemplate**
sei	**All the flowers**
fai sei koai, fai sei mois	**Which flower ? It's the one that is called 'The Month**
de Marieogu paki gi Gomen	**of Mary' This flower is my bouquet**
	This bouquet has lead me to Gomen,
gi dunga savé nickel	**my place of work**
	There where nickel is worked.
Goa oti ifo idinéi	**Goodbye my friends, Goodbye my brothers and**
domadoè fai mako fékité tantéhi-	**sisters**
na fékité balua	**Our song is ending**
	Goodbye.

(For the direct French translation see p. 268.)

The *Masina* song.

Ouvéa has two languages and yet dances and music do not seem to differ between the two linguistic areas. In fact their music seems close enough to that of the other Loyalty Islands which have also experienced Polynesian immigrations. Based on the current Ouvéa situation the hypothesis could be advanced that once intercultural contact has been established cultural exchange is easier and expresses itself sooner in dance and music than in language.

CHAPTER 8

KANAK DANCE AND MUSIC IN A PACIFIC CONTEXT

A great diversity in Kanak dance and music has become apparent during this study. Features common to the whole of New Caledonia are few, although some regional generalisations can be made. A consideration of New Caledonia's Kanak culture, its geography and its more recent history may contribute to an understanding of the diversity.

The round-dance of the *Grande Terre* is quite informal. It is open to everyone, does not require the learning of special steps or movements and traditionally, is performed without an audience. It is accompanied by bark-clappers, stamping-tubes and a pair of singers. It occurs all over the centre and north of the *Grande Terre* where it is the culminating ritual of exchange ceremonies and all sorts of festivities.

The mimetic dances are war dances, very clearly so in the centre and north of the *Grande Terre*, less clearly but still really so, on the Loyalty Islands and the Isle of Pines. War dances in which the dancers are positioned in a square and where short sequences are performed one after the other, occur all over New Caledonia. They are the only sort of mimetic dance in the centre and north of the *Grande Terre* but on the Loyalty Islands and in the south of the *Grande Terre* other forms of mimetic dances occur. These are the theatrical dances where dancers are arranged in a circle, in a simple line or in a less fomal way, or, when no formation is apparent, the dance becomes a scenic play.

In Hoot ma Whaap and sometimes in the Bourail region mimetic dances are accompanied by percussion instruments, but in the Paicî-Cèmuhî region they are unaccompanied except for whistles and voice sounds. In the centre and north of the *Grande Terre* some, at least, were once accompanied by singing which has disappeared. In the Loyalty Islands they are accompanied by singing performed by a mixed seated choral group who strike leaf parcels and the songs recount historical subjects, especially past battles.

The ritual dance movements carried out during the 'speech given from a tree', known from the centre and north of the *Grande Terre*, are accompanied by percussion instruments and participatory noises of those present while the voice of the speaker from high up is concerned with the rhythmic recitation of poetry.

The various trade-dances are known only from the centre and north of the *Grande Terre* but it seems likely that they were originally to be found throughout New Caledonia. They encapsulate the traditional relationship of ceremony, trade and dance.

Lullabies are sung throughout New Caledonia and the Kanak flute from the *Grande Terre* is a melodic instrument which was often played alone and in private. However the most typical and significant Kanak music is singing accompanied by percussion, which itself accompanies dancing.

Throughout New Caledonia there are classes of songs in which a large number of texts and a number of melodies can be used together independently. These include the *wejein* from Lifou, the *waueng* from Maré and the *ae-ae* from the centre and north of the *Grande Terre.*

In the *ae-ae* songs each singer of a pair uses the same register. Some songs are antiphonal and where the singers sing together, including overlapping sections where singing is frequently in unison or in interupted bourdon, a short section in counterpoint may also be created.

In the mixed choral singing of the Loyalty Islands very old dance songs (*fehoa*) have a restricted range, seldom over m3 and often limited to a rapid repetition of a short musical theme.

More recent composition in the Loyalty Islands is very strongly influenced by European music.

Melanesian dances

Ethnochoreological research in Melanesia, in the modern sense, lags behind the attention paid to Polynesia. From what can be gathered from modern ethnological studies of, for example, Guiart (1956), Dean (1977), Coppet and Zemp (1978), Rossen (1987), Crowe (1990), Thomas and Takaroga (1992), Melanesian dances are an important part of ceremonies and rituals, and may be described in ethnological studies in relation to a particular ritual (Strathern 1985 ; Gondale 1995 and others). The following points taken from Kaeppler (1983:9) give a general idea of Melanesian dances.

- In a Melanesian dance all may join in[1] and there is no separate audience.
- Basic movements are primarily legs and swaying bodies rather than arms and hands.
- Dancers often form a moving group which may progress in a circle, in single or multiple lines or in columns.
- Melanesian dance has a spontaneity that does not require long and arduous training.

Besides these particular characteristics of Melanesian dances, Kaeppler (1993:62) distinguishes two kinds of dances : those of "impersonation" and those of "participation".

In the dance of impersonation, the dancers take the roles of mythical or ancestral beings celebrated in the oral literature. The dancer or dancers can wear masks and costumes. They behave like mythical figures, they do not talk and movements are made by legs and swaying bodies.

The dances of participation are an extension of ceremonies. Individuals

[1] However, if the dance makes part of a venerated ritual woman are generally excluded.

can take part in such dances celebrating, for example, head-hunting, warfare etc. They are often accompanied by drumming. If words are associated they are repetitious and do not seem to tell a story.

Much of the Kanak dance and music repertoire agrees well enough with the characteristic Melanesian dance and music given above. However there is also a good deal of Kanak dance and music which requires further explanation and this is attempted below.

The Melanesian cultural context of dance and music

The principal function and notion of Kanak ceremonies, the alternation of giving and receiving material goods or food between two groups, is symbolised in many ways. Often the alternating movement of the wooden needle which fixes the roof and wall paperbark thatch to the wooden framework of a *case* (Leenhardt 1922:263), is said to symbolise the alternation of exchange between two groups. The same symbol can be seen. in the zig-zag lines often carved on the wide wooden posts (*chambranles*) on each side of the door of a traditional *case* ❶ and which also appear frequently on incised bamboos.

Music performed during a ceremony consists of two elements : singing and percussion. Singing is performed in pairs and in the *ayoii* songs the two singers sing in alternation. The *rythme du pilou* that accompanies these songs, consists of the alternation of two different beats and the percussion section itself is divided into two groups beating in alternation. The two main instruments (the stamping-bamboos and the bark-clappers) each traditionally consists of two separate instruments. The notion of two similar but distinct elements acting in alternation is fundamental to the structure of many of the components of Melanisian ceremonies.

However, not every element of a traditional ceremony can be explained as being a symbol of an alternating or hocketting series. In the mimetic dances such structures are less obvious. In the Loyalty Islands vestiges of customary exchanges are still to be found at weddings, especially when members of a *chef*'s family are concerned, but patterns of alternation are less obvious than on the *Grande Terre.* Music there represents, above all, accounts of the history to be found in legends.

Furthermore there seems to be another element interacting with the pair of alternating elements which appears to be undefined, free or even chaotic. For example, while the music of the round-dance is full of symbols of alternation, the choreography of the dance is quite free. The chaotic element is also present in the whistles, hisses and phrases that can be added without any order to the structured beats of the percussion and the singing. Even the *rythme du pilou* consists of an 'exact' beat and one of a more liberal, arpeggio-like or less coordinated beat.

Only parts of the musical repertoire can be explained as an expresssion of alternation. In lullabies, for example, an alternating or hocketting structure seems to be absent and only some music from the centre and north of the *Grande Terre* can be interpreteted in this way. However the structuring of ceremonial music in the same way as the ceremony as whole appears in other places in Melanesia.

❶ These door posts can also be interpreted as a net in which dead bodies were wrapped, because heads are carved on the upper part of these posts.

Coppet and Zemp report this from the 'Are'are on Malaita (Solomon Islands). In the chapter "musical structures and social structures" ("structures musicals et structures socials") they explain that the 'Are'are divide their ceremonies into two groups : the first consists of the important ceremonies, where two ceremonial partners exchange large amounts of money, and the second group consists of less spectacular exchanges, where there is a continuous circulation of small amounts of money. Coppet and Zemp associate with the second group a small number of musical pieces, consisting of only a single section repeated an indefinite number of times, plus a specific final formula.

With the more important ceremonies Coppet and Zemp associate a great number of musical pieces which consist of two to several sections differing melodically. The structure of these musical pieces corresponds to the structure of the ceremony itself which consists of an exchange of money between two partners. Each receives four times and gives four times and at the end a ninth giving and receiving action is added. The accompanying ceremonial music consists of two pairs of sequences, each one repeated (2 x 2 x 2) and to this composition an end piece is added.

Coppet and Zemp say "Corporal measurements, amounts of money, melodic segments, pieces of music and ceremonial sequences follow the same principle of order by twos and fours which are also found in the explicit polyphonic structure of the four types of Panpipe ensembles and in the position of the musicians arranged face to face"❶ (De Coppet/Zemp 1978:119).

The 'Are'are distinguish keenly between odd and even numbers. Whereas the first few even numbers measure the different parts in music and ceremonies etc, the odd numbers are a sign of immovability. The relationship between odd and even numbers is both friendly and hostile. However, the odd number at the end of an exchange cycle is needed to preserve the continuum of the ceremonial relationship between the partners❷.

Coppet and Zemp close the chapter by stating "In their attempt to master time, that is to say human passions confronted by the reality of death, the 'Are'are have constructed on one and the same arithmetical base both music and society"❸.

Like the 'Are'are and the Kanaks in the centre and north of the *Grande Terre*, the Iatmul from the Middle Sepik (Papua-New Guinea) express basic cultural notions in their ceremonies and in their ceremonial music.

Musical instruments of the Iatmul in the Middle Sepik are always played in pairs. The transversally played flutes used in rituals are no exception. The flutes are made from a piece of bamboo and they vary in length from 60-300 cm, and have no finger holes. Two flutes of unequal length form a unity; the longer is the male flute, the shorter is the female.

❶ "Mesures du corps, mesures monétaires, segments mélodiques, pièces de musique et séquences cérémonielles suivent ce même principe d'ordre par deux et par quatre que l'on retrouve également dans l'organisation polyphoniques explicite des quatre types d'ensemble de flûtes de Pan et dans la position des musiciens rangés face à face".

❷ This may be compared with the fact that in a ritual exchange between Kanaks, one partner is obliged to give more than the other (see chapter on the round-dance) so that the exchange can be continued on another occasion.

❸ "Dans leur tentative pour maîtriser le temps, c'est-à-dire des passions humaines confrontées aux rigueurs de la mort, les 'Aré'-aré ont construit sur une même arithmétique la musique et la société".

The two flute players stand close together, facing each other, and play in alternation each one a tone, using the overtone scale from the second up to the sixth partial-tones. The alternation of each musician playing a tone, can be visualised as a hocketting pattern.

The unequal length of the two flutes *Mariuamangi* in the village Kandingai, shifts the partial-tone scale of the shorter female flute about a major second higher than that of the longer male flute. To play the scale of these flutes from the lowest to the highest tone, demands an alternation of one tone by each flute. The ceremonial music pieces played with this flute also consist of a complex pattern of alternation of different musical themes (Spearritt 1979 [unpubl.]/ Ammann 1989 [unpubl.]).

Gordon Spearritt (1983:106-125) has pointed out that the dual system in music can be attributed to the dual system in which the society of the Iatmul as a whole functions. The Iatmul class every phenomenon and object in nature and culture in one of the two moieties : sun/heaven (*nyoui*) and mother/earth (*nyame*). In many aspects the two moieties are hierarchically organised, *nyoui* is stronger than *nyame*. The interaction between the two moieties is traditionally determined and ensures the continuation of social life.

Gregory Bateson describes the Iatmul pattern for name giving as follows : "A man takes his father's names (a child receives names varying from two to six or eight in number) and applies them to his own sons. Similarly he takes his father's sisters' names and applies them to his daughters" (Bateson 1931:273). The same system appears in the 'age grade system' of the Iatmul and in the way that two clans exchange women for marriage (Bateson 1931:279). Even in the plan of a typical Iatmul village an interlocking or alternating notion is obvious. The centre of a Iatmul village is formed by the long ceremonial place *wompunau,* with the men's house at its end. Each side of the *wompunau* is reserved for one moiety and each clan has its place following the clan hierarchy in its moiety, also in alternation.

It seems that John Blacking's (1973:25) often cited sentence fits perfectly in the Melanesian world of music and dance : "We can no longer study music as a thing in itself when research in ethnomusicology makes it clear that musical things are not always strictly musical, and that the expression of tonal relationship in patterns of sound may be secondary to extramusical relationships which the tones represent".

Geographical position : isolated yet a meeting point

Although somewhat isolated in its geographical position within the western South-Pacific, New Caledonia has received emigrants from both Melanesia and Polynesia.

Southern Vanuatu, the closest islands to New Caledonia, provided Melanesian immigrants and trading voyages over centuries. Emigrants from western Polynesia sailing to the West reached the Loyalty Islands which form an outer barrier to the *Grande Terre* in several migratory waves, but only a small number of migrations landed directly on the *Grande Terre.* Some immigrants who arrived first on the Loyalty Islands continued on their way to the *Grande Terre.* Generally it can be said, that the Loyalties were more exposed to the outside world than was the *Grande Terre* and that this exposure included cultural influences, especially those from Polynesia.

Moyle (1991:48) sums up the characteristics of Polynesian dances as follows : "..., Polynesian dance typically involves a more-or-less stationary group of performers who make their formal presentation to a separate audience. Most Polynesian dances are performed together with singing (by either the dancers, or a separate group of musicians, or a combination of both) and, indeed, the dance movements are intended to enhance and thereby intensify the allusions in the song poetry". The dancers are mostly positioned in lines, round-dances do not exist at present in Polynesia[1]. Kaeppler (1993:12) confirms Moyle's summary and points out the most important feature of Polynesian dance in one sentence : "..,Polynesian dance is intimately associated with language and poetry, which it conveys in the form of storytelling".

Dance and music in the Loyalty Islands show some features similar to those of the islands of both southern Vanuatu and western Polynesia. In contrast the *Grande Terre* was more isolated from external influences and developed or kept its own Melanesian world of dance and music including the unique musical instruments the Kanak flute and bark-clappers along with the unique polyphonic *ae-ae* songs, which are quite distinct from present-day Polynesian polyphonic songs. In the centre and north of the *Grande Terre* the round-dance shows strong Melanesian elements although the mimetic dances are not typically Melanesian.

A general comparison between features of Kanak dances and those of Polynesia and Melanesia, shows that the Loyalty Island dances are close to Polynesian dances in as much as they are accompanied by singing and that the dancers mime subjects described in the dance songs. Yet the very old Loyalty Island dances (*pehua, bua,* and *fehoa*) are round-dances, a dance form which is very rare or even inexistant in Polynesia. There are several ways in which the round-dances of the Loyalty Islands could have developed. They may have been inspired by the round-dances of the *Grande Terre* and from southern Vanuatu, for example, from the *nupu* dance of Tanna[2] (Lindstrom 1996:127). On the other hand they are not typically Melanesian because they are not open to all-comers and the dance performance demands a learning period. In addition the term *fehoa* suggests a Samoan origin and the seated mixed choir is typically Polynesian. It seems as if the Loyalty Islanders have made choices among the different elements brought by various immigrants and visitors, and adapted them according to their own cultural ideas.

Conclusion

New Caledonia, although geographically a somewhat isolated group of islands, was an area in which, in precolonial times, different cultures had already met and foreign elements had been absorbed. Both typical Melanesian and typical Polynesian elements can be easily detected in Kanak dance and music, but a third factor, perhaps the principal one, lies in the way in which the Kanaks have reacted to these diverse elements. They have created their own particular dances and music which today are difficult to classify as belonging to either one of the big cultural areas of Melanesia and Polynesia.

[1] confirmed by Burrows (1940:343) and Beth (1968:65) but in contrast to Poort (1975: 12).

[2] The line dance on Tanna, called *toka* (like the ceremony itself) may on the other hand be in relation with the *toka* dance from the Polynesian outlier island Futuna (Vanuatu) from where it is reported by (Thomas/Takaroga 1992).

Throughout their history the people of the Loyalty Islands have been exposed to new cultural forms. Perhaps this long experience, as well as a softer colonisation than on the *Grande Terre*, allowed the Loyalty Islanders to take advantage of the later European influence to bring those new elements too, into their dance and music.

Most external influences on the *Grande Terre* were filtered through the Loyalty Islands which acted as a buffer until colonial times when the land of the *Grande Terre* appeared far more favorable than the coral of the Loyalties to potential colonists from Europe. During its long period of comparatively isolated cultural development the *Grande Terre* saw a rather specific form of Melanesian culture emerge in which the notions about nature, man and life, essential for the practical and psychological well-being of any human group, were strongly expressed symbolically in dance and music, among other cultural forms. It could be that faced with the disruption of the last 150 years, the people on the *Grande Terre* preferred to abandon their dance and music when they could not be hidden, instead of modifying them in such a way that the all-important symbolism would be lost.

(David Becker/A.D.C.K.1995, Lifou)

APPENDIX

Translations of words or texts in Kanak vernacular languages, whether published or given by informants, are always into French. English translations in this book are based on the direct French translations which are given below.

Ayoii song from Hiengène (see p. 135)

veda ven mala yé tamé ru Hoot ma Hwaap	**Voici le jour où ils arrivent de Hoot et Hwaap**
Yélu tamé vha nynyami ngen aman pé nethuugi	**Eux deux arrivent pour se remémorer les choses qui sont oubliées**
Ai Wéga dani ngen naii men paguui	**Pour qu'il y ait un chemin pour nos enfants et petits-enfants**
Thui ai wé nei téna	**Raconte pour que nous écoutions**
Yélu tamé thui ven hun mooé ven nga	**Eux deux arrivent, racontent la manière d'être de la maison**
Ngê ngen jinu ngen duu kahok né ven kaémoo Kalédoni	**Maison des ancêtres-esprits des vrais hommes du pays de Calédonie**
Thui na néi maan daahma maan daahma	**Raconte-leur, à eux deux grands-chefs,**
Drubéa ma Kapuné	**eux deux grands-chefs de Drubéa et Kaponé**
Ai wéga jinu men mwii	**Pour que les ancêtres-esprits et puissances**
ai wéa balei wéga thôôwéragi ven Kanaky	**donnent la force pour faire le tour de l'île de Kanaky**
wéga thôôwéragi ven Pacifik	**Pour faire le tour des îles du Pacifique.**

Kutera dance from Maré (see p. 184-185)

Bee bee nood ea	**frappez frappez le peuple *ea***
rue haicahan ea	**deux jeunes gens *ea***
rue haerow ea	**deux jeunes filles *ea***
'ngee komeej ? ea	**« pourquoi sommes-nous ici *ea***
xeyu a ngai (e) ea	**ornés de *bugny* ? » *ea***
theitheicoon ea	**ils tirent (par secousses saccadées) *ea***
iaa theicoon ea	**ils tirent toujours**
ha cara ti ri hnawe	**ils tombent avec les filles à Hnawe**
hna-nue-rune wedr	**à l'endroit où on jette les feuilles de pandanus**
ha sere lo hula	**Ils se tiennent debout à l'est**
hnaee lo huli	**ils volent vers l'ouest**
cahane biengo dridri	**Les hommes papillons noirs**
hnaee lo huli	**Ils volent vers l'ouest**
rue waxeje drera ea	**Deux petites frégates rouges**
hnaee lo huli	**volent vers l'ouest**
ca lenec a rue beti ea	**entre les deux îles**
ha ruu lu so hulu ea	**elles plongent au fond**
ha sei thea ni koko	**là où les ignames ont débarqué**

bee bee nood ea	frappez frappez le peuple *ea*

bee bee nood ea	frappez, frappez le peuple *ea*
wamiiratene	Wamirat
si o re adra - are	casse une branche d'*are* pour faire signe
areona hadri ea	fait un signe au sud
rue sia i ore	les deux filles du matin
areone hadri ea	fait un signe au sud,
karenin ni shokaw	le coude de Shokaw,
e so hna karenin	a toujours le coude (levé)
wanaacashuba	Wanaacashuba
e so hna karenin	lève toujours le coude
tiri-uc-i-yaac	la brochette de poulpes des *yaac*
e so hna karenin	lève toujours le coude
sei kediudrone	avec Kediudrone
dede wano ti lo	saute en tournant
Ima re thothobene	Le crépuscule de poussière rouge
inoo gurewene ea	comme l'arc-en-ciel *ea*
ci tho tho jo huni	font voler la poussière au nord
gua ta idraro ea	à la petite place des *idraro ea*
ci tho tho jo huni	font voler la poussière au nord
gua ta idraro ea	à la petite place des *idraro*
ci tho tho jo huni	font voler la poussière au nord
o waimadrane	Waimadrane
de lu ko re nood	détruit le peuple
hnakuyadrone	Hnakuyadron
rue cahan i po	les deux hommes de Po
theicoone yawe	arrachent encore
hna-be ni yaac	au lieu de danse des *yaac*
theicoone yawe	arrachent encore
waete i gec	au mur de pierre de Gec
ha ru luso hulu ea	plongent au fond
sei thea ni koko	là où les ignames ont débarqué
bee bee nood ea	frappez, frappez le peuple

bee bee nood ea	frappez, frappez le peuple
loi adraejuni	c'est bien pour Adreajune
Lew o hna egoon	d'avoir dit « oui » (pour le mariage)
loa sicoone lo	elle monte sur la vague et s'enfuit
ile ci seroo lene	se trouvent sur mon chemin
wajaea ne numanum	Wajaea et Numanuma
theicoone yawe	ils arrachent encore
sei rabatetone	chez Rabatetone
loa sicoone lo	elle monte sur la vague et s'enfuit
cacane tadrane	l'homme Tardane (lui dit)
zikozikone lo	« Fais vite vite »
ca ienece ca reu beti	elle passe entre les deux îles
hna ru lu so hulu	plonge au fond
sei thea ni koko	là où les ignames ont débarqué
bee bee nood ea	frappez, frappez le peuple
a bee bee nood	frappez, frappez le peuple
cahane megenine	l'homme Megenine
se loo i nie	se tient debout à Nie
theede kaaduo	glisse (sur la vague) vers l'ouest
nacawa keludre	à Nacawakeluedr
theede kaaduo	descend vers l'ouest
coocoo ri rue gunin	il va aux « deux plages »
ri ta re-te wanod	aux récifs
namaea i siwene	le courant de Siwen
ha hna ro renood ea	c'est là où le peuple s'est enfoncé
rue biengo dridri	les deux papillons noirs
tica-dedone lo	arrachent et s'envolent
ha sasa dodon	on fait la danse *sasa* (devant) Dodon
bee bee nood ea	frappez, frappez le peuple *ea*

Kutera dance from Maré (see p. 189-190)

be ko be ae	**frappez donc, frappez, *ae***
be ko ba	**frappez donc, frappez**
be i kaze ri woc	**Frappez du *kaze* de la brousse**
itranine lu ko	**liez-le bien (le *kaze*)**
yengu ri hnawawa	**le vent est sur le champ de bataille**
wawane ruecil	**on va à Ruecil**
wawane lu Pakad (a)	**on descend à Pakad(a)**
theitheicoon	**on arrache encore, et puis encore**
ci hai pawaroi	**on contemple Pawaroi**
theitheicoon	**on arrache encore**
ci hai padewia	**on contemple Padewia**
watyaluma	**Watyaluma**
raba, raba, raba	**guette, guette, guette**
raba makalua	**guette Makalua**
trotro nineko	**« Où dois-je aller ? »**
hwako nineko	**« Je suis monté là-haut. »**
gurewoe parac (a)	**Gurewoc et Parac**
nue lu parapeu	**laissez Parapeu**
tha te lui loi ya	**(*intraduisible*)**
kukuama celam	**(*intraduisible*)**
noda yeco	**au pays des yeco**
ukesinane lu	**faites la torche**
ne sineunamaea	**et incendiez la maison**
uke lu ri mayo	**détachez là-bas**
lo na ithithir	**(...) qui a hérité**
doku ni Ketiwan	**la chefferie de Ketiwan**
ha iru iru kom	**a combattu, combattu ici**
sia i wayaw	**envoyé à Wayaw**
ha i-sia ko dreudreu	**a envoyé Dreudreu**
me lue padaw (a)	**et les deux Padaw(a)**
ke cie hna wedreng	**(*intraduisible*)**
ru lu i Adong (o)	**s'enfonce à Adong(o)**
wewe lu anga yo	**Ils descendent là-bas**
eraba eonin	**épient ensemble**
there no linen	**cherchent**
hnei sa i wayaw	**par un de Wayaw**
there no linen	**cherchent**
hnei sa i wayaw	**par un de Wayaw**
rue Malanyim	**les deux Malanyim**
i kaze ri woc	**le *kaze* de la brousse**
i wawa ri eng (o)	**va (ou combat) sur le vent**
there la anuma	**cherche le sentier**
tha numa numa ko	**cherche, va, va,**
ea wahmirat	**Wamirat**
Wewe lu Lolong (o)	**Va à Lolong(o)**
thede lu yewe	**reviens en glissant (planant) sur la vague**
ale ale ri woc	**nage, nage dans la forêt**
gurepedibaroi	**morceau de petite anguille**
kome uni tronem (u)	**Ici est Tronem(u)**
hna uni weliehme	**On a trouvé Weliehme**
Di re hne dra era	**Plume, reste chant de sang**
tice naca-xeje	**la grande frégate s'en va**
he a e ie ie o	***he ae*, il dit celui qui**
be i kaze ri woc	**frappe du *kaze* de la brousse**
hanga ? Ngai !	***hanga ? Ngai !***

Wayai dance song from Maré (see p. 196)

Hoiyee hoiyee...	**Eh Washongoshongone**
Ca washongoshongone	**D'où viens-tu ? D'où es-tu ?**
sere o ? Kio ehme ?	
Inu serei Kiam (u)	**Je viens de Kiam(u)**
Mama da kaio nu,	**grand frère, appelle-moi**
da hna ti lu o re iei,	**donne-moi du feu**
co shengi o re oreg (o)	**pour réchauffer mon estomac**
Inu ha leulebu(e)	**j'ai froid**
co hue i Deceiri	**d'aller à Deceiri**
co there o re warog (o)	**prendre mon filet à langoustes**
We ! cenge shukeli	**Hé, le panier de fougère *shukeli* (piège à poissons)**
ome ci sere te ole	**tiens la barre**
Ca washongoshongone !	**Eh Washongoshongone**
Hoiyee hoiyee...	
ma ona yahu(e) wayaw	**Quand ils auront trouvé *Yahue wayaw***
nine wala i re yeng (o)	**la mouche reviendra avec le vent**
Ha ahnga ? - Ngai !	

Children's game song from Maré (see p. 206)

Hielo, Hielo, Hielo, Hielo, Hielo, maitutune	**Donnons la main, donnons la main**
Guakoutre i Popu	**Petit manteau de Popu**
Hnegu hna ci kokoeon	**que j'ai porté**
So so so e navaso kapiri so	**(*mots neutres intraduisibles*)**
Wa kumala, wa kumala	**petite patate douce, petite patate douce**
Wa kamarade ne suri	**petit copain de la souris.**

Waueng songs from Maré (see p. 207-208)

Yesu keriso kabanulo ri node om	**Jésus Christ, emporte-moi de cette terre**
Ma ci nia du nu kei wa thu hulo lia	**Cette ingrate m'a fait tant de mal.**

Kolo ci ranelo re cekole ci kurulo	**Quel beau souvenir que ce joli lever de lune**
Ci nerenonelo re parowo ni wacanor	**qui éclaire le doux visage de ma bien-aimée.**

---

le du cecene ni bo me ci ane dunene ni inu	**À ton père qui me garde rancune, Dis-lui**
Ko inu co hue ne bo ke dekote ma hmani bo	**Que je sortirai avec toi, mais sûrement pas avec ta mère.**

Kinikinibot' ore gunine i Asicen	**Creuse, creuse, le sable de Asicen (*plage*)**
Bane ci iedi oiru ko guhnegu ne wanacor	**En souvenir de ma bien-aimée.**

Nuelu ore yelego ri pon'ore yele ni bo	**Écris mon nom auprès de ton nom**
Efase cileboto yele ni hna marie ne bo	**Et raye à jamais celui de ton conjoint.**

Three *uke hajin* from Lifou (see p. 214)

kölö eneila hi,	**je pense maintenant**
eneila hi kölö	**je pense maintenant**
ngo tha	**et jamais**
loi ngo tha	**certainement jamais**
ngo tha elanyi, elanyi macak	**jamais demain**

---

hnimi modeti pi hë ni,	**je pense à toi mon amour**
pi hë ni, lo e hna	**toujours et toujours**
e hnaifego,	**tu es je ne sais où**
ne hnagejë	**sur la mer**

---

kölö itre mama,	**je pense à vous mes grands frères**
itre mama koloi nyiné	**mes grands frères à quoi sert,**
lo nyiné,	**à quoi sert**
nyiné ouela,	**à quoi ça sert**
ouela uke jia	**la trique ?**

Modern song composition from Maré (see p. 203)

Se yeretiti co laenatan'ore ya nore nodei	**Un mythe raconte**
ia	**la traversée des animaux.**
hna ekote ha thu co ya, ha thu co ya	**Ils ont convenu de se rendre**
jew'ose nod	**ensemble dans un pays.**
pakone kore toka koe, meni hna ie inu	**La buse sera le commandant.**
paelatre	**« Je serai le pilote, a dit la chouette,**
inu ha ul'ore pathe,	**Car je sais où se trouve la passe,**
hne pathe ri bet'omelei	**la passe de cette île ».**
paelatre i meni, ha paekoc,	**Mene le pilote se tait subitement,**
wala ya i mene ha kalekal	**Mene le guide est pris de sanglots.**
ha rewerewe kei toka koe, ha te ri peda	**Le commandant regrette,**
kore koe.	**le bateau est sur le récif.**
Ma hna nuebot'ore nod,	**Ils quittèrent l'île**
hna ya ri ridin' ore ridri	**pour partir en pleine nuit,**
hna ethedone co paelatre, ca sererekane	**mais on se disputa le pilotage du navire.**
koi meni	**Mene fut finalement choisi.**
meni ci kaie :	**Il cria alors :**
nue icelu, nuelu ome,	**« Par ici, par là ! »,**
ha ci kuru te kore cekoe	**quand en même temps se levait la lune,**
ri naca koe, paelatre ha adreadre	**éblouissant le pilote à l'avant**
	du navire.
Ta hnatale, yan'ore koe,	**Les marchandises, enfouies dans le bateau,**
sio ne hamu ne drera	**les richesses**
hna hmutilu ri hne pathe, hnen'ore hna	**furent englouties au fond de la passe,**
walaya i Meni	**par la faute de Mene.**
Cengeni me hma re thuben, ha hna luzion	**Pierres précieuses,**
ha gupako kore hna ruace, koe ha kapa,	**perdues à jamais.**
ka matelo ha etha sic.	**Efforts vains,**
	le bateau s'est brisé
	et les matelots se sont enfuis.
Numu se ya inomelei,	**Souvenez-vous de cet autre voyage :**
ya nore rekokonien	**celui des apôtres.**
hna loaze i Gethesemani, hna pareu ne	**Égarés à Gethsémani,**

rewerew	**pris de peur et de regret,**
hna loaze i Gethesemani, hna pareu ne	**égarés à Gethsémani,**
rewerew	**pris de peur et de regret,**
Ca ha hna 'oreci une,	**trahison et mensonge,**
hna wakewi ne hna cacere	**ils se sont enfuis,**
hna sice, ka Yesu di,	**abandonnant Jésus**
odene ri satauro.	**seul sur la croix.**

Wayai dance song from Maré (see p. 200)

Pe rue cakoe	**Sur les deux rougets de nuit**
Watini hidra i Thoon ea Pe rue cakoe	**L'eau douce de Thoon**
Walalu i Hnakingen (i)ea Dai hnide lo	**Sur les deux rougets de nuit**
te	**La descente de Hnakingen(i)**
Ice n'garangara lo	**Retournez-vous un peu**
La hne tha waw	**Montez à pic**
Karenione lo	**Au sentier où on lance la balle**
Si Gi ne Si Puan	**Levez le coude**
Wadrarepien	**Les si Gi et les si Puan**
Token ore Yaac	**Wadrarepien**
Rue Waithorone	**Chef des dieux**
Wabubu re Waitru	**Les deux Waithorone**
Ice lo i Ngarangara	**L'extrémité de Waitru**
Gurewala ni Yaac	**Montez à pic à Ngarangara**
Dukewi ne Wadusa	**Le petit sentier des génies**
Ceceni Hnawanyo	**Dukewi et Wadusa**
	Le père de Hnawanyo
Pe rue cakoe	
Oiaa he i waiyawe	**Sur les rougets de nuit**
Ha pe rue cakoe	**(*exclamation*)**
	C'est sur les rougets de nuit
Hanga ? - Hai !	

Fehoa dance song from Lifou (see p. 229)

Upine une	**Entrailles de serpent**
Upine une	**Entrailles de serpent**
Xelene une	**Intestins de serpent**
Zöhuni jë la goe tro lue	**Zöhun regarde vers les deux enfants**
Jö mina ha ciwë e Tama	**Le soleil est à l'ouest à Tama**
Sasaqe tro ange hmaeë	**Vite dépêchons**
Drulima ha e hnine etë	**Drulima est dans le tas de pierres**
Kapa pi hë Zike Ukewetr	**Porte le Zike Ukewetr**
A wetrë ukeineqë jë	**Il est notre viande**
Qalikötre jë Kicima	**Kicima se tortille**
Traqa i angetre atresi	**À l'arrivée des atresi**
A nyinyapëne hë Ngazoeo	**Ngazoeo court à leur rencontre**
Ea jë la ketre wene peiny	**Prends un œuf de serpent**
A thithingë hë la koi Wahel	**Mon offrande à Wahel**
Hlegehlege hnameci	**Il a dépouillé le cadavre**
Hadredreu cia pi kö ni e catr	**Éclatante ma force a surpassé**
Aeng uthe Lösi	**Aeng neveu de Lösi**
A nanë hë nyupë e Xumoz	**Toi garde le passage à Xumoz**
Kötrene ju pë hë	**On t'abandonne**
Kötre wa hë ge ca	**Le boiteux fuit par les brousses**

Thaa hë e Huluialo	**Ne crie pas à Huluialo**
A koho e Huilati	**Là-haut à Huilati**
A hmekë ni ju pë hë	**Prenez soin de moi**
Wamitu me Sapotr	**Wamitu et Sapotr**
E kohië a Hnamek	**Là-bas à Hnamek**
Ke matre gaa co jon	**Car il y a moins de sagaies**
Upine une	**Entrailles de serpent**
Upine une	**Entrailles de serpent**
Xelene une	**Intestins de serpent**

Seloo song from Ouvéa (see p. 250)

Tehi ogos bong seventrin k'ame khöp tö cica me Kope, k'ena hiöu biju. More inyka-nyua auuuh ! k'amena khula, li dekö iöhmun	**Le 17 août, papa et Kope débarquent, et toi tu n'y es pas. More est à l'étranger, auuh ! nos larmes coulent.**
E sangbetenge ânyâm mök, una mokcu hon gatin m'öhmun na hnyi delûôuju	**Émouvante est ta mort, puisses-tu mourir chez nous,** **pour que nous puissions te porter.**
Ohmuna hnyi delûöuju me me na khula deköi iöhmun ka hnyi ûlâiâm	**Pourvu que l'on te porte aussi, pour que nos larmes coulent sur ta poitrine.**
Ohmune na he kana khaû hlitr, ae na hiö More biju hnyi anyihmun bunyen	**Nous allons nous vêtir tout en noir, parce que More est absente de notre bande.**

Wahaihai dance song from Ouvéa (see p. 243)

dénéa é missi hano	**Qui va doucement va sûrement**
ma mounagé dé wésel	**Premier coup de sifflet est donné**
godé wésel o Vito	**C'est le signal donné par Victor**
go Vito ma Kapua	**Par Victor et Kapua**
é tapa fafiné	**Rassemblement de toutes les femmes**
o hano ni mako	**Pour la répétition de chant et de danse**
ni mako mai Tonga	**Rassemblement dans la tribu de Tonga**
idé poo madé Ao	**Nuit et jour**
gidé Asso odé Sehnyün	**Pour le jour de la fête**
dénéa é missi hano	**Qui va doucement va sûrement**
Lékiné mai dé Atua	**Tribu de Lékiné premier sujet pour la construction**
Faga tai dé Fofonau	**Toute la tribu se réunit sous le regard du Seigneur**
Tou agé Waboula	**Waboula sujet important dans la tribu**
O Mounéa daou Mouna	**donne la parole**
tahina Mao Mai	**Vous les hommes dans la tribu**
gégou nago Mounéa	**supportez les travaux**
dé Bongon odé Huliwa	**et vous les femmes**
Tangata faga tafa	**vous allez contribuer**
Fafiné oukataué	**vous allez aider**
Soli lima kéou oti	**On se donne la main**
dénéa é missi hano	**Qui va doucement va sûrement**
Go Thamoa dé Makéké	**Thamoa est le petit chef de Lékiné**
go dodadoü döhnu	**C'est lui le soutien moral technique et physique**
lima i a taou néi	**de la population dans le travail**
Péna péna ina oti	**La force est considérée comme notre bien**
Amoa gé dé Fatou	**pour accéder à l'objectif**
Névéagé dé Belai	**Cinq ans de préparation**

Saon Saoua dé Oné *Goa paré dé Koloa*	Aujourd'hui tout est prêt, cailloux, caillasse, sable Tout le matériel est là
dénéa é missi hano *Kéliagé mala tranché* *Soukiagé mala Oumou* *Saounagé mala poteau* *Toukiagé dé kofrage* *Lingiagé dé béton* *Goa siai ogou Méne* *Goa Malingi dé Kakava* *Goudé kai Madé Sasa*	Qui va doucement va sûrement Un ordre est donné Creusez les tranchées Préparez le béton Plantez les poteaux Coffrez et coulez Les linteaux (lignages) le béton Plus de repos La sueur coule On mange dans la poussière
dénéa é missi hano *Goa Toukia dé Kapa* *ogou ngala gidé langi* *Déma goia tou dé Kourousé* *idé clocher* *Touagé à Victoria* *Tapagé à Doumai* *dénéi dogu bouquet* *Goa fétapa dé Fao* *Godé aso Alleluia*	Qui va doucement va sûrement Je contemple le ciel les hommes clouant les tôles La croix est déjà à sa place au clocher Victoria sujet important par respect pour le chef l'appelle pour lui présenter un bouquet La cloche nous appelle C'est jour de fête
dénéa é missi hano *Godé 29 juin* *Lékiné toagué dé Foé* *Ouvéa, Lifou et Maré* *Calédonie oti oti* *Ekétiagé de Vaka*	Qui va doucement va sûrement Le 29 juin fête patronale de Lekiné Ouvéa, Lifou et Maré et toute la Calédonie Montez dans le bateau
Saint-Pierre idé langi *Ihoagué a Gagnière* *Merci l'évêque Pierre Martin*	Saint-Pierre pensez à Gagnière Merci à l'évêque Pierre Martin

Seloo song from Ouvéa (see p. 249)

Walaang ötinaa löng ge bongon Jurop *Walee ke thaan hnyi Jomen jia Guillaume ien* *Ame penapena tajee unyi hnâân ûâât* *Baïonnette hele ûâât kuha ame cuha*	Écoutons les nouvelles venant d'Europe. Il s'agit d'un roi allemand, Guillaume est son nom. Il prépare l'armement pour la guerre. La baïonnette, le couteau de guerre et le fusil éclatant.
Walaang anyin ke metâ ame penapena *Ame kunâ je sumara ka he eû hnyin köiö* *Heka koû je hu walee jee mââniwââ* *Eti gaan sangbetenge ge at ame na laus*	Voici une de ces inventions qu'il projette, il envoie les sous-marins sous l'eau pour couler les navires qui sont des bateaux de guerre. Beaucoup de tristesse à l'égard de l'homme qui meurt.
Walaang hnen hnaûnykûme hnyi ûnykûmënen *Ame na weeny he ka ûâât me Paris* *Hnyi anyin tang metâ me anyin tanghwe-ge* *Kene oo but ame na ûâât ge hele me kuha*	Voici ce qu'il envisage dans son projet. Il veut entrer en guerre contre Paris, dans son intelligence et sa force, jusqu'à ce qu'il combatte au couteau et au fusil.
Walaang jee thauzan aa hiaa but *Hnen anyidrin jee metâ a e na kong obiny* *Ana bâ but at hwadeeny hnen je poizin* *Aeropilan, hele, kuha ame cuha*	Des milliers ont disparu à cause de ses inventions aux fins tragiques. Beaucoup d'hommes on disparu à cause de ses poisons, aéroplanes, couteaux et fusils éclatants.

Modern song from Ouvéa (see p. 252)

Masinaé oku ifo dou fai mataekité otina go mala fai sei	**Lune, j'aimerais bien avoir tes yeux pour pouvoir regarder et contempler toutes les fleurs.**
fai sei koai, fai sei mois de Marieogu paki gi Gomen	**Quelle fleur ? C'est celle qu'on appelle « mois de Marie ». Cette fleur est mon bouquet. Ce bouquet qui m'a conduit à Gomen, mon lieu de travail**
gi dunga savé nickel	**là où on travaille le nickel.**
Goa oti ifo idinéi	**Adieu mes amis**
domadoè fai mako fékité tantéhina fékité balua	**adieu mes frères et sœurs notre chant prend fin adieu.**

Wejein song from Lifou (see p. 237)

Ka jë hë pikok,	**Où es-tu pikok,**
ke ma, ke matré trona	**pour que je puisse chercher**
ngénu thel, e ciejë é Noumea, the,	**une place à Nouméa**
thei mama, ketré loi.	**chez les gens aisés ?**

BIBLIOGRAPHY

Unpublished Material

AMMANN, Raymond, 1989. *Flötenmusik am Sepik.* Universität Basel, Ethnologisches Seminar (Lizentiats-Arbeit).

DUBOIS, Marie-Joseph, 1969. *Dictionnaire maré-français, pene nengone (Nouvelle-Calédonie),* vol. I-IV. revised version in 1980.

DUBOIS, Marie-Joseph, 1973-1974. *Dictionnaire francais-belep (Nouvelle-Calédonie).*

DUBOIS, Marie-Joseph, undated. *Lexique de la langue kwenyii (île des Pins).*

GORODÉ, Waia, 1979. *Mon école du silence.* Manuscript.

KASARHEROU, Christiane, 1991. *L'Histoire démographique de la population mélanésienne de la Nouvelle-Calédonie 1840-1850.* DEA- thesis in history, Université de Paris I, Panthéon-Sorbonne.

MONTAGUE, Paul, D., undated. *Ethnographical Notes from the Houailou Valley.* Extrait : Social Organisation and Customs. Manuscrit v : CUMAA, 0A2/9/7 (Brx 97). Concerning the years 1913 and 1914.

OHLEN, Carole, 1987. *Iconographie des bambous gravés de Nouvelle-Calédonie.* Maîtrise - thesis in ethno-esthétique et sciences de l'art, Université de Paris I, Panthéon-Sorbonne.

Rapports manuscrits de prêtres sur "les fêtes païennes" pour la première Conférence Ecclésiastique du Vicariat Apostolique de Nouvelle-Calédonie (see Montrouzier 1885).

SALOMON-NÉKIRIAI, Christine, 1993. *Savoirs, savoirs-faire et pouvoirs thérapeutiques. Guérisseurs kanak et relation de guérissage dans la région centre-nord de la Grande Terre.* Mémoire - thesis of E.P.H.E., section Sciences religieuses, Paris (written by request of the A.D.C.K., Nouméa).

SAND, Christophe, 1994. *La Préhistoire de la Nouvelle-Calédonie, Contribution à l'étude des modalités d'adaption et d'évolution des sociétés océaniennes des un archipel de Sud de la Mélanésie.* Thesis in archeology, Université de Paris I, Panthéon-Sorbonne.

SPEARRITT, Gordon, D., 1979. *The Music of the Iatmul People of the Middle Sepik River (Papua New Guinea) with Special Reference to Instrumental Music of Kandagai and Aibom.* University of Queensland, St. Lucia (Ph.D. Dissertation).

Published Material

AMMANN, Raymond, 1993. "An Introduction to Kanak Dances". In *Who We Are* : VIth Festival of Pacific Arts - Rarotonga - Cook Islands - 1992 : Delegation of New Caledonia. Nouméa : A.D.C.K., pp. 30-49.

AMMANN, Raymond, 1993b. "Les Musiques de danse traditionnelle". *Mwà Véé* (Nouméa : A.D.C.K.) 2:10-11.

AMMANN, Raymond, 1994. *Les Danses kanak: une introduction.* Nouméa : A.D.C.K.

AMMANN, Raymond, 1994b. "La Musique et les Danses de l'aire paicî". *Mwà Véé* (Nouméa : A.D.C.K.) 5:9-10.

AMMANN, Raymond, 1995. "La Renaissance de la flûte kanak". *Flûtes du Monde, de l'Océanie à Madagascar,* Revue Culturelle de l'Association *Flûtes du Monde.* Belfort : A.F.M.

AMMANN, Raymond, 1995. "Les trois flûtes" and "le pilou photographié". In *Studio Canaque, Histoire Kanak.* Cataloque de l'exposition du Musée Territorial de Nouvelle-Calédonie, Nouméa.

anonymous, 1967. *Airs. Mélodies des cantiques de l'Église évangélique en Nouvelle-Calédonie et aux îles Loyauté.* Nouméa : Église Évangélique, nouvelle édition.

anonymous, 1991. *Nuevare. Danses traditionnelles.* Catalogue du Festival de Danses Traditionnelles, 26 octobre - 11 novembre 1991. Nouméa.

ANDERSEN, Johannes, C., 1934. *Maori Music with its Polynesian Background.* Polynesian Society Memoir, 10, New Plymouth : Avery.

ARAMIOU, Sylvain & EURITÉIN, Jean, undated. *Peci rhe. Taperas mere A'xe A'jie.* Houaïlou : Fédération de l'Enseignement Libre Protestant, Collection Bweweye (Allée Centrale) 3.

ARCHAMBAULT, Marius, 1908. "Sur les chances de durée de la race canaque". *Bulletins et Mémoires de la Société d'Anthropologie de Paris* (Paris) 5/19:492-502.

BATESON, Gregory, 1931. "Social Structure of the Iatmul People of the Sepik River" . *Oceania* 2:245-291.

BAUDOUX, Georges, 1952. *Légendes canaques.* I : *Les vieux savaient tout.* Paris : Nouvelles Éditions Latines.

BAUDOUX, Georges, 1952b. *Légendes canaques.* II : *Ils avaient vu des hommes blancs.* Paris : Nouvelles Éditions Latines.

BEAUDET, Jean-Michel, 1984. "Les Instruments de musique kanak / Kanak Musical Instruments". *Pacific 2000* (Nouméa) 6:25-34.

BEAUDET, Jean-Michel, 1984b. "Un air de flûte". *La Case* (Nouméa : O.C.S.T.C.) 2:20-21.

BEAUDET, Jean-Michel, 1986. "Les Chants de type ayoii". *La Case* (Nouméa : O.C.S.T.C.) 5:54.

BEAUDET, Jean-Michel & TEIN, Kaloombat, Gilbert, 1985. "Musique de Hienghène". *La Case* (Nouméa : O.C.S.T.C.) 4:2-25.

BENESH, Rudolf & Joan, 1956. *An Introduction to Benesh Dance Notation.* London : A & C Black Ltd.

BENESH, Rudolf & Joan, 1983. *Reading Dance. The Birth of Choreology.* London : Souvenir Press. (First published : 1977).

BENSA, Alban, 1983. "Le Masque dans la région de Touho (aire linguistique cèmuhî), Nouvelle-Calédonie". In *Océanie : le masque au long cours.* ed. François Lupu. Rennes : Ouest-France, p. 67-68.

BENSA, Alban, 1990. *Nouvelle-Calédonie, un paradis dans la tourmente.* Histoire 85, Paris : Gallimard.

BENSA, Alban, 1996. "L'Auto-sacrifice du chef dans la société kanak d'autrefois". In *Les Cahiers d'Arcanes.* Paris : Arcanes, pp. 101-120.

BENSA, Alban & RIVIERRE, Jean-Claude, 1976. "De quelques genres littéraires dans la tradition orale paicî (Nouvelle-Calédonie)". *Journal de la Société des Océanistes* (Paris : Musée de l'Homme), XXXII/50:31-65.

BENSA, Alban & RIVIERRE, Jean-Claude, 1982. *Les Chemins de l'alliance. L'organisation sociale et ses représentations en Nouvelle-Calédonie.* Langues et Cultures du Pacifique. Paris : SELAF.

BENSA, Alban & RIVIERRE, Jean-Claude, 1990. "Une poésie paicî : la mort du chef Céu". In *De jade et de nacre. Patrimoine artistique kanak.* Paris : Réunion des Musées Nationaux, pp. 198-205.

BENSA, Alban & RIVIERRE, Jean-Claude, 1995. *Les Filles du rocher Até. Contes et récits paicî.* Patrimoine kanak de Nouvelle-Calédonie 1. Nouméa/Paris : A.D.C.K./Geuthner.

BERNARD, Augustin, 1895. *L'Archipel de la Nouvelle-Calédonie*, Paris : Librairie Hachette.

BLACKING, John, 1973. *How Musical is Man ?* Seattle : University of Washington Press.

BOITEAU, Pierre, 1981. *Flore de la Nouvelle-Calédonie et dépendances.* Tome 10, *Apocynacées.* Paris : Muséum National d'Histoire Naturelle.

BOULARD, Jean-Claude, 1992. "Premières rencontres : sens et contresens". In *Nouvelles-Calédonies... d'avant 1914.* Paris : Association Pacifique, pp. 52-61.

BOULAY, Roger, 1984. *La Grande Case des Kanaks : documents autour de l'architecture traditionnelle.* Nouméa : O.C.S.T.C.

BOULAY, Roger, 1993. *Le Bambou gravé kanak.* Arts témoins. Marseille/Nouméa : Parenthèses/A.D.C.K.

BRAINNE, Charles, 1854. *La Nouvelle-Calédonie. Voyages. Missions. Mœurs. Colonisation (1774-1854).* Paris : Librairie Hachette et Cie.

BROU, Bernard, 1987. *Préhistoire et société traditionnelle de la Nouvelle-Calédonie.* Nouméa : Société d'Études Historiques de la Nouvelle-Calédonie 16. (First published : 1977).

BROU, Bernard, 1992. *Histoire de la Nouvelle-Calédonie. Les temps modernes : 1774-1925.* Nouméa, Société d'Études Historiques de la Nouvelle-Calédonie 4. (First published : 1973).

BROWNING, Mary, 1973. "Micronesian Heritage". *Dance Perspectives* 43. New York : Éditions Selma Jeanne Cohen.
BURCHETT, Wilfred, G., 1942. *Pacific Treasure Island, New Caledonia. Voyage through its Land and Wealth. The Story of its People and Past.* Melbourne : Cheshire F.W.
BURROWS, Edwin, G., 1940. « Polynesian Music and Dancing ». *Journal of the Polynesian Society* 49:331-46.
BURROWS, Edwin, G., 1945. *Songs of Uvea and Futuna.* Honolulu : B. P. Bishop Museum Bulletin, 183.
CANÉ, Edmond, 1948. "Infiltration des Polynésiens dans les îles voisines de la Nouvelle-Calédonie". *Études Mélanésiennes* (Nouméa), 3:14-17.
CHILKOVSKY, Nadia, 1978. *Introduction to Dance Literacy.* Roodespoort : International Library of African Music.
CHRISTENSEN, Dieter & KOCH, Gerd, 1964. *Die Musik der Ellice-Inseln.* Berlin : Museum für Völkerkunde.
CODRINGTON, R., H., 1972. *The Melanesians : Studies in their Anthropology and Folklore.* New York : Dover Publications. (First published : 1891, Oxford : Clarendon Press).
COPPET, Daniel de & ZEMP, Hugo, 1978. *'Aré'aré, un peuple mélanésien et sa musique.* Paris : Seuil.
COURANT, Victor, 1931. *Le Martyr de la Nouvelle-Calédonie. Blaise Marmoiton, frère coadjuteur de la Société de Marie, 1812-1847.* Lyon-Paris : Librairie catholique Emmanuel Vitte.
COURTIS, Christine, 1984. *Après 1878 : les souvenirs du capitaine Kanappe.* Nouméa : Société d'Études Historiques de la Nouvelle-Calédonie 35.
CROWE, Peter, 1981. "After the Ethnomusicological Salvage Operation - What ?" *Journal of the Polynesian Society* (Wellington) 90/2:171-182.
CROWE, Peter, 1990. "Dancing Backwards ?" *World of Music* (Berlin) 32/1:84-98.
CROWE, Peter, 1995. "Des tambours à fente au Vanuatu". *Percussion* 39:24-29.
CROWE, Peter, 1996. "La Musique au Vanuatu". In *Vanuatu, Océanie, Arts des îles de cendre et de corail.* ed. Bonnemaison, Huffman, Kaufmann. Paris : Réunion des Musées Nationaux, pp. 146-159.
DEAN, Beth, 1968. *The Many Worlds of Dance.* Sydney : Murray.
DEAN, Beth, 1977. *Three Dances of Oceania.* Sydney : Sydney Opera House Trust.
DEAN, Beth, 1978. *South Pacific Dance.* Sydney : Pacific Publications.
DELACOUR, Jean, 1966. *Guide des oiseaux de la Nouvelle-Calédonie.* Neuchâtel : Delachaux & Niestlé.
DELBRIDGE, A.(ed.), 1988. *The Macquarie Dictionary, Second Revision.* Macquarie University, NSW : The Macquarie Library Pty Ltd. (First published 1981).
DELLENBACH, Marguerite, 1936. "Bambous gravés de la Nouvelle-Calédonie". *Archives Suisses d'Anthropologie générale* (Genève) VII/3:259-276.
DOUGLAS, Bronwen, 1970. "A History of the Balade People of New Caledonia 1774-1845". *The Journal of the Polynesian Society* (Wellington) 79:2, pp. 180-200.
DUBOIS, Marie-Joseph, 1951. "Be-be-nod, danse de Maré". *Études Mélanésiennes* (Nouméa) 5:145-146.
DUBOIS, Marie-Joseph, 1968. *Géographie mythique et traditionnelle de l'île de Maré.* Paris : Institut d'Ethnologie.
DUBOIS, Marie-Joseph, 1975. *Mythes et traditions de Maré (Nouvelle-Calédonie) : les Eletok.* Paris : Société des Océanistes 35.
DUBOIS, Marie-Joseph, 1977. *Les Chefferies de Maré (Nouvelle-Calédonie).* Paris : Champion.
DUBOIS, Marie-Joseph, 1981. *Histoire résumée de Maré (îles Loyauté).* Nouméa : Société d'Études Historiques de la Nouvelle-Calédonie 27.
DUBOIS, Marie-Joseph, 1984. *Gens de Maré : Ethnologie de l'île de Maré, îles Loyauté, Nouvelle-Calédonie.* Paris : Éditions Anthropos.
DUBOIS, Marie-Joseph, 1989. "Be be nod : chant guerrier de Maré (Nouvelle-Calédonie)". *Flamboyant Imaginaire* (Nouméa) 2:15-25.
DUBOIS, Marie-Joseph, 1990. "Maré contre Hitler, le chant de Vahnara, Maré (îles Loyauté), poème et chant guerrier traditionnel. Un péan de 1946 ". *Bulletin de la Société d'Études Historiques de la Nouvelle-Calédonie* (Nouméa) 84:3-16.
DUBOIS, Marie-Joseph & NAGIEL, Véronique, 1992. "La Danse des pêcheurs fantômes de Wapâng (de l'île des Pins)". In *La Fête.* Nouméa : Actes du Colloque C.O.R.A.I.L. 1991, pp. 189-211.
DUBOIS, Marie-Joseph, 1996. "Le Vanuatu vu de Maré". In *Vanuatu, Océanie, Arts des îles de cendre et de corail.* ed. Bonnemaison, Huffman, Kaufmann. Paris : Réunion des Musées Nationaux, pp. 82-85.

DURAND, Jules, 1900. "Chez les Ouébias en Nouvelle-Calédonie". *Le Tour du Monde* (Paris), VI/42-43.

EDGE-PARTINGTON, James, 1895. *An Album of the Weapons, Tools, Ornaments, Articles of Dress etc. of the Natives of the Pacific Islands, etc.*, vol. 2. Manchester : J. C. Norbury.

ELLISON, Suri, 1980. *Ten Traditional Dances from Solomon Islands.* Honiara : University of the South Pacific.

EMERSON, Nathaniel, B., 1909. *Unwritten Literature of Hawai'i. The Sacred Songs of the Hula.* Washington : Bureau of American Ethnology Bulletin, 38.

FAGOT, 1948. "Relations familiales et coutumières entre les chefferies aux îles Loyalty". *Journal de la Société des Océanistes* (Paris : Musée de l'Homme) IV/4:87-96.

FISCHER, Hans, 1983. *Sound-Producing Instruments in Oceania.* Trad. Philip W. Holzknecht. Boroko : Institute of Papua New Guinea Studies. (First published in German : 1958. *Schallgeräte in Ozeanien.* Strasbourg-Baden-Baden : Heitz).

FORSTER, Georg, 1966. *Georg Forsters Werke, sämtliche Schriften, Tagebücher, Briefe.* 3. Band. Reise um die Welt II. ed. Gerhard Steiner. Berlin : Deutsche Akademie der Wissenschaften zu Berlin, Akademie Verlag.

FOUCHER, Philippe, 1984. *Nomenclature cartophile de Nouvelle-Calédonie : cartes postales anciennes 1900-1945.* Marseille : Éditions du Premier Mai.

FRANKS, A., H., 1963. *Social Dance, a Short History.* London : Routledge and Kegan Paul.

GARDNER, Robert & HEIDER, Karl, G., 1968. *Gardians of War. Life and Death in the New Guinea Stone Age.* New York : Random House.

GARNIER, Jules, 1990. *Voyage à la Nouvelle-Calédonie.* Nouméa : Éditions du Cagou. (Première publication : 1978). (Facsimile of *Le Tour du Monde*, t. 16, 2e sem. 1867, pp. 155-208, et t. 18, 2e sem. 1868, pp. 1-64. Paris : Librairie Hachette).

GARRETT, John, 1992. *Footsteps in the Sea : Christianity in Oceania to World War II.* Suva/Genève : Institute of Pacific Studies of the U.S.P./World Council to Churches.

GASSER, Bernard, 1992. "La Fête canaque sur la Grande Terre vue par les Européens, dans la littérature d'inspiration calédonienne". In *La Fête.* Actes du colloque C.O.R.A.I.L. 1991. Nouméa : C.O.R.A.I.L., pp. 121-145.

GASSER, Bernard, 1993. "Le Contact entre Européens et Canaques dans les nouvelles de Georges Baudoux". In *Voyage, découverte, colonisation.* Actes du colloque C.O.R.A.I.L. 1992. Nouméa : C.O.R.A.I.L., pp. 145-164.

GODARD, Philippe, 1978. *Le Mémorial calédonien. 1. 1774-1863.* Nouméa : Nouméa-Diffusion.

GOODALE, Jane, C., 1986. "Gender, Sexuality and Marriage : A Kaulong Model of Nature and Culture". In *Nature, Culture and Gender.* ed. Cormack & Strathern. Cambridge : University Press, pp. 119-142.

GOODALE, Jane, C., 1995. *To Sing with Pigs is Human : the Concept of Person in Papua New Guinea.* Seattle : University of Washington Press.

GORODÉ, Déwé, 1994. "Introduction à la littérature orale du pays paicî". *Mwà Véé* (Nouméa) 6:10-11.

GORODÉ, Waia, 1990. "Le Grand Deuil". In *De jade et de nacre. Patrimoine artistique kanak.* Paris : Réunion des Musées Nationaux, 1990, pp. 170-188 (extract of the unpublished manuscript 1979).

GOUBIN, Benjamin, 1985. *Lifou Pacifique-Sud : une chronique de la Nouvelle-Calédonie, de 1876 à 1916, d'après la correspondance de Benjamin Goubin, missionnaire et ardéchois.* ed. Jean-Luc Chaulet. Colombier le Cardinal : Jean-Luc Chaulet.

GOURLAY, Kenneth, A., 1975. *Sound-Producing Instruments in Traditional Society : A Study of Esoteric Instruments and their Role in Male-Female Relations.* New Guinea Research Bulletin, 60. Port Moresby/Canberra : Australian National University.

GRACE, George, W., 1975. *Canala Dictionary (New Caledonia).* Canberra : The Australian National University, (Pacific Linguistics. Series C/2).

GUIART, Jean, 1952. "Les Origines de la population d'Ouvéa (Loyalty) et la place des migrations en cause sur le plan général océanien". *Études Mélanésiennes* (Nouméa) 6:26-35. (First published : 1950. *Bulletin de la Société des Études Océaniennes* (Papeete), 8/4:149-159).

GUIART, Jean, 1953. *L'Art autochtone de Nouvelle-Calédonie.* Nouméa : Éditions des Études Mélanésiennes.

GUIART, Jean, 1953b. "Mythes et chants polynésiens d'Ouvéa (îles Loyalty)". *Journal of the Polynesian Society* (Wellington) 62:93-117.

GUIART, Jean, 1953c. "Nouvelle-Calédonie et îles Loyalty. Carte du dynamisme de la société indigène à l'arrivée des Européens". In *Un siècle d'acculturation en Nouvelle-Calédonie 1853-1953, Journal de la Société des Océanistes* (Paris : Musée de l'Homme) IX/9:93-97.
GUIART, Jean, 1956. "Notes sur une cérémonie de grade chez les Big Nambas". *Journal de la Société des Océanistes* (Paris : Musée de l'Homme), XII/12:227-243.
GUIART, Jean, 1957. *Contes et légendes de la Grande Terre.* Nouméa : Éditions des Études Mélanésiennes.
GUIART, Jean, 1959. "Le Dieu porteur de masque en Nouvelle-Calédonie". In *Le Masque.* Paris : Édition des Musées Nationaux, pp. 30-32.
GUIART, Jean, 1963. *Structure de la chefferie en Mélanésie du Sud.* Travaux & Mémoires de l'Institut d'Ethnologie, LXVI. Paris : Institut d'Ethnologie.
GUIART, Jean, 1977. "Maurice Leenhardt inconnu : l'homme d'action". *Objets et Mondes. La Revue du Musée de l'Homme* (Paris) t. 17, 2:75-84.
GUIART, Jean, 1987. *Mythologie du masque en Nouvelle-Calédonie.* Paris : Société des Océanistes 18. (First published : 1966). (includes a reprint of Leenhardt 1933, pp. XI-XIX).
GUIART, Jean, 1992. *Structure de la chefferie en Mélanésie du Sud*, vol. 1. Paris, Institut d'Ethnologie. (revised and updated edition of 1963).
HADFIELD, Emma, 1920. *Among the Natives of the Loyalty Group.* London : MacMillan.
HAUDRICOURT, André-Georges, 1963. *La Langue des Nenemas et des Nigoumak. Dialectes de Poum et de Koumac, Nouvelle-Calédonie.* Te Reo Monographs. Auckland : Linguistic Society of New Zealand.
HAUDRICOURT, André-Georges & OZANNE-RIVIERRE, Françoise, 1982. *Dictionnaire thématique des langues de la région de Hienghène (Nouvelle-Calédonie) : pije - fwâi - nemi - jawe.* Lacito-Documents, Asie-Austronésie 4. Paris : SELAF.
HAUSER-SCHÄUBLIN, Brigitta, 1977. *Frauen in Karrarau, Zur Rolle der Frau bei den Jatmul.* Basel : Basler Beiträge zur Ethnologie 18.
HOLLYMAN, Kenneth, Jim, 1966. "Un nouveau manuscrit sur la Nouvelle-Calédonie : le travail de J. Mauger". *Journal de la Société des Océanistes* (Paris : Musée de l'Homme) XXII-22:111-113.
HOLLYMAN, Kenneth, Jim, 1987. *De muna fagauvea I : dictionnaire fagauvea-français.* Te Reo Monographs. Canberra : Linguistic Study of New Zealand.
HOWE, Kerry, R., 1977. *The Loyalty Islands : a History of Culture Contacts 1840-1900.* Canberra : Australian National University Press. (translated into French : 1978. *Les Îles Loyauté. Histoire des contacts culturels de 1840 à 1900.* Nouméa : Société d'Études Historiques de la Nouvelle-Calédonie 19).
HUFFMAN, Kirk, 1996. "Flûtes en bambou". In *Vanuatu, Océanie, Arts des îles de cendre et de corail.* ed. Bonnemaison, Huffman, Kaufmann. Paris : Réunion des Musées Nationaux, pp. 152-155.
HUMPHREYS, C., B., 1926. *The Southern New Hebrides : An Ethnological Record.* Cambridge : Cambridge University Press.
HUTCHINSON, Ann, 1973. *Labanotation or Kinetography Laban. The System of Analyzing and Recording Movement.* New York, Theatre Art Book. (First published : 1954).
IHAGE, Weniko, 1992. *La Tradition orale à Lifou.* Nouméa : Éditions du Niaouli/A.D.C.K.
IRWIN, Geoffrey, 1992. *The Prehistoric Exploration and Colonisation of the Pacific.* Cambridge : Cambridge University Press.
JONASSEN, Jon, 1991. *Cook Islands Drums.* Rarotonga : Ministry of Cultural Development, Government of the Cook Islands.
JOWITT, Glenn, 1990. *Dance in the Pacific.* ed. John Hart & Kath Joblin. Auckland : Longman Paul.
KAEPPLER, Adrienne, L., 1980. "Polynesian Music and Dance". In *Musics of Many Cultures - An Introduction.* ed. Elizabeth May. Berkeley : University of California Press, pp. 134-153.
KAEPPLER, Adrienne, L., 1983. *Polynesian Dance with a Selection for Contemporary Performances.* Honolulu : Alpha Delta Kappa.
KAEPPLER, Adrienne, L., 1993. *Hula Pahu, Hawaiian Drum Dances*, vol. I. *Bulletin Anthropology* 3. Honolulu : Bishop Museum Press.
KAEPPLER, Adrienne, L., 1993b. *Poetry in Motion : Studies of Tongan Dance.* Tonga : Vava'u Press.
KASARHEROU, Emmanuel, 1990. "Les Saisons et les Jardins". In *De jade et de nacre. Patrimoine artistique kanak*, pp. 50-66. Paris : Réunion des Musées Nationaux.

KASARHEROU, Emmanuel, 1990b. "Le Masque". In *De jade et de nacre. Patrimoine artistique kanak*, pp. 143-151. Paris : Réunion des Musées Nationaux.

KASARHEROU, Emmanuel, 1990c. "La Hache ostensoir". In *De jade et de nacre. Patrimoine artistique kanak*, pp. 152-154. Paris : Réunion des Musées Nationaux.

KASARHEROU, Emmanuel, 1993. *Le Masque kanak.* Arts témoins. Marseille/Nouméa : Parenthèses/A.D.C.K.

KEITSCH, Frank, 1967. *Formen der Kriegsführung in Melanesien.* Inaugural-Dissertation. Tübingen : Eberhard-Karts-Universität.

KNOBLAUCH, Ferdinand & al., [1988]. *Six textes anciens sur la Nouvelle-Calédonie.* Nouméa : Société d'Études Historiques de Nouvelle-Calédonie 42.

LA HAUTIÈRE, Ulysse de, 1980. *Souvenirs de la Nouvelle-Calédonie.* Nouméa : Hachette-Calédonie. (Fac-similé de 1869, Paris : Challamel Ainé).

LAINÉ, Hélène, 1942. *Pioneer Days in New Caledonia. A Story of Pacific Island Settlement.* ed.and transl. H. E. L. Priday. Nouméa : Imprimeries Réunies. (translated from 1942, *Hommage filial. Documentaire calédonien*).

LAMBERT, Pierre, 1985. *Mœurs et superstitions des Néo-Calédoniens.* Nouméa : Société d'Études Historiques de la Nouvelle-Calédonie 14. (Facsimile of 1900, Nouméa : Nouvelle Imprimerie Nouméenne).

LARSEN, May & Henry, 1961. *The golden Cowrie : New Caledonia, its People and Places.* Edinburgh/London : Oliver and Boyd.

LAVILLE, Jean, 1949. "Les Trois Districts d'Ouvéa". *Études Mélanésiennes* (Nouméa) 4:16-18.

LAVILLE, Jean & BERKOWITZ, Joseph, 1944. *Pacific Island Legends : Life and Legends in the South Pacific Islands.* Nouméa : Librairie Pentecost.

LEENHARDT, Maurice, 1922. *La Grande Terre, mission de la Nouvelle-Calédonie.* Paris : Société des Missions Évangéliques. (revised edition of 1909, *La Grande Terre*).

LEENHARDT, Maurice, 1933. "Le Masque calédonien". *Bulletin du Musée d'Ethnographie du Trocadéro* (Paris) 6:3-21 (republished in Guiart 1966/1987, pp. XI-XIX. and in Leenhardt 1971, pp. 5-30).

LEENHARDT, Maurice, 1935. *Vocabulaire et grammaire de la langue houaïlou.* Travaux et Mémoires X. Paris : Institut d'Ethnologie.

LEENHARDT, Maurice, 1945. "Mawaraba Mapi. La signification du masque en Nouvelle-Calédonie". *Journal de la Société des Océanistes* (Paris : Musée de l'Homme) I/1:29-35. (republished in Leenhardt 1971, pp. 31-39).

LEENHARDT, Maurice, 1946. *Langues et dialectes de l'Austro-Mélanésie.* Travaux & Mémoires XLVI. Paris : Institut d'Ethnologie.

LEENHARDT, Maurice, 1953. Mythe du masque. In *Ethnologie de l'Union française*, t. 2, *Asie, Océanie, Amérique.* Paris : P.U.F., pp. 763-765.

LEENHARDT, Maurice, 1971. *La Structure de la personne en Mélanésie.* ed. H. J. Maxwell et C. Ruga-fiori. Maussiana I. Milan : S.T.O.A. (includes a reprint of Leenhardt 1933, pp. 5-30 and Leenhardt 1945, pp. 31-39).

LEENHARDT, Maurice, 1980. *Notes d'ethnologie néo-calédonienne.* Travaux & Mémoires VIII. Paris : Institut d'Ethnologie. (Facsimile of 1930).

LEENHARDT, Maurice, 1985. *Do Kamo, la personne et le mythe dans le monde mélanésien.* TEL 95. Paris : Gallimard. (First published : 1947).

LEENHARDT, Maurice, 1986. *Gens de la Grande Terre, Nouvelle-Calédonie.* Nouméa : Éditions du Cagou (Facsimile of 1937, Paris : Gallimard).

LEENHARDT, Raymond, H., 1978. "Figures mélanésiennes : le grand chef Amane des Poyes de 1898 à 1917". *Journal de la Société des Océanistes* (Paris : Musée de l'Homme) XXXIV/58-59:23-35.

LEMIRE, Charles, 1884. *Voyage à pied en Nouvelle-Calédonie et description des Nouvelles-Hébrides.* Paris : Challamel. (Facsimile 1979, Papeete : Les Éditions du Pacifique).

LENNIER, Gustave, 1896. *Description de la collection ethnographique océanienne qu'a offerte à la ville du Havre M. Le Mescam, négociant de Nouméa.* Le Havre : Imprimerie du journal *Le Havre.*

LENORMAND, Maurice, H., 1948. "Fehoa : danse et chant de guerre de Lifou". *Études Mélanésiennes* (Nouméa) 3:25-28.

LENORMAND, Maurice, H. & SAM, Léonard, Drilë, 1993. *Lifou. Origine des chefferies de la zone de Wé. Quelques éléments de la société traditionnelle.* Points d'Histoire 9. Nouméa : C.T.R.D.P.

LINDSTROM, Lamont, 1996. "Représentations matérielles et mentalité locale dans une île sans traditions artistiques importantes : Tanna". In *Vanuatu, Océanie, Arts des îles de cendre et de corail.* ed. Bonnemaison, Huffman, Kaufmann. Paris : Réunion des Musées Nationaux, pp. 124-129.

LOBSIGER-DELLENBACH, Marguerite & Georges, 1951. "Deux flûtes néo-calédoniennes". *Archives Suisses d'Anthropologie Générale* (Genève) XVI:165-170.

LOVREGLIO, Jacqueline & Janvier, 1989. *Mes chers canaques. La Nouvelle-Calédonie telle que je l'ai connue. Du Mans à Nouméa.* Paris : Téqui. (Publication of the recollections of Marthe Lion, from the period 1872-1876).

LYNNE, Hanna, Judith, 1987. *To Dance is Human, a Theory of Nonverbal Communication.* Chicago : University of Chicago Press. (First published : 1979).

MACKEE, Hugh, S., 1985. *Les Plantes introduites et cultivées en Nouvelle-Calédonie.* Paris : Muséum National d'Histoire Naturelle.

MALM, William, P., 1977. *Music Cultures of the Pacific, the Near East, and Asia.* 2e ed. Englewood Cliffs, N. J. : Prentice-Hall. (First published : 1967).

MANGEMATIN, Loïc, 1976. "Sisiwanyano et la fille du vent du nord". *Bulletin de la Société d'Études Historiques de la Nouvelle-Calédonie* (Nouméa) 29:45-49.

MARIOTTI, Jean, 1950. "Pilou filmé en Nouvelle-Calédonie". *Journal de la Société des Océanistes* (Paris : Musée de l'Homme) VI/6:252.

MARIOTTI, Jean, 1953. *Nouvelle-Calédonie : le livre du Centenaire 1853-1953.* Paris : Horizons de France.

MAYET, Henri, [1959]. *Mœurs et coutumes des indigènes.* Nouméa : Imprimeries Réunies. (Publication of the author's reports of interviews with Adrien Millet in 1929).

McFEE, Graham, 1992. *Understanding Dance.* London : Routledge.

McKESSON, John, A., 1990. "In Search of the Origins of the New Caledonian Mask". ed. F. Allan Hanson & Louise Hanson. In *Art and Identity in Oceania.* Bathurst : Crawford House Press, pp. 84-92.

McLEAN, Mervyn, 1974. "The New Zealand Nose Flute : Fact or Fallacy ?" *Journal of the Galpin Society* 27:79-94.

McLEAN, Mervyn, 1994. "Diffusion of Musical Instruments and their Relation to Language Migrations in New Guinea". *Kulele* : Occasional Papers on Pacific Music and Dance, 1. Port Moresby : Cultural Studies Division, National Research Institute.

McLEAN, Mervyn, 1995. *An Annoted Bibliography of Oceanic Music and Dance.* Michigan : Harmonie Park Press (First published : 1977).

McPHERSON, Gordon & TIREL, Christiane, 1987. *Flore de la Nouvelle-Calédonie et dépendances.* Tome 14, Euphorbiaceae 1, Paris : Muséum National d'Histoire Naturelle.

MEAD, Margaret, 1934. "Tambarans and Tumbuans in New Guinea". *Natural History.*

MENENGO, Théophile, 1985. "Réflexion et enquête sur la musique traditionnelle". *La Case* (Nouméa : O.C.S.T.C.) 3:3-7.

MÉTAIS, Éliane, 1979. *Art néo-calédonien.* Paris : Nouvelles Éditions Latines 4.

MICHEL, Louise, 1988. *Légendes et chants de gestes canaques.* Paris : Éditions 1900. (First published : 1885. Paris : Kéva).

MISSOTTE, Philippe & TJIBAOU, Jean-Marie, 1984. *Kanaké, Mélanésien de Nouvelle-Calédonie.* Papeete : Les Éditions du Pacifique. (First published : 1976). (English translation : 1978. *Kanaké, the Melanesian Way.* Papeete : Les Éditions du Pacifique. Première publication : 1976).

MONCELON, Léon, 1886. *Les Canaques de la Nouvelle-Calédonie et des Nouvelles-Hébrides. La colonisation européenne en face de la sauvagerie locale.* Paris : Jouve. (paper given on 3rd December 1885 to the 'Société Française de Colonisation').

MONFAT, P., A., 1925. *Dix années en Mélanésie. Étude historique et religieuse.* Paris : Librairie Catholique Emmanuel Vitte.

MONTROUZIER, Xavier, 1885. *Les Fêtes païennes.* Compte rendu des Conférences Ecclésiastiques du Vicariat Apostolique de la Nouvelle-Calédonie, fasc. 1. Nouméa : Imprimerie Catholique.

MORRISON, Boone & CHUN, Malcolm, Naea, 1983. *Images of the Hula.* Hawai'i : Summit Press.

MOULIN, Jane, Freeman, 1979. *The Dance of Tahiti.* Papeete : Gleizal/Les Éditions du Pacifique.

MOULIN, Jane, Freeman, 1994. "Music of the Southern Marquesas Islands". *Occasional Papers in Pacific Ethnomusicology* 3. Auckland : University of Auckland, Department of Anthropology.

MOYLE, Richard, 1988. *Traditional Samoan Music.* Auckland : Auckland University Press/The Institute for Polynesian Studies.

MOYLE, Richard, 1989. *The Sounds of Oceania : An Illustrated Catalogue of the Sound-Producing Instruments of Oceania in the Auckland Institute and Museum.* Auckland : Auckland Institute and Museum.

MOYLE, Richard, 1990. *Polynesian Sound-Producing Instruments.* Princes Risborough : Shire Publications.

MOYLE, Richard, 1991. *Polynesian Music and Dance.* Auckland : Centre for Pacific Studies, University of Auckland.

MOYLE, Richard, 1995. « Singing From the Heart ? ». In *The Essence of Singing and the Substance of Song, Recent Responses to the Aboriginal Performing Arts and other Essays in Honour of Catherine Ellis.* ed. Linda Barwick et al. Sydney : Oceania Monograph 46, University of Sydney, pp. 53-58.

MOYSE-FAURIE, Claire & NECHERO-JOREDIE, Marie-Adèle, 1986. *Dictionnaire xârâcùù-français (Nouvelle-Calédonie).* Nouméa : Edipop.

MOYSE-FAURIE, Claire & RIVIERRE, Jean-Claude, 1992. "Langues". In *Nouvelles-Calédonies... d'avant 1914.* Paris : Association Pacifique, pp. 36-43.

Mwà Véé, Revue Culturelle Kanak. 1995[10] / 1995[11] / 1996[13]. Nouméa : A.D.C.K.

NEVERMANN, Hans, 1942. *Kulis und Kanaken, Forscherfahrten auf Neukaledonien und in den Neuen Hebriden.* Braunschweig : Gustav Wenzel und Sohn.

OPIGEZ, Octave, 1886. "Aperçu général sur la Nouvelle-Calédonie". *Bulletin de la Société de Géographie* (Paris), 7:403-451.

O'REILLY, Patrick, undated. *Dancing Tahiti.* Paris : Nouvelles Éditions Latines.

O'REILLY, Patrick, 1946. "Quelques disques loyaltiens et calédoniens enregistrés en France". *Journal de la Société des Océanistes* (Paris : Musée de l'Homme) II/2:101-107.

O'REILLY, Patrick, 1978. *La Nouvelle-Calédonie vue par le photographe Allan Hughan il y a cent ans.* Paris : Nouvelles Éditions Latines.

O'REILLY, Patrick & POIRIER, Jean, 1953. "L'Évolution du costume". *Journal de la Société des Océanistes* (Paris : Musée de l'Homme) IX/9:151-169.

O'REILLY, Patrick & POIRIER, Jean, 1959. *Nouvelle-Calédonie : Documents iconographiques anciens.* Paris : Nouvelles Éditions Latines.

OZANNE-RIVIERRE Françoise, 1984. *Dictionnaire iaai-français (Ouvéa), Nouvelle-Calédonie.* Langues et Cultures du Pacifique 6. Paris : SELAF.

OZANNE-RIVIERRE Françoise & MAZAUDON, Martine, 1986. *Lexique nyâlayu (Balade), Nouvelle-Calédonie.* Notes et Documents. Paris : Lacito/C.N.R.S.

PANNETRAT, Martin, 1993. "1856. Au pays des alikis". *Bulletin de la Société d'Études Historiques de la Nouvelle-Calédonie* (Nouméa) 96:17-47. (First published : 1857. Le Havre : *Le Journal du Havre,* 7, 8 et 10 mai).

PARDON, Daniel, 1986. *Tahiti et les mers du sud / Tahiti and the Southern Seas, Portraits et Danses.* Villeurbanne/Papeete : Joie du Monde.

PATOUILLET, Jules, 1873. *Voyage autour du monde. Trois ans en Nouvelle-Calédonie.* Paris : Dentu.

PISIER, Georges, 1975. *Les Aventures du capitaine Cheyne dans l'archipel calédonien 1841-1842.* Nouméa : Société d'Études Historiques de la Nouvelle-Calédonie 7. (translation and edition of extracts of Cheyne, Andrew, 1971. *An Account of Trading Voyages in the Western Pacific, 1841-1844.* ed. Dorothy Shineberg. Pacific Series 3. Canberra : ANU Press).

PISIER, Georges, 1980. *Le Témoignage de Ta'unga ou la Nouvelle-Calédonie vue par un "teacher" polynésien avant l'implantation européenne.* Nouméa : Société d'Études Historiques de la Nouvelle-Calédonie 25. (translation and edition of extracts of Ta'unga o te Tini, 1968. *The Works of Ta'unga. Records of a Polynesian Traveller in the South Seas, 1833-1896.* ed. Ron et Marjorie Crocombe. Canberra : ANU Press).

PISIER, Georges, 1985. *Kounié ou l'île des Pins. Essai de monographie historique.* Nouméa : Société d'Études Historiques de la Nouvelle-Calédonie 1.

POORT, W. A., 1975. *The Dance in the Pacific : A Comparative and Critical Survey of Dancing in Polynesia, Micronesia and Indonesia.* Katwijk, Netherlands : Van Der Lee Press.

RAU, Éric, 1944. *Institutions et coutumes canaques.* Paris : Larose.

RALLU, Jean-Louis, 1990. *Les Populations océaniennes aux XIXe et XXe siècles.* Travaux et Documents, Cahier n° 128. Paris : Institut National d'Études Démographiques/Presses Universitaires de France.

REPORT of the I.F.M.C. Study Group for Folk Dance Terminology, 1972. 1974. « Foundations for the analysis of the structure and form of folk dance : a syllabus ». *Yearbook of the International Folk Music Coucil.* Vol.6, International Folk Music Council, Department of Music, Queen's University, Kingston, Ontario.

RIVIÈRE, Henri, 1881. *Souvenirs de la Nouvelle-Calédonie, l'insurrection canaque.* Paris : Calmann-Lévy.

RIVIERRE, Jean-Claude, 1981. "Linguistique". In *Atlas de la Nouvelle-Calédonie et dépendances.* Paris : ORSTOM, pl. 19.

RIVIERRE, Jean-Claude, 1983. *Dictionnaire paicî-français (Nouvelle-Calédonie).* Langues et Cultures du Pacifique 4. Paris : SELAF.

RIVIERRE, Jean-Claude, 1994. *Dictionnaire cèmuhî-français.* Langues et Cultures du Pacifique 9. Paris : SELAF.

ROCHAS, Victor de, 1862. *La Nouvelle-Calédonie et ses habitants. Productions, mœurs, cannibalisme.* Paris : Sartorius.

ROSSEN, Jane, Mink, 1987. *Songs of Bellona Island (No Taungua o Mungiki).* 2 vol. Acta Ethnogaphica Danica, 4 : Language and Culture of Rennell and Bellona Islands. Vol. 6, Copenhagen : Forlaget Kragen.

ROUVRAY, Louis, Loriot de, 1946. *Un homme de cran. Guillaume Douarre, premier évêque missionnaire de la Nouvelle-Calédonie.* Paris : Beauchesne et ses fils.

ROUGEYRON, Pierre, 1995. *Abrégé de la vie d'Hippolyte Bonou, chef de la tribu de Pouébo en Nouvelle-Calédonie.* Nouméa : Grain de Sable 2. (text written in 1868).

ROZIER, Claude, 1990. *La Nouvelle-Calédonie ancienne.* Paris : Librairie Fayard.

SACHS, Curt, 1937. *World History of the Dance.* transl. Bessie Schoenberg, New York : W. W. Norton and Company. (First published in German : 1933. *Eine Weltgeschichte des Tanzes.* Berlin : Dietrich Reimer/Ernst Vohsen).

SACHS, Curt & HORNBOSTEL, Eric von, 1914. "Systematik der Musikinstrumente". *Zeitschrift für Ethnologie* XLVI:553-590.

SAM, Léonard, Drilë, 1980. *Lexique lifou-français.* Nouméa : C.T.R.D.P.

SAM, Léonard, Drilë, 1995. *Dictionnaire drehu-français (Nouvelle-Calédonie).* Langues Canaques 16. Nouméa : C.T.R.D.P./C.P.R.D.P. des Îles Loyauté.

SAND, Christophe, 1993. *Archéologie en Nouvelle-Calédonie, État des recherches au début des années 1990 et perspectives d'avenir.* Nouméa : A.D.C.K./C.T.R.D.P.

SAND, Christophe, 1995. *"Le Temps d'avant". La préhistoire de la Nouvelle-Calédonie.* Paris : L'Harmattan.

SARASIN, Fritz, 1917. *Neu-Caledonien und die Loyalty-Inseln, Reiseerinnerungen eines Naturforschers.* Basel : Von Georg.

SARASIN, Fritz, 1929. "Ethnologie der Neu-Caledonier und Loyalty-Insulaner". In *Nova Caledonia, Forschungen in Neu-Caledonien und auf den Loyalty-Inseln.* München : Kreidel.

SARASIN, Fritz, 1931. "Neu-Caledonien". In *Aus den Tropen, Reiseerinnerungen aus Ceylon, Celebes und Neu-Caledonien,* pp. 144-194. Basel : Helbing und Lichtenhahn.

SAUSSOL, Alain, 1979. *L'Héritage. Essai sur le problème foncier mélanésien en Nouvelle-Calédonie.* Paris : Société des Océanistes 40.

SCHAEFFNER, André, 1980. *Origine des instruments de musique. Introduction ethnologique à l'histoire de la musique instrumentale.* Paris/La Haye/New York : Mouton. (First published : 1968).

SCHMID, Maurice, 1995. *Fleurs et plantes de Nouvelle-Calédonie.* Papeete : Les Éditions du Pacifique/Times Editions. (First published : 1981).

SHENNAN, Jennifer, 1981. "Approaches to the Study of Dance in Oceania: Is the Dancer Carrying an Umbrella or not?" *Journal of the Polynesian Society* (Wellington) 90/2:193-208.

SHENNAN, Jennifer, 1985. *Some Examples of Movement Notation (Kinetography Laban).* supplement to "The Maori Action Song". Wellington : Council for Education Research.

SHINEBERG, Dorothy, 1983. "Un nouveau regard sur la démographie historique de la Nouvelle-Calédonie". *Journal de la Société des Océanistes* (Paris : Musée de l'Homme) XXXIX/76:33-43.

SIRON, Jacques, 1994. *La Partition intérieure, jazz, musiques improvisées.* Paris : Éditions Outre Mesure. (First published : 1992).

SPEARRITT, Gordon, D., 1983. "The Pairing of Musicians and Instruments in Iatmul Society". *Yearbook of Traditional Music* 14:106-125.

SPEISER, Felix, 1990. *Ethnology of Vanuatu : an Early Twentieth Century Study.* Bathurst : Crawford House Press. (First published in German : 1923).

SPEISER, Felix, 1924. *Südsee, Urwald, Kannibalen : Reisen in den Neuen Hebriden und Santa-Cruz-Inseln.* Stuttgart : Strecker und Schröder.
SPENCER, Paul, 1988. *Society and the Dance. The Social Anthropology of Process and Performance.* Cambridge : Cambridge University Press.
STÖHR, Waldemar, 1987. *Kunst und Kultur aus der Südsee, Sammlung Clausmeyer Melanesien.* Köln : Rautenstrauch-Jöst Museum für Völkerkunde.
STRATHERN, Andrew, 1985. "A Line of Boys. Melpa Dance as a Symbol of Maturation". In *Society and the Dance.* ed. Paul Spencer. Cambridge : University Press, pp. 119-139.
TATAR, Elisabeth, 1993. *Hawaiian Drum Dances,* vol. II. The Pahu, Sounds of Power. *Bulletin in Anthropology* 3. Honolulu : Bishop Museum.
TCHOEAOUA, Eloi (ed.), 1982. *Contribution à l'histoire du pays kanak.* Nouméa : Association pour la Fondation d'un Institut Kanak d'Histoire Moderne.
TEIN, Kaloombat, Gilbert, 1984. "Le Pilou et le Jado". In *La Grande Case des Kanaks : documents autour de l'architecture traditionnelle.* ed. Roger Boulay. Nouméa : O.C.S.T.C., pp. 102-105.
TEIN, Kaloombat, Gilbert, 1984b. "Une histoire de Panié". *La Case* (Nouméa : O.C.S.T.C.) 2:22-23.
THOMAS, Allan, 1981. "The Study of the Acculturated Music in Oceania : 'Cheap and Tawdry Borrowed Tunes ?'" *Journal of the Polynesian Society* (Auckland) 90/2:183-191.
THOMAS, Allan & TAKAROGA, Kuautoga, 1992. "Hgorofutuna Report of a Survey of the Music of the West Futuna, Vanuatu". *Occasional Papers in Pacific Ethnomusicology* 2. Dep. of Anthropology. Auckland : University of Auckland.
THOMAS, Julian, 1886. *Cannibals and Convicts: Personal Experiences in the Western Pacific.* London : Cassel & Company.
TURNER, George, 1984. *19 Years in Polynesia, Missionary Life, Travels, and Researches in the Islands of the Pacific.* Papakura : R. MacMillan. (First published : 1861. London : John Snow).
TURPIN de MOREL, M., 1949. "Mœurs et coutumes canaques : le pilou". *Études Mélanésiennes* (Nouméa) 4:32-36.
TRYON, Darell, T., 1971. *Debu-English Dictionary.* Canberra : Australian National University 6. (First published : 1967).
VERMAST, A., [1902]. *Chez les Canaques de la Nouvelle-Calédonie. Aventures d'une famille de colons.* Gand : Vanderpoorten.
VILLARD, Jean-Albert, 1946. "Autour de la musique des Néo-Calédoniens, une audition de musique vocale néo-calédonienne". *Journal de la Société des Océanistes* (Paris : Musée de l'Homme) II/2:93-100.
VIEILLARD, Eugène & DEPLANCHE, Émile, 1862-1863. "Essais sur la Nouvelle-Calédonie". *Revue Maritime et Coloniale* (Paris), 6(1862):52-85, 203-235, 475-498, 615-656, 7(1863):81-100.
VOIS, Paul, 1939. "La Musique des vieux". *Études Mélanésiennes* (Nouméa) 2:10-13.
WALLIS, Mary, 1994. *The Fiji and New Caledonian Journal of Mary Wallis 1851-1853.* ed. David Routledge. Suva : Institut of Pacific Studies.
WEIRI, Lionel, 1986. "Confection d'un battoir". *La Case* (Nouméa : O.C.S.T.C.) 7:15-18.
YAYII, Phillip, Lamasisi, 1983. "Some Aspects of Traditional Dance Within Malanggan Tradition of North New Ireland". *Bikmaus* IV/3:33-48.
ZELZ, Caroline, Eliot, 1995. *Masken auf Neukaledonien.* Münster : Lit Verlag. Kulturanthropologische Studien 23.
ZEMP, Hugo, 1971. "Instruments de musique de Malaita (I)". *Journal de la Société des Océanistes* (Paris : Musée de l'Homme) XXVII/30:31-53.
ZEMP, Hugo, 1972. "Instruments de musique de Malaita (II)". *Journal de la Société des Océanistes* (Paris : Musée de l'Homme) XXVIII/34:7-48.

Discography

Music cassettes

AMMANN, Raymond, 1994. *Iaai 1. Chants traditionnels des îles Loyauté.* Nouméa : Centre Culturel Yeiwene Yeiwene/A.D.C.K.
AMMANN, Raymond, 1994. *Drehu 2. Chants traditionnels des îles Loyauté.* Nouméa : Centre Culturel Yeiwene Yeiwene/A.D.C.K.

AMMANN, Raymond, 1994. *Nengone 3. Chants traditionnels des îles Loyauté.* Nouméa : Centre Culturel Yeiwene Yeiwene/A.D.C.K.

BEAUDET, Jean-Michel, 1992. *Cada et ayoii : chants de Hienghène.* Nouméa : A.D.C.K.

Long play records, 33 rpm

Musiques canaques de Nouvelle-Calédonie. CLA MIA (collection particulière).

ZEMP, Hugo, 1972. *Flûtes de Pan mélanésiennes. 'Aré'aré,* vol. 1-3. Collection Musée de l'Homme. Paris : Vogue LDM 30104-6.

Compact Discs

AMMANN, Raymond, 1997. *Nouvelle-Calédonie / New Caledonia, Danses et musiques kanak / Kanak Dance and Music.* AIMP XLVIII, Musée d'Ethnographie, Genève. VDE CD-923.

BEAUDET, Jean-Michel, 1990. *Chants kanaks : cérémonies et berceuses.* Collection C.N.R.S./Musée de l'Homme. Le Chant du Monde LDX 274909.

CROWE, Peter, 1994. *Vanuatu (Nouvelles-Hébrides / New Hebrides), Singing-Danis Kastom/ Musiques coutumières / Custom Music.* AIMP XXXIV, Musée d'Ethnographie, Genève. VDE CD-796.

ZEMP, Hugo, 1990. *Polyphonies des îles Salomon : Guadalcanal et Savo.* Collection C.N.R.S./Musée de l'Homme. Le Chant du Monde LDX 274663.

ZEMP, Hugo, 1996. *Les Voix du monde : une anthologie des expressions vocales.* Collection C.N.R.S./Musée de l'Homme. Le Chant du Monde CMX 3741010-12.

Filmography

AMMANN, Raymond, 1994. *Danse de Ti.Ga.* 18', Nouméa : A.D.C.K.

anonymous, 1954. film without title. Archives A.D.C.K.

BIRONNEAU, Michel, 1990. *Le Cricket en Nouvelle-Calédonie.* 12', Nouméa : C.T.R.D.P.

BOUSSAT, Marc-Arnaud & AMMANN, Raymond, 1993. *La Danse de Wetr.* 26', Nouméa : A.D.C.K.

CIDOPUA, Auguste, 1992. *Danser avec les lutins.* 15', Nouméa : A.D.C.K.

CONNOLLY, Bob & ANDERSON, Robin, 1992. *Black Harvest.* 90'.

DAGNEAU, Gilles, 1995. *Levée de deuil à Tiaoué.* 20', Nouméa : A.D.C.K./R.F.O.

DAGNEAU, Gilles, 1995b. *Chants kanak : ayoii et cada.* 58', Nouméa : A.D.C.K./R.F.O.

DAGNEAU, Gilles, 1996. *Remember New Caledonia.* Nouméa : R.F.O.

LALIÉ, Jean-François, 1992. *Jèmââ.* 19', Nouméa : A.D.C.K.

PEU, Élie, 1992. *La Légende de Mwaxrenu.* 16', Nouméa : A.D.C.K.

RAVAT, Georges & CHANEL, Guy, 1975. *Mélanésia 2000.* 17', Chanel Production.

ROUEL, Alphonse, 1931. *Nouvelle-Calédonie, terre missionnaire.* 37', Société de Marie.

TRAVANT Brigitte, 1994. *Ae-ae se chante la nuit.* Nouméa : A.D.C.K.

WHAAP, Brigitte, 1992. *Mwakheny.* 17', Nouméa : A.D.C.K./Comité du Festival des Arts du Pacifique.

WHAAP, Brigitte & RAVEL, André, 1994. *Les Danses drui et trutru aho.* 11', Nouméa : A.D.C.K./Centre Culturel Provincial Yeiwene.

WHAAP, Brigitte & RAVEL, André, 1994b. *La Danse bua.* 10', Nouméa : A.D.C.K./Centre Culturel Provincial Yeiwene.

WHAAP, Brigitte & RAVEL, André, 1994c. *La Danse Drengeju cileje trohemi.* 15', Nouméa : A.D.C.K./Centre Culturel Provincial Yeiwene.

WHAAP, Brigitte & RAVEL, André, 1994d. *La Danse tchap.* 10', Nouméa : A.D.C.K./Centre Culturel Provincial Yeiwene.

ZEMP, Hugo, 1979. *Tailler le bambou.* 36', Paris : SERDDAV/C.N.R.S.

ZEMP, Hugo, 1979. *Musique 'Aré'aré.* 2 h 30, Paris : C.N.R.S. Audiovisuel.

GLOSSARY

ae-ae : traditional songs of the centre and north of the *Grande Terre* ; performed by two singers and accompanied by percussion instruments.

apouéma : the Cèmuhî word for 'mask'. It has often been used in ethnographical and other literature as a generic term for the New Caledonian mask.

ayoii : traditional songs of the Hienghène region performed by two singers and accompanied by percussion instruments.

bagayou : New Caledonian term for a penis sheath.

be be nod : one of the oldest dances on Maré, that is still performed.

bèèmä : mimetic dance of the Paicî-Cèmuhî region.

bwinji-bet : Iaai word for the 'leaf parcel'.

blackbirders : Australian and Fijian seamen who hired (sometimes kidnapped) natives on Pacific islands to work on sugar cane plantations in Queensland and Fiji from the 1860s onwards.

boria : Ajië name for the round-dance. It was used by Leenhardt as a general term for the round-dance on the *Grande Terre.*

bua : war dance from Lifou.

buru : a 'sling' or 'propelling string' on Maré.

bwan-jep : name of the concussion bark-clapper in some languages of the north of the *Grande Terre.*

bwénaado : Cèmuhî term for the exchange ceremony generally referred to as the *pilou-pilou.*

cäbu tabéâ : Paicî term for the round-dance.

cada : traditional songs introduced to the Hienghène region, performed by two singers and accompanied by percussion instruments.

cap : a cheerful and popular dance on Lifou where a boy and girl may dance together.

case : traditional Kanak house, conical in form with a central post (*poteau central*). The wooden structure is covered entirely with straw on the Loyalty Islands, on the *Grande Terre* the walls are covered with niaouli (*Melaleuca quinquenervia*) bark.

chef : chief (*petit chef* : lesser chief ; *grand chef* : high chief). Traditional Kanak society is hierachically structured with the *grand chef* at the top. This does not mean that he has absolute power. Frequently the *grand chef,* or a forebear, originated as a stranger who was adopted and invited to become the *grand chef.* He is surounded by people of high social status. A *grand chef* may be the head of a district containing several *petit chefs* or simply *chefs* with their subjects. A *petit chef* may be the head of a *tribu* or the head of a clan or lineage.

chefferie : In New Caledonia, a *chefferie* refers to all the subjects of a *chef,* or the *chef*'s family and also to the piece of land which he administers which may correspond to an administrative district. *Chefferie* is also used to refer to the houses, land and courtyard where the *chef* or *grand chef* resides.

ceremonial axes, in French *haches ostensoires,* the jade (nephrite) axes symbol of the *grand chef,* were called so by Catholic missionaries because of the (superficial) resemblance to their own ritual monstrances.

cèto (Cèmuhî spelling) - women's dance from the north of the *Grande Terre.*

club with long points (in Leenhardt 'casse-tête à longues pointes') : special kind of club probably used in many women's dances of the *Grande Terre* ; today it is used in the women's dance *cèto.*

coutume (custom) : The word *coutume* has many different meanings and it may include various actions for which there are specific terms in Kanak languages. On a basic level, the *coutume* may be translated as custom, something that is part of tradition and justified by time. The *coutume* can also be a gift consisting of a length of material on which are laid cigarettes, chewing tobacco, matches and paper money. Important *coutumes* may include yams, mats, or other material goods. A small *coutume*, perhaps consisting of only a few coins, is offered, for example, when entering the house of someone to whom one is not related, for the first time. *Coutumes* of great importance occur during weddings when members of the same lineage bring together goods and money to offer to the members of another lineage. A *coutume* may be offered when asking for forgiveness or when asking something from somebody etc. There are various reasons and ways of how and when to present a *coutume* and regional differences exist. The receiver of a *coutume* has to give back a *coutume* either of equal size or of a well accounted different size. With the *coutume* a delicate diplomatic affair of debt accumulation and prestige is played. A non-respect of certain rules can cause difficulties in the relationship between partners involved in a *coutume* and it is always possible to refuse a *coutume* which results in the public humilation of the person who has offered it.

colons : French settlers in New Calédonia.

daro : old traditional songs from the Houaïlou region.

doh : religious polyphonic songs of the Protestant church, notated in a particular system.

drui : generic term for the dances of the people from Drueulu (Lifou). Drui is the only dance today where a masked figure appears.

Eletok : Ancient chiefs and land owners on Maré, according oral history, they were eliminated in a revolution that lasted from the end of the 18th century to the middle of the 19th century.

era : Nengone word for 'song' and 'to sing'.

faimanu : dance with synchronised mouvements from Muli (Ouvéa).

fehoa : venerated dances of Lifou, similar dances on Maré are called *pehua* and on Ouvéa *fehuô*.

four-beat rhythm : a particular 'rhythm' that accompanies several mimetic dances. The percussion part of the 'rhythm' consists of a pattern of four beats, indefinitely repeated.

hae hae : lullabies and songs sung to children on Maré.

haze : magic stone on Lifou

heterophony : "The superposition on a melody of its own variations. The variations are most frequently improvised and consist of small diversions from the melodic line which can be modulations, grace notes or shifts in rhythm" (Siron 1992/1994:245) [translated from the French].

hneen : mimetic dance from the north of the *Grande Terre.*

hocket : "Partition among several musicians of overlapping melodico-rhythmic lines, often with a polyrhythmic character" (Siron 1992/1994:730) [translated from the French].

hyavic : the name for bamboo in several langagues of the north of the *Grande Terre.* As many Kanak musical instruments are made of bamboo, this term has been extended to music in general.

'Iahnithekeun' : a dance festival held at Luecila (Lifou) on 28 and 29 October 1995.

idiophone : a musical instrument in which it is the body itself which vibrates to produce the sound.

jèkutä : generic term in Paicî for all kinds of tales including mythological stories, fictitious stories, historical stories or present events and stories in a conversation.

jèmââ : a) synonym for *jèkutä* , b) generic term for a group of specific recitations about events which were important in the creation of the world and those concerning the mythological world of the clans.

kaneka : contemporary music of young Kanaks. *Kaneka* bands attempt to create a fusion between traditional Kanak music and popular modern music styles. The kanak element in *kaneka* is typically identified in the percussion group which is part of every *kaneka* band, while the songs are compositions in various international music styles. All *kaneka* bands are electrically amplified, and all have a similar collection of musical instruments. Besides the traditional Kanak percussion there are : a synthesiser of rudimentary quality (good ones are too expensive), electric guitars and rock-type drum kits.

kaze : magic stones on Maré.

kot : means 'to sing' or 'song' in several languages of the north of the *Grande Terre.*

kutera : generic term on Maré for venerated dances accompanied by singing of a mixed choir.

L.M.S. (London Missionary Society) : a British protestant missionary society founded 1795 by Pastor Haweis.

Ma : mysterious place in the Pacific, from whence the 'real' yam is said to have been introduced to Maré.

major-minor tonal system : "The way in which the different scales are organised around the major mode and the minor mode. The system is that which was used by composers of the Renaissance until the end of the 19th century and includes the baroque, classical and romantic periods. It has continued in Western popular music" (Siron 1992/1994:197) [translated from French].

manou : waist cloth : a piece of fabric that is worn by men fastened around the waist and descending to the knees. A *manou* also has symbolic value as part of the *coutume.*

'medicine' : in French : *médicament*, special plants or vegetable substances. The incorporation of a 'medicine' can heal or help to fulfill a certain activity.

'Melanésie 2000' : The first major festival representing Kanak culture in New Caledonia, held in Nouméa in September 1975.

momoa : one of the names of the drui dance mask. In the Fagauvea language this word means 'mask'.

monnaie kanak : Traditional Kanak 'money', a fine artistic handicraft including specially made flat beads threaded onto a string.

mother hubbard : in French : *robe mission*, "a woman's loose flowing gown, like that proper to the nursery heroine" (Chambers Dictionary 1993). It is the daily clothing of Kanak women since the time of introduction at the end of the 19th century.

mwakheny : a spirit or spiritual being from the north of the *Grande Terre.*

mwaxrenu : theatrical dance from the *tribu* of Touaourou.

nata : Protestant Loyalty Islanders sent on missionary work to the *Grande Terre.*

nêêkiipâ : mimetic dance from the Paicî-Cèmuhî region.

nodal cross wall : the transverse wall across a hollow stem occurring at a node, commonly found in bamboos and reeds (see node).

node : level on a stem where a leaf is inserted (attached) (see nodal cross wall).

notu : the notu pigeon (*Ducula goliath*). An endemic pigeon of the forest of the *Grande Terre.*

nyäbi : Paicî word, generic term for chant or song.

nyäbi kârâ èpo : Paicî term for children's songs.

ôdobwia : mimetic dance of Paicî region.

ololo : Paicî term for lullabies.

ouaï : a type of trade-dance described by Lambert, probably related to the *hwâi* dance and 'rhythm' of the north of the *Grande Terre.*

padoku : Nengone term for chefferie on Maré.

pehua : a group of venerated dances on Maré. The name is derived from the Lifou word *fehoa.*

Pidjeuva (also Pidjeupatch) : a mask and spiritual being from the centre of the *Grande Terre.* This spiritual being is the leader of the *boria* dance in the world of the ancestor spirits.

pilou : refers today to the round-dance of the *Grande Terre*, where all may join in.

pilou-pilou : general term for ancient kanak ceremonies with food and good exchange of speeches and dance performances.

piré : 'silent' exchange system which existed between coastal people and those living in the mountain ranges.

popai : Paicî term for 'speech'. As a generic term *popai* covers several kinds of speeches, each of them reserved for a specific occasion.

popai görö upwârâ : Paicî term for the ceremonial speech given from a tree.

pwêêti : Paicî word for 'dance tassel'. Dancers on the *Grande Terre* as well as on the Loyalty Islands hold a dance tassel in their hands during performances. The dance tassel is the strongest symbol of the mimetic dance.

'Pwolu Jenaa' : dance festival held at Touho-Mission during 11-13 November 1994.

'rencontre préparatoire au VIe Festival des Arts du Pacifique' : dance festival held in Nouméa on 31 July and 1 August 1992.

R.F.O. : Radiodiffusion Télévision Française pour Outre-Mer.

rythme du pilou : 'rhythm of the pilou'. Kanak music which accompanies dancing and singing. The *rythme du pilou* consists of a percussion part and a voice part and has become an acoustic symbol for Kanak music in general.

sasa : a men's dance on Maré. The dancers, strongly camouflaged, imitate the furious behaviour of warriors.

seï : mimetic dance of the *tribu* of Pothé, with the subject of compulsory labour.

seloo : song genre from Ouvéa.

seleweilewei : dance from Héo in the north of Ouvéa.

speech given from a tree : in French *discours sur la perche*, ritual speech from the centre and north of the *Grande Terre*, in which the speaker stands in an elevated position.

taperas : religious polyphonic songs of the Protestant church.

ténô : Paicî term for a poem that can be performed in either a rhythmical recitation or in a song.

thuruket : ancient dance from Maré.

Ti.Ga. : Cultural Association at Poindimié, not to be confused with the island of Tiga.

tribu : 'tribe'. Whereas a tribe in ethnological literature is a group of related persons, a *tribu* in New Caledonia, refers today rather to a settlement or a 'village' where the inhabitants are not necessarily related to each other.

tsianda : trade-dance described by Lambert.

uke hajin : genre of songs on Lifou performed before a major event.

ururua : old Kanak songs from the Houaïlou region once performed inside a *case.*

wahai : Leenhardt's term to refer to theatrical pieces or interludes during mimetic dances.

wahaihai : women's dances of the Iaai language area on Ouvéa.

Wamirat : mythological hero of Maré's oral history.

wayai (or ***waiai***) : Fagauvea and Nengone term for traditional women's dances.

waueng : song genre, performed by young men on Maré.

waxejeon : Nengone term for the basic position of the *fehoa* dancer on the Loyalties.

wejein : song genre performed by young people on Lifou.

xumwong : Iaai word for 'singing'.

yaac : Spiritual beings in the Mythology of Maré.

yaace : a) Spiritual beings in the Mythology of the Isle of Pines, b) name of a dance from the *tribu* of Wapan (Isle of Pines).

INDEX